DOCTOR WHO: THE UNFOLDING TEXT

Doctor Who
The Unfolding Text

John Tulloch
and
Manuel Alvarado

St. Martin's Press   New York

First published in the United States of America in 1983.

Library of Congress Cataloging in Publication Data

Tulloch, John.
  Doctor Who.

  Includes index.
  1. Doctor Who (Television program) I. Alvarado,
Manuel. II. Title.
PN1992.77.D6273T84   1983   791.45′72   83-16143
ISBN 0-312-21480-4 (pbk)

Contents

The interior of the Tardis during the Fourteenth Season

The interior of the Tardis

Acknowledgements

We would like to thank the Drama Department of the BBC for allowing initial access to production of *Doctor Who*, and in particular John Nathan-Turner for his unfailing help, courtesy and openness in the months that followed. For giving their precious time to often lengthy interviews we should like to thank Verity Lambert, Barry Letts, Philip Hinchcliffe, Graham Williams, John Nathan-Turner, Terrance Dicks, Douglas Adams, Eric Saward, Peter Grimwade, Christopher Bailey, Jon Pertwee, Peter Davison, Richard Todd, Nerys Hughes, Simon Rouse, Adrian Mills, Lee Cornes, Janet Fielding, Sarah Sutton, Matthew Waterhouse, Peter Logan, Peter Howell, Dick Mills, Malcolm Thornton, Jeremy Bentham, Ian Levine, David Saunders, Gary Russell, Deanne Holding; and for taking the trouble to explain personally why he did not want to be interviewed, Patrick Troughton. Although the subject of audience reception is only touched on in this book, we should also like to thank the many audience groups of television professionals, performers, school, college and university students, *Doctor Who* Appreciation Society (London, Liverpool and Sydney), science fiction fans, young mothers and many others whose incredibly varied appreciations, interpretations and discussions of identical *Doctor Who* episodes constitute an (almost) hidden background to some of our thinking and discussion here, but which we hope will be properly articulated later. We are very grateful to all of them for giving up as much as three hours of their time, even though there is no space to mention the hundreds of names here. In that context we should also like to thank Anne Davies and Elizabeth Stone, our untiringly efficient research assistants on the audience project, and Maureen Kelleher for the huge task (always cheerfully performed) of transcribing audience tapes and typing the manuscript. We would also like to thank the Audience Research section (especially Dennis List) of the Australian Broadcasting Commission for access to their qualitative 'Television Program Appreciation' research, and valuable time given to discussing it.

Finally, we would like to say a very special thank you to Jeremy Bentham who compiled Appendices I and II. Jeremy Bentham was among the two million children to have watched the very first episode of Doctor Who in November 1963 and, as such, was a pioneer of behind-the-sofa viewing. He co-founded the Doctor Who Appreciation Society in 1976 and later spent three and a half years as Associate Editor and writer for the commercial publication *Doctor Who Monthly*.

Sydney and London   J. T.
May 1983   M. A.

The publisher wishes to thank the BBC for kindly providing the cover photograph of the BBC Television Centre and for providing all the photographs which appear in the text.

Terms

I. In/on television there are considered to be three predominant forms of fiction – the single play, the series and the serial. The single play is an obvious category and one that is derived from the theatre and cinema. The distinction series/serial is, however, more complex and thus far has generally been handled with a certain imprecision in media analysis. Because of *Doctor Who's* uneasy overlapping of both areas of television production we briefly offer a suggested typology to be of use in future media research:

1. Continuous serial
2. Episodic serial
3. Sequential series
4. Episodic series

1. The **continuous serial** is characterised by the fact that it can run infinitely and that it possesses multiple narrative strands which are introduced and concluded in different temporal periods. There are therefore multi-layered narrative overlaps; the programmes *Coronation Street, Crossroads, Emmerdale Farm, Brookside* are examples of this format.
2. The **episodic serial** is the category to which *Doctor Who* belongs. It is characterised by there being narrative continuity, but for a limited and specified number of episodes. The viewer has to see all the episodes encompassed within one title to understand fully the narrative structure and closure. It is not a very common form but includes programmes such as *Out* and *The Prisoner* (GB). It is questionable as to whether a continuous serial which 'fails', for example *The Cres*, becomes, through its failure, an episodic serial!

3. The **sequential series** is close to the *episodic serial* but does nevertheless constitute a separate category. It is character- ised by the fact that while each episode constitutes a complete narrative structure and experience there will invariably be an enigma posed at the end of each episode. *Dallas* is the classic example but there are a number of others, for example *Fox, Dynasty, Knott's Landing*.

4. The **episodic series** is television's most common and endur- ing fictional format and is perhaps the one fictional mode it can claim to have invented (with cinema now beginning to copy it with series like the *Superman* films). Each episode consists of complete and discrete narratives with only the main protagonists and main locations (offices/ homes) providing continuity between episodes. Examples of episodic series abound in the television productions of many countries of the world, for example *Starsky and Hutch, Minder*, etc., etc.

The first three categories all require the posing of an enigma at the end of most episodes (with a consequent lack of nar- rative closure), thereby using narrative structure to draw an audience back for the next episode — the fourth uses audience identification with protagonists/stars to maintain high viewing ratings.

II.   Throughout this book we have generally used the term 'cliffhanger' to describe those moments of narrative break that occur at the end of an episode of a serial and which are designed to keep the audience in a position of suspense until the next episode — 'How will the protagonist escape?' is the question one is left asking. It is a term that would seem to date from the period when serials were a common cinematic form and where each episode ended with the hero in mortal danger.

However, while the term 'cliffhanger' has entered the com- mon parlance of the television professionals who worked on *Doctor Who*, we find the term somewhat crude, particularly when applied to those narrative breaks which don't hold the life of the hero in balance. In some of the adventure stories of *Doctor Who* this is the case, but there are also stories which are more subtly concerned with the complex problems of human emotional relations and which will simply encourage questions such as 'What will happen in the next episode?' or 'How will that problem he resolved?' In those situations we would prefer to use the term 'suspended enigma' and on certain occasions we do.*

---

* A problem that one encounters when the term is used in relation to discussions of a programme like *Coronation Street*, where lives are rarely, if ever, at stake at the end of an episode. Cf. Christine Geraghty, 'The continuous serial — a definition', in Richard Dyer *et al.*, *Coronation Street* (BFI, 1981). See this piece also for an extremely useful and extended definition of the continuous serial.

Louise Jameson as Leela

Introduction

It is highly appropriate that the world's most famous Time Lord should also be BBC Television's longest-running series. It is also appropriate that the world's largest broadcasting organisation – an organisation that is Great Britain's most powerful and influential cultural institution – should have created a programme which has itself become something of an institution within British cultural life. These alone are valid criteria for writing a book that offers a description, an historical account, and a critical analysis about this enduring phenomenon.

What this book represents is the first attempt to chart and unpack a programme which, because of its long history – twenty years – and massive number of episodes, has become a very complex and dense text. In fact, while this book treats the *Doctor Who* programmes as texts – cultural artefacts which require forms of textual analysis – it will also engage with *Doctor Who* as commodity – the programmes as a series of artefacts which undergo the stages of production/circulation/consumption. How will the book engage in this project?

Doctor Who: the unfolding text

At the date of this book's publication, *Doctor Who* will be twenty years old, and its anniversary will be marked by a variety of events. The main reconstruction of its history will be via the programme's fictional world itself, as successive episodes in the twentieth season rehearse characters and events out of its past. Its story will also be told in other formats (television 'documentary', picture book, etc.), each adopting a detailed and intensive view of the programme. *Doctor Who* will be excavated for its history, the true 'facts' told, 'classic' incidents and characters re-revealed, relevant producers, performers and production staff interviewed. Probably the results of much of this research will be a reduced version of work already done by the programme's own scholars, the *Doctor Who* Appreciation Society, who cherishingly and with painstaking accuracy have revealed and debated it in all its minutiae during the last few years. An outstanding example of this work is the 'Cybermark Services' series, *Doctor Who — An Adventure in Space and Time*, co-ordinated by Jeremy Bentham, which, with a remarkable attention to programme history (and unashamedly outright value judgements), has set itself the task of detailing, reviewing, discussing every *Doctor Who* episode ever made and which, at the time of writing, is still immersed in the Hartnell years. For absolute archivist competence in the intensive history of *Doctor Who*, this work is second to none.

Our book quite deliberately takes a different — extensive — approach to the history of *Doctor Who* — by which we mean an investigation in terms of the industrial, institutional, narrative, generic, professional and other practices which, originally existing outside the programme, have operated in different ways to shape it. Whereas the intensive approach investigates *Doctor Who* as a found object, with its own 'essence' which is the source of analysis, the extensive approach examines the programme as a site of intersection, a nexus, where codes (implicit in the programme's determination as BBC television institution, as science fiction, as narrative, etc.) meet. Hence the object of analysis, *Doctor Who*, is not cherished as a personal possession, domesticated, loved for the comforting store of intimate secrets it reveals to the afficionado. Rather, it is deconstructed, made to reveal its other secrets — the material practices and discourses which have determined its institution and its unfolding. Our book is therefore a 'history' which examines the programme as a text that unfolds according to a wide range of institutional, professional, public, cultural and ideological forces. It examines, for instance, the programme's origins in the BBC's attempt to compete with commercial television, its early designation as both 'educational' (history) and 'popular' (science fiction), its ability to draw on a variety of stars and codes of performance, as well as a range of genres (from the Gothic Horror coding which brought it into confrontation with Mary Whitehouse's National Viewers' and Listeners' Association to the 'meta-science fiction' coding under the influence of Doug Adams (author of *Hitch Hiker's Guide to the Galaxy*) which brought it into confrontation with the hard-line fans), the current 'return' to cliffhangers and action drama in the drive for an American market, the new policy of big name guest stars, and so on. These and other material determinants have established *Doctor Who*, over twenty years, as an 'unfolding text', subtly shifting its ground in response to social and professional pressures, yet vindicating television's recipe for success: something different but something the same.

As writer and script editor Terrance Dicks says (of a show he has been associated with since the late 1960s):

> *Doctor Who* is like a saga. Every few years there will be a new something. There will be a new companion. There will be new writers. There will be new script editors. There will be new producers. And every chunk of years there will be a new Doctor. So all of the these things bring change, which is absolutely to the good. Of course when Barry Letts and I left and Philip Hinchcliffe and Bob Holmes did it slightly differently, we went around mumbling 'things aren't what they were in the old days'. But they shouldn't be, and now that John Nathan-Turner and his script editor Eric Saward have taken over, *they* will do it differently, and it is quite right that they should. They should not do it the way I would do it, that is the whole point. And I think that is really the answer to what has kept *Doctor Who* alive — it's this continuous input.

Despite these unfolding events, there is a central professional continuity. *Every* producer and script editor would agree with Dicks's description of the essentials of the programme:

> The brief is to get a good, entertaining, fast-moving story. Now given that, which is the bottom line, the more pluses that you can get in, the more depth, the more texture —

Buddhism, ecology, people's obsessions and worries — the better. They all add up to make the soup richer, making *Doctor Who* more interesting than *Star Trek*.

The fact, then, that this *continuity* of professional concern has nevertheless provided *Doctor Who* with a *variety* of signatures needs accounting for. Stark contrasts (that between Graham Williams's 'send-up' era and John Nathan-Turner's 'cliffhanger' one is the most debated) need to be explained in terms of forces much more powerful than individual whim or intention.

To narrate an 'extrinsic' history of *Doctor Who* is nothing less than to examine television itself as an institution in society. So this book is designed not simply as a case study of a long-running television series, but also as a textbook of television studies, which, for the teacher and student of the media, will examine and offer a practical demonstration of the value of current critical and theoretical concepts through their application to *Doctor Who*. Thus each chapter in turn examines different issues of current television study: television as discourse and cultural institution; narrative and series/serials; science fiction and fantasy as genres; authorship and organisation; stars, satellites (the Doctor's companions) and circulation; conditions of production and performance. This last chapter, which is based on an extensive period observing all phases of production at the BBC and on interviews with artists and production staff involved with *Doctor Who* since 1963, makes this the first case study of a television programme which combines textual analysis based on a range of theoretical work together with an examination of the production practices of television.

Our commitment to this book as a text in television studies has also influenced our choice of a few episodes of the programme for detailed analysis, since it is hoped that in due course these few (rather than many) *Doctor Who* episodes may be made available for serious study at secondary and tertiary level. At the same time we hope that the commitment of one of the authors to *Doctor Who* ever since its first episode in November 1963 will provide an overview of the programme to counter the 'bias' of selection.

The uniqueness of 'Doctor Who'

There are reasons other than the longevity and popularity of *Doctor Who* which make it a unique programme for investigation and analysis. First, it is possibly the only programme intended for children which has become as popular with adults as children without losing its child audience. We will discuss this matter further in Chapter 1, but will here offer one observation about how this might have come to be the case. It strikes us that *Doctor Who* is one of the few television programmes that doesn't patronise or insult the intelligence of children – and therefore is adult enough to appeal to 'grown-ups' – but thereby ensures that it maintains high child audience ratings, an audience that regenerates much faster than an adult audience. The combination of 'fast-moving story' plus 'texture' that Dicks describes has a lot to do with this.

Second, the complexity and variety of *Doctor Who* is the result of its use of a range of different genres – Science Fiction/Historical Romance/Comedy/Gothic Horror/Adventure, etc., which together with the regular phoenix-like reincarnation of the Doctor himself (allowing a range of different actors with different personalities and personae to play the role) make for another aspect of its uniqueness and another reason for its durability.

Third, as a programme intended for children *Doctor Who* might have had a fairly low status among television workers interested in 'graduating' to more prestigious areas of programme production. Conditions of production at the BBC (which are described in Chapter 1), however, encouraged writers and directors originally not to see *Doctor Who* as 'second-class work'. And today writers like Christopher Bailey argue that *Doctor Who* is a unique television space for experimenting with ideas and narrative style. It has now also achieved the status of a severe testing ground for those about to make the 'big time' in television – if directors and producers can handle *Doctor Who*, they can handle anything.

One can therefore say that in terms of the production context, range of characters and characterisations, generic form, range and size of audience, *Doctor Who* represents a site of

endless transformations and complex weavings as well as a
programme of increasing institutional stability and public
popularity. It is also a production that has one of the best-
organised fan club followings of any television programme in
the world. Programmes like *Coronation Street* stimulate huge
audience followings and attract thousands of letter writers
but they don't seem to give rise to the highly organised fan
club structures and detailed fan club magazines and conventions that *Doctor Who* enjoys.

'Doctor Who': writing the book

In writing any book authors are obviously going to encounter
problems — we will briefly list a few of what we considered
to be the important ones we experienced.

One aspect of our analysis is the substantial use we make
of interviews and conversations conducted by John Tulloch
with a large number of people who have worked in different
capacities on the programme over the years and also with
leading members of the British *Doctor Who* Appreciation
Society. The account and analysis are, of course, by and
large our own (as teachers and researchers in media theory).
But we felt it was crucial that those concerned professionally
with *Doctor Who* should 'speak' through this book, both
directly through interviews and through their observed professional practices. Without their co-operation much of the
analysis of professional work could not have been done.
Without exposure to their usually implicit (sometimes unconscious) values of practice, analysis of their 'professionalism'
would have been simplistic. The question of the production
of this text via the debate of 'professional' and 'theoretical'
discourses is taken up in Chapter 4. Here we should say we
would have been naïve if we had not anticipated their statements to be sometimes contradictory, often critical and, on
occasion, acrimonious! Given that we did not wish or intend
to write a gossip-column account of *Doctor Who*, we have
attempted to pick our way carefully through a potential
minefield of people's emotions and feelings about one another.
We have used quotations where people are critical of others

only when it was crucial for the making of an important general point. We don't necessarily share, agree with or support such subjective statements but we do recognise their value in terms of aiding a clearer understanding of the complexities that make up *Doctor Who*. We don't think we have included anything that is likely to be offensive or to offend anyone but in an industry as public as television (and where many workers are freelance), it often seems that the only way of ensuring that one causes no offence is to write a totally anodyne book.

Another area of concern in writing any book is with the use of language. The issues we raise are ones determined by the current debates within media studies, rather than directly via the concerns of 'hands-on' professionals. But we hope that what is said here will be of interest to television professionals as well as to many fans of *Doctor Who*. For this audience (but not for students of the media) occasional terms (such as 'discourse': 'a process of construction of social realities and imposition of these realities upon other members of the communication process', Carswell and Rommetreit) may be unfamiliar. But they do have a precise meaning: the fans' much communicated dismissal of Graham Williams is, for instance, 'discourse' not 'fact', since it depends on their social assumptions and values (their adherence to programme 'continuity' which Williams breached). And the fact that such terms do have as pecise and useful a meaning as 'jargon' terms within the television industry (such as 'shoot off' and 'wild track') suggests that the much-noted hostility between 'theorists' and 'practitioners' of the media will not begin to improve until people in both camps (and both are in fact practitioners within an industry, whether television, publishing or teaching) take a little more care in visiting the locations and concepts of the other. Only at that point will fruitful debate start.

A different matter of language is the use of non-sexist (and non-racist) language, to which we have paid close attention. For example, we use the term 'performer' because of the negative and often derogatory connotations of the word 'actress'. This is also of particular concern when writing about television because of the fundamental questions that are

raised about the representation *and* employment of women
in the media. This is a matter that will be addressed later in
the book but there are a couple of points we wish to clarify
in this introduction.

As far as the representation and employment of women in
Doctor Who is concerned there are many problems. On the
one hand there would seem to be some positive aspects of the
programme. For example, the first producer was a woman;
Leela was a female companion designed to break the dominant
stereotype of women in adventure fictions; Ursula Le Guin
has been an important source of inspiration in a programme
analysed here. On the other (and much more damaging) hand
of that listing are the facts that all subsequent producers have
been male; that in the first nineteen years of the show there
have been only two female writers (Lesley Scott and Barbara
Clegg) and a handful of women directors (Julia Smith, Patricia
Russell, Fiona Cumming and Mary Ridge); that the companions are still only 'companions' (and the majority have been
'screamers'); that generally and dominantly *Doctor Who* has
maintained the male view of the world to which most 'Sci-Fi'
subscribes despite the influence of a writer like Le Guin. In
fact, in terms of the roles women occupy within the series
one would have to argue for the extreme narrative conventionality of *Doctor Who*.

This leads into what is perhaps one of the major disappoint-
ments of the series, which is that for all the innovativeness
with which *Doctor Who* is justifiably associated it ultimately
is narratively highly conventional and also adopts the 'classic
realist mode'.[1] This might initially seem a strange statement
to make given that *Doctor Who* blatantly uses non-realist sets,
allows different performers to play the title role, engages
with a remarkably wide range of genres and would generally
seem to be fairly experimental as far as most television fiction
is concerned. However, we would argue that in terms of the
narrative functions, structures and progressions it deploys,
the modes of representation it adopts and in particular its
acceptance of the classic realist mode ('realism' understood as
a form as well as a content) *Doctor Who* clearly operates
within the constraints of the dominant aesthetic of the vast
bulk of television production.

Recently John Fiske has elaborated on this problem in his useful article 'Doctor Who: Ideology and the Reading of a Popular Narrative Text'.[2] We would agree with much that he says there, and in particular with his concern for the role of the reader in negotiating meaning in relation to the preferred narrative design. For this very reason, however (and because Fiske only analyses one story), we feel that our examination of the greater complexity of discourses determining *Doctor Who* reveals a potential that is open to some 'readers' (carried especially by the Romantic–Gothic coding of the text itself) to unsettle the realist/consensual narrative. And we would suggest that the enjoyment of *Doctor Who* by, for instance, university students (particularly in the Baker period) owes more to its self-referentiality and tendency to the 'bizarre' and fantastic than to the linear drive of a moral 'scientific' wisdom. Symptomatically, of course, it was the Gothic and self-referential tendencies which aroused most hostility towards the programme, too, from Mary Whitehouse in the first instance, and from the fans in the second.

Reading 'Doctor Who'

One of the areas which this book does not cover, but which we hope to offer an account of in the future, is that of the audience and the notion of differential readings. Media research has increasingly become concerned not just with the ways different sectors of the audience experience programmes but also with the way in which programmes construct different subject positions for those different sectors, thereby encouraging (albeit unwittingly) differential readings. A couple of small and minimal examples are offered later in this book:

> The discussion here was framed by the discourse of television professionals — about 'gripping' writing, cliffhangers, time-slotting, target audience and so on — but even with this degree of in-group knowledge, for some members the pleasure in the show adhered to its 'adult' reference to 'our own times'. In contrast, an infant school audience found 'The Monster of Peladon' comprehensible and enjoy-

able by focussing on a series of actions (such as the continuity of 'tricks' played by the Doctor – against the monster, against the guard, etc.) and concrete details (noticing, for instance, that the cup of wine given to the Doctor after his rescue was shaped like the monster's horn). While not understanding the political references, these children were working to establish a different register of relevance and coherence – and therefore a different 'memory' – for the show.

A group of Asian undergraduates at the University of New South Wales who were Buddhist and quite aware of the meaning of 'dikkha', 'anatta', 'anicca', etc. still did not 'read' the episode of 'Kinda' in which they appeared in a Buddhist way. Concerned to appropriate 'Western' professional values and skills to take back to their countries, these students found *Doctor Who* of no interest because 'too imaginative and unreal', and preferred shows which gave them a 'realistic' understanding of Western culture, such as news, documentary, current affairs and drama reflecting 'more down to earth problems'. Consequently they did not consider *Doctor Who* sufficiently close to their interests to begin to assign relevance and codes of coherence to their understanding of it. This for them was *Western* television (and therefore was not considered as a forum for Buddhist ideas). Hence the Buddhist clues (played down by the production team. . .) were not appropriated to generate a reading: the students' 'Western' professional orientation overlaid the producer's 'action-drama' signature to efface the Buddhist allegory.

This is clearly an important area for future media analysis and research and one which, when engaged with in terms of the differentials of class, sex and race (as well as in terms of age, as indicated in the first example above), will prove to be theoretically, analytically and politically crucial.

It is also becoming an urgent project in terms of the increasing international circulation of texts (to be intensified with the technological developments of video, cable and, in particular, satellite transmission). To take our area of investigation,

Doctor Who, having become a British television phenomenon and what amounts to a domestic institution, has now also become an international success. It is now sold to more than thirty-eight countries and enjoys a huge following across the world — a *Doctor Who* convention held in Chicago in June 1982 attracted 10,000 fans. Clearly the cultural specificities of the programme and the cultural differences of the readings of it will further compound the difficulties of attempting to conduct research into the decoding process within any one national boundary.

William Hartnell

Chapter 1

Mystery: Television Discourse and Institution

On Saturday 23 November 1963 at 5.25 pm the *Doctor Who* theme music was heard on television for the first time, and just under twelve minutes later William Hartnell appeared through the London fog as the first Doctor. It was the birth of an institution – in terms of its wide-scale public currency as well as longevity. When *Doctor Who* writer Christopher Bailey said that he conceived of his audience as stretching 'from seven year olds up to university professors', he was underestimating the span of a programme which certainly attracts children as young as 2 and adults over 65, has an audience crossing all classes[1] in Britain and is transmitted in nearly forty countries around the world.

The programme has become so well known that the BBC Radiophonic Workshop, servicing every BBC department and with over two hundred different commitments a year, tends to be known primarily for the *Doctor Who* theme music it created. When the Queen was introduced to Radiophonic Workshop members at the Centenary Conversazione of the Institution of Electrical Engineers at the Royal Festival Hall, her response was, 'Ah, yes, *Doctor Who*'.[2] In 1981 Madame Tussaud's in London announced its special *Doctor Who* exhibition with a huge street banner carrying the words 'Who's Next? Doctor Who. Who Else?' in full confidence that the public would know the popular television programme to which it referred. And in January 1982 when *Doctor Who* was moved

away from its Saturday transmission slot for the first time by
the BBC, the 'quality' newspaper, *The Guardian*, thought fit
to devote an editorial to the failure of the BBC to recognise
the programme's status as an institution among all sections of
the British people.

Together with its liberal critique of the Israelis for deliberately provocative 'annexation' policies against the Arabs, and
of the conservative Mrs Thatcher for her misuse of productiv-
ity statistics, *The Guardian* chided the BBC for ensuring that
the 'Tardis lands on the wrong day'.[3]

> All those who have grown up or grown old with *Doctor
> Who* (for some who watched it in the early days, trembling-
> ly, from around the safe cover of a friendly armchair are
> now men of destiny and captains of what industry this
> country still has left) know it to be essential a part of a
> winter Saturday as coming in cold from heath, forest, or
> football, warm crumpets (or pikelets, if preferred) before
> the fire, the signature tune of Sports Report, and that
> sense of liberation and escapist surrender which can only
> come when tomorrow is a day off too. These conditions
> cannot be created on Mondays and Tuesdays. Saturday
> will be smitten by the destruction of an essential ingredient,
> and *Doctor Who* will be destroyed by this violent wrenching
> from its natural context. If Mr Alasdair Milne is not to
> forfeit the hope that has been riding on him since his recent
> appointment to the Director-Generalship, he must intervene
> now and order that this sacrilege be stopped.

In terms of *The Guardian*'s editorial narrative, the *Doctor Who*
item functions rather like those humorous or sporting items
which often end the news, ensuring, as Richard Collins has
said, that whatever political and economic crises come and go,
'the rule governed rituals of daily life — cricket in the summer,
soccer in the winter — go on'.[4] Indeed, the *Doctor Who* item
appeals directly to that guarantee of a fundamental orderliness
— of *Doctor Who* forever on a winter Saturday afternoon —
which stands against the destruction of industry by Mrs
Thatcher which the earlier editorial comment (and the *Doctor
Who* item itself) points to.

So, while obviously tongue-in-cheek, the item is also deadly serious in its appeal to a cultural unity: on weekday nights, it complains, *Doctor Who* will be lost equally to those 'still homeward bound in their chauffeur-driven Jaguars' and to those travelling home on 'such commuter trains' as the railwaymen's strike 'is currently permitting to run'. After all, the cultural unity of middle-class forest rambles and working-class football is dear to *The Guardian*'s liberal-reformist stance, which is fundamentally threatened by hawkish and ultra-conservative politics at home and abroad.

Yet despite *The Guardian*'s appeal to the unity of a typically 'British' culture and to the cosy stability of the Saturday 'liberation' from Thatcher-destruction of the working week, the success of *Doctor Who* has by no means relied on unity and stability alone. Some of its success as a television institution has been due to its ability to divide its viewers into different audiences, and to threaten the stability of its own 'scientific' world view. If it has achieved a form of unity — and this is a kind of which *The Guardian* would certainly approve — it is the 'democratic' one of a sectional pluralism.

The particular 'quality' of *Doctor Who* to mean different things at different levels was immediately apparent during one week in November 1981 when Sarah Hayes, writing about children's science fiction in *The Times Literary Supplement*, said that 'it is the thrill of a known fear that doesn't linger in the mind that enlivens the best of *Doctor Who*',[5] while Nigel Robinson, addressing a 'sophisticated' adult leisure market in *Time Out*, spoke of good scripts, excellent performances, exemplary direction and 'mind-boggling concepts' which show 'just how good a *Doctor Who* story can be'.[6] That audience span — from childish 'fear' (the inflection for instance of the Madame Tussaud's exhibition) to intellectual 'concepts' — has been the hallmark of *Doctor Who* from its inception, and has enabled various aspects of the programme to be inscribed in different institutional and entertainment forms.[7]

This appeal to child and adult audiences is perhaps *Doctor Who*'s most remarkable quality as a television institution, and can be ascribed — in so far as it was an almost instantaneous phenomenon — partly to its mode of television address and partly to the programme's insertion within the departmental structure of the BBC.

'Normal and uncanny': 'Doctor Who' as television discourse

On 22 November 1963 President Kennedy was assasinated,
and the following day a new, and minor, science fiction
mystery series was launched in the midst of extraordinary
'here-and-now' television drama. Yet *Doctor Who*'s initial
signature as 'mystery' was not entirely opaque to that sense
of documentary drama. Unlike a lot of popular science fiction,
the diegetic world of its characters was not simply 'displaced'
in some other time or place. It was located, insistently, in the
present: London, 1963.

From the beginning *Doctor Who* established itself as
familiar, but different, normal and uncanny. As the first
producer, Verity Lambert, said of the opening visuals, which
were so important in hooking the audience and establishing a
foretaste of what was to come: 'I just wanted it to look
familiar but odd.' And before even those first visuals, the
Radio Times located its narrative mystery — 'Doctor Who?' —
in the 'ordinary' Britain and among the 'ordinary' people of
1963. If the face of William Hartnell which stared out from
page seven of the *Radio Times* (21 November 1963) was
aesthetically intense and elusively professorial, his colleagues
were earmarked more prosaically as 'normal' teachers.

The *Radio Times*, in fact, established a preferred reading
which the programme was to take up two days later.

> Doctor Who? That is just the point. Nobody knows precisely
> who he is, this mysterious exile from another world and a
> distant future . . . He has a granddaughter Susan, a strange
> amalgam of teenage normality and uncanny intelligence . . .
> It begins by telling how the Doctor finds himself visiting
> the Britain of today: Susan (played by Carole Ann Ford)
> has become a pupil at an ordinary British school, where
> her incredible breadth of knowledge has whetted the
> curiosity of two of her teachers.

The 'naturally' rational curiosity of a teacher of science and a
teacher of history was to be the point of audience identification, inscribing viewers within the foregrounded hermeneutic
code (the code of puzzles and mysteries) of the new program-

me. At first Susan, too, was to be an 'ordinary' schoolgirl, but writer Anthony Coburn insisted that she should be the Doctor's granddaughter, with, as producer Verity Lambert put it, 'all the irresponsibility of a child, but having superior knowledge to the humans. That gave us an added dramatic effect.' The drama, indeed, opened with the investigation of Susan, not the Doctor; and it continued by displacing 'mystery' into the 'scientific' and 'historical' worlds of the schoolteachers, without ever solving that of the Doctor. As the *Radio Times* article said:

> They may visit a distant galaxy where civilisation has been devastated by the blast of a neutron bomb or they may find themselves journeying to far Cathay in the caravan of Marco Polo. The whole cosmos in fact is their oyster.

And in that cosmos the narratives of *Doctor Who* would ensure that only the Doctor remained a puzzle.

The nomination of Susan as 'teenage normality and uncanny intelligence' was virtually a description of the Doctor himself, in so far as Verity Lambert also saw him as a combination of childishness and brilliance. But it was also an alibi for *not* naming him, since this was to be a character without 'essence', composed of oppositions and contradictions.

> *Verity Lambert*: The original conception was that here was a total mystery and he was not predictable in any kind of way. He was irascible as well as being kindly. He was dangerous ... and ... there was this childlike quality about him as well ... That unpredictability was very much part of him, and I had seen William Hartnell do two things that really impressed me. One was a really awful, nasty sergeant in *The Army Game* where he was tough and strict and angry and cross, and the other was as the old talent scout in *This Sporting Life* where he was very vulnerable and sad. I thought, 'if we could just get that combination!' ... So that just as you were getting cross with Doctor Who, he suddenly turns and is gentle, and suddenly you feel that this old man is vulnerable.

A sense of defining the unknown by means of the contradictory (imperious old age and childlike vulnerability, colossal scientific wisdom and irresponsible irrationality) was central to Verity Lambert's conception of the Doctor. The normal (the similar, the identifiable) estranged by the different: this was to be the initial definition of *Doctor Who*. It began with that first episode in November 1963 when the audience had to wait for 11¾ minutes for his first appearance — time for the programme to establish the tension between banality and difference which in fact was his character.

We will begin by looking at those opening minutes of a twenty-year-old institution.

Signature tune

The instant signature of the *Doctor Who* theme music was on the one hand its rhythmic, repetitive melody, and on the other hand its strangeness. Repetition — both of musical motifs within the piece, and of the theme itself, day after day, year after year — is obviously an important feature of long-running television institutions like *Coronation Street* and *Doctor Who*. As with the opening music and sound of the daily news, it pronounces that the programme remains stable and the same, whatever the changes elsewhere. As Christine Geraghty says of *Coronation Street*, 'the familiar signature tune alerts us to the fact that the serial is about to begin. It does not disappear "until the autumn" or "until the next series" '[8] — part of that sense of cultural continuity to which *The Guardian* appeals.

Signature tunes have to establish an almost immediate familiarity if they are to do their job — hence the repetition of musical motifs and, in some cases, their similarity/difference from familiar popular tunes. Marion Jordan has noted the 'haunting' similarity of the *Coronation Street* theme to 'Thanks for the Memory'.[9] In contrast to this 'nostalgia for vanished virtues', the *Doctor Who* theme promoted its weekly ritual in terms of contemporaneity — the combination of repeated base beat and pizzicato swoop in the *Doctor Who* signature tune had become a very conventional one in pop

music by 1962. At the same time it inflected contemporaneity
'futuristically' by means of the special Radiophonic Workshop
sound which gave the *Doctor Who* theme instant recognition.

Verity Lambert was conscious from the start that she
needed a recognisable melody which promoted a sense of
familiarity, but was also 'different', both from other theme
tunes, and, in so far as it was melody, from other SF electronic
music.

> *Lambert*: I had wanted to use music — whether electronic
> or by some other means — that had a melody, rather than
> just musique concrète . . . There was a group of French
> musicians that I had seen . . . who played music on glass
> rods — a very curious sound. I talked to the head of that
> group and asked him if he would do something. He was
> terribly busy and couldn't do it.

Verity Lambert then turned to the Radiophonic Workshop,
who suggested Ron Grainer, whom Lambert readily accepted
because he had already proved himself with television signature tunes like *Maigret*, *Steptoe and Son* and *Comedy Play-
house*.

> *Dick Mills*: Ron wrote the music and left the manuscript
> with us at the Radiophonic Workshop which we put to-
> gether using sound equipment. There are no instruments at
> all on the original *Doctor Who*, not even synthesisers
> because they hadn't been invented then. It was done
> literally by choosing frequencies, recording them the right
> length, and sticking all the separate notes together.

Interestingly, the mark of 'mechanical' similarity versus
'human' difference which, as we shall see, became a defining
theme of *Doctor Who*, was inscribed in the signature tune at
that stage.

> *Mills*: It soon became quite obvious that we could make
> a science fiction signature tune using sound equipment
> that didn't need to be played in an acoustic over a micro-
> phone. There was a certain robotic quality, a sterile quality,

which, if you like, could only be found in outer space where there's no atmosphere, and no colouration . . . If you were to write a piece of music, and realise it just in physical terms by cutting tape and joining them together, there's no reason why it shouldn't be perfect. It could be too perfect. It would be so predictable that the rhythm and the happenings in the music would perhaps be uninteresting. It's very easy to listen to musicians — they bring a piece of music to life by putting their own performance on it. And although they are in rhythm 99% of the time, it is the little 1% that makes it a human being playing it and not a machine . . . So when we did the *Doctor Who* music we tried to creep in one or two, not wrong notes, but imperfections, like a little bit of tremolo in the tune. We may have shifted the beat slightly just to make it sound as though it was played by somebody with feeling, rather than a stitched together music job . . . The *Doctor Who* tune swoops up, it doesn't go up in precise notes. It sort of slides up from note to note, and it does give it a bit of a spacey feel.

It was this contrast between 'normal' human imperfections and the unfamiliar, robotic and alien world of 'space' that determined the musical theme, rather than any 'time' concept, which Dick Mills felt could better be carried by the incidental music.

Mills: It would be very difficult to imagine how to devise a signature tune that would encompass all the time scales through which the Doctor travels . . . I think really to help this time travel business the incidental music plays a far bigger part, because obviously when the Doctor lands in Venice or Rome he will encounter music being played by travelling musicians of the time or the incidental music will reflect that time and people. All the signature tune could do was give an unearthly feel, a sort of space feel, give a bit of mystery and spookiness, but not necessarily time travel.

The difference in concept between the signature tune and incidental music in *Doctor Who* marks its difference from

Coronation Street. 'Time' music in *Doctor Who* conveys the density of a particular social milieu, reflecting 'that' time and people in the future or past. Because *Coronation Street* evokes a sealed-off world of day-by-day social interaction, its nostalgic location can be conveyed by the signature tune. The same function – for a variety of closed-off worlds – is attempted by *Doctor Who*'s incidental music. But the programme itself was designed to work out of, and away from, the domesticated 'Social Realist' formula of *Coronation Street*. Hence its theme music emphasised not social density, but 'human' difference.

The time travel concept *was* carried by the opening titles (which were composed to the music), but again, this was subordinate to the principle of 'familiar but odd'.

Opening titles

The first visual of *Doctor Who* in November 1963 was of an upward shooting probe, similar in a schematic way to conventional representations of space craft taking off. But this upward probe immediately broke up and tilted over to merge with forward rushing 'clouds', which themselves then merged with the 'bleeding' image out of which first 'Who'[10] and then 'Doctor Who' appeared. A visual tension was established as 'Doctor Who' receded backwards against forward rushing clouds, finally vanishing as the swirling clouds themselves became billowing mist in the first representational image.

The idea for the title sequence came to Verity Lambert from Mervyn Pinfield, who had been appointed as Associate Producer to add a technical competence required by the new 'sci fi' show. Pinfield had himself got the idea from an experimental director at the BBC who had formed a group to examine the potential for electronic effects in drama. They had discovered what Verity Lambert saw as the 'extraordinary' and 'odd' picture break-up effect when a camera shoots its own monitor. She employed Bernard Lodge to control the effect and make the 'Doctor Who' badge 'bleed'.

> *Lambert*: I think it just looked so very strange and different from anything else. I didn't want it to just look like

'time' — I wanted it to look familiar but odd, which is
what the *Doctor Who* theme was.

The title sequence, 'familiar but odd', was to establish the
mood of the first representational sequence that followed,
and of the episode generally.

Policeman

The visuals proper begin with a policeman shining a torch
outside a junkyard (prefiguring the mystery of Ian with *his*
torch inside the junkyard later). The sequence and iconography is familiarly *Dixon of Dock Green* — the policeman
coming to camera, the 'seedy' location, the fog — but made
different by the gates which open by themselves as the policeman turns away. The opening junkyard gates reveal — as the
title music fades — a familiar London sight of 1963, a police
box, but here coded as 'strange' by its location inside the
junkyard, and by the dominating hum which replaces the
music. Eighteen years later, in 'Logopolis', the last Tom Baker
story, a policeman and police box would again provide the
opening sequence. But then it was a self-referencing device,
relying on the institutionalised longevity of the programme
to delight *Doctor Who* buffs by recalling its own origins and
mythology. In November 1963 there was a different function.
These were the very first images of *Doctor Who*, and they
were there to establish its new identity as 'familiar but odd'.
The hum now covered the transition to the first ever story
title, again announcing the usual that was unusual: 'An Unearthly Child'.

School

That this (as yet unseen) child is part of the banal daily
environment of teenage 'normality' is immediately established
as we fade out from the unusually located notice on the police
box and into the notice-board of Coal Hill School, with its

lists of the 'everyday': football, athletics and house news. '1963' is established by the 'contemporary' clothes (school uniform is avoided) and make-up of senior schoolgirls coming down a corridor. This sequence consciously establishes *Doctor Who* in terms of the everyday 'normality' and folk wisdom of its main target audience: school-children. In contrast to the 'police genre' coding of the previous sequence, these visuals are coded as 'document'. But they are not there to document a particular school or to investigate 'school' sociologically. An 'everyday school' is there to establish the television contemporaneity which the programme *Doctor Who* will work on to make strange.

In their analysis of a similar establishing sequence in a *World in Action* documentary. Stephen Heath and Gillian Skirrow write:

> It is not merely by chance that the images themselves are all moments of passage — school children going through doorways, coming down corridors — since they are there minimally, to be appropriately ('in school') insignificant . . . The space is entirely that of a passage, of the succession of images for a time (or times: of the commentary, of television), not that of the analysis of a reality.[11]

That television 'time', as they point out, is the present instantaneous — the immediate, intimate and yet mass communicated image of the world, presented 'here-and-now' especially for me as viewer, and drawing for its credibility on the 'truth' that 'the camera doesn't lie'. It is only in relation to that truth that the image of the gates that open by themselves connotes 'mystery'. 'Strangeness' depends on the certainty of the empirically perceived. 'The empirical rule of the dominance of the picture is a rationalisation of the ideology of the document, the window on the world; the image *must be* the cause, the initiator.'[12] What we 'know' is what we see; and what we see is 'instantly' communicated to us by television. The 'knowable' becomes the ceaseless, arbitrary (i.e. untheorised) pattern of 'here-and-now' events with which the screen is constantly filled.

Little matter in this respect what is communicated, the crux is the creation and maintenance of the communicating situation and the realisation of the viewer as subject in that situation. The subject of television is a citizen in a world of communication; he or she is called — and occupied — there, for that world. 'Immediacy, intimacy, and mass communication': television here and now, for me personally, for me as the unity of everyone.[13]

The effect in television news, current affairs and documentaries is to convert all history, all 'knowledge' into the constant passage of the present tense and therefore into the world of drama: the 'drama' of the Kennedy assassination and its aftermath, carried 'live'. 'Interpretation' then becomes a matter not of social and historical analysis, but of 'balance' between carefully selected 'representative' (and always 'up-to-the-minute') viewpoints. So, Heath and Skirrow argue, what is technically specific to television — the possibility of the 'live' broadcast, the present electronic production of the image — actually becomes the alibi for its self-enclosure of knowledge and its 'proposition of the intelligible'.

This was the television ground rule of instantly reproducible, 'documentary' knowledge which — especially in the week of President Kennedy's assassination — the initial *Doctor Who* episode was working with and against. It was not just the 'everyday' reality (of school) of the target audience, but the everyday television reality (what the target audience does when *home* from school) that was the basis of the 'familiarity' out of which *Doctor Who* initially constructed its 'difference'.

Susan

After the 'normality' of children in school, two representative teachers meet at the end of a representatively 'terrible day' among the familiar test-tubes of the school science lab. But the daily events are there to introduce a mystery:

> *Ian*:   Susan Foreman — is she your problem too? You don't know what to make of her? Fifteen . . . she knows more science than I'll ever know!

Susan's other mystery — where does she come from? — is also revealed:

> *Barbara*: A big wall on one side, houses on the other and nothing in the middle. And this nothing in the middle is number 76 Totters Lane.

After establishing the mysterious 'absence' of her home and her character the narrative ostentatiously *reveals* Susan-as-spectacle. Reminiscent of the visual rhetoric of TV pop music shows, the camera tilts up and down her maturing body as she listens to the current electric guitar 'hit' on the radio. The transistor is a sign of 1960s youth culture, and Susan herself resembles one of the teenage 'pop' star products of that culture, Helen Shapiro. In contrast to this insistent contemporaneity, Susan's gesture, ostensibly motivating the camera movement, reveals a mysteriously 'different' teenager who follows the familiar beat of the music in very unfamiliar ways.

Contrasts of the 'familiar but different' now come thick and fast: the expected loan by the teachers of a large tome on the French Revolution which she says she will read in one evening; the conventional offer of a lift home which she refuses: 'I like walking in the dark — it's mysterious'; the ominous music and Susan's strange knowledge as she opens the book on the French Revolution; the flashbacks revealing Susan's mysterious understanding of time and space compared to Ian's constant resort to a 'rational' explanation and Barbara's hope that the mystery of 'walking in the dark' is the 'wonderfully normal' one of meeting a boy; the extreme close-up of Susan as a schoolgirl chewing sweets, juxtaposed with the close-up of a split skull, a premonition of the horrific 'cave of skulls' adventure to come.

The narrative is driven along by a constantly shifting series of puzzles, all premised on the same opposition between the banal and the unknown. And each new move is motivated by the tension established between acceptance of the everyday explanation (Ian's 'I take things as they come') and the schoolteacher's 'rational' desire to explore further: 'The truth is, we are both curious about Susan, and we won't be happy until we know all the answers.' But the programme — *Doctor Who*?

— will not supply the answers. Instead it will constantly turn puzzles into actions.

Junkyard

The 'junkyard' is a significant location in modern science fiction. Patrick Parrinder has noted that in recent SF it has come to represent a satirical comment on the technological utopianism and galactic imperialism of the earlier genre. The universe as 'an enormous junkyard' shows:

> The hopelessness of man's historical and biological situation. Technological determinism leads to the nightmare of a world of machines which is a stereotyped parody of the human world . . . Evolutionism, on the other hand, leads only to the nightmare of entropy — of the running-down universe in which everything is falling into disuse and decay.[14]

Recent science fiction has satirised the confident positivism of the nineteenth-century opposition between the universe as ordered machine open to human thought and the entropic universe. *Doctor Who's* 1981 story, 'Logopolis', draws on that opposition also — though here inflected in idealist terms, the universe is held together by the power of the human mind — and addresses the original H. G. Wellsian conflict between human mental power and material collapse more directly, reserving its satire for the Doctor's time machine rather than science in general.

In 'An Unearthly Child', too, the time machine in a junkyard draws on the Wellsian notion of human mental aspiration in the midst of the time-bound density of the mundane world.[15] But here the junkyard also signifies in a more specific way. It is the banal site of a greater mystery. Beyond the 'creepy' conventionality of its apparent mystery — its darkness, its skulls, its lurking places — there lies another mystery, defined only in contrast to the densely depicted world of the junkyard. The junkyard may consist of objects that connote 'mystery' — but in themselves they are concretely nominated.

This is a vase, that is an old picture frame which the Doctor picks up, and against which his own mystery and elusive character is evasively defined. It is that *interplay* between opaque behaviour and concretely defined objects which will mark the 'otherness' of *Doctor Who*; and it is a mark of Ian Chesterton's prosaic and 'commonsense' misunderstanding that he cannot recognise that definition of the 'other' lies in the articulation of opposites. For him here is a junkyard and there a scientific discovery, each containing an independent, substantive and essential meaning. In fact the Doctor is defined, from his first appearance, as 'other' in terms of what is already visually and aurally established. His clothes — an eccentrically stylish bricolage — locate him less in a particular milieu than in contrast to the cluttered and broken objects around him. And his signifying sound — the monotonously distancing Tardis hum — establishes his presence by negating the ominously rising musical scale of the 'junkyard' motif which had accompanied the 'mystery of Susan' sequences.

Tardis

From the beginning the Tardis was conceived as something concrete and familiar, fitting in naturally with its environment, and yet narratively defined as 'odd' and 'incongruous'.

> *Lambert*: Initially the Tardis was going to change its shape in relation to its surroundings — so that it could change into a tree or it could change into whatever on the outside. What happened was that we had a very small budget, and we couldn't afford to keep building new exteriors to the Tardis. But that turned out, I think, to be a positive advantage because there was a kind of incongruity of this police telephone box appearing in the French Revolution and the middle of Neanderthal man.

Even in its first and 'natural' location in London of 1963, it was important to make the familiar police box exude 'difference' (its unusual location, its hum), which Ian then tried to explain (his search for a hidden power source). This 'plausibility' coding not only defined *Doctor Who* in terms of what it was *not*, but also generated a constant series of puzzles and actions which enabled the serial never to investigate its own absence, Doctor Who?

For instance, as Ian and Barbara inspect first the junkyard and then the Tardis before the Doctor's arrival, the narrative draws on conventional codes of children's mystery and adventure tales to establish a puzzle. The Doctor is perhaps, in Ian's understanding, an evil old sorcerer, a Doctor Caligari, who has abducted Susan and hidden her in this cabinet. There is, in fact, a mystery in the box but the puzzle of the Tardis is not a matter of action-adventure coding at all, but a science fiction one: it is bigger on the inside than on the outside.

The desperate final resort to 'plausibility' of Ian and Barbara is that all is an illusion — some optical trick motivated by a psychological sickness on the part of Susan and the Doctor. But, of course, the Tardis is also a place where the Doctor holds people against their will — Ian and Barbara are themselves trapped there — and it is this constant displacement of the hermeneutic code by the proairetic, of the puzzle by the action, which, as a narrative strategy of the early *Doctor Who*, allows the Doctor's pseudo-explanation to suffice:

> You say you can't fit an enormous building into one of your small sitting rooms. But you've discovered television haven't you. Then, by showing an enormous building on your television screen, you can do what seemed impossible, couldn't you?

Television's own discourse of the world made intimate and instantaneous is deployed here to draw attention away from the 'plausible scientific explanation' which Verity Lambert says that she and Anthony Coburn tried but failed to find. In fact, it was precisely its refusal of 'realism' in explanation and its reliance on it in action, its shifting rhetoric of televisual codes ('police', 'document', 'pop', 'mystery adventure') in the search for 'science fiction', its status then as an 'absence' adhering to the conventional, that became the signature of the programme.[16]

This definition of the Doctor as 'absence' and 'mystery' was lost, Verity Lambert believes, when later producers provided him with a 'presence', a world of his own, on Gallifrey.

Lambert: I have never been particularly keen on the Time Lords actually, on actually seeing them. I just think it would have been better not to see them. I think some things are better kept as a mystery. I believe certain areas you should explain as little as possible.

Verity Lambert's success in explaining as little as possible depended on the 'success' of the narrative in continuously displacing the puzzle with the action, and thereby upholding the dominance of the hermeneutic — Doctor Who? — by never asking that question of him, but only of others whose puzzles and problems *he* resolved. The centrality of the Tardis as 'place', as signifying the 'other' world of the Doctor, was constantly displaced on to the worlds of action where it materialised, and where all the companions (Ian and Barbara as well as Susan and the Doctor) are 'other'. The importance of the Tardis as 'place' relates to the nature of *Doctor Who* as series: it provides a point of coherence, ritualised recognition and exchange in much the same way that the 'Rover's Return' does in *Coronation Street*. But it is a place which is constantly displaced as the Tardis materialises in a series of social terrains. This narrative strategy of displacing the hermeneutic 'place' to the world of action is typified in the first episode by the Doctor's response to Ian's bewilderment at the Tardis' interior: 'You don't deserve any explanation. You pushed your way in here uninvited and unwelcome', then, 'The point is not that you don't understand, but what is going to happen to you.' The alibi for the constant lack of understanding (Who is this Doctor? And what is the explanation of the Tardis?) was precisely the action-drive of his 'what's going to happen to you?' carried week after week, month after month, by the narrative's own 'lacks', its suspended enigmas ('cliffhangers') and its resolutions. In resolving this endlessly displaced series of puzzles, the Doctor's own mystery remained intact.

The Doctor

Every story enacts a tension between the setting of enigmas (who did the crime?) and their resolution. Our interest today is not so much in whether the Doctor will prevail, but in the detours and complications that the Master places along the way. Hence the hermeneutic code (of puzzles) organises the code of actions in the narrative. In addition, in a long-term series, as Richard Paterson and John Stewart point out,[17] an audience's acquired stock of knowledge gives it a competence in reading inflections and innuendos in particular narratives which are not specifically articulated, but rely on the 'memory' of the programme. Thus in 'Logopolis' the killing of the policeman by the Master outside a police box is both an obstacle to the Doctor and a reference back to 'An Unearthly Child'.

In the continuing stories of a series the narrative is also organised by other codes: sub-cultural codes — for instance, the Doctor's 'liberal' values of anti-violence and racial tolerance; and connotative codes, which determine the developing complication of the characters (actants) in the narrative.

The narrative 'character' is no more than a space containing a tension between expansion of meaning (for instance, the Doctor was initially represented as 'strange' then 'crochety', 'arrogant', 'absent-minded', 'caustic', 'nostalgic', 'gentle', 'whimsical', 'selfish', 'merciless') and repetition of meaning (the programme's repeated emphasis on the Doctor's intuitive quality which endlessly defeats the villains). In melodrama the expansion of meaning is usually in terms of repetition, in so far as 'villainy' is characterised by a series of actions which are metaphors for each other.[18] More 'serious' drama, on the other hand, is marked by a density, or even contradiction, of expansions generating the sense of 'reality', whereby the narrative is often motivated by internal inconsistencies and puzzles within the main characters themselves.

In its first episode, however, *Doctor Who* neither emphasised melodramatic repetition nor 'realist' expansion of character-meaning. And, as a first episode, it could not draw on its audience's stock of knowledge of individual character-texts to generate pleasurable or puzzling references to the programme's own past. Instead, it took seriously its own nomination — Doctor Who? — and allowed the hermeneutic code to dominate the narrative. Certainly the character of the Doctor was a space for expansion and repetition, but each expansion was at the same time a repetition of the fundamental 'mystery' coding. The Doctor's character development is not, in fact, delayed by his late entry into the narrative. It is composed in his absence by the repetition of the puzzle: what is the mystery in this everyday and banal environment? Successively the proairetic sequences unfold as a process of naming — 'the policeman', 'the school', 'Susan', 'the junkyard', 'the Tardis' — which is at the same time the nomination of difference — the mystery of the policeman, the school, Susan, the junkyard, the Tardis. The sequences are codified generically — 'police drama', 'document', 'pop', 'children's mystery adventure' — allowing for a visual rhetoric of 'differences', so that both visually (as a mode of address) and thematically the programme describes the Doctor as 'difference', 'mystery', 'absence' in his absence.

To some extent the Doctor's threat to the process of classification and naming was, as Lambert saw it, in his consciously anti-establishment character, which was lost (she believes at great cost) when Pertwee's Doctor became 'very moral, very upright, very dependable', and 'always ringing up heads of state'. So the concept of the Doctor as uncontradictory patriarch and law-giver was consciously avoided by the programme's first producer' and, as we have seen, she chose William Hartnell for the part to represent ambiguity and contradiction.

But more important than this positive identification was the definition of the Doctor as 'absence' before his arrival, and the displacement of his 'presence' when he did finally arrive into an eternity of adventures in space and time. His question inviting his own demystification: 'Have you ever thought what it's like to be travellers in the fourth dimension? To be exiles?', in fact, immediately becomes the action-filled future of the Earth companions. The question, 'exiles from where?' is displaced and answered in surrogate, as Ian and Barbara become exiles-in-action, and the 'mystery' becomes 'how to return them to their own time and space'.

The foregrounding and yet displacement of the enigma is also carried by the camera style. As well as the conventional mixture of camera set-ups (2-shots, 3-shots, small group shots combined with mid close-ups (MCU's) of single characters for dramatic effect), 'An Unearthly Child' deploys a particular repertoire to connote the mystery and difference of the unknown. This camera strategy consists of extreme close-ups (ECU's) of the Doctor and Susan, which, either by contrast via cuts (e.g. the first conversation between Ian in MCU and the Doctor in ECU) or by means of slow zooms in to ECU (especially in the sequences signifying the mystery of Susan) mark the time travellers as 'different'. Similarly, although the conventional shot/reverse shot style of editing is adhered to, with cuts motivated by dialogue, 'difference' is marked by slow zooms in to ECU's of objects and faces (e.g. Susan's eyes over the ECU of the book on the French Revolution) and by shifts from persons to objects, establishing mystery by contiguity and homology (as in the pan from the ECU of Susan chewing sweets in the junkyard to the ECU of a split skull).

The dominant visual strategy thus establishes the difference and 'otherness' of the Doctor and Susan in terms of contrast to the conventional camera style.[19] This camera rhetoric of 'difference' can then be borrowed for other characters where appropriate. Thus in the entire episode there is only one ECU of Barbara, when she is first amazed by the inside of the Tardis, and of Ian as he explains of Susan: 'Nothing about this girl makes sense!'

Once established, these markers of 'otherness' can be used to signify (without explaining) the absent world of the Doctor and Susan which, now immune from investigation, serves simply as a transition to the world of action — as we see at the end of episode one, where ECU's of Susan and the Doctor are superimposed over the repeated 'space/time' opening visuals, and are followed by a shot of the tilting and lonely Tardis in a new and alien world. As the mysterious hum of the Tardis is replaced by the 'realistic' windswept sound of a landscape on the edge of an ice age, an ominous humanoid shadow falls across the shot, acting as suspended enigma out of the episode, and signifying a new mystery in a new world of threat which it will be the task of the series to replicate continuously, thereby displacing endlessly the mystery of the Doctor and Susan.

This camera rhetoric, contrasting eyeline MCU's of Ian and Barbara with angled ECU's of Susan and the Doctor, also establishes the school-teachers as interrogators, interpreters (and guide) in pursuance of the mystery. This is signified not only by their narrative relationship with the Doctor and Susan but also by the visual register. Charlotte Brunsdon and Dave Morley note in their analysis of a current affairs programme a 'tendency to move in for bigger close-ups of subjects who are revealing their feelings, whereas the set-up for the . . . interviewer' is 'the breast-pocket shot'. The relation here is between what Stuart Hall calls 'the ideology of personalisation' which 'highlights the face and eyes, the most expressive parts of the body' as the 'truth' (the 'human point of the item') and the myth of the neutral observer 'in search of truth', named by the camera as our objective representative.[20]

In 'An Unearthly Child' the cuts from 'interviewer' MCU to 'expressive subject' ECU operate in a similar way, but here the 'essence' revealed is nothing other than 'mystery'. To Ian's question, in offering her a lift home, 'Where do you live?', Susan replies in ECU that she prefers to walk because 'It's mysterious'; to Ian's question as to what the dimensions are that prevent her doing her geometry problem in a normal way, the answers are 'Time' and, on a zoom in to ECU, 'Space'; to Barbara's interrogation insisting that she is a normal child, Susan replies in ECU 'I was born in another time, another world'; and to Ian's incredulous 'Your civilisation?' the Doctor replies in ECU that they are exiles, wanderers in the fourth dimension: 'Susan and I are cut off from our planet, without friends or protection. But one day, we shall go back. Yes, one day.'

Home

It is clear that what is being interrogated here is not simply a mysterious knowledge, but the lack of a home, and, in the odd asymmetry of grandfather and child, lack of a 'normal' family. Set in a family viewing slot, an initial 'difference' the programme reveals is the loss of domesticity. The absence which *Doctor Who* interrogates, the lack which it establishes, is only partly a 'science fiction' one. It is also that of the 'normal' home where the other school-children are going at the end of a 'normal' day. As 'responsible' teachers, *in loco parentis*, Ian and Barbara seek to restore — and indeed in their ensuing adventures themselves fill out — the sphere of domesticity and the unity of the family scene. In an important sense the enigma — Doctor Who? — is left open only because the action/adventure worlds are re-inscribed in terms of 'family life'.

The constant displacement of puzzle into action which upheld for years the original mystery — Doctor Who? — was legitimated and made 'responsible' by this 'parental' function, and by the 'schoolmasterly' discourse of the first episode — Ian-as-teacher-of-science constantly reiterating, 'There's got to be a simple explanation', and Barbara's condescending comment to the wayward child, 'Can't you see that this is all an illusion . . . It's a game that you . . . are playing.' Because in a sense the time travellers arbitrary materialisations were a game, and in the worlds of action that they visited Ian's 'simple' explanations were more plausible than in the 'absent' world of the Doctor.

The subverted 'rational' explanation is a familiar device of fantasy and horror; but in *Doctor Who* the role of the school-teachers as 'rational' and 'human' was also valorised by the action. It is Ian, for instance, who prevents the Doctor from selfishly and unpredictably killing a wounded cave man in episode three of the first story.

In things other than the mystery of the Doctor, the dis-course of school-teacher as hero often prevailed. Ian Chesterton was conceived as a hero — not simply because William Hartnell was old and unable to play an action lead, but also because, as Verity Lambert explained, the Doctor was in some ways an irresponsible and childish anti-hero. Symptomatically, a well-known television action-hero 'star', William Russell, was cast in the part of Ian.[21]

If the Doctor was anti-establishment, like the imputed audience, so too was he childish, like the audience, and a dominant discourse of the programme was to lead him away from an immature solipsism, guided by the parent/teachers, to a galactic responsibility. The 'lack' in his character, represented in the first episode, where, as Verity Lambert puts it, 'In a *totally* irresponsible way he takes away these two people that he knows he has no means of actually getting . . . back again', is redressed by the good that he does in the universe, through the agency and persuasion of the school-teachers. And eventually, after the Daleks are defeated for a third time, and not only the Earth has been rescued, but the Doctor himself has been saved from the ultimate solipsism of being an external exhibit in a space museum. Ian and Barbara return to their home, their task of educating the Doctor to maturity and responsibility apparently over.

On the one hand, then, *Doctor Who* operated as a distinctive television discourse of regularity and flow,[22] similarity and difference, constructing its special status as 'science fiction mystery' as an absence/displacement of television's 'here and now' (whether as 'factual' document or as a fictional succession of genres). On the other hand, this difference in *Doctor Who*, first located safely in terms of television discourse, was then confidently tied down within the institutionalised and paternalistic pedagogy of the BBC.

Education and entertainment: 'Doctor Who' as BBC institution

Audiences outside Britain often comment that *Doctor Who* is 'very British, very BBC'. The Doctor is frequently described as 'very much the English gentleman', while one Australian academic described the programme as somehow revealing the last dilettante farewell of a ruling class culture.[23]

Doctor Who is, of course, a BBC institution — its longest running television series. But it is also part of the BBC as institution — and the BBC has for much of its history been deeply implicated in the transmission of British ruling culture. As Raymond Williams says, by the time of the establishment of the BBC in the 1920s as a public broadcasting corporation:

A dominant version of the national culture had already

been established, in an unusually compact ruling-class, so
that public service could be effectively understood and
administered as service according to the values of an existing public definition, with an effective paternalist definition
of both service and responsibility.[24]

The nature of appointment was by delegation from above,
rather than by any kind of public debate or election (either
within the BBC by producers and other broadcasters, or outside the Corporation). This ensured that a notion of 'national
interest' defined in terms of a pre-existing cultural hegemony
was maintained, even while allowing for a greater flexibility
within the BBC in relation to short-term party interests than
some European state-controlled broadcasting systems achieved.

As Williams points out, the secret of the BBC's 'autonomy'
from direct political control has been its appeal to a public
'consensus'.

It depends, finally, on a consensus version of the 'public'
or 'national' interest: a consensus which is first assumed
and then vigorously practised, rather than a consensus
which has ever been openly arrived at and made subject to
regular open review.[25]

A major feature of the ruling cultural hegemony was the
notion that the BBC existed — not to disclose class contradictions — but to narrow the 'cultural' gap that existed between
the élite and the masses. As former BBC producer, Krishnan
Kumar observes, in the early days the current emphasis on
'professionalism' as the prime virtue of a broadcaster was by
no means so dominant:

In the time of Reith at the BBC . . . professional skills
would have been assumed and cultivated. But there would
never have been any question but these technical skills
should be quite subordinate to the overriding goals of the
BBC as Reith had conceived them: the goals of lifting the
British nation to new moral and cultural heights.[26]

As Kumar argues, a new institutional space was carved out in British society. Unlike broadcasting organisations in almost any other country in the world, the BBC came to be 'thought of in terms usually reserved for the venerable institutions . . . Parliament, the Civil Service, the Law Courts, the colleges of Cambridge and Oxford'. The BBC achieved this institutional status by clearly demarcating its 'place'. It avoided political controversy (generally giving way when it became embroiled in it, as over the General Strike of 1926); and it avoided economic controversy by agreeing not to compete with the commercial press in news-gathering.

The BBC's place as 'national institution' was to be in the domain of 'Culture'.

Reith interpreted the injunction of the BBC's Charter, to inform, educate, and entertain fully in the spirit of Matthew Arnold. It was through its classical music, plays, poetry, talks, discussions — as well as its comedies, reviews and dance music — that the BBC established itself as a distinctive and finally authoritative national cultural institution.[27]

The 'popular' was included in the bill of fare to lure the 'mass' into the broadcasting channels which would then educate them into the 'Cultural'. This self-conscious centrality of the BBC as a national institution has been 'the source at once of its proverbial caution and conservatism, as well as of its need and ability to fend off identification with the other national institutions'.[28]

One symptom of its concern for the 'Cultural' and separation of its identity from the 'lowbrow', was the BBC educational section's concentration on children's 'classics'. Programming of this kind was part of the BBC's self conscious centrality as a national institution. The transmission to children of 'Britain's heritage' — in terms of its distinctive imperial history and literature — has often been a source of especially bitter hegemonic struggle between ruling class and 'mass' commercial interests. In Australia in the 1920s, for instance, it became the subject of extremely contentious debate at a Royal Commission into the American 'take-over' of the cinema industry, which was threatening, it was said, the proper education of

'British' children. Girton-educated Beatrice Tildesley complained of children being exposed to films by 'wholesale clothiers who have extended their energies from the purveying of reach-me-down suits to the providing of drag-me-down entertainment'; while conservative women's associations called for state intervention to ensure the exhibition for children of films out of Britain's heritage: of 'great lives' and 'good books', such as Nelson, Rudyard Kipling and *Puck of Pook's Hill*.[29]

That tradition of 'good' literature on film and television was still upheld at the BBC in 1963, but the position of the BBC as a British national institution was beginning to change. Its control over national broadcasting had been lost in 1955 with the establishment, under American advertising pressure, of a British commercial television channel. BBC audience figures were to slump by the late 1950s to 27 per cent compared to ITV's 73 per cent. The result was, as Sir Hugh Greene, Director General of the BBC later described it, that 'the BBC had to become more competitive and had to shake off a lot of its old-fashioned ways'.[30] The more competitive responses tended to come from the less conservative departments. The BBC had established a world-wide reputation for the 'accuracy' of its news, and for its 'Cultural' leadership enshrined for adults in the concept of the Third Programme (now, Radio Three) and for children in its 'classics' oriented children's department. Kumar observed that:

> Characteristically the breakthrough in the BBC came not from the conservative news division but from the new 'Current Affairs' complex, with the launching in 1957 of *Tonight*, a topical daily programme with a magazine format that won great popularity, and whose form was instrumental in shaping a whole new range of news and current affairs programmes.[31]

Similarly the new and quickly successful concept in children's programming, *Doctor Who*, came not from the conservative children's department but from the drama department with its new head, recently appointed from ITV, Sydney Newman. With him he brought other commercial television personnel, including the first producer of *Doctor Who*, Verity Lambert.

> *Lambert*:   I think that Sydney felt that children's drama
> was very firmly based in a certain area which was drama-
> tisations of children's books, and it was perhaps slightly
> old-fashioned. He was trying to find something which took
> into account the new things that fascinated kids, like space
> and other planets, and certainly he felt that he wanted a
> programme which, while not necessarily educational as
> such, was one which children could look at and learn
> something from. In the futuristic stories they could learn
> something about science and in the past stories they could
> learn something about history in an entertainment format.

This was very close in conception to Alasdair Milne's notion
of *Tonight*, when he argued that in a new competitive age the
programme set out to 'entertain in order to inform'.[32]

Despite wanting to pick up audiences which ITV's successful *Robin Hood, Ivanhoe, William Tell* and *Rob Roy* had
established,[33] the BBC's 'cultural' and 'educational' hallmark
was certainty not lost, even if now located within a new
'more competitive', framework. Indeed 'education' was the
source of *Doctor Who*'s determinedly pedagogic discourse.

'Doctor Who' and education

> *Lambert*:   *Ivanhoe* and *Rob Roy* and all those sorts of
> things were very much in the children's classic series or
> series/serials slot, which still goes on. We tried to approach
> it slightly differently, because we really did try to approach
> it accurately from an historical point of view. So that
> when we took something like Marco Polo . . . the only
> thing that was inaccurate in it was the presence of our
> good people. But the actual things that happened within
> the story were historically accurate, and we spent a lot of
> time and trouble making sure that they were. What was
> fulfilling was that we did get a lot of letters from teachers
> saying . . . that they were very grateful that we were not
> trying to bend history.

At the beginning *Doctor Who* was seriously concerned with helping to teach history[34] and science. It was no coincidence that two of the first four main characters were teachers — of history and science — that another was their pupil who had a superior knowledge in each of these two areas, and that the fourth, the Doctor was there to teach them all the value of open-minded enquiry. Like *The Eagle* comic of the previous decade, which is likely to have been in Newman's mind as an example, *Doctor Who* sought to entertain in a 'responsible' and educative way; and also like *The Eagle* (which was the only comic allowed in many state schools of the 1950s), it drew much of its public legitimacy from the published authority of the state's educators.

Twenty years later, *Doctor Who*'s producer was still adopting this 'responsible' approach to history and education. At the end of 'The Visitation' (1982), the Doctor has a fight with terileptils, and these are burnt to death when a gun explodes and starts a fire.

Nathan-Turner: The Doctor jumps into his Tardis, and the last image we have is of the Tardis disappearing revealing the sign 'Pudding Lane'. So actually I think we *have* distorted history, but only to people who are intelligent enough not to be confused by it. I think that if the Doctor had said, 'That's the start of the Great Fire of London', that would be very dangerous for the younger viewers. But because it is something that adults can draw from, it is acceptable . . . It's a wry smile at the end of the thing.

The problem of science 'education' through *Doctor Who* has proved more difficult. The programme has not been surrounded by the plethora of professional and university scientists that the early science fiction magazines in the USA had on their editorial boards.

Producer Graham Williams admitted that 'our general knowledge about science is pretty peripheral . . . only a couple of steps out of *The Reader's Digest*'.[35] But the general policy has been as script editor Terrance Dicks put it, that: 'You don't make childish errors in atomic structure or molecular theory or anything like that because although 90% of the audience won't know, the other 10% will, and the whole show will lose credibility.'

To an important degree *Doctor Who* has avoided the 'science as education' problem by drawing on the 'soft' socio-cultural scientific speculation associated with its Wellsian time-travel model. This tended to direct *Doctor Who* towards the investigation of different cultures through space and time, rather than seeking an involvement with hard science and this was why the first episode was documented 'Britain 1963'. It was an established point in time from which to go forward and back.

Just as Wells's original *The Time Machine* was based in his own period, and was his projection of what he saw as unhealthy contemporary problems into a catastrophically divided and exploitative future society, so the original Daleks represented the extrapolation of contemporary militaristic, racist and illiberal obsessions into a terrible future mutation. The contrast in *Doctor Who*'s first 'future-science' world, between the evilly warped intelligence of the Daleks and the Thals who were represented as 'tall, blond, blue-eyed . . . Aryan symbols of racial purity',[36] evoked a Nazi problematic which is familiar in popular science fiction, and which the creator of the Daleks, Terry Nation, has consciously pursued in the programme ever since. But the deeper theme, spoken by Ian Chesterton in that first 'science' story — 'A dislike for the unlike . . . They're afraid of you because you're different from them' — is of a 'responsible' cultural perspectivism. As a long-running institution *Doctor Who* has consistently sympathised with the sentiments of Mena in the 1980 story, 'The Leisure Hive', when she explains the purpose of their games to the Doctor:

Mena: The purpose is to promote understanding between life forms of all cultural and genetic types. There must be no more such wars . . . Even the games and our experiential grid explore alien environments. Each race learns to understand what it is like to be the foreigner.

As a 'responsible' and 'quality' children's programme from its first inception, *Doctor Who* has drawn on 'soft' socio-cultural

SF to promote its liberal discourse of 'tolerance' and 'balance' against the militaristic tendencies of the Bug Eyes Monster (BEM) syndrome.

Nevertheless, the new competitive position of the BBC and Verity Lambert's self-confessed lack of a 'scientific mind', ensured that the BEM syndrome did get in.

Lambert: Sydney Newman, when I first did the Daleks, was absolutely furious with me, because the one thing he'd said to me was 'I don't want any BEM's.' When the Daleks came up there was a *kind* of scientific factor of this planet having been radiated and the Daleks having to build these machines to put around them in order to move because they had been so seriously mutilated by the effects of radiation. But when it came to anything more complicated than that I was just lost. We did *try* to put some kind of scientific thing in, but the stories were much more purely entertainment I think than science.

However, the embattled position of the BBC meant that 'entertainment', even without 'education', was allowed to prevail in the scientific stories. A 'balance' could, after all, be maintained by upholding education in the alternating historical stories. Though Donald Wilson, head of series/serials, also hated the Dalek story, Lambert went ahead on the grounds that the next planned story, 'Marco Polo', was not ready.

Lambert: At this point everything seemed to be very expensive because we were starting off, and you have to amortise costs. I think the BBC just got very,very nervous and said, 'What is this peculiar thing which seems to be costing a lot of money and doesn't seem to be really good? So we will stop it.' They wanted to stop it after the first eight, and I said, 'You can't stop it after the first eight because this is a seven part serial', and there was a sort of moment when it hung in the balance. But we recorded quite close to our time of transmission. We were only, I think, about two weeks behind. So the first Dalek one went on, and by the second Dalek episode it was an absolute runaway success, and the BBC said, 'Well, right — go on.'

At that point Verity Lambert was also having problems with the BBC Visual Effects Department, who refused to work on *Doctor Who* in protest at the influx of commercial television personnel, with the result that the Daleks were made by an outside firm.

In its early days *Doctor Who* was negotiating new and difficult terrain in terms of BBC children's television — with a stress on science fiction 'entertainment' under the guidance of 'commercialising' Sydney Newman, but incorporating the BBC's traditional concern for 'education', which Newman himself clearly took seriously. Given the concern to be 'serious' about science, and the limitations on doing so, it was perhaps inevitable that *Doctor Who* should draw, consciously or otherwise, on conventions from a preceding children's science fiction institution, 'Dan Dare' of *The Eagle* comic. Although the negotiation of a terrain that was at once 'cultural' and 'competitive' was new to BBC children's programming, it was not new in the broader world of children's popular culture.

Responsible entertainment: 'Dan Dare' and 'Doctor Who'

Many of *Doctor Who*'s young adult audience in 1963 are likely to have been addicts of 'Dan Dare' in the previous decade. Like the *Doctor Who* of the 1960s, *The Eagle* comic of the 1950s brought together a serious educational design — much praised by teachers — with a new science fiction adventure format in its lead feature, 'Dan Dare, Pilot of the Future'. Although 'Dan Dare' was mainly Vernian-type 'boys' adventure' in space, ocean and underground, its narratives were combined with 'hard science' blueprints,[37] and augmented by *The Eagle*'s other main colour strip: the historical 'Great Men' series. This juxtaposed the themes of Christian heroes (like St Paul and St Patrick) with heroes of British imperialism (like Winston Churchill), while others, like David Livingstone, quite overtly combined the two.

As well as being 'responsible' and 'educational' *The Eagle* was also, like *Doctor Who*, a phenomenal 'entertainment' and marketing success with sales and merchandising royalties of £1 million a year. Of the commercial marketing of 'Dan Dare', James Slattery writes:

> The young fanatic could skip out of his Dan Dare pyjamas, into his Dan Dare slippers and dressing gown, brush his teeth with Calvert's Dan Dare toothpaste, all before checking that it was time (on his Dan Dare watch) to kit up in his Dan Dare T-shirt, belt, scarf, spacesuit, etc.[38]

Similarly, Jeremy Bentham writes of the mid-1960s *Doctor Who* fan:

> Awake in bedroom decorated in Dalek wallpaper. Put on Dalek slippers (Furness Footwear Ltd) and go to bathroom to wash with Dalek soap (Northants Assoc for the Blind). Do daily exercises with inflatable Dalek (Scorpion toys) as punchbag before setting off for school sporting Dalek mini-badge (Woolworths) on jumper.[39]

During the rest of the day the young fan could happily purchase and consume Dalek comics, books, sweet cigarettes, records, slide shows, and so on and on.

These two 'similar but different' accounts simply represent the formula of the commercial exploitation of leisure, and the recognition of consumer spending in the new-found 'youth culture' in the years after the post-war austerity. 'Dalekmania' replaced the marketing of Dan Dare, and by mid-1966 the Daleks themselves were being replaced by *Batman* and *The Man from UNCLE* as heroes of the toyshop.

'Dan Dare' and *Doctor Who* also had a unique similarity as national institutions. Each quickly became famous for drawing in differentiated (and frequently 'prestigious') audience groups — Slattery's claim that 'Cabinet ministers along with Rhondda Valley schoolboys' read 'Dan Dare' was supported by medical scientist Kit Pedler, who said that his hospital hierarchy discussed each storyline in detail.

Later Kit Pedler was to create *Doctor Who*'s other successful mechanical monsters (after the Daleks), the Cybermen, and these physically resembled the Mekon's electrobots in the 1957 Dan Dare 'Reign of the Robots' story. Pedler makes the link between 'Dan Dare' and *Doctor Who* quite specifically:

> The first television writing I did while I was still an academic was for *Doctor Who* and during the creation of twenty-four episodes I invented some monstrous creatures called the Cybermen . . . At the time I was obsessed as a scientist by the differences and similarities between the human brain and advanced computer machines and I was thinking that although I could easily imagine a logical machine reasoning to itself and manipulating events outside it, by no stretch of the imagination could I visualise a machine producing a poem by Dylan Thomas. And so the Cybermen appeared. They were an ancient race on a dying planet who had made themselves immortal by gradually replacing their worn out organs and limbs with cybernetic spare parts. They had become strong in the process and always behaved logically, but had lost their feelings and humanity as they became more and more machine driven – very much like the Treens and Mekon against whom Dan and Co waged their longest battle.[40]

In the absence of a 'serious' science, the emphasis on human values and aspirations *against* the mechanistic rationalism of science was taken over as a central theme of *Doctor Who* from its predecessor. So, in the first 'Dan Dare' story, in August 1951, Dare tells the assembled Earth leaders:

> It is true that the Treens have gone way ahead of us scientifically. But on the way they've lost quite a lot of qualities we value . . . Our illogical human love of things for their own sake, and not for their practical value – the impulse that makes a man sail a yacht in a world of diesel engines. Or ride a horse in a world of motor cars – the love of silent soaring flight that makes a pilot fly a glider when he could have a jet.

And in the 1982 *Doctor Who* story 'Earthshock' the Doctor
tells the completely logical Cybermen:

> Emotions . . . enhance life. When did you last have the
> pleasure of smelling a flower, watching a sunset . . . For
> some people small, beautiful events are what life is all
> about.

The aestheticism and moralism of this position — Pedler's
'poetry' against 'logical machine reason' — is a familiar one in
science fiction, and derives (as described more fully later)
from the influence of Romantic discourse on the genre. As
David Morse has shown, the Romantic discourse laid waste
the Lockeian sense of a human consciousness based mechan-
istically on sense impressions — the abject empiricism to which
the Doctor refers in 'Time Flight' (1982) as 'To be is to be
perceived — a naïve eighteenth-century philosophy.'

> Locke's stress on empirical processes of learning, whereby
> similar influences could be expected to have the same
> effects in all circumstances and all contexts . . . made the
> idea of the individual seem paradoxical . . . for the produc-
> tion of knowledge could only make difference or idiosyn-
> crasy appear as some kind of defect or fault.[41]

It is for this human 'difference' and idiosyncrasy, of course,
that the Mekon derides Dan Dare, and the Master sneers at
the Doctor's 'predilection for the second-rate'. And it is this
same 'human' idiosyncrasy which always defeats the mechan-
istically rational villains. It is precisely because Dare and the
Doctor are fallible that the narrative grants them, as the
Romantic discourse insisted, the possibility of being individual
— and therefore the potential to defeat bureaucratic rationalism. This celebration of the 'human' as spontaneous, fallible,
arbitrary and idiosyncratic was the position of Sterne, Blake
and other Romantics long before it was that of Dan Dare and
the Doctor, whose appeal to the 'illogical' and 'poetic' human
love of things for their own sake was directly prefigured by
Blake's rejection of neo-classical rationalism which destroyed

the 'uniqueness and singularity of every object in the universe'.[42] The concept of the subject in process, endlessly responding and maturing in relation to his experiences — the concept which above all defines the Doctor — now opposed that of the subject authoritatively and finally located in the universe of reason.

And that debate, as Morse notes, was over: 'The way in which the individual's concern for himself, his freedom and capacity for self-realisation are bound up with a cosmic struggle against abstract principles of universality, which are themselves a means of oppression'.[43] Once relocated in the nineteenth-century SF genre, this discourse could easily be deployed in socially moralistic narratives: renegotiated for instance in terms of Britain's crumbling Empire in *The Eagle* in 1950, and the BBC's crumbling hegemony in *Doctor Who* in 1963.

The distinction between 'logic' and 'poetry' which Pedler found alike in 'Dan Dare' and *Doctor Who* is, then, not surprising: it was deeply determined by science fiction's Romantic discourse. But as well as these similarities, there were crucial differences too between 'Dan Dare' and *Doctor Who*. Despite his distinction between machine logic and human poetry, the hero that Pedler admired in *The Eagle* could never, as he admitted, ever have been a poet, as the Doctor claimed to be in helping Shakespeare with the prose style of *Hamlet*. As Pedler said, 'Someone called Dan Dare just has to have a bounding, masculine, clean-cut charisma and could not possibly be a tweed-suited poet with a floppy bow-tie.'[44] And it is the latter, not the former, which has been the image of the Doctor. Dare was always an *insider*, with the code of honour and refusal to lie that was the mark of the English ruling 'Public School' culture. The Doctor, in contrast, was (from his first conception in the *Doctor Who* pilot episode)[45] an alien, an outsider, with an egocentric and often solipsistic aestheticism that was especially marked in his first story.

Whatever the generic similarities, Dan Dare and the Doctor were located in different historical conjunctures, and in particular in the different circumstances of their respective mass entertainment forms.

'The Eagle': commerce and Christianity

The Eagle, which was born in 1950, combined a 'United Nations' inflection of the British imperial ideal with Protestant evangelism. It was founded by the Rev Marcus Morris as a successor to his low circulation Christian magazine The Anvil, with the idea of increasing his flock through the agencies of monopoly capital and science fiction. Looking for a more effective voice for his 'Society for Christian Publicity', Morris decided on carrying the message through an exciting strip cartoon comic with 'professional' production values. At one point in the deliberation, Dan Dare was to be a 'trouble-shooting flying padre', but this was thought to be too close to The Anvil's direct preaching, and the 'clean-cut space colonel' appeared instead.

The concept was sold to Hulton Press (later taken over and merged with the IPC combine), but the original Protestant emphasis was not lost. The 'Eagle' title and insignia were taken from the eagle lecterns in Anglical churches, and the back cover story — balancing in colour the new SF front cover — began as a series of long-running Biblical and Christian 'Great Adventures'. Dan Dare himself — and his space fleet controller, Sir Hubert Guest who called on the world to pray when threatened with destruction[46] — was a Protestant hero of action, dramatising in numerous narratives the values which The Eagle spelt out in its moralising editorials.[47]

Overt Christian moralising is nothing new to SF: its founding Romantic discourse was historically conjoined, as Morse notes, with Protestantism. However, what differentiates The Eagle from what went before or after it, was its insertion in the culture of post-imperial, austerity Britain.

The new, post-war 'UN'/'world government' image of order and consensus in the early Dare stories is laid directly on top of the iconography of Britain's imperial past — not only in the fusion of 'Agincourt' mythology with that of the Mounties and the Sikhs in the first great battle with the Treens, but also in the assumption that the struggle against dictatorship is to preserve 'typical' English culture as represented by the village cricket match (overlooked by its Anglican church and squireochracy) between Nether Wallop and Picrust Parva still taking place just before the battle in 1996. Here the generic theme of 'human' emotional wholeness and brotherhood against 'alien' rationalism and exploitation is inflected in terms of the 'natural' bond between comical Hampshire villagers and their gentry.

The Eagle located its heroes very much in terms of the Second World War and the effect this had on Britain as a world power. There was much talk in 'Dan Dare' of the failure of 'appeasement', and the iconography of space battles tended to be that of the Battle of Britain (the recently updated Agincourt theme) with space cruisers weaving like fighters in aerial dog fights, and the hero's call of 'beware raiders diving out of the sun'. While Hitler was shrieking on the back page of *The Eagle* in 'The Happy Warrior' (the story of Winston Churchill) 'We will conquer Europe, Asia, the World! The hour is at hand', on the front page the Mekon, having already conquered the world, was coolly telling Dan Dare:

> *Nothing* matters but power . . . To use it all, I must possess all! First the planets, then beyond, and beyond — and *beyond.*

Only Winston Churchill and Dan Dare stood In their way. And while David Livingstone was protecting the innocent blacks of Africa from slave traders in order 'to make an open path for commerce and Christianity' on the back page, Dan Dare was freeing the innocent, peace-loving Mercurians from Treen slave labour on the front.

A special feature on the Duke of Edinburgh — 'Our Sportsman Prince'[48] — as 'All-Round Cricketer', 'Sailing Helmsman' and 'Polo Pivot', bound together the 'healthy' Protestant action and 'Empire and Monarchy' orientation of *The Eagle* in precisely the terms that Dan Dare (whom the Prince resembled uncomfortable closely in his lead photograph) offers as the true 'human' qualities that will defeat the Treens:

> Our illogical human love of things for their own sake and not for their practical value — the impulse that makes a man sail a yacht in a world of diesel engines. Or ride a horse in a world of motor cars . . . Our 'waste of time'

indulging in sports for the sheer fun of it — these are out
trump cards now.[49]

The Bournemouth cricket ground where the Duke is shown
leading out his team to play Hampshire is only a few miles —
ideologically as well as geographically — from Dan Dare's
Nether Wallop.

The relationship between British SF and imperial decline
has been noted by various writers.[50] But in contrasting this
generic specificity with SF in other countries at the time, it
is important to consider the particular institutional insertion
of SF in popular culture forms. In the case of *The Eagle* this
was to be mass circulation Protestant proselytism inscribed as
peculiarly 'British' — *The Eagle* was to be 'a Rolls Royce
among rusty old bicycles'[51] — and defined in terms of the
'missionary' zeal of Empire. It relied on an appeal to a 'lived
consensus', which for Marcus Morris was gloriously marked
by the moment (celebrated by a special colour spread in *The
Eagle*) where the head of the Protestant church in England
invested the new Queen 'of the Commonwealth and Empire'.
Morris's message to his readers as 'the Queen's young protect-
ors' was 'keep the old Union Jacks flying', shout their allegi-
ance and remember their good fortune in having, in addition
to the Queen, 'as first gentleman in the land HRH The Duke
of Edinburgh, a keen and first class all-round sportsman'.[52]
By 1963, when *Doctor Who* was born, that sense of a ruling
class cultural consensus which *The Eagle* drew on so readily,
was in crisis.

'Doctor Who': BBC populism

By the 1960s, as Kumar says:

> Politicians, moralists and sociologists on all sides were
> talking about the break-up of 'the consensus' that had
> been the underlying force in the stability of the political
> and social system — and so of the BBC — up to the end of
> the 1950s. Whether or not such a consensus existed and if
> so, whether or not it has broken up . . . the point is that

the BBC believed it, along with many others. This meant that it could no longer speak to the one great national audience in the same firm and rather aloof manner that it had adopted for so long.[53]

The notion of 'Cultural' leadership depended on that idea of national 'consensus', and with its loss a new terrain had to be negotiated. Facing a consciously sectionalised audience, with often contradictory demands, the BBC now appealed to a 'professional' rather than moral image. The BBC was now, in the words of David Attenborough, Director of Television Programmes: 'To be like a theatre in the middle of a town, and the broadcasters . . . are part of the theatre staff. And it's the job of that staff to find from society . . . a whole selection of voices . . . and to enable those voices to be heard in that theatre.'[54] As Kumar argues:

> More than ever before the BBC cannot afford to be identi-
> fied with any sectional interest in the society – even some-
> ting as indefinite as 'high culture . . . What keeps it on an
> even keel, increasingly, is the 'management' function per-
> formed by the professional broadcasters. It is in their
> stance, through their style and presentation, that the BBC
> tries to keep its autonomy and ward off the clutching
> embraces from all around.[55]

The BBC must therefore air the 'voices' of 'Left' and 'Right' (within a now much broader and vaguer notion of 'democratic' consensus), but must not be seen to stand *for* any of these voices. It has favoured a general 'populist' stance against the big forces of 'Left' ('the unions') and 'Right' ('unscrupulous' big business, fascism, etc.) and its new champions of institutional 'neutrality' are the presenters with whom audiences are expected to identify. Their sceptically aggressive attitude towards the 'official' leaders whose arguments they present has become the hallmark of the BBC's 'integrity'.

The BBC handbook defined this new presentational style in its successful *Tonight* programme as 'quizzical, amused, slightly sceptical'; and Kumar notes that his compound of 'aggressiveness, scepticism, irony and detachment' has been carried over as the presentational mode of nearly all the BBC's new heroes of 'factual' discourse — the presenters, the 'link-men', the chairmen of live discussions, the regular anchor men. But what has not been noticed is that the BBC's new hero of 'fiction' — in the science fiction programme comparable in its 'breakthrough' qualities with *Tonight — Doctor Who*, was constructed in terms of those same quizzical, amused, sceptical, aggressive ironic and detached qualities. Whereas the 'Romantic' inflection of the Doctor's persona has varied in its force over the years, he has consistently adopted exactly that liberal-populist role in criticising 'sectionalist' forces of 'Left' and 'Right', and in rebuking the 'official' and the powerful, whether in big business, the military, government or 'militant' unions. That is possibly why Verity Lambert intuitively was uneasy with the third Doctor who lost his 'anti-establishment' character and was at risk of becoming identified with the needs of the military and government.

David Attenborough's 'theatre' metaphor was well chosen, because the role in current affairs programmes of the 'neutral' presenter is primarily a dramatic one. By orchestrating conflict between representatives of preconceived 'opposite' positions, or by 'devil's advocate' questions to single celebrities, his (and it usually is 'his') role has been continually to invoke the 'drama' of public life. 'Conflict', when it works in these terms, is synonymous in the professional discourse with 'good television'. 'Realism' in the television industry correlates with the dramatic juxtaposition of opposing 'points of view'.

Doctor Who operates 'politically' on an identical principle. In discussing 'The Monster of Peladon', a 1974 *Doctor Who* story which — in the year of the British miners' union confrontation with the Heath government — had the Doctor discussing miners' 'grievances' and siding with the 'moderates' against both the 'hot-heads' and the upper class, producer Barry Letts and script editor Terrance Dicks clearly revealed the implicit connection between the breakdown of the imperial consensus, the new 'neutral'/'realistic' role of the BBC professional, and the 'drama' of conflict.

Dicks: We weren't making a direct comment on the miners' strike that was happening in real life. We couldn't because it wasn't our place to. But obviously that kind of issue was in the air, and . . . you can't just do a kind of old imperial story whereby the galactic federation is coming to Peladon and is bringing the simple natives the benefits of civilisation, like *Sanders of the River* bringing law and order to Africa. This isn't how people think anymore, and you can't do a story like that, even with a children's adventure story or a family adventure serial. We are all well aware now that what happens when an advanced race meets a primitive race is not always to the benefit of the primitives. So you have got the conflict of the different factions. It is simply a kind of realism. Obviously the miners would resist the technology because it wouldn't be what they were used to and they would be frightened by it and it might put some of them out of work . . . Obviously the ruling establishment would try and latch on to the technology and try and see what benefits were going to come from civilisation . . . This is the kind of thing that now happens in real life.

Letts: Drama is concerned with conflict between people, and if it becomes mechanical and it's only a plot situation with cardboard characters . . . the whole thing falls right down . . . It is very easy when one is thinking of stories for a long-running series like this to slip into the stereotypes, slip into the clichés of story-telling, and especially science fiction story-telling. It is very useful and very helpful, quite apart from showing a certain amount of integrity, to relate it to what is going on in real life . . . It's a realism. It's saying what does actually happen.

When confronted with the argument that this was a *view* of 'realism' Barry Letts conceded the point, and tied it into the general position of 'creative' people at the BBC.

Letts: Ultimately it is *our* view and the writer who was working with us. Obviously . . . each incarnation of the Doctor . . . will reflect the personalities of the producer and the script editor concerned . . . I agree with what Terrance is saying, but what he is not admitting is that to

take that position is in fact to take a political position . . .
If you get a collection of intelligent . . . people together,
especially creative people, they will tend to be liberal/left
of centre, because that is the most intelligent position to
take . . . So to be extreme is automatically to put oneself
in an almost indefensible position, in my opinion.

Terrance Dicks, while preferring to call his position 'realist'
rather than 'political', also supported the creative BBC position of standing between (and in the case of 'The Monster of
Peladon' orchestrating) the 'tragic' drama of extremes. And
this was, as he saw it, precisely the position of the Doctor
too.[56]

> *Dicks*: I would say it is a kind of general liberal consensus
> that in any strike there are rights and wrongs on both sides
> . . . It is never heroic capitalist against strikers, and it is
> never heroic strikers against evil capitalists. You have got
> two parties with conflicting opinions, and there is always
> right on both sides. That is the tragedy of it really. On
> Peladon the high priest wanted to preserve the old ways,
> and the leader of the miners wanted to look after his
> people . . . The tragedy is that they both think that they
> are right, and they both think the other person is totally
> wrong. And the Doctor is very much a person who can
> step back. The Doctor always plays this role.

While we would question Dicks' views on 'realism' it is clear
that the Doctor as 'neutral' presenter was symptomatic of the
BBC's new (and competitively induced) 'integrity'.

Spanning the audience

Doctor Who then, contained an appropriate and familiar (yet
mysteriously unfamiliar) hero of the BBC in the particular
conjuncture of the 1960s, when the Corporation was faced
by competition from commercial television and the breakdown of its legitimising consensus. As a 'space and time'
character, he was 'new' and competitive in ratings terms. And

yet, like the BBC itself, he could 'step back' from (and at the same time orchestrate) the 'tragic' drama of conflict. As with the BBC presenters, this position could allow 'safe' entry into the dangerously sectionalised world of the 'social' and 'political' — which is one reason perhaps for *Doctor Who* being taken as a 'serious' programme, attracting an adult as well as child audience.[57] Another reason was that the genre of science fiction itself provided an appropriately conventional format for its BBC debate of democratic liberalism and cultural perspectivism.

A third reason was more specific to the debate about 'children's television' within the BBC. In selecting Verity Lambert as the new producer for the show, Sydney Newman was replacing one concept of 'high culture' (that traditionally associated with 'children's classics' and the old moral 'consensus') with another, deriving from the now residual category of 'serious drama' with which both ITV and the BBC now marked the permanently sectionalised nature of their audience. Verity Lambert came to *Doctor Who* straight from ITV's prestigious *Armchair Theatre*. But though in an historical sense residual, 'serious' drama was still associated with 'cultural prestige' (now representing for the BBC its new policy of 'balance' and for commercial TV a guarantee of franchise renewal) and carried with it very different conditions of production and notions of audience 'competence' than *Doctor Who*. The transition for Verity Lambert was not easy and influenced what *Doctor Who* became. Lambert pointed out that, used as she was to the 'fairly literate' conventions of *Armchair Theatre*, she found it hard to come to terms with the 'ugh' and 'gugh' of 'An Unearthly Child'; and that her own lack of knowledge of children confirmed the suspicions of the BBC's children's department that *Doctor Who* would not be tailored specifically for 8- to 14 year-olds.

> Although the kids liked it, and still do, it also — which I happened to think was a plus — got in a much older audience of 18 to 25 to 30 year olds . . . There were no pressures on me in the drama department to do that. I had no children . . . It's perhaps because I *had* no knowledge of kids that . . . made it span those two groups.

That, Newman's decision to place it in a family viewing slot of 5.15 pm on Saturdays, and the programme's consistently unpatronising address to children, launched *Doctor Who* as an institution which has continued to span various age groups ever since; so that in 1979 its British audience breakdown was:[58]

5– 7-year-olds	14.7%
8–11-year-olds	18.8%
12–15-year-olds	12.9%
16–19-year-olds	7.3%
20–29-year-olds	16.4%
30–49-year-olds	17.1%
50–64-year-olds	8.0%
65+ -year-olds	4.8%

It was not, however, just the coincidence of Verity Lambert having 'no experience of children' that made *Doctor Who* the new style, all-audience programme that it became. Sydney Newman's choice of Lambert for the part was a symptom of a new self-confidence among television drama professionals. Shaun Sutton, a later head of BBC drama, describes the early 1960s as an especially innovative time in TV drama. For the first time 'original' drama, written especially for television, was being produced in quantity, and with critical success. It was not just children's television drama that was now seen as outmoded, but the drama department's own traditional policy of reproducing successful stage plays. As Sutton described it: 'Sydney Newman . . . burst into BBC Television Drama at its moment of expansion, seized the opportunity, and set a match to a dramatic bonfire that has warmed us all since.'[59] In the list that Sutton provides of 'today's top directors' who first made their mark at that time is Warris Hussein, first director of *Doctor Who*; and in his list of trail-blazing 'original' play series is, of course, *Armchair Theatre*, from which *Doctor Who* got its producer.

Yet, despite their consciousness of being dramatists of a new kind, it is clear from Sutton's account that the traditional values of 'good' theatre prevailed. Most of the bright new

directors came from the theatre, not from film, and although
Sutton mentions the pioneering importance of the new weekly
TV series format, he derides, on conventional 'high art'
grounds, 'the very sameness of the situation and the characters,
their predictable actions and reactions'. In 'a format born of
the necessity for audience loyalty . . . abrupt changes of
character were frowned upon'.[60] A very few of the early
series, however, 'while following this intractable formula,
managed to rise above it', and became, in Sutton's view, as
'fine' television drama as was being provided by the 'serious'
one-off plays.

It is precisely in this context of a new and 'serious' series
drama concept, in which characters were unpredictable and
subject to 'abrupt change' that we can understand Verity
Lambert's insistence that for the part of the first Doctor
'unpredictability . . . was something that I wanted'. With
concepts carried from the new brand of 'serious' original
drama, located in the new popular series format, and blended
with 'the grace of technical, electronic and engineering
genius'[61] with which BBC drama was just then experimenting,
Doctor Who entered a select field of 'serious' popular drama
designed especially for television. In this formative period of
the early sixties, Sutton recalls: 'There was no stigma in the
mind of the writer or the director against the weekly series —
it was not considered a second-class work, by any of us'. So 'A
philosophy and foundation were laid, establishing the place
of serious drama in the schedules, its respect for the written
word and the writer, and for those who carried those words
to the screen.'[62] It was in this kind of company that *Doctor
Who* was projected: a children's format, but with a wider
provenance.

To some extent, once institutionalised, *Doctor Who*'s various audiences have continued to exist by weight of inertia.
But they have also been held by conscious programme manipulation. Incoming producers make judgements as to which
audience groups they feel the programme is under-serving
when they are considering what their own particular 'signature'
will be. So, for instance, in 1975 Philip Hinchliffe moved
away from the 'current day' and 'establishment' orientation
of Pertwee's Doctor and consciously towards a 'Gothic Horror'

style, largely because of his concern to build up the adult audience.

> *Hinchcliffe*:   I felt that the show had become a bit too childish . . . I wanted to try and win over more adults to the audience as well as keep the children. So the whole thing became a little bit more scary and a bit more convincing, a bit more plausible.

Whatever the particular inflection of the programme has been, Hinchcliffe's 'try and win over more . . . as well as keep . . . ' formula has been a central and continuous production strategy. Once established as an institution with a variety of 'levels' and audiences, *Doctor Who*'s producers could quite consciously play around with a whole range of conventions — 'Gothic', 'psychological', 'social', 'send up' (rather as directors of the Western genre had done earlier) — as 'bonuses' in order to hold audiences 'above the bedrock'. As producer Graham Williams saw it: 'We reckoned that we had a bedrock audience loyalty that we should feed and take notice of . . . between six and eight million viewers . . . The rest of the audience we reckoned we could grab on the wing as it were, by tapping into various popular areas.' Williams consciously exploited current generic tendencies orienting *Doctor Who* according to a succession of short-term trends — historical romance, 'epic' science fiction, 'buff' cinema and so on, in his own version of the 'similar but different' formula.

It was the longevity of *Doctor Who* as a BBC television institution that encouraged this typically 'generic' strategy. But the fact that it became an institution with these characteristics has to be understood in terms of other institutions, more profound than *Doctor Who* — of television as a medium, of the BBC, and the location of both within British culture. These were determining discourses which intersected with others to construct the narratives of *Doctor Who*, as we shall see in following chapters.

Patrick Troughton

Chapter 2

Regeneration: Narrative Similarity and Difference

In 'The Krotons' (1968), Patrick Troughton as the second Doctor and his mini-skirted companion Zoe run frantically fourteen times. Running away to outflank the enemy was Troughton's forté. Jeremy Bentham, historian of the Appreciation Society, says his Doctor was one of high nervous energy and pace in a world of: 'Smartly run installations peopled by disciplined, officious staff. Into these scenes would wander the Doctor, looking very much like an eager child let loose in a sweet shop.'[1]

Troughton's facial make-up, trampish clothing and consistent 'little man creates havoc with the system' repertoire was borrowed from silent cinema. The large bow tie, vagabond's dress (with baggy pants tucked into boots) and spotted handkerchief were modelled by the designers after Chaplin, whose bowler they replaced in the initial episodes with a lop-sided stove-pipe hat. From Chaplin there came the seedy tramp's pride, the refusal to give way to power when logic suggested he must be defeated, the strategy of taking to his heels and returning to fight another day, the sense of timing amidst hideous traps and misfortunes, the ability to be confused by props, and, especially, the strong moral purpose in challenging those who abused and humiliated the weak. There was also something of Keaton in the heavy make-up and turned-down mouth, the sad — until it smiled — passive face which, in fact, connoted a patience to endure and devise some effective if illogical solution; the contrast between his small scuttling form and the monstrous size and power of machines. Essentially the rhythm of the Troughton stories drew on the 'confrontation-run-chase-chaos-conquest' scenario and pace of early silent comedy; and in many places Troughton's Doctor would not have seemed very different had the film been run fast, whereas Hartnell's arrogant and rather static Doctor certainly would.

The transition from Hartnell to Troughton was bound to be traumatic, and very many regular viewers of Doctor Who were appalled as they saw the second Doctor dancing like a leprechaun with his recorder past monsters and boiling mud pools. But Troughton quickly captured an audience, and ratings picked up after declining badly in the last Hartnell series. The BBC had considered cancelling Doctor Who, but opted instead for more 'guts' and a younger lead. It was not, however, the impact of 'younger blood' that saved the series[2] so much as the 'difference' of a new dramatic coding. Under Troughton the hermeneutic dominance was lost — as Bentham notes disapprovingly, there was little play on the mysterious background of the exiled time traveller until the final story of the 1960s, 'The War Games', when all was revealed and Troughton left the series. In the place of 'mystery', there came the 'cosmic hobo', an idea that, according to Troughton, came from Sydney Newman.

Troughton had been considering playing the second Doctor as a 'rather tough, seafaring man'. But the 'cosmic hobo' concept had the advantage of continuity as well as difference — the Doctor as wanderer was still emphasised, even if the character was changed. The check trousers of Hartnell were retained, if now clownishly baggy;[3] and the big silk handkerchief supposedly had the co-function of 'symbolising the magician quality'[4] which had been there from the beginning. Yet the action narrative now carried a 'silent comedy' sub-text signified not only by codes of dress, make-up, expression and theme, but also by the degree of 'business' and timing of the lead actor.

Patrick Troughton was chosen for the part as a versatile character actor,[5] much concerned with the skills of his trade. In an important sense the mystery of the Doctor's character was replaced by the 'professional' mystery of performance. Elizabeth Burns has noted that: 'Professional secrecy and the creation of professional mystique are implicit in the writing and utterances (in interview) of many actors.'[6] And she quotes Gielgud's belief that, 'It is more seemly that these mysteries should remain a secret.' Patrick Troughton, unlike the other Doctors, has consistently refused to be interviewed, and gave the authors this explanation for it: 'I believe there's too much "going behind the scenes" nowadays. It spoils what actors try and do!'[7]

Since the first traumatic regeneration, the Doctor's lead has been changed three more times. Each Doctor has been the site of intersection of different codes, and each one has been encouraged to foreground the rhetoric of 'difference' — the Edwardian grandfather, the clown with recorder and baggy pants, the dandy, the 'student' bohemian with long trailing scarf, the vulnerable action-hero — although fundamentally working for similarity and continuity to establish programme identity, orderliness and stability.

The success of the programme (its audience size and logevity) must depend on this other 'success' (its tension between novelty and sameness) — the latter's terms defined according to the 'good television' discourse of television professionals. In this precise context — the rule-of-thumb assumptions of producers and television hierarchy that 'something similar but different' is required to re-invigorate a 'tired' format and ensure the success of time-slot scheduling — the changes of persona of the Doctor are no different in principle from the replacement of *The Sweeney*'s Jack Regan by *Hazell*'s James Hazell.[8] The initial drive of the producers of *Hazell* to anchor its interiorised 'talk' format — replacing the 'chase' scenario of *The Sweeney* — within the conventions of 'film noir' depended on the same professional assumptions that secured the new in *Doctor Who* — the change from 'hermeneutic' to 'performance' coding — within the old and established *television* convention of 'silent comedy'.

These professional assumptions of 'something similar but different' relate causally to what Heath and Skirrow have called the central fact of television experience, 'flow and regularity'; or, as Jeremy Isaacs said of British television's

Channel 4, 'The programmes will be different, but not too
different'.[9] But the very gesture to novelty-within-convention,
even while seeking its guarantee in consistency and 'realism',
may at the very same time open up the possibility of intertextual references which create complexities unintended by
the producers. In *Hazell* the 'film noir' signature, carrying
its own conventions of the 'strong and fatal' woman type,
compromised the producer's own, and different, concern for
'authentic' female parts. In the case of *Doctor Who*, the
Troughton Doctor was enfolded 'realistically' in the text in
terms of the repetition and expansion of nominations. Thus
the initial 'hobo' dress is filled out coherently with 'tramp'
behaviour and characteristics, just as the third Doctor's
'style' is soon seen to be consistent with his knowledge of
wine, his flowing cape and his swordsmanship. But the 'silent
comedy' coding also threatened to generate its own discourses
– for instance, Chaplin's conscious class inflection which
served a very different audience from that of modern television.
And Chaplin's own clown drew on the much older tradition,
whereby as Burns notes: ' "Playing the fool" is a standard
device for disrupting the conventions which maintain the
symbolic universe'.[10]

In long-running series like *Doctor Who* a shared typification as to the 'reality' and 'continuity' of the show is built
up. It is not the case, as some screen theorists have argued,
that the audience is necessarily inscribed naïvely in the world
of the drama by the 'transparency' effect of 'realism'. Audiences, as Richard Dyer has argued: 'May be fully aware of
how the media construct reality without thereby being particularly concerned to change the dominant definitions of
reality enshrined in those constructions'.[11] And, as Elizabeth
Burns notes, the audience's 'recognition of the "double
occasion" '

> Of theatrical performance pre-supposes a readiness to
> accept, for the time being, the code . . . and the world
> of social relevance established for the duration of the
> performance . . . The simplest actions or exchanges of
> the ordinary social world – forms of language, and gesture
> used for greetings, partings, declarations of love or an-

nouncements of death — seem to acquire quotation marks.[12]

During the gathering accretions of a long-running series, a devoted audience becomes acutely aware of, and jealous to preserve, the particular signification of these 'quotation marks'. Thus the repeated greetings gesture in the Nathan-Turner era of '(arm outstretched) "This is the Doctor"', while perhaps irritatingly obtrusive to less devoted followers of the programme, satisfied the fans because, apart from being enfolded 'seriously' and 'realistically' in the narrative, it emphasised the coherent 'memory' of the programme, the refusal to forget its originating hermeneutic. As programme 'historian' Ian Levine expressed it:

> Doctor Who was not called Doctor Who, but 'the Doctor'. *Doctor Who* is the title of the programme, meaning Doctor Who? . . . In one story called 'the War Machines', he had the computer saying 'Doctor Who is required. Bring him here'. That is just one of the most unforgiveable things that you wouldn't get now with John Nathan-Turner. He was never Doctor Who. The Doctor Who bit arose from a line in the second episode where Barbara says 'Doctor Foreman', and Ian says, 'That's not his name. Who is he? Doctor Who?'

It is precisely because they *are* aware of the fictionality of the programme's 'realism' that the fan's pleasure resides less in his/her inscription within the diegesis than, as Sheila Johnston has said of *Crossroads*, in 'the creation and slow consolidation of a complex fictional world'.[13] Ian Levine was perfectly clear about this process, and argued that the programme — and the fans pleasure — had sunk to an all-time low when Graham Williams was producer, because he:

> Didn't care about the programme, didn't care that a fact that had been established one year should be adhered to the following year. *Doctor Who*, although it is a fiction — it is like you took the American series *Dallas*, for instance, and you tried to contradict a fact that happened a year

before. All the fans of the programme would be in an
uproar because they follow it avidly. The same with a
show like *Coronation Street* in Britain — millions of people
watch it every week, and they remember what happened
ten years ago. You can't change the basic facts . . . I think
it is an insult to the intelligence of the viewer if facts that
are given in one story clash grossly in the next. For instance,
we are told in one story that only the Doctor can fly the
Tardis, and in the next story he has got the savage Leela,
who had no grasp of electronics at all, asking what the
co-ordinates were and going to fly the Tardis herself . . .
I could never forgive Graham Williams for the regeneration
scene with Romana. First of all, any producer must make
sure they know whether their artists are going to carry
on the following year before they let their contract expire,
or, if they are going to leave, make sure that they have
written up the series properly, rather than be left in-
between seasons with Mary Tamm leaving and not having
written her out. Instead he had that awful scene in the
Tardis with Lalla Ward in 'Destiny of the Daleks', where
she . . . tries on six or seven new faces before she settles
on the one which she wanted . . . Now it has been clearly
established that a Time Lord can only have twelve regenerations. So how can they have some supposedly responsible
female Time Lord . . . wasting six regenerations? . . . It is
that sort of non-attention to the series that gives me no
regard for Graham Williams at all.

Levine's opinion, shared by many *Doctor Who* fans, that
Williams was displacing the coherent fictional world of the
programme for comedy indicates the potential problem that
Patrick Troughton faced when he too inflected *Doctor Who*
in terms of comedy, in so far as a 'Chaplin' coding could
have destroyed the shared typification of 'reality' and 'continuity' of actor and audience.

Against the threat of dissolution an actor — and a text —
must work hard. Two kinds of convention — what Burns
calls the 'authenticating' and the 'rhetorical' — must be
preserved. Authenticating conventions — 'representations of
the agreements that exist between people in ordinary life'

— are understood by television professionals in terms of 'plausibility'. Would this kind of character act in this kind of way in this kind of situation? Actors in *Doctor Who* consistently plot their intepretation of parts minute by minute according to this attachment to plausibility. Rhetorical conventions involve the tacit agreement of 'rules of the game' between producers and audience — based on the 'realist' illusion that the characters are acting only for each other in a real world, and not for the audience. In contrast to the 'realist' illusion of the diegesis and the active character/ passive audience convention of traditional drama, Tom Baker's Doctor was to appeal to the newer Pinteresque rhetoric, 'that of the clown, the buffoon, who challenges the social reality of the audience'.[14] And it was that traditional audience reality which Ian Levine was defending when he complained: 'Graham Williams just sent the series up and turned it into mock comedy, whereby instead of depending on good plots, he depended on Tom Baker . . . fooling around and making pop-eyes and pinning pink rosettes on K-9.'

Whereas the repeated introduction of Peter Davison as 'This is the Doctor' was acceptable to fans, because contained within traditional rhetorical and authenticating conventions, Baker's breezy and pop-eyed 'Hullo, I'm the Doctor, this is K-9, what a nice little place you have here' routine was not, because it emphasised the comic performance of the actor, not the character. Tom Baker's notion of how to 'surprise people' and refurbish predictability with 'fun', was a self-referencing accent on performance. Patrick Troughton, faced with the same risk attached to his performance coding, was very careful to locate it in the 'humanity' of the character: 'In the beginning I played him very clownish. But I mellowed him as the series progressed. He was always off-beat, but I tried to make him human.'[15] The 'invisibility' of Troughton's acting — even while coding a part predominantly in terms of performance — is what has made him so highly respected as a character-actor within his profession. In one episode of *All Creatures Great and Small*, for instance, whereas there were noticeable continuities between Peter Davison's per-fromance as Tristan and the part he played later as the Doctor, Troughton was almost impossible to recognise, even though he again played a 'tramp'. Here the slow-speaking and seriously 'working-class' performance was closer to the 'tough seafaring man' that he originally planned to play in Doctor Who.

The success of the Hartnell/Troughton transition, however, relied on rather more than the 'genius' of the actor. The 'invisible' location of Troughton's performance itself relied on the continuous inscription of the Doctor as 'human' within the programme's narrative. It was this, above all, that protected Doctor Who from the disintegrating effect of the Chaplin discourse.

Like Chaplin, Troughton subordinated the vocal components and body movements of his act to the dominance of gesture, facial expression and pose. Troughton's ingratiating voice, his merry jigs, his recorder's 'mood' music and his frantic running away were themselves primarily coded as gesture — they expressed changes in his mental state. Also like Chaplin, the dynamic of Troughton's dramatic figure was strongly determined by what Mukařovský[16] calls the 'interference' between 'gesture-signs' — the 'social' gesture of Chaplin as self-assured social climber, of Troughton as universally competent Time Lord — and 'gesture-expressions' — the emotional complex of inferiority of Chaplin-the-beggar, and of panic of Troughton the mistake-prone galactic tramp.

However, in Chaplin, the dramatic hierarchy of textual codes was entirely subordinate to the structural organisation of the star's gestural code. As Mukařovský says, the Chaplin narrative was no more than a series of events functioning to promote the dynamic sequence of incompatible gestures (the drama of 'interference'), and it was this play on gestural contradiction which promoted the socially critical discourse. This presupposed 'an almost unbelievable economy in all the other components' of the text, any one of which (and the narrative flow in particular) could, if less redundant, have challenged the dominant gestural structure. With Troughton, in contrast, though the code of gestural 'interference' was strong, the narrative was stronger. Gesture, ultimately, served the plot. It was not the Chaplinesque 'social paradox' of the 'beggar with social aspirations' which motivated the gestural 'interference'. Rather, it was the narrative. Troughton's gestural contradiction between 'fear' and 'mastery' was a function of his ultimate narrative control.

Narrative: science fiction similarity as essence

Images

In 'The Krotons' Patrick Troughton's Doctor encounters most of his action in the underground caves of the backward Gonds and the advanced space machine of their oppressors, the Krotons. *Doctor Who* is frequently enacted in these two enclosed spaces: the caves and tunnels of other planets (a Nature defiled by science, but also threatening defilement); and, homologously, in the rooms and corridors of space stations, space ships, and industrial/research centres (a culture signifying progress, but also potential defilement). These two claustrophobic spaces — at once places of human quest and threat, of precarious safety and eternal defilement — draw on a central paradox of science fiction as a film genre: that human culture is godlike as it scientifically probes and masters the universe; and yet at the same time it has a terrible fragility, in terms of the 'unknown' both in nature and itself.

Over the last few decades popular science fiction has generated two dominating images, emphasising one or other pole of this 'human' paradox. The first image, which draws on the 1940s confidence of Asimov, Clarke and Heinlein in human probing and ingenuity, is one of precious fragility. A space-suited figure hangs in a void, floating outside its ship to which it is attached by an umbilical cord, while the blue-green Earth floats in the blackness beyond. Humankind, embryonic in space, is passively dependent for its life-services and systems on the mother ship and then, ultimately, on mother Earth itself to which it must return to survive. Although located in a scenario of optimistic anticipation, the narrative trajectory most often played on is the 'lack' of man in space (human fragility) and the 'plenitude'[17] of return to Earth.

The second image – drawing on the 1950s concern with flying saucers and nuclear holocaust, and later, the 1960s fears of Ballard and Ellison about ruthless machine control – is one of ominous power. Scientific technology has become fearful, as computers take control (*2001*), or the screen above our heads is crushingly filled by the enormous, slow-moving wedge of the *Star Wars* space cruiser. The danger of machine control from the skies in the form of super-rational, emotionless aliens (*The Thing* 1951, *War of the Worlds* 1953) tended to be replaced, as the film genre developed, by machine-like dehumanisation from within (*Invasion of the Body Snatchers* 1956, *Village of the Damned* 1960, which set the precedent for 'An Unearthly Child'), and concomitantly the narrative threat to Earth has become a threat to the 'essence' of humankind. This Romantic *doppleganger* motif has more recently still been projected across the entire universe, and in the *Star Wars* cycle the human spirit (or 'Force'), identified as always with the 'free world', has become the quest and final reward.

The *Star Wars* image is twenty-five years later than the first one. The pencil-shaped, fragile looking space ship has gone, as has its area of exploration, the nearer planets. Science fiction as genre depends on temporal as well as spatial displacement, so that as limited space exploration becomes the subject of a 'factual' and 'on-the-spot' television discourse, the content of SF is displaced from solar to galactic systems. If the first image promotes 'female'/maternal connotations, the second image advances itself as virile and 'male'. Earthmen become frontier sheriffs, cleaning up the space wilderness and making the universe safe for democracy and the human spirit. But the displacement has been more than one of time and space. Crucially for *Doctor Who*, there has been a tendency to shift from the physical to the mental and moral frontier, from the fragility of Earth's precious garden to the fragility of the human spirit. Both aspects have always been present. The 1982 *Doctor Who* story 'Four to Doomsday', for instance, includes both the image of the Doctor adrift from his Tardis in space and of Monarch the universal law-giver. But the emphasis has been displaced from the opposition of garden and wilderness to that of human knowledge and the will to power.

Locations

Kitses has pointed out that the Western myth is part of a great imperialist theme.[18] In America the frontier was linked with a sense of Manifest Destiny and Christianising mission, and was located in the Western myth as a purifying place — a site drawing out pure male virility and achievement in contrast to the westward creeping softness and ascriptive corruption of Eastern civilisation.

Henry Nash Smith has suggested that the Western legend grew in the space between these two poles: on the one hand the notion of the frontier wilderness purging the effete and corrupt civilisation of the East; on the other hand the civilising and Christianising notion of converting the wilderness to a garden.[19] Kitses, in turn, has suggested that this opposition — because of the ambivalence in each of its terms, 'garden' and 'wilderness', and each of its sub-terms, 'West'/'East', 'Nature'/'Culture', 'Individual'/'Community' has created a shifting and living corpus out of which very different Western meanings could be derived. Thus the 'wilderness' could signify a spectrum of values ranging from individual freedom to self-interested solipsism, from purity to savagery, and likewise the 'garden' could signify cultural restriction or civilised community, corruption or humanity.

SF as a film genre is less ambivalent than the Western in its inflection of this particular opposition. By and large the Earth is garden, space is wilderness, and that's that.[20] The early spaceships were precarious and transitory homes, questing out but always physically and emotionally tied to mother Earth which, significantly, tended to be remembered as a location of beauty and fecundity rather than of ultimate technology and industry. And when located in space, the frontiersmen were always hampered — in contrast to the free flowing and uncluttered masculinity of the Western hero — first by the fragile space suits and air bubbles they lived in,

and later by their own evil id and doppleganger (e.g. *The
Forbidden Planet* 1955). The emphasis was seldom on the
frontier as humanising, spiritualising and authentic location.
The ultimate trajectory was always back to what was known
and experienced, to an eternally beautiful mother of green
fields and blue waters.

The emotional and normative dominance in science fiction
of the garden over the wilderness reproduced many of the
values of its medieval progenitor in poetry and painting, the
walled garden. 'Paradise' is the Persian word for 'walled
enclosure', a concept drawn on directly in *Doctor Who*'s 'The
Face of Evil' (1977) where Leela says 'God' dwells 'within
the black wall wherein lies Paradise'. This notion of the ideal
place made safe by its wall was a central medieval icon (as
it was later in *Doctor Who*'s 'Kinda' (1982) and 'Face of Evil')
for a spirituality safe from the threatening lusts of the dark
unknown places beyond. There were animals and birds in the
garden, but like the flowers they existed for human pleasure.
Each element of this gentle microtheos existed symbiotically,
emphasising a higher spirituality through the peaceful fusion
of humankind and nature.

Science fiction's Earth, with its frequently overt religious
references, is a renewed representation of that walled paradise,
protected by its atmosphere, and standing in its anthropocen-
tricity for that same spirituality against which all outside
creatures and forces are basely material and materialistic. The
ultimate threat is the take-over of the human/spiritual by the
alien/material, the adulteration of the pure stock of Earth.

People

The garden/wilderness opposition is not, then, the basis of
ambiguity and 'authorial' variety in science fiction narrative.
But this is not to say that SF is less 'dense' than the Western.
It *is* founded on a deep ambivalence — in humankind itself,
on the one hand, as fragile 'organic' centre of the universe,
and on the other, as powerful and 'intellectual' definer of its
wilder limits. Fundamentally, SF narrative works on this
shifting principle of centreing and diffusion, of centripetal

and centrifugal forces, of a universe located in human fragility, and a universe defined as extension of 'man's' outward questing intellectual forces. This generic opposition has informed the title sequences of *Doctor Who* since the time of Patrick Troughton.

The opening titles of *Doctor Who* establish a preferred reading by underlining generic context: 'This is science fiction'. In doing so they reproduce visually the centripetal/centrifugal opposition fundamental to SF's play of meaning. The changing shots of the title sequence — for instance of the Doctor, of the Tardis, or of the hole in time, each in turn at the centre of centrifugal lines of force — are structured visually on SF's principle of centreing and diffusion. The Doctor is both human centre and, through the hole in time represented by the vortex (or the star field), a ceaseless explorer and peacekeeper of the universe. In Descartes the vortex, the rotary movement of atoms of matter around an axis, accounts for the formation of the universe; and the opening image of *Doctor Who* from the time of Troughton on, with lines of force spreading outwards from his forehead, potently recalls the idealist principle that the universe exists because man thinks it exists: 'I think, therefore I am'.

In contrast, *Doctor Who* defines its villains' relation with the universe as a matter of power and will: 'I will therefore I am'.

Doctor: You exist only because your will insists that you exist. But your will is all that is left of you.

Omega (cry of anguish) It is not true. I am Omega, creator of this world. And I can also destroy — therefore I must exist . . . If I exist only by my will, then my will is to destroy. And all things shall be destroyed . . . All things . . . All things.

('The Three Doctors')

The Tardis is crucial to this dual image of man: grand, scientific and powerful on the inside; absurdly idiosyncratic on the outside, and human in its tendency to error — like the Doctor himself.[21] The Tardis' function is to materialise

inside other objects (space craft, caves and tunnels on the
other planets) changing those places by its presence, creating
new patterns, transforming nature into culture, or perhaps
alien culture into pure, human-like culture. In 'The Krotons',
for instance, the transformation is from the slave-like culture
of the Gonds, determined by the inhuman law of the Krotons,
into a culture of freedom, inquiry and love. This transformation parallels, but with an entirely opposite valuation, the
other central theme of Doctor Who — the materialisation of
alien matter and anti-matter in the human organism, the
taking over and transformation of human culture by powerfully antagonistic and impure forces, as in the draining of
the humanoids' mental energy to recreate the Kroton
machines. But though valued differently, that parallel constantly points to the system of similarity and difference, or 'I
think therefore I am' and 'I will therefore I am'. Their direct
relationship — as in the Krotons' 'We don't think — we only
obey' — is the continuing goal of the narrative.

Much of the emotional resonance of SF derives from this
play between identification and alienation, between (organic)
spirit as 'free' thought and decision and (machine-like) will,
between the human heartland (home/body/spirit/culture)
threatened by befouling aliens and 'man's' own imperial pride
and will (potently carried by the theme music of 2001) as he
himself conquers a universe. In the 'Ark in Space' (1975)
serial of Doctor Who, for instance, the futile struggle of the
space station leader, Noah, to 'guard' his body from being
taken over by monstrous insects is ironically counterpointed
on the soundtrack, which gives us the heroic speech (recorded
long ago) of the Earth High Minister — itself premised on the
contrast between human pride and fragility:

> Our great undertaking — the salvation of the human race —
> has been rewarded with success. You have slept longer
> than the recorded history of mankind, and you stand now
> at the dawn of a new age. You will return to an Earth puri-
> fied by flame. A world that we cannot guess at. If it be
> arid, you must make it flourish. If it be stony you must
> make it fertile. The challenge is vast, the task enormous.
> But let nothing daunt you . . . Remember, citizen volun-

teers, that you are the proud standard bearers of our entire race . . . You have been entrusted with a sacred duty — to see that human culture, human knowledge, human love and faith shall never perish from the universe. Guard what we have given you with all your strength.'

Different Doctors

This episode of Baker's 'Ark in Space' draws, like Troughton's 'Krotons', on the SF genre's unusually complete Manichean division of actants into the pure and the polluted. Because of this emotional investment, audience identification in SF films has tended to be pre-set and carried by action and event, rather than the star-identification common in 'realist' texts. However, because it is a relatively low budget programme, and by design as well, *Doctor Who* avoids the grand events of space opera. In counter-balance star-identification is heavily inscribed. The programme is publicised in terms of its success through 'stars': 'The formula for the Troughton years proved a great success';[22] 'Pertwee had a huge following of six million',[23] and under Baker 'we had gone up to about twelve million.'[24]

One of the successes of the programme has been its ability to replace not just the Doctor but also the 'star' several times. There has been an attempt to avoid conflict and division within the seamless firmament of 'stardom' by emphasising contrast. There has been a regular alternation of Doctors — straight/comic/straight/comic/straight[25] — each star, we suppose, has his own sphere. Pertwee's 'Grand Prix' dare devil signature had the advantage of making the Doctor profoundly different from Troughton's timid tramp, while not threatening the programme as institution with the effect of Pertwee as 'star-text',[26] because he was popularly known for his comedy parts.

In addition, there is in *Doctor Who* a potent narrative design which works to protect textual coherence. The reason for the successful replacement of the Doctor depends, above all, on the ideological project of the programme, which is to found human 'essence' or 'spirit' in the un-typical, unmachine-like, unbureaucratic, quirky and often flawed response to situation and change. And given this definition of the ex-perientially 'human' as subject to freedom and the process of change, the transitions in the Doctor could be further secured by the myth that human change depends less on social process than on biology. The different Doctors could then be seen as 'naturally' different, because of vastly different ages.

Central to the Doctor's definition, and constant throughout all his different forms, has been science fiction's definition of the 'human' as powerful but fragile, rational but irrational, material but spiritual too. Troughton's Doctor was brave but frightened, and irrational in the cause of an oblique logic. And as the fourth Doctor's scientific companion Romana tells him: 'You're capricious, arrogant, self-opinionated, irrational, and you don't even know where we are going.' However, in the light of the evil Black Guardian's threat to hunt them through the universe, the Doctor's capriciousness in fitting a randomiser to the Tardis guidance system appears entirely rational. As he replies: 'If I knew where I was going, there'd be a chance the Black Guardian would too.'

If humanity is defined as much by its intuitive randomness as by its scientific system, then the apparently random alter-nation of Doctors is both appropriate and supported by the central emotional investment — that is, with being human — of the programme, which has certainly been its emphasis since the Hartnell years. When Romana adds to the Doctor's 'now no one knows where we are going', her exasperated comment 'Not even us', only one shot remains to conclude the epic 'Key to Time' season. It is of the Doctor, responding to her comment by looking full into the camera and breaking into his boyishly 'human' grin. If the close-up of the horrified expression of the Doctor has been a consistent suspended enigma of serial episodes, this grin has equally been established — especially with Troughton, Baker and Davison — as a marker of serial resolution. 'The Krotons', 'The Armaggedon Factor' and 'Castravala' which open with the plenitude of the Doctor as the mental centre of the universe end with this other human quality of intuitive idiosyncrasy and fragility. The 'lack' of the narrative (signified by the Doctor's shocked gaze) has been played out especially to mark this trajectory of 'human' difference.

Themes

In 'The Krotons', the parasitic draining of human mental energy is matched by the Doctor's determination to free Gond thought. There are two recurring themes in *Doctor Who*: the threat of human defilement which is opposed by the liberation of the oppressed. As the Doctor says in 'The Sun Makers': 'I want you to scatter through the city and tell the people what's happened. Remind them that they're human beings, and tell them that human beings *always* fight for their freedom.' Both themes have the same project: the naming of what it means to be human, and they are metaphorically related, since each depends on the materialisation of one life-force inside another with a view to changing it. But they are also related syntagmatically[27] in so far as they define the linearity of the narrative which develops from 'lack' (defilement of the human body) to 'plenitude' (balance and freedom in the universe). Whole series, and within them single episodes, follow this trajectory from lack to plenitude in which emotional involvement is generated by the narrative disgression spun out by the codes of puzzles and actions. This is typical of traditional narrative. What is particular to *Doctor Who* is that the narrative quest is also to prove that the intellectual law-giver is, after all, 'spontaneously' human. *Doctor Who* debates at its centre the key notion of the science fiction genre: the anthropocentric principle. Humanity is defined as something between the brutish beasts and the angels. Brutes can do only evil, angels only good. But humans have the power to choose. The story of 'Kinda' (1982) where, on the planet of Deva Loka ('world of celestial ones'), the Doctor mediates (by mistakes as much as by reason) between forces of pure good and evil, is only an overt form of this underlying *Doctor Who* theme. It is that precarious balance choosing sometimes evil, sometimes good (with the Troughtonesque capacity both to innovate powerfully and to make mistakes foolishly) which, rather than any permanent and bureaucratically designed balance, is the only truly human harmony, based as it is as much on intuition as reason, on the irrational and random choice as much as on scientific knowledge.

The authentic balance is a 'natural' one: every being has its place, provided it does not usurp the space of another being. The sin of the monstrous forces which try to take over human beings in *Doctor Who* is that they do not keep to their own place, where, as the Doctor insists, they have their own right to live. The fundamental villainy, as every audience group recognises, is the Krotons'/Daleks'/Ice Warriors'/Cybermens' etc determination to take over every other space and control an entire world or galaxy.

Near the end of 'The Key to Time' season (1978–9) the Doctor, for a moment, plays with the 'mad scientist' persona of human pride and ambition:

> We have the power to do anything we like, absolute power over every particle in the universe, everything that has ever existed or ever will exist — as from this moment. Are you listening to me Romana . . . because if you're not listening I can make you listen, because I can do anything. As from this moment there's no such thing as free will in the entire universe. There's only my will, because I possess the key to time.

In response to Romana's anxious, 'Are you all right?', the Doctor drops this rolling-eyed spoof of madness for his conventionally idiosyncratic, matter of fact, near-nonsense persona: 'Well of course I'm all right. But suppose I wasn't all right . . . this thing makes me feel in such a way that I'd be very worried if I felt like that about somebody else feeling like this about that. Do you understand.' Not quite nonsense, however, because the key to time can stop the entire universe and enable the Guardians to 'restore the natural balance between good and evil' throughout it. And it would be, as the Doctor observes, 'a terrible tragedy for the universe' if it fell into the wrong hands. The Black Guardian reveals his true character when he says that the individual human being who makes up the sixth segment of the key of time must remain imprisoned for ever rather than endanger the fate of the whole universe by dismantling the key. The White Guardian, the Doctor observes, 'would never have had such a callous disregard for human life'. And yet it is the Doctor himself who is accused by Sarah in 'Pyramids of Mars' (1975) of having an 'inhuman' disregard for individual human life in his galactic struggle with Sutekh. The Black Guardian represents the sin of pride and ambition in the Doctor's 'human' quest for 'freedom'.

In 'The Genesis of the Daleks' (1975) the Doctor holds in his hands two cables which, if touched together, will destroy at source the most potent force for evil in the universe — Daleks. He ponders whether that future order, harmony and happiness in the universe would justify even this one destructive action.

> Listen, if someone who knew the future pointed out a child to you, and told you that that child would grow up totally evil, to be a ruthless dictator who would destroy millions of lives — could you then kill that child?

Let us here juxtapose another text:

> Imagine that it is you yourself who are erecting the edifice of human destiny with the aim of making men happy and giving them peace and contentment at last, but that to do that it is absolutely necessary . . . to torture to death only one tiny creature . . . would you consent to be the architect on those conditions?[28]

This second text is Dostoyevskii's *The Brothers Karamazov*. In Dostoyevskii and *Doctor Who* it is disdain for individual human life which defines the sin of a power lust disguised as the quest for ultimate social order. To accede to it would be to enter the world of machines programmed for survival, conquest and ultimate power — the world of the Daleks and the Krotons:

> *Doctor*:   And everyone uses these machines?
> *Selris*:   When they are young, yes. That is the law.

Doctor: Whose law, Selrig?
Selrig: Our law — the Gonds'.
Doctor: But I thought you said all your law was given
you by the Krotons?
Selrig: Yes, all our science, all our culture, everything we
have has come from the machines.
Doctor: I see — a sort of self-perpetuating slavery.

If the system of social stratification is allusively that of class
control, and the discussion is potentially that of hegemonic
transmission via the machines of cultural reproduction, that
possible reading is systematically closed off by the narrative
of science fiction and its quest for human 'essence'. The
narratives of Doctor Who are invariably about 'slavery', but
the narrative struggle is always for the restoration of 'balance',
where each kind has its natural place. As in conventional
narrative, there is always an initial plenitude — and in Doctor
Who it is human freedom — which is 'naturally' ongoing
(despite the caste nature of the Gonds' freedom in 'The
Krotons') until the reconnaisance of the villain.

This recurrent theme is stretched across the narrative interplay of actants which various theorists of popular culture
have isolated ('heroes, villains and fools',[29] 'professionals,
bureaucrats and amateurs',[30] white and black fathers, white
and black children'[31]). Jerry Palmer's categories of professional, bureaucrat and amateur, for instance, seem especially
appropriate to Doctor Who. The weakness of the amateur —
as in the case of Doctor Who's many freedom fighters, such
as the Gonds — is in acting over-intuitively, improvising
inappropriately (which, as this is science fiction, usually
means an unprogrammed attack with technologically inferior
weapons). The weakness of the bureaucrat is in being too
programmed to handle sudden changes of plan — the very
'secret' of human success over the Daleks which is extracted
from the Doctor in 'The Day of the Daleks' (1972). The
strength of the bureaucrat is massive scientific and technological precision; that of the amateur is entrepreneurial
initiative and spontaneity.

The 'professional' hero — the 'Doctor' — synthesises the
strengths of each without the weaknesses. Like the bureau-

crat he is scientific; like the amateur he is spontaneous and entrepreneurial. But he is neither too rash nor too programmed. This 'professional' mode is a deeper motivation for Patrick Troughton's 'comic' signature as the Doctor than personal intentionality or acting style, and is what ties the 'Chaplin/Keaton' inflection into programme continuity. When it is rash to attack, he runs away; but his most arbitrary response always contains an unexpectedly outflanking rationality. As the cliffhanger to episode 2 of 'The Krotons', Troughton cowers in terror, hands in front of his face, at the mercy of a Kroton killing machine. But in the next episode we learn that covering his face has disturbed the machine's face-print guidance system, and it kills an 'amateur' Gond instead. As the Doctor says: 'It was programmed to kill once — me — stupid machine.' The interaction of the heroically rash Gond who tries to kill the machine with his axe, the spontaneously rational Doctor, and the bureaucratic Krotons for whom all human 'waste matter must be dispersed — that is procedure' is one rehearsed continuously not only throughout the history of *Doctor Who*, but in many areas of popular fiction.

As an example, Palmer quotes the case of James Bond in *From Russia With Love*, where Bond's execution is planned with machine-like precision by a chess Grand Master. He is to be killed by a single bullet through the heart at an exact moment at a specific place. However, Bond innovates by surreptitiously slipping a silver cigarette case contained in a pocket-book over his heart. This initiative gives him the surprise he needs to defeat his equally powerful, programmed opponent. An almost identical incident occurs in 'The Sontaran Experiment' (1975), where Tom Baker's Doctor appears to have been killed by a ray to the heart; but he too has secretly placed a deflecting device there, again giving him the advantage of surprise.

In his analysis of *The Sweeney*, Geoff Hurd[32] has noted the familiar structuring of the fictional world in terms of:

Professional	v.	Organisation
Authority	v.	Bureaucracy
Intuition	v.	Technology

and has usefully drawn on Westergaard to explain these
oppositions as displacements of class contradiction. As
Westergaard points out, the representation of supposedly
'universal' divisions, as between age and youth, intellectuals
and masses, pensioners and wage-earning unionists, professionals and 'organisation' men, constructs the expected drama
of conflict within modes of cultural reproduction, such as
the media, without in any way threatening the hegemonic
consensus.[33] These divisions are, after all, changeable within
the system — either by reform, by recourse to the 'law' against
irresponsible strikers, or simply by the process of the young
getting older and wiser. And so a myth of classlessness and
the potentially just society is generated.

Troughton's signature as an acute professional especially
opposed to 'disciplined, officious' bureaucracy, draws on
this mythology. But it is coded, as we have said, in terms of
science fiction which, as well as further displacing class
contradiction in terms of 'human' universals, creates at the
same time its own ambiguities and contradictions.

Narrative: TV series and 'difference'

In an article on *Crossroads*, Sheila Johnston rightly points
out that while analysis of a variety of media texts for their
narrative 'sameness' is important, it also leads to an impasse,
leaving 'only one strategy open — routine denouncement,
criticism as exposé'. 'An approach that gives primacy to the
sameness of all mainstream drama has nothing to say about
it other than that it performs reflexive ideological operations
in a mechanical and wholly uninteresting way.'

So where, given the popularity of these programmes, 'are
we to look for the "difference" of soap opera, the points at
which it deviates from the norms (if norms there be) of
narrative fiction?'[34] Johnston's answers relate to the nature
of long-running television serials, and so are important to our
discussion of *Doctor Who* — though we shall argue that the
nature of SF narrative itself as 'difference' is more central.

Johnston isolates several ways in which the audience
experience of soap opera may contest 'the contention that

the viewer is entirely passive', the 'poor dupe of television' who, for Heath and Skirrow is 'carried along . . . summoned . . . held . . . into the programme'.[35]

> The Great Threat Now Facing Doctor Who: If the new season fails to attract figures of around 10 million or more, then a serious possibility exists that the programme will end at its twentieth anniversary.

(Doctor Who Fans' *Freesheet*, 1982)

The long-running form of the series delays endlessly the 'return to order'. Not only is there no final narrative closure, but 'the audience knows, hopes even that there is none' — as is clear from the anxiety of *Doctor Who* fans in early 1982 (and as has to be the case for the unfortunate members of the British *The Prisoner* Appreciation Society). For them, as Johnston says, the primary source of pleasure is to be found not in 'the closed and comforting symmetry' of narrative, but in the 'long-arch' story-line which allows the 'creation and slow consolidation of a complex fictional world'. Indeed, fans in the *Doctor Who* Appreciation Society displayed a desire to open out the final closure of 'Kinda' (1982), to turn serial into series, by seeing in Tegan's dazed expression the potential reappearance of the beast 'from inside' in a later season. Yet, there is a 'closed and comforting symmetry' none the less: for long-term fans the endless unfolding of the show's mythology is pleasurable only if the continuity of *Doctor Who* as institution is upheld.

Johnston argues that in soap operas like *Coronation Street* the episodic and parallel sub-plot construction of the narrative opens the way to ambiguity and even contradiction of attitudes and values. Hence a variety of positions is constructed for the viewer. In *Doctor Who*, which as an episodic serial insists on audience involvement with each and every episode, the emphasis is on linear rather than multiple plot lines. The Doctor and companions may get separated, but their narrative function is tied to the central melodrama of hero versus villain. Occasionally in a *Play of the Month*[36] story like 'Kinda', the 'realistic' complexity of a social world is attempted (an opposition between a patriarchal, linear-progressive, militaristic society and a peaceful, non-interfering matriarchal one). In this case audiences can enjoy the complexity of themes, though even here with a firm sense of conventional narrative enigma and closure. Here, and generally in *Doctor Who*, the threat to 'any secure sense of what constitutes the status quo' tends to stem less from multiple plot lines than from the Romantic/Gothic discourse operating to generate a 'difference' within the narrative.

> If, in the crime series, the transgressors appear so briefly that they remain anonymous or, alternatively caricatured, their extended period of tenure allows all soap opera characters a measure of continuity and development, a chance to assert themselves in diverse dramatic roles. Even villains can occasionally be victims, and friends may turn out to be foes . . . So viewers are denied a secure and enduring perspective (the 'dominant specularity' supposedly afforded by the classic text). Constant adjustment is called for as the story lines move slowly on and actants are realigned in different dramatic modes. Nor can this be recuperated as subtle, complex psychology . . . Not exactly realist, not quite stylised, this hybrid quality makes these programmes oddly intractable to traditional tools of analysis.[37]

In *Doctor Who* there is quite another threat from 'within'. Though very occasionally a familiar friend becomes a foe (as with Captain Yates of UNIT), the villainy is instantly re-cuperated. Yates was 'brainwashed' and returns in a later story ('Planet of the Spiders', 1974) to exonerate himself, even if now as an outsider. Indeed, Yates susceptibility to villainy is a result of his sensitivity: a valued 'human' charac-teristic which in itself distinguishes him from the (machine) villain. Equally rarely, as in Bailey's 'Kinda', there is an attempt by a writer to shatter the viewer's secure perspective by showing a constant 'villainy' lurking beneath the surface of a companion, but this was suppressed before recording. However, there is a continuing threat to the status quo from 'within', which derives from the SF narrative's hybrid quality as 'realism' and allegory, action-drama and intertextual mode of address.

> The reason 'Logopolis' succeeded is because rather than your average *Doctor Who* story where they go out and land on an alien planet and get involved in events there, events in 'Logopolis' revolved around the myth itself of *Doctor Who*. In other words the whole story started because the Doctor wanted to change his broken chameleon circuit, which has been broken ever since the very first story — and we even got referred back to Totters Yard to explain it. That's how it started, and add to that the return of the Doctor's arch foe, the Master. By bringing in anything from the series' past you get my vote anyway. The Doctor's arch foe comes along and tries to mess things up, so you have a staggering mind teaser. The Doctor tries to land around a real police box to measure the dimensions, but the Master has already landed around it first and disguised his Tardis as a police box. So you have got the three identities within one another. And this whole thing led to the Doctor then going to Logopolis to try and fix his chameleon circuit with the Master on board. The entire plot of 'Logopolis' arose inside the myth of *Doctor Who*, rather than taking the myth of *Doctor Who* to an outside planet.

> (Ian Levine)

A committed audience, as Geraghty points out about *Coronation Street*, has an accumulated knowledge and clear memory of a programme's past. On the other hand, Johnston argues that the 'immediacy' quality of the soap opera, and its 'inconceivable' lacks of repeats, creates a 'defective' memory in more casual viewers. This difference in knowledge leads to a variety of viewing experiences, encouraging producers to play with the past in differential ways. Geraghty says that in a long-term radio serial like *The Archers*, the past can be openly invoked to allow a younger audience to hear of key events in the programme's mythology; or it may simply be implied elusively and by resonance for audiences with more knowledge. So, 'the kind of work the audience can do has greater potential in the serial than in other narrative forms'.[38]

The implication, however, that fans work on 'Logopolis' for their pleasure, while others, as 'poor dupes of television' are carried off by the 'good, pacey story', ignores the fact that the 'memory' associated with a long-running show is by no means only intra-diegetic. In the first place, it is not the case with *Doctor Who* that repeats are 'inconceivable',[39] and any half enthusiastic fan of the programme can easily secure an accurate 'memory' by subscribing to magazines and fanzines which run regular synopses of past programmes, discussions of continuity, profiles of past performers and so on. This is not to say that there are not a variety of viewing experiences associated with the show, but again we will argue this relates more significantly to the programme's authenticating and rhetorical conventions, which themselves may change during a long-term series for 'professional' reasons.

Secondly, the fact that *Doctor Who* carries with it an audience which has grown up with the show, may produce a 'defective' memory of another kind, arising from a different range of competences appropriated by the viewer as adult than as child. Programme 'knowledge' can change its register within any one long-term viewer. One Cambridge student ascribed this shift in register entirely to the evolution of the programme: 'Whereas in every *Doctor Who* programme they once had the only response they wanted was pitiless fear, now . . . it's a reference game. The whole metaphysical thing in "Kinda" is a reference game if you happen to get the references in it.' Yet, though there *have* been changes in the programme in terms of more external references, this is by no means new — 'The Green Death' (1974) and 'The Monster of Peladon' for instance made references out to political events (Chamberlain's speech, multi-nationals, 'ecology', the miners' strike, 'women's lib' etc) in the early 1970s. An audience group of television professionals discussed 'The Monster of Peladon' in terms of its political references, and although framed by in-group considerations about 'gripping' writing, cliffhangers, time-slotting, target audience and so on, some members drew pleasure in the way the show adhered to its 'adult' reference to 'our own times'.

I think this alien society really can be interpreted as our own society in any generation . . . For instance, when you take a look at those workers, the oppressed workers, I thought of Russia in 1917 prior to the Revolution.

I thought of Poland today.

Alright, Poland today. When you look at that chancellor, that's bureaucracy today. In other words I think what I'm saying is that what *Doctor Who* really is, is a reflection of our own times . . .

Doctor Who's your real hero, because he is, if you like, the light at the end of the tunnel. He's the one person who is saying, 'Well, you know, there is an answer if you will listen to it.'

The voice of reason.

He's offering you peace in a sense . . .

He's obviously a goody, and there were morals rammed down one's throat, even if not platable. That's how I saw it and I was quite fascinated. I wanted to watch another episode . . .

He was a definite 'small-l' liberal — *for* miners, women's lib and reason.

It's today in a different guise.

I think that's what helps adults to watch it.[40]

In contrast, an infant school audience found 'The Monster of Peladon' comprehensible and enjoyable by focusing on a series of actions (such as the continuity of 'tricks' played by the Doctor — against the monster, against the guard, etc.) and concrete details (noticing, for instance, that the cup of wine given to the Doctor after his rescue was shaped like the monster's horn). While not understanding the political references, these children were working to establish a different register of relevance and coherence — and therefore a different 'memory' — for the show.[41]

Thirdly, the constant search for 'good stories' in a long-

term series, in conjunction with the wish to gain 'bonus'
audiences, leads to variations of ideological and rhetorical
position over the years, inscribing different audiences and
different modes of 'work'. Though (as a 'children's' show and
because of its dominating patriarchal discourse) *Doctor Who*
rarely touches on what Johnston calls soap opera's traditional
concern 'with the troubling and explosive issue of sexual and
. . . to a lesser extent . . . class politics', its need for 'novel'
plots as a series did allow the subject of female sexual repression to get as far as rehearsal stage in 'Kinda'[42] and class
politics to be raised (in a muted, small 'l' liberal form) in 'The
Green Death', 'The Monster of Peladon' and 'The Sun Makers'
(1977). As script editor, Eric Saward put it, 'political' continuity is much less important than stories that 'work'.

> In my job I don't see myself as a censor. If somebody has
> written a good story and it works, that is the way it comes
> out. The continuity is only for the regular people. If the
> story is good and it has a left-wing bias – well splendid.
> I mean, I'm not a Buddhist, but if a writer wants to use
> Buddhist fables and tales, splendid.

The 'pacey' action format, Saward would argue, is there for
the 'bedrock' fans; the 'left-wing' or 'Buddhist' ideas are a
bonus for more sophisticated audiences; and continuous
references to the show's history are for the buffs. This makes
the programme, for Saward, a 'specialised show' with 'many
different levels'. *Doctor Who*, because of its longevity, has
created its own specialised audiences who recognise and work
on different conventions within the show.

For instance, the first response of the Liverpool branch of
the *Doctor Who* Appreciation Society as to why they liked
'Kinda' was to appeal to the history of the show:

> It impressed me. Can I compare it to the other two stories
> we have had so far – I thought it was superior to 'Castra-
> valva' in that all the explanations were given, and we were
> fairly familiar with a lot of the concepts involved such as
> telepathy and dreaming and block-transfer computation,
> where you would have had to have seen 'Logopolis' and

videoed 'Logopolis' and spoken to the person who wrote
'Logopolis' . . . But yet it had more to think about really
than 'Four to Doomsday'. And I like a lot of the visual
imagery — for example, the chess game.

In contrast, Peter Holland, Cambridge University lecturer in
English (and also a keen follower of *Doctor Who*) mainly
liked its references out — the 'Shakespeare' reference of
the 'chess' game, and the socio-historical 'contemporary'
reference.

It doesn't seem to be saying that the *whole* of civilisation
will collapse . . . as 'The City of Death' does. It is suggesting
that there are *local* cycles of civilisation collapse. And that
seems to me more disturbing because it's less intergalactic
and more personal. We are watching something like the
effect of colonial powers on a culture which is far more
sophisticated than we are prepared to recognise; and our
own unawareness of the effect on the culture of, say, the
Brazilian Indians or whatever which is being destroyed
by the process of colonialisation. In fact these other
societies are *far more sophisticated* than we give them
credit for. This story seems to be blatantly saying that
these societies are complex ones, in which the prophet/
older women/seer is a complex figure, and in which you
can have a matriarchal society and working telepathy . . .
and where suddenly one of the men speaks and the surprising thing is that he should speak. The man who speaks
is the indication of the end of that civilization.

There are, then, a number of ways in which *Doctor Who*
can 'flaunt' its own tradition and conventions. It can play on
its own history in order to seal it off as an ever denser mythic
reality, enclose its longevity within its continuity — a tendency
to in-group hermeticism and closure which gives obvious
pleasure to fans. It can draw on its 'universe in peril' convention to localise it, innovate on it, create difference out of
similarity — and in doing so draw on its reputation with other
audiences for 'reflecting our own times'. In contrast to this
greater density of authenticating devices, it can play on its

own (or other popular fictional) themes and iconography in order to 'send them up'. Clearly, though, there are complexities to *Doctor Who's* mode of address which allow for a variety of readings. One answer to Johnston's question of where to find 'points of resistance' to narrative 'sameness', and how to locate the mobilisation of diverse pleasures in popular television can be found for *Doctor Who* by reference to 'differences' within its narrative. It is on the basis of competing discourses within SF narrative that varying audience readings and pleasures are mobilised.

Narrative: similarity and difference

The major weakness of 'professional/bureaucrat', 'white father/black father', 'hero/villain' approaches, is that while offering a rudimentary classification of narrative actants, none of them adequately considers the development of narrative through its play on difference. It is true that each offers a basic narrative model in the Greimasian sense[43] of classifying narrative structure at a level before the transformation into specific discourse:

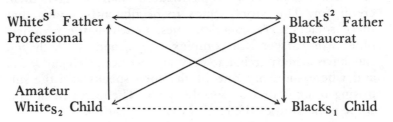

We can also draw on Fredric Jameson's understanding of the role of the 'donor' as supplying the 'asymmetrical force' that generates the 'storiness' of the story, making it 'interesting to tell'. The donor (for example, the Doctor's quirky innovativeness) is the point of interest that resides between our knowledge that the hero will prevail in the end and our later knowledge of how he does prevail:

> We may restate the necessity for the existence of the donor . . . by pointing out that in the beginning the hero is never strong enough to conquer by himself. He suffers

from some initial lack of being: either he is simply not
strong enough or not courageous enough, or else he is too
naïve and simple-minded to know what to do with his
strength. The donor is the complement, the reverse, of this
basic ontological weakness.[44]

This formulation is important in distinguishing between those
actants who are already (or naturally) puissant or wise (the
donors) and those who only become wise or powerful during
the course of the narrative. Hence the Doctor is donor rather
than hero. The recurrent freedom-fighters seeking their
precious object (their princess in 'The Monster of Peladon',
but more generally their freedom as in 'The Krotons') are the
heroes of the tale. So we can reformulate our previous
model thus:

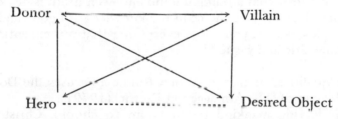

However, this classificatory use of Greimas' actantial model
(whereby he simply sets out narrative according to four
abstract categories) still does not tell us much about the process by which narratives become digressive stories. Jameson
suggests that, after isolating the deep structure of narrative,
the value of Greimas' model would be to mediate on the
differences between the four categories. In other words, what
are the possibilities for lures, traps and equivocations in the
narrative process due to the play between similarity and
difference as between Donor, Villain, Hero and Desired Object?
The stories of narrative are generated by the differences
between, and resolution of the value contradictions of, these
four fundamental actants. In *Doctor Who* the narrative digression between initial lack and final plenitude depends on the
successive play of similarity and difference between the
Doctor and the Krotons or Daleks, the Doctor and the Gonds
or other freedom-fighters, and so on.

If we return to the intertextual relationship of 'Genesis of the Daleks' and *Brothers Karamazov*, we can trace one of these narrative dimensions ($S_1 \longmapsto\!\!\!\!\longrightarrow S_2$, Donor $\longmapsto\!\!\!\!\longrightarrow$ Villain) further. After Ivan Karamazov tells Alyosha that future harmony cannot be bought at the cost of even one individual (the theme of the final episode of 'The Key to Time'), he narrates his 'Legend of the Grand Inquisitor'.

The Inquisitor accuses Christ of leaving man in a state of free will, when he wants only material comfort and spiritual slavery.

> I tell you man has no more agonising anxiety than to find someone to whom he can hand over with speed the gift of freedom with which the unhappy creature is born . . . did you forget that a tranquil mind and even death is dearer to man than the free choice in the knowledge of good and evil . . . instead . . . you chose everything that was exceptional, enigmatic and vague.[45]

The qualities, in fact, of which Romana accuses the Doctor at the end of 'The Armaggedon Factor' (1979).

In leaving mankind the freedom to choose, Christ had rejected the things that were Caesar's — the power of authority and control. Now the Inquisitor's own élite have taken 'the sword of Caesar and proclaimed ourselves the rulers of the earth, the sole rulers'. They had been hindered by rebellions, easily put down, but which temporarily have forced them underground into caves and catacombs.

> This work is only beginning, but it has begun. We shall have to wait a long time for its completion and the earth will have yet much to suffer, but we shall reach our goal and be Caesars.[46]

The Daleks are also trapped in tunnels underground.

> We are entombed here, but we still live on. This is only the beginning. We will prepare. We will grow stronger. When the time is right, we will emerge. We shall build our city.

We shall rule Skaro. The Daleks will be the supreme power in the universe.

The Grand Inquisitor says that when he has put on Caesar's robes:

A world state and universal peace will have been founded. Then men will 'no longer rise in rebellion nor exterminate one another, but will be at peace.

Similarly, Davros, inventor of the Daleks, tells the Doctor:

When the Daleks are the supreme power of the universe then we shall have peace. All wars will end. The Daleks are the power not of evil but of good.

As in Dostoyevskii the debate is about science and evolutionism within the parameters of human choice, individualism and sacrifice. *Doctor Who* is premised on alternative forms of evolutionism, defined essentially according to whether they do or do not sacrifice human martyrs and human choice. For Davros, villain of villains:

History shows that co-operation between different species is impossible. One race must survive all others, and to do this it must dominate ruthlessly. Now I intend . . . that the supreme victors shall be our race, the Daleks.

In contrast, one of his 'freedom fighter' opponents argues:

What Davros has not made clear is that there is another way . . . We can destroy the genetically conditioned creatures and allow the mutation to follow its own course. Our race will survive if it deserves to survive. But they're to have all the strengths and weaknesses that we have. Compassion and hate. They're to do good things and evil. But we cannot let it become an unfeeling, heartless machine. That is our choice.

This debate marks the difference between the 'inhuman'

villain and 'human' freedom-fighter/heroes. But there is a
further difference which motivates the following action. The
donor, the Doctor, is absent: the freedom-fighters lack
Davros' knowledge and power, and as in 'The Krotons', many
of them die for it. The donor will, of course, arrive (or
return) and re-equip further freedom-fighters with the power
to destroy the Krotons or Daleks. But, crucially, this donor is
not only sometimes absent but also permanently tainted as in
the Doctor's 'inhumanity' in 'Pyramids of Mars'. A central
emphasis of Doctor Who is on the pride of 'man' as scientist
— grappling, sometimes with the best of motives (replenishing
dwindling energy supplies), sometimes the worst motives
(racial or capitalist greed), with forces which are beyond
comprehension and control.

One of the recurrent motifs of Doctor Who is of the planet,
once organic, where flora and fauna existed in symbiotic
relation, but now riddled with mining shafts and tunnels; a
dead hulk living on merely as material energy or wealth for
invaders. And these invaders are human as often as they are
alien. The threat of defilement to 'pure' people and 'organic'
planets comes from the exploratory principle ('science') itself,
which is all the more problematic in Doctor Who because
the donor is himself a scientist. He, like the villains, materialises
in those claustrophobic locations, making them a dramatic
mise-en-scène for a romantic melodrama of quest and defilement; sometimes, as in 'Kinda', threatening the garden purity
of their world. In episode one of 'Kinda', in the sunlight of
the forest, Tegan comes round from behind the Tardis to
discover Adric and Nyssa (to whom she is an outsider as both
watcher and human) playing draughts. The Doctor then
enters from behind her on the left of screen and converses
with her. Later in the same episode, Tegan, now located in
the blackness of the 'wherever', follows an identical path
around a Tardis-shaped but mysterious energy machine to
discover again a male and female playing a strange board
game. The players are now old not young, and the strangeness of their dress is different from the non-Earthly clothes
of Adric and Nyssa. But again Tegan is an outsider (as watcher
and as human), and again a dominating male, the evil Dukkha
enters from behind left and converses with her. The play

between the syntagmatic and paradigmatic planes of the *Doctor Who* narrative is presented as a play of similarity and difference between the donor and villain. The linear development of the narrative generates the heroic discourse 'knowledge ◄─────►liberation':

Plenitude	Lack	Plenitude
First image of Doctor: Knowledge as centre of universe: 'I think therefore I am.'	Exploitation/ Defilement by aliens: 'I will therefore I am.'	Liberation: the final (human) face of the Doctor.

But the metaphoric relation of the two major themes of defilement and liberation (the repeated function 'penetration' by the Doctor/by the aliens) generates a much less optimistic resonance, which in turn creates the narrative space for some of the most 'articulate' (and ambiguous) sequences in the programme (e.g. 'Have I the right . . . the responsibility is mine and mine alone': 'Absolute power over every particle of the universe . . . I can do anything'). The narratives of *Doctor Who*, deeply based on a hybrid form of SF, threaten to generate their own 'resistance'. The syntagmatic and paradigmatic play between similarity and difference, purity and defilement, quest and hubris, thought and will, science and power is formally presented as a play between a 'realistic' and an allegorical form. Fletcher has said that in the sense that asceticism is defined by desire, the natural theme of allegory is temptation.[47] We cannot, in other words, know what purity is without sin and defilement, nor what 'true' science is without its misconception as power. Science fiction allegory relocates human ambivalence by projecting outwards on to separate personifications of good and evil (Doctor/ Dukkha, Doctor/Dalek, Doctor/Davros) emotional states and psychological dispositions which are internal and inseparable. It depends on the parallel yet different paths of hero/donor/ villain, the latter tracing what the former are in their 'other' selves, and throughout the journeys and unendingly final confrontations the hero (or donor) is endlessly tempted to become one person again. The text in other words offers the

constant temptation of serious dramatic 'realism' — the temptation of Christopher Bailey's 'Kinda' — that is, to populate
the diegetic world with 'complex' and 'psychologically dense'
beings containing both good and evil.

By the same token the donor/hero of SF can only survive
if he resists this defilement and continues to displace on to
'other' monsters his own innate temptations. This is the play
of similarity and difference of narrative digression. SF allegory
creates a narrative by projecting outwards certain 'inauthentic'
qualities of the human spirit, and making them threaten the
now purified hero through quest and combat. The paradigmatic threat to the actant 'hero'/'donor' is at the same time a
threat to the meaning of the 'relentless forward flow' hero of
the narrative since it seeks to expel the difference through
which he is defined. In this sense the Krotons, Dukkha, the
Daleks, the Master, all eternal travellers like the Doctor, are
monsters from his Id who battle his Super Ego across the
terrain of the narrative.

At the end of his era as the Doctor, Patrick Troughton
finally revealed his 'home'. As it was revealed (and as it has
grown and developed since then) the Time Lord home of
Gallifrey turned out to be that very source of inhumane and
bureaucratic science which has been the Doctor's continuous
enemy.

> There are always procedures to be followed, pre-set tasks
> to be performed and files to be amended. The rituals of
> record housekeeping are eternal and there is always some-
> body wanting items of information . . . Nothing ever
> goes wrong — no breakdowns, no faulty machinery —
> not a single fault to upset the ordered calm of this, the
> central city of the Time Lords. Yet, this itself has contri-
> buted to the state of atrophy. For if nothing ever goes
> wrong, if all the machines and technological wonders
> perform strictly according to function then there is no
> need to understand the principles upon which they were
> first built. Up above the Time Lords live and work, serene
> in their ordered, procedurised lives, while deep beneath
> their feet the machinery that maintains their balanced
> existence hums away in everlasting motion.[48]

The home to which William Hartnell says, in episode one, he will one day return has been found. The home of 'friends and protection' for which he yearns is also the procedurised world of his greatest foe.

In his analysis of *The Sweeney*, Phillip Drummond has argued that the nature of the series format is to drive out 'difference'. The narrative:

> Unites a paradigm of representatives of the law against an episodically varied repertory of representatives of the world of crime. Since the forces of law and order predominate, Regan, Carter and Haskins ... form an almost perpetual ensemble versus opponents inevitably characterised by fictional ephemerality; intruding into the fictional, non-regular characters are much more likely to be transgressors — expelled from the contest, they are expelled from the fiction. In other words, while the *actant* 'villain' remains essential within the opposition, its *actorial* expression is constantly in flux.[49]

In *Doctor Who* this is far less certainly the case. Both in the metaphoric parallel of the function 'penetration' and in the continued reappearance of the same villains, *Doctor Who* as SF narrative never finally expels its 'difference'. Indeed, it is the female companions and the actorial expression of the Doctor himself who are regularly expelled in the programme's search for idiosyncrasy and human individualism in the face of ratings and rationalism. But it is less the nature of the programme as an episodic serial that creates this 'resistance', than *Doctor Who*'s profound reliance as narrative on the discourses of science fiction and Romantic Gothic.

Jon Pertwee

Chapter 3

Establishment: Science Fiction and Fantasy

'*Doctor Who* won its reputation as a top science fiction series during Jon Pertwee's time in the role.'[1] As the third Doctor, Pertwee adopted a 'stylish' action-persona, centred on his mode of dress and his stunts. 'Spearhead from Space', his first story, inaugurated a period of location-based pyrotechnics, hardware and acrobatic set-pieces featuring teams of stunt men. Pertwee's own physicality replaced Troughton's running away, and ruffed shirts and ornate flowing capes displaced the clown in baggy check pants. Compensating for the less fanciful locations of the now Earth-based Doctor was the emphatically 'visual' action-style and the fact that this was the first Doctor in colour. Pertwee wore his grandfather's evening suits, supplementing them with red, blue and green velvet smoking jackets, changing each season — 'almost the stereotype', the *Doctor Who Monthly* remarked, 'of the English Dandy'.[2]

Pertwee signified 'adventure in style' partly because he personally liked that kind of life, partly because the production team wanted to co-opt the success of the 'Swinging Sixties' and the world-wide marketing of 'liberated' affluence via Carnaby Street and Biba (the programme had a considerable audience among 'up-market' 17 to 19-year olds). There were also intertextual reasons. Pertwee and his producer were adapting *Doctor Who* in terms of the popular 'chase' and 'karate' action mode of James Bond ('The Daemons' actually using exploding helicopter footage from a Bond film), and Bond was a stylish dresser. At the same time the Victorian cut of his cloak and the deerstalker hat worn by Pertwee in 'Spearhead from Space') contributed a Sherlock Holmes dimension which Pertwee felt was important. It was dignified and more in keeping with the established age of the Doctor than the Bond image. So the new 'fashion' persona of the third Doctor lay at the intersection of a variety of personal, economic and generic determinants.

But as well as co-opting current 'up-market' fashion and media successes, there was also a strong element of programme continuity. With the exception of the Troughton era, *Doctor Who* has fundamentally adhered to the original brief of Verity Lambert and David Whittaker that the Doctor should appear as 'a citizen of the universe, and a gentleman to boot', the latter signified by Hartnell's Edwardian gentleman wardrobe, Pertwee's dignified 'Holmesian' style, Baker's bohemian upper-class persona out of Toulouse-Lautrec, and Davison's 'Regency' and gentleman-amateur cricketing gear.

The 'gentleman' image has always been a central part of the Doctor's style — described by a hostile Australian audience member as an 'extremely irritating and patronising South-East English self-indulgent shot at the rest of Britain'. In Pertwee's case, this was the ability to carry essentially upper middle-class English accents, mores, mannerisms and 'cool' to, for instance, working-class Wales in 'The Green Death', and various other out-of-the way places which are represented as naturally 'inferior' and frequently inflected in terms of the English class system. Occasionally this allowed reference to the inequities of class, but generally *Doctor Who* stepped back from this and displaced stratification through the Doctor's wit and action into a cool 'establishment' superiority. It is this extension of British colonial sang-froid and humour from the Indian to the galactic frontier which allowed Pertwee's Doctor to draw so easily on the Bond action-chase scenario — since James Bond was also inhabited by the British gentleman's 'cool'.

So under Pertwee the Doctor's 'citizen of the universe persona was an extension of the English gentleman one, with self-professed 'old fashioned' virtues very different from the

'student rebellion youth challenging authority' persona which
Philip Hinchcliffe ascribed to Tom Baker. But the persona
was also crossed by a necessary 'SF' coding. As we have seen
the 'citizen of the universe' image was taken very seriously in
1963, with the hermeneutic coding determining the narrative
at least as much as the action and events which later came to
dominate in the Pertwee years from 1970—4. As the *Doctor
Who Monthly* noted: 'Hartnell was given one extra item to
make him look out of place even in pre-First World War
Brighton: a flowing main of silver hair which looked totally
incrongruous on a gentleman of his supposed age'.[3] Actually
the flowing hair was much more than an 'item' added on top
of the wing collar and silk scarf. It was coded 'aesthetically' (in
the first Hartnell story there is a prolonged close-up of the
unconscious Doctor, his face lit to accentuate the narrow
features, the high cheek bones, the noble brow and thrown
back silvery hair of a stereotyped representation of some
nineteenth-century composer); and Romantically — the
Doctor as a wanderer and outcast of immeasurably superior
culture. That early tension between the 'everyday' and the
'alien', the professional gentleman and the citizen of the
universe, 'realism' and 'SF', has continued to define the semic
density — the parameters of character development — of the
Doctor.

This tension and contrast has been dramatised by means
of the Doctor's relationship with his companions, most of
whom have been taken from Earth, and as such have tended
to carry the 'here-and-now' of contemporary fashions, mores
and events. Katy Manning, as the third Doctor's female companion Jo Grant, like Pertwee adopted the 'action-style'
repertoire, wearing on her fingers her own fourteen rings,
dressing from Biba, and doing some of her own stunts, just
as Pertwee did. She was replaced by Elisabeth Sladen, as
Sarah Jane Smith, who wore clothes 'geared to make her look
somewhat tomboyish — overalls, leather jacket and a variation
on the Robin Hood Lincoln Green'.[4] And in the 1980 Janet
Fielding, representing an 'independent' woman from a super-
sonic age, wore the formal mauve of an air hostess.

In terms of economic and professional values, these codings of dress are easy to understand. Television as a medium

aspires to 'here-and-nowness' (the second Doctor's Beatle
haircut, Sarah Jane Smith's 'women's lib' gear, Tegan's air
hostess in a series which was the first BBC show ever to gain
access to the '£30 million a day prop', Concorde;)[5] and long-
term serials in particular co-opt contemporary events in their
endless search for 'motivation' and 'good drama'. Unlike that
other long-term institution, *Coronation Street, Doctor Who*
as science fiction is generally unable to co-opt contemporaneity by means of reference to 'events' — the Royal Wedd-
ing, the Queen's Jubilee, the change to decimalisation and so
on. But it can co-opt current 'style' and it can locate these in
current 'movements' such as 'women's lib' or environmental-
ism, or as Hinchcliffe said of Tom Baker, the student movement.

Contemporaneity is reached for indirectly. Pertwee's
producer, Barry Letts, felt that his current audience would
take more easily to the 'women's libber' Sarah Jane Smith
than to the somewhat passé mini-skirted and '1960s' Jo
Grant, but she had to fulfil the same 'dramatic' role. The
journalist Sarah Jane was brighter than Jo, and, as a professional news gatherer, inquisitive and therefore likely to get
into the 'necessary' scrapes for more positive reasons. To
flesh out this change in persona but not in dramatic motivation, the producer's values helped extract 'Women's Lib'
from the 'here-and-now'. Appropriate 'tomboyish' clothes
were designed in accordance with the dominant media representation of feminists, and Sarah Jane Smith stepped out as
a gentle reproof to the aesthetically and morally traditional
Doctor. BBC television was adopting its conventional pattern
of extracting 'drama' from the 'balance' of contrasts.

In comparison, the later companion Nyssa, as the daughter
of an aristocratic non-Terran class that lived 'intelligently and
without evil', adopted a mode of dress with so little of the
'here and now' about it that it became quite dysfunctional on
location and was replaced by a (still 'stylish') velvet trouser
suit. As a 'science fiction' character from another galaxy,
Nyssa's initial clothes signified 'strangeness', 'gentleness' and
the sylvan preoccupations of her class. As an 'SF character' a
universe of styles was available, but intertextual reference
provided a convenient shorthand: a vestimentary coding

drawn from the aristocratic woodland dalliance of *A Midsummer Night's Dream* seemed appropriate.

The infinitely various possibilities for 'estrangement' of a science fiction hero can pose problems of contextualisation and credibility for a short (twenty-five minute) and episodic programme dependent on ratings and instant identification — unless, as was shrewdly done in the very first episode, strangeness is itself emphasised as the 'problem' of the narrative. But as a number of producers have commented, 'You can't keep the Doctor a mystery forever'; and Pertwee's Doctor took the bull by the horns in locating the action on Earth and co-opting, as far as was possible within budgetry limitations, the fast-pace, 'Bondian "action-fantasy" genre', located in 'realistic' settings. None the less, Pertwee had always to be the SF Doctor as well and the introduction of his alter-ego, the Master (or 'Moriarty in space'), was an attempt to emphasise the SF concept at a time when the Doctor himself was becoming least distinguishable from the Earth élite.

This narrative conjuncture between 'realism's' here-and-now and an estranging 'other' world is typical of science fiction as a genre. But how are the 'realistic and the (science) 'fiction' plausibly conjoined?

SF as semiotic practice: the absent paradigm

Marc Angenot has made the following comparison to distinguish between 'realist' and science fiction discourses.

1   A young lady with a blue merino dress trimmed with three rows of frills came to the doorstep. She introduced Mr Bovary in the kitchen, where a big fire had been kindled. (Flaubert *Madame Bovary* 1856)

2   Around the swimming pool were strangely shaped chairs made of blentos. . .Over her discoll she was wearing an iridescent gown fashioned of vovax and adorned with bernital inlays. (Bruss *Complet Vénus Terre* 1963)

The juxtaposition here of a 'realist' and an SF text confronts us with a question: 'How to differentiate a "blue merino dress trimmed with three rows of frills" from an "iridescent gown fashioned of vovax and adorned with bernital inlays"?'[6] How to differentiate Tegan's functional air-hostess uniform (or Sarah Jane's 'feminist' overalls) from the fairy diaphony of Nyssa?

The answer appears simple at first: the difference is a matter of the strange 'neologism' introducing items of clothing. Yet, Angenot argues: 'A reader not versed in the frivolities of fashion in the first half of the nineteenth century would have some trouble in making any distinctions. He might find words like "merino" and "frills" just as queer as "vovax" and "bernital".'[7] And equally a viewer not versed in the modish dress-style of the late 1960s may not have been able to distinguish that Katy Manning dressed from Biba, while young 1980s viewers tend not to associate Sarah Jane's knee breeches with 'feminism'. In their own context, the 'realistic' and the 'SF' clothes all *signify*, and depend, for their 'transparent' appropriation by an audience on the latter being 'competent' in the same cultural codes. All 'reading' — whether of 'realist', SF or whatever genre — requires a code.

What then is the difference? 'Realist' fiction, in contrast to the 'estranging' quality of SF, is coded according to the norms, conventions and taken-for-granted assumptions of the reader's 'empirical' world. Yet this itself is a social construction, determined by discourses of 'knowledge' carried by dominant knowledge institutions such as the media (the emphasis on 'up-to-dateness', the constant passage of the present tense) and the school system (the emphasis on facts as authentic knowledge — the 'voice of authority' carried by television quiz shows as by the early 'historical' *Doctor Who*'s). Pertwee's frills, like those of Madame Bovary, are coded in terms of current constructions of knowledge: for those who 'know' Jo's gear comes from Biba, and even for those lacking this kind of specialised intellectual capital, the broader connotations of 'difference' and 'swinging style' may be clear because represented as the 'latest and mostest' in a variety of television presentations. Similarly, the dress of Marco Polo, Nero, Troilus and other characters in the early 'historical' *Doctor Who* stories, were coded according to a 'known' narrative of facts and events, as familiarly described in schools throughout the country.

Equally in the 'hard' science fiction period which some claim Pertwee's to be, *Doctor Who* now drew on the *SF* discourse of the empirical present interrupted suddenly and fearfully by alien invaders: the 'sleepy villages and cities of England attacked by alien virus and war machine' syndrome of H. G. Wells's *War of the Worlds* which had recently achieved wide public currency through the BBC television success *Quatermass*. In the first Pertwee story 'Spearhead from Space' (1970), *Doctor Who* directly borrowed the Wellsian theme of a 'shower of meteorites' from outer space which in fact presage alien invasion. This tended to be followed alternatively by threats to the 'empirical' present from the interior and/or past of the Earth ('The Silurians', 'Inferno', 'The Daemons', 'The Sea Devils') and further threats of mechanical and monstrous extra-terrestrial invasion, ('The Ambassadors of Death', 'Terror of the Autons', 'The Claws of Axos', 'The Day of the Daleks'). In *Doctor Who* Daleks and Cybermen had already been seen invading the 'realistic' terrain of Westminster Bridge and St Paul's Cathedral. These had been successful stories and, for many long-term *Doctor Who* fans, number among the 'classics' of the programme. The 'London of today laid waste by some nameless unknown terror',[9] the images of the Daleks advancing smoothly across Westminster Bridge and the Cybermen descending mechanically (with thanks to *Battleship Potemkin*) down the steps in front of St Paul's, are treasured icons of the fans and programme buffs who speak nostalgically in the BBC Television Centre bar of the days when that kind of location work was still possible. Many would presumably agree with Jon Pertwee's justification for his preference for an Earth-based 'science fiction James Bond', that a 'Yeti on the toilet seat in Tooting Bec' is more frightening than in its native Himalayas. Terrance Dicks, script editor during the Pertwee/Letts era, had marked his debut in that position with the classic Cyberman story, 'The Invasion' (1968), a signature which was to dominate in years ahead.

Each of these discourses (of television, of school history,

of science fiction) firmly fixed the current empirical world as the more authentic and 'natural' in the face of threat. But as a 'quality' programme *Doctor Who* has also tried to locate its aliens in their culture — which for the Daleks was a terrain of high-minded science cut short by warfare, irradiation, bestial metamorphosis and degeneration; a narrative of events which drew loosely on the tradition of SF social and cultural perspectivism, first popularly focused by Wells's *The Time Machine*. This notion of the Dalek 'tragedy' as a possible future scenario for Earth potentially opened out on to a different SF discourse — of science fiction as conjecture — as sources of potential Terran tension and conflict — race, sex, class, and (because this is SF) kind — are projected on to other worlds and times as a conjecture of what might be possible although located elsewhere. Sometimes the stories can signify very specifically the contradictions of the 'contemporary', as in the representation of miners' grievances in the 1973—4 Pertwee stories, 'The Green Death' and 'The Monster of Peladon'. Though here, the perspectivism is little more than simplistic projection of current English problems, consensually coded, on to terrains signified as alien merely by the surface data of hair colour, dress and curious monsters.

In contrast, in more 'literary' science fiction, such as Ursula Le Guin's *The Word For World Is Forest*, (and to a reduced extent its *Doctor Who* spin-off 'Kinda'), entire alternative cultures are constructed, according to which Terran 'problems' (in Le Guin's case the Vietnam War) are located in a more radical perspective.

This latter kind of science fiction is, as Angenot argues, 'a conjectural genre in two respects. Its aesthetic goal consists in creating a remote, estranged, and yet intelligible "world". The narrative about such a world itself requires a conjectural reading. It does not call for the reader to apply the norms, rules, conventions, and so forth of his empirical world, but instead assumes a paradigmatic intelligibility that is both delusive and necessary.'[10]

As an example of this dual conjecture in 'serious' science fiction, we can take the moment in Le Guin's *The Word For World Is Forest* when the brutal American-marine-in-Vietnam type, Captain Davidson, is pinned on his back to the ground by one of the alien 'creechies' who then sings over him, having already participated in the killing of all Davidson's men. In the first place, the narrative creates the remote world of 'New Tahiti', intelligible immediately by its Earth-ascribed name, resonant in the memory of familiar narratives about the original Tahiti and the destruction of its 'paradise' culture by European colonisation, and resonant too with the then current American colonialism in Vietnam, as buttressed by Davidson's ruthless Social Darwinism.

> Get enough humans here, build machines and robots, make farms and cities, and nobody would need the creechies any more. And a good thing too. For this world, New Tahiti, was literally made for men. Cleaned up and cleaned out, the dark forests cut down for open fields of grain, the primeval murk and savagery and ignorance wiped out, it would be a real paradise, a real Eden. A better world than worn-out Earth. And it would be his world.[11]

The narrative brings its 'meaning' to the fore: it is 'about' colonisation and genocide which are all too familiar in the reader's empirical world, just as *Doctor Who*'s 'The Green Death' in its novel form[12] is 'about class exploitation.

> The memory of the General Strike in 1926 was still with many of them. For seven bitter months the coal miners had remained on strike until finally they were defeated because they had no food.'
>
> 'I was only a boy in those days', said Dai Evans quietly, remembering the humiliation of the miners' defeat.
>
> 'I learnt that sometimes you have to give in.'
>
> 'Even if it means you are being exploited? asked Professor Jones.'
>
> 'The workers have always had bosses', said Dai Evans, 'people who live off our backs, so we might as well accept that.'[13]

But in Le Guin's novel there are further levels of meaning:

in contrast to the 'maggot' monsters of 'The Green Death',
we learn that the 'creechies' of Athshe 'use a kind of ritualised
singing to replace physical combat' and, like many Earth
animals, for them the act of prostration and exposure of the
belly to an aggressor terminates the fight. The creechies'
alien/alternative culture is revealed: 'Rape, violent assault,
and murder virtually don't exist among them'.

This, however, is still the 'paradise' discourse of Earthmen,
inflected in 'academic' terms by the anthropologist, Dr
Lyubov:

> They're a static, stable, uniform society. They have no
> history. Perfectly integrated, and wholly unprogressive.
> You might say that like the forest they live in, they've
> attained a climax state.[14]

Similarly in 'Kinda' we have the 'academic' explanation by
Todd:

> The clown stroke jester is a familiar figure, anthropologic-
> ally speaking. He performs the function in a non-coercive
> social grouping of diffusing potential sources of conflict
> through mockery and ridicule.

To finally recognise the essential 'otherness' of Le Guin's
world, the reader has to slowly interpret the Athsheans' own
speech and culture values (a development which never properly takes place for the Trickster in 'Kinda').

> "Sometimes they talk of their dreams, the healers try to
> use them in healing, but none of them are trained, or have
> any skill in dreaming. Lyubov, who taught me, understood
> me when I showed him how to dream, and yet even so he
> called the world-time 'real' and the dream-time 'unreal', as
> if that were the difference between them".[15]

In contrast, Selver:

> Feared that he was cut off from his roots, that he had gone
> too far into the dead land of action ever to find his way
> back to the springs of reality.[16]

Whereas in 'The Green Death', 'The Keeper of Traken' and 'Kinda' we are shown that 'reality' lies in the Doctor's world of action, and not among the passive working, aristocratic or primitive classes, in *The Word for World is Forest* we slowly understand that the 'real' world is the land of dreaming. It is through dreaming that men and women recognise and resolve the contradictions within themselves. In contrast the Earthmen project their inner conflicts outwards.

> Therefore they go about in torment killing and destroying, driven by the gods within, whom they will not set free but try to uproot and deny. If they are men they are evil men, having denied their own gods, afraid to see their own faces in the dark.[17]

By the end of the novel, the narrative has inscribed the reader within an alternative cultural perspective: the 'yumens' (Earthmen) are hardly human bacause they do not 'sing' or 'dream', but instead kill and rape — each other, their own Earth, and this new planet whose word for world is forest. The originally foregrounded perspective, signifying the exploitation of the environment and of primitive peoples (which in 'The Green Death' was consumed in action) has here been consumed by an 'other', more estranging one in which the world of action — whether of Davidson's aggression or even of Lyubov's study and conservation — is 'unreal'. Le Guin wrote in 1976: 'It is not only the Captain Davidsons who can be found in the unconscious, if one looks. The quiet people who do not kill each other are there, too, It seems that a great deal is there, the things we most fear (and therefore deny), the things we most need (and therefore deny). I wonder, couldn't we start listening to our dreams.'[18]

In contrast, in *Doctor Who*'s 'Kinda', where a conscious attempt was made by the writer to draw on the sustained conjectural mode of 'serious' science fiction, the production team's emphasis on TV action, effects and programme continuity combined to defeat his attempt to inscribe the audience in the dreams of an 'other' culture. Despite the similarity with Le Guin in the representation of the psychologically unstable military/colonial mind, the 'scientific' but

Earth-bound understanding of alien forms by an anthropologist, and the communal/environmental harmony of the natives, in the end the narrative 'alternative' is reduced to the threat of a snake-like monster, and the audience is offered a world from within its conventional stock of knowledge: the garden of Eden.

Le Guin's science fiction, on the other hand shifts us from the syntagmatically unfolding sequence of the plot (a tale of colonial exploitation) to a paradigmatic 'elsewhere'. An alternative world of words, customs, institutions and values is built by the work of the reader. Potentially this 'other' world of science fiction is, as Agnenot points out, a place, that (though 'fictive' and 'delusive') offers a coherent and utopically estranging light on the audience's empirical world. Its series of 'absent paradigms' — the building up of entire imaginary cultures from the foregrounded use of unfamiliar words like 'vovax' and 'bernital' or the unfamiliar use of familiar terms like 'sing' and 'dream' — may offer the audience its own empirical world more 'realistically'.

> SF functions in its semiotic axioms as a paradigmatic 'phantasm', shifting the reader's attention from the syntagmatic structure of the text to a delusion which is an important element of the reader's pleasure. In this regard, SF is a u-topia (no place) both through its ideological influence and in its mode of decipherment. As in a utopia, the reader is transported from a locus or place — the actual syntagnatic sequence — to a non-locus or no place, the paradigmatic 'mirage' which presumably regulates the message. . . SF is not determined by any direct relationship between its fictional given and the empirical world, but by the relations — inherent in any fictional discourse — between syntagm and paradigm.[19]

For Angenot 'authentic' and 'artistic' science fiction estranges the reader from his or her taken-for-granted environment in order to see beneath its surface more 'realistically' — a tendency which is compounded by the anti-individuating and 'epic' character of science fiction, its desire to speak about entire cultures and worlds, and the fact that science characters are 'never individuals but representatives of groups or species'. In contrast, he argues, there is a strong tendency in a great deal of popular science fiction — in comics, in films and on television — in the direction of cultural non-estrangement. The 'species' characteristic of science fiction is then inflected in a right-wing, militaristic (the Communists as BEM syndrome), or liberal-consensual (as in *Doctor Who*'s 'The Keeper of Traken') direction. But in either case audience 'work' is negated, and pleasure inscribed in the dominant action-chase scenario.

Angenot derives an 'imminent aesthetics' of the science fiction genre for these contrary tendencies: 'If the mechanical transposition of "this-worldly" paradigms is sufficient to account for every narrative utterance, we have a witless, even infantile, type of science fiction. If, on the contrary, a maximum distance is maintained between the empirical and the "exotopic" paradigm, although the alien rules tend to organise themselves into a consistent whole, the reader's pleasure increases.'[20]

Angenot's 'reader' is clearly of a specific 'high culture' type; and there is a danger in his simply dichotomised formulation of missing the differences — and subversive potentialities for pleasure — within popular science fiction. Certainly examples of the 'infantile' science fiction are easy to find: the 'mechanical transposition of this-worldly paradigms' is common in *Doctor Who* — especially in the Pertwee era. But as we tried to show in the previous chapter, an estranging and unsettling negation of the familiar and the conventional of liberalism, as well as militarism, of tolerance and rationalism as well as fascism — also often operates at the paradigmatic level. The comfortable trajectory of 'democracy' and 'liberation' is threatened by an 'other', which is incoherent and defined only as a negation.

In the era of *Doctor Who* immediately following that of Pertwee, when Philip Hinchcliffe was producer and Tom Baker was the new star, quite a different SF intertextuality was favoured in place of the Bondian inflection of the 'monster on the toilet seat in Tooting Bec'. Hinchcliffe, who was seriously interested in SF 'ideas' and 'myths', challenged the notion that the Pertwee era, with its 'soldiers running around

on Earth and kiddy monsters' had been real science fiction.
On the one hand he wanted to get away from the 'establishment' figure of Pertwee, and felt that the 'bohemian' 'student
rebellion' features of Baker better represented the 'general
whittling down of Britain's world role after Macmillan and
Eden'. Baker was 'youth challenging authority' and 'reflected
what was going on in England after Suez and the decline of
Empire'. On the other hand, Hinchcliffe wanted to 'take the
programme back into fantasy', with a less moral and 'more
ambivalent' human/unhuman hero conducting 'the audience
on strange voyages to really give them something fantastic'.
By strongly emphasising the Gothic concept of possession
Hinchcliffe felt he could evince the drama of horror: 'One,
by concentrating on the person being possessed, the twin
personalities fighting for control, etc., and two, by showing
the reactions of those around him to that developing horror'.[21]
The possession' theme could relate to the organic ('plant
power' in 'The Seeds of Doom' (1976) which played on current environmentalist discourses) or to the mechanistic ('robot
revolution' in 'The Robots of Death' (1977), playing on a
traditional theme in SF. But above all (and in place of what
Hinchcliffe and his script editor, Robert Holmes, saw as the
Star Trek liberal moralism of the Pertwee/Letts era) it drew
on the Gothic 'fantasy' origins of science fiction.

Hinchcliffe: What we went for was a very powerful concept. So we borrowed from science fiction. . .and we
borrowed from established horror themes and Gothic. . .
'Planet of Evil' originally grew of an idea to have a Jekyll
and Hyde planet . . .In fact we also pinched a bit from
Forbidden Planet because we had a sort of monster of the
Id. . .We did another Gothic thing with a mummy story,
about mummies that wake up and take you over — robot
mummies. . .And we did a Frankenstein story, 'The Brain
of Morbius'. . .And then we did a Jack the Ripper story,
'The Talons of Weng Chiang'. . . We did quite a few Gothic
ones, because I like the trappings. What I liked to do was
to go to a literary convention or a science fiction convention. . .and borrow the trappings of it, and then re-dress

that up within the *Doctor Who* format. That seemed to me a device that worked very well.

Hinchcliffe's approach tended to start from an initial SF/Gothic concept such as the Jekyll and Hyde of 'Planet of Evil': 'So that half the time everyone was normal and Jekyll-like, and when it gets dark they all become Hydes. I think I didn't know any more about it than that'; then to consult very early with designers in order to think up frightening and fantastic visual effects, such as the weird red jungle and the travelling eye of the same story; and to move from there to the construction of very tight disturbing 'space melodrama' story-lines with the script editor and the writer. Even when it began as a visual concept, like Hinchcliffe's idea of doing a story set in the time of the Borgias after he had been to Port Meirion and felt it would make a good Renaissance Italian location, the Gothic element was lurking closely beneath the surface with the science of Da Vinci's era threatened – and the maiden Sarah Jane threatened as was symptomatic of the Gothic – by the dark monkish practices and endless catacomb corridors of 'The Masque of Mandragola' (1976).

Hinchcliffe's successful era as producer of *Doctor Who* suggests that the 'phantasm' which estranges the linear development of the narrative is not necessarily the realist construction of an alternative culture symptomatic of Angenot's 'absent paradigm'. The 'phantasm' may be generated by fantasy. In the remainder of this chapter we will look at the 'absent' paradigm in terms of two alternative constructions available within SF as genre, emphasising respectively the signifieds and signifiers of science fiction. This will lead to an examination of the two dominating discursive practices which have operated within the SF genre – and help account for the 'super technology' and 'Gothic' inflections respectively of the Pertwee/Letts and Baker/Hinchcliffe eras: Wellsian Scientism and the Romantic Gothic.

SF and realism: estranging the signified

One discursive practice of *Doctor Who* is its cultural perspectivism, based especially on the privileged viewpoint of its intellectual hero. In the Wellsian tradition the Doctor, by means of his movements and intellectual experience, establishes a vantage point outside the historical worlds of social, racial and sexual stratification which he visits, and from which their moral values can be criticised. Often, as in Pertwee's 'The Monster of Peladon' and 'The Green Death', this world of stratification is a close approximation to the viewer's empirical world (miners versus government, multinationals, feminism, federation), which the Doctor's intellectual distance then estranges through analysis.

As Darko Suvin has argued, the necessary condition for SF is its introduction of a *novum* — a cognitive innovation 'super added to or infused into the author's empirically "known" — i.e. culturally defined — world'.[22] In *Doctor Who* of course, as in Wells' *The Time Machine*, the novum is the possibility of time travel and the experimental and estranging 'wisdom' this allows the time traveller. The 'essential tension' of SF, then, is between the reader trapped in his/her own time and 'the Unkown introduced by the novum'. The innovation may be of varying degrees of magnitude and relevance, varying from the minimum of one discrete 'invention' (such as the multi-national corporation whose polluting waste literally becomes monstrous in 'The Green Death') to the maximum of deriving not only the spacio-temporal locus, but also the writing 'voice' from an 'other' time, place and social group, as in Le Guin's *The Word For World Is Forest*.

If the novum is the necessary condition of SF, its sufficient condition is 'the validation of the novelty by scientifically methodical cognition'.[23] It is important to note that Suvin's definition of 'science' is not confined to 'hard science' and the 'really possible'/'near future' variants of the genre. Indeed, he believes that the 'better' SF has drawn more on the 'soft' social and human sciences such as anthropology, ethnology, sociology and linguistics. This is the SF of 'ideal possibility' in the sense 'of a conceptual or thinkable possibility the premises of which are not in themselves or in their consequences internally contradictory'.[24]

Hence time travel in *Doctor Who* is a novum allowing for a variety of social interactions, each in themselves relying on the conditions of causal motivation and plausibility even

if the novum itself is not. The novum is introduced as a
'mental experiment' which, once postulated, adheres to
'accepted scientific, i.e. cognitive, logic'. It is precisely this
necessary condition of scientific logic, as a bedrock of serious
SF, which allowed *Doctor Who* script editor Douglas Adams
to parody the genre in *Hitch Hiker* by motivating events with
a spaceship's 'improbability drive' that, for instance, turns
two undeviatingly aggressive nuclear missiles into 'a bowl
of petunias and a very surprised looking whale'. The satire
works because SF as genre — whether 'hard' or 'soft' — stops
short of acknowledging metaphysical agency, 'in the literal
sense of an agency going beyond *physis* (nature), beyond the
ideal possibilities of physics or any other science'.[25] For
Suvin it is the 'presence of scientific cognition — not only
and not even primarily in the guise of facts and hypotheses
but as the manifestation and sign of a method identical
to that of the philosophy of science' that differentiates SF
'from the "supernatural" genres or fantasy in the wider sense,
which include fairy tales, mythical tales, moral allegories and
so on, over and above horror or heroic "fantasy" in the
narrower sense'.[26]

'Cognitive novelty' then is the necessary and sufficient
kernal (or 'conceptual premise') of SF. Further, the novelty
has to be located:

In concrete (even if imaginary) terms, ie in terms of the
specific time, place, cosmic and social totality within
which it is acting, and especially in terms of its effect on
the (overtly or covertly) human relationships upon which
it impinges . . . This means that, in principle, SF has to be
judged — in some ways like naturalistic fiction and quite
unlike the supernatural genres — by the density, objects
and characters described in the microcosm of the text . . .
One could easily set up a Hegelian triad, where the thesis
would be naturalistic fiction, which has an empirically
validated effect of reality, the antithesis would be the
supernatural genres, which lacks such an effect, and the
synthesis would be SF, in which the effect of reality is
validated by a cognitive innovation.[27]

Following Lukács, Suvin's distinction between on the one
hand the 'trivial sensationalism' of 'naturalism' and, on the
other, 'realist' SF, is based on the device of estrangement
from the everyday, which offers a better 'vantage point' from
which to comprehend and comment on 'the author's collective
context'. Thus in Wells' *The Time Machine* and *Doctor Who*'s
'The Green Death', the density of the objects and characters
— and in particular the representation of 'monsters' creeping
out from tunnels and mines underground — is not simply for
the effect of sensational adventure. In each case the monsters
are themselves an effect of the economic relations of capitalism.
In 'The Green Death' the death of the miners at the hands
of monsters created by a profit-oriented multi-national
corporation, Global Chemicals, is contextualised not only
by an environmentalist discourse, but also in relation to the
'exploitation' of workers by bosses (in the novel, the history
of the working-class struggle and the General Strike of 1926),
and the overt relating of Global Chemicals to the world of
fascism.

Lukács noted of Flaubert's historical novels that they
simply offered, in their density of naturalistic detail and
trivial exoticism, an escape from analysis of the degraded
relations of capitalism.[28] Similarly, Suvin allows the use of
historical and mythological stories in SF only if the 'innovation is to estrange the implied readers' familiar conventions,
and . . . thus . . . reflects back to his world'. While not
adopting Lukács' epistemology or aesthetic, Suvin does
draw on his important distinction between 'naturalism'
and 'realism', and his implication that the recent narrowing
down of the concept of 'estrangement' to interrogation of
the signifier and not the signified is a misappropriation of its
original usage in Brecht.

For Angenot and Suvin SF situates itself within the
'general alternative of liberation versus bondage, self manage-
ment v. class alienation, by organizing its narrations around
the exploration of *possible new relationships*, where the
novelty is *historically* determined and critically evaluable.
Thus the understanding of SF — constituted by history and
evaluated in history — is doubly impossible without a sense
of history, a sense that this genre is a system which changes

in the process of social history.'[29] Consequently they place both naturalism (with its acceptance of the 'trivial' and 'sensational' surface of empirical events) and fantasy (with its rejection of cognitive analysis of empirical events) on the side of the literature of 'bondage'. And they would also criticise theorists of the fantastic, like Tzvetan Todorov and Rosemary Jackson for their ignorance of anything but the most gross understanding of the historical mediation of generic forms.

As a matter of principle, Angenot and Suvin argue for a symptomatic reading of SF. They criticise 'motif' definitions of genre (the notion that SF is defined by its content of space travel, alien planets and robots) and argue that the SF text is constituted and marked as much by what it excludes as by what it includes — the exclusion for instance of labour (or its displacement into conflicts between the 'individual' and 'society'), the exclusion of power (or its displacement into natural catastrophes or into individualised, manic psychology) and the exclusion of history (or its displacement into 'cyclical' theories where the future is just a weird repetition of the past). Hence 'true' SF, by their definition, is that which avoids these exclusions but rather employs its 'cognitive novelty' to throw new light on them.

It would, of course, be easy to find examples of all these exclusions in *Doctor Who*. But, as 'The Green Death' example illustrates, it is also possible to find *Doctor Who* stories where they are included, and even underlined. 'The Robots of Death', for instance, in which an effete profit-hungry ruling élite is decimated by a robot revolution led by Taren Capel draws overly on Karel Capek's *RUR*, where the threat to human existence is generated by capitalist industry and implemented by its robotic workforce. As in *RUR*, in 'The Robots of Death' the Doctor represents the 'middle class' resort to humanity against 'alienation' and 'revolution'.

In a programme as long-running as *Doctor Who* a whole variety of inflections are possible, and it is much more useful to cite these in terms of their specific historical, professional and material practices than to distinguish between *Doctor Who* episodes in terms of 'true' and 'false' SF. However, Angenot and Suvin's analysis is important in its insistence that an SF text, in its absences as much as by its inclusions, is always an interpretation of the extra-textual universe. For Angenot and Suvin the object of 'scientific' criticism — as of 'good' SF — is to demystify ideology through cognition, and to expose the 'real' relations of human exploitation beneath the surface of appearances.

It is not, however, to adopt the stance of empiricism or 'objectivism'. The 'realist' position adopted here agrees with 'conventionalist'[30] analysis that interpretation of the world is theory-bound and can therefore never be neutral. As Angenot and Suvin note: 'All knowledge is inescapably co-determined by its subject's point of view as well as by its object. The mystification comes about when this historically located construct and heuristic choice, which is basically an "as if" grows like a djinn from the bottle, into a trans-cendental entity and metaphysical essence. Such mystifying criticism installs a blind spot, a conceptual fetish degrading it into ideology instead of cognition, at the centre of its vision.'[31]

Angenot and Suvin's realist theory of SF occupies a place between what Dyer has called unreflexive 'realism' and solipsistic conventionalism[32] in a way which is homologous with the location of SF between naturalism and fantasy. Indeed in their heuristic choice — their 'as if' — they are adopting the very *novum* which they see as central to SF as genre, and to the post-Baconian scientific method, which is the 'only horizon that incorporates the viewer (experimenter, critic) into the structure of what is being beheld (experiment, text). It is therefore the only horizon which permits the provisional method situated within it to be integrated into social practice and to become self-corrective on the basis of social practice, and which has a chance — if used intelligently — to show realistically the relationship of people and the material world.'[33]

Suvin separately argues that: 'Science is since Marx and Einstein an open-ended corpus of knowledge, and all imagin-able new corpuses which do not contravene the philosophical basis of the scientific method', are valid as SF[34] — and by implication, valid as criticism. To counter the charge of 'eclecticism' he argues against conceptual 'fetishism' — the fault of any theoretical discourse, whether Marxist, psycho-analytical, author-centred or whatever — which ignores that knowledge is co-determined by the subject's point of view and its object. Such fetishising analysis replaces the object's material conditions with its own point of view as 'a universal, eternal axiom'. Hence any theory of genre which fails to take due account of historical determinations — specifically the conditions of production, circulation and reception of SF texts — as well as its own discursive framework, is in danger of fetishism.

Suvin's contribution, has been to argue for a socio-historical and relational definition of science fiction. On the one hand, he has argued, like Todorov,[35] for a theoretical rather than empirical definition of genre: the need to define SF 'negatively' via its relationships with other literary genres (such as naturalism and fantasy) among which it develops. On the other hand, unlike Todorov, Suvin argues for a definition of SF 'positively' as well, determining the 'specific domain' of SF as a genre without lapsing into the empiricism of robot spotting. Hence Suvin's definition of the 'necessary and sufficient conditions of characteristics whose presence identifies a fictional story as SF'.[36]

While agreeing fundamentally with Suvin's realist position, it has to be said that there are weaknesses in both the 'negative' and 'positive' areas of his analysis of SF. By collapsing together the fantastic and the marvellous, Suvin misses a crucially important potential for narrative play within the genre, and within *Doctor Who* in particular, as we have suggested. And further, Suvin's failure to locate historical and material analysis of SF within the generic possibility of science fiction (SF as a site of intersection for the deter-mining discourses of Positivism and Romanticism) draws attention away from analysis of the 'traditional and con-temporary' mediations which he and Angenot argue is essential to any adequate account of the genre. Indeed, their own 'history' of the genre amounts to little more than a broad 'reflection' theory, relating alternating 'utopian' (Bellamy to London, and the 1961—73 work of Le Guin, Dicks, Delany *et al.*) and 'occulted' (Burroughs and Asimov, and post-1973) SF directly to socio-political events.

In these last half dozen years, the utopianising thrust of
ca 1961—73 has mostly run dry in response to socio-
political backleash and disappointment. This is why we
find a wave of demoralisation, of co-mingling anti-cognitive
fantasy with SF, or irrationality or banality, surging back
into even the more significant SF texts.[37]

Certainly the tendency towards 'fantasy' and 'irrationality'
needs analysis in socio-historical terms. But Angenot and
Suvin's 'history' would offer a very mechanistic explanation
indeed of the rise of overt 'class', 'feminist' and 'ecological'
issues in the early 1970s Doctor Who, and their subsequent
replacement by cycles of bizarre and sensational adventure
in the later Williams/Adams era. This discussion of SF, in
which Doctor Who marks a stage beyond the Burroughs-
style 'Dan Dare' of the 1950s, is certainly relevant to our
account: there was in fact a 'drive to utopianism' in the first
episodes of Doctor Who (marked, however, as much by the
Romantic-aesthetic coding of the Doctor as by his cultural
perspectivism) which differentiated it from the technological
mastery of sensational conflict displayed in 'Dan Dare'. But
to leave the analysis at that level would be to ignore in this
history both the generic and intertextual continuities between
these two periods (between, for instance, Dan Dare and Pertwee's Doctor), and the differences locating themselves in
the conditions of production and reception.
    There are many forms of 'popular' SF, and to dismiss
them all as unified 'bourgeois' texts is to fall for a gross
economic determinism. Some modern SF writers (Ursula
Le Guin, Christopher Bailey in Doctor Who's 'Kinda') work
through 'mystical' themes in questioning the 'mythical'
certainty of dominant ideologies and the 'scientific' ideologies
which carry them. And the fact that in Bailey's case this
questioning is not carried through because of the material
conditions of production itself raises questions about Angenot/
Suvin's thesis, since they seem to posit realist SF texts as
coherent wholes, rather than as complexes of competing
discourses.[38]
    As we shall now see in examining H. G. Wells' location
in science fiction, tensions and contradictions within SF texts

were founding principles of the genre. This was not least because SF as genre was never either simply 'bourgeois' or 'subversive', but was strongly influenced by intra-class tensions within modernising capitalism, between the possessors of intellectual and material capital.

H. G. Wells: SF as scientific realism

When in November 1963 the scientific but whimsical Doctor returned to his time machine for the first time, dressed as a turn-of-the-century gentleman, the salute to H. G. Wells' scientist/time traveller, who similarly had 'more than a touch of whim among his elements', was appropriate. Not only because Wells to all intents and purposes established time travel as a generic theme of science fiction — and *Doctor Who*, as its first producer said, was based 'more than loosely . . . on *The Time Machine*' — but also because the genre's central ambivalence about a godlike yet not always benign science came via Wells, rather than its other 'founding father' Jules Verne.

To place *Doctor Who* in direct line from H. G. Wells and his *The Time Machine* is not to seek a simple origin for the programme, to adopt in other words a familiar 'high art' discourse which finds behind the 'imitation'· of television the 'creativity' of a real artist. It is, however, to suggest that *Doctor Who* and other popular SF 'texts' are marked by a generic inflection of SF influenced by Wells. H. G. Wells did not create the genre: but the genre of SF was 'certainly influenced by the interplay of socio-biographical, aesthetic and production codes which between them generated 'H. G. Wells'.

Despite Angenot/Suvin's belief that the originally radical potential of SF was betrayed by its 'absorpition of bourgeois ideology' somewhere around 1910, any account of the 'subversion' potential of SF must take into account contradictions within the bourgeois class. As regards 'general' bourgeois ideology, Wells's scientific training and early 'socialism' alienated him from the idle rentier class and what he regarded as their false ideology of Social Darwinism. On the other hand, Wells was also socially (as teacher and 'scientist') and culturally (as successful author and owner of an architect designed house) mobile, and was able to move into a prestigious élite. His rise from the petit-bourgeoisie and his ambivalent class position generated not only a density of social representations in his literature as part of his critique of capitalist class relations but also, as Parrinder has noted, an 'hysterical uncharity' against the 'threatening, anonymous crowd around and below'.[39]

What this depended on was not only the emergence of new social-technological roles within capitalism, but also on new conditions of artistic production. 'Scientific' realism marked the literary intellectual's emergence from the Romantic 'madness' of isolation (caused by his shift from the security of patronage to the insecurity of the market) into a new security, and a new elite role, as professional savant and social engineer. SF, as part of the wider movement of scientific realism (as represented by Zola and Chekhov) was captured, in terms of authorship, product and audience, by the fraction of the middle class whose wealth consisted in their education, and who were by no means always in accord either with the owners of capital or with the proletariat.

Late nineteenth-century literary realism, as in Zola, Chekhov and Wells, was substantially endowed with the positivistic materialism and evolutionary determinism which had become the capital of the 'educated'.[40] As a 'scientific' realism, it fought its war on two fronts. On the one hand it opposed the 'subjective' revolutionary apocalypse which ignored the scale and system of human evolution, and on the other hand the paralysing 'objectivism' of those who accepted or justified current exploitation on the basis of the immutable laws of history. The representation of the vicious subterranean class of Morlocks and the effete leisure class of Eloi in *The Time Machine* was not just a fanciful inversion of the predator/prey relationship of bourgeois and proletarian classes in Victorian Britain. It also used the ideology of Victorian capitalism — Social Darwinism — against itself to predict degeneration, rather than complacent progress, within the ruling class. According to Wells's thesis, loss of initiative and vigour (as technology progressively took over) would transform the leisure class into 'cattle' for the Morlocks, the brutalised subterranean descendents of nineteenth-century workers who had been forced to remain vigorous in tending the machines.

Wells early SF was radical insofar as it condemned class exploitation (via inversion in *The Time Machine*) and imperialist racism (as in *The War of the Worlds*). The conservative reader's identification of 'us' against the alien 'them', could be radically disturbed by reversals such as when, in *The First Men in the Moon*, it suddenly became apparent that the narrator's description of the monstrously 'functional' culture of the Selenites was in fact a comment on the social reproduction of the English class system – a Wellsian inversion reproduced in *Doctor Who*'s 'Ark in Space' (1975).

By means of Wells' narrative convention – a story within a story – of a complacent 'normal' society invaded by a monstrous alien world (in 'Ark in Space' the brutally functional world of Earth survivors taken over by the Wirrn) which is finally no more than the brutal underside of that self-same civilised world, Wells stressed the connection of civilisation with ruthless exploitation. He therefore demystified the urbane and closed upper-class society and, at the same time, laid waste its optimistic and legitimating Social Darwinist 'philosophy'. Humankind had, in Wells' opinion, to work to retain its culture, and *The Time Machine* is an allegory of what happens when that work is absent. Without it, an artificial human culture is swept aside by bestiality.

In his sociological study *Anticipations*, Wells was more positive predicting that there was indeed a social group equipped to adapt to and master the necessary 'scientific' work of the modern age. Side by side with the effete 'shareholder' class which was steadily becoming 'unfit' for co-operative defence of its class interests, and the 'disintegrating cells' of the working class drifting 'inexorably, towards the 'abyss', there was also a positive process in which 'men, often of the most diverse parentage and antecedent traditions, are being segregated into a multitude of specific new groups'.[41] These varied from sanitary, electrical and mining engineers to doctors, agronomists and irrigation experts, but all were marked by a new and unique competence – the ability to understand and control the age of industrial technology and science. Wells predicted that in the shadow of the scientific wars which would inevitably be generated by international capitalism's greed for profit, it would become apparent 'that the whole apparatus of power in the country is in the hands of a new class of intelligent and scientifically educated men'.[42]

The new rulers would be like its new kind of soldiers – each a 'sober, considerate, engineering man – no more of a gentleman than the men subordinate to him or any other self-respecting person'.[43] In place of the selfishness of monetary control, with its cliques of advertisers and its controlled newspapers, there would be a 'common "general" reason' in things linked through 'the agency of great and sober papers. In England *The Lancet*, and *British Medical Journal* and the already great periodicals of the engineering trades, foreshadow something, but only a very little, or what these papers may be.'[44]

This would be neither a racist society – 'white, black, red, brown . . . efficiency will be the test' – nor a class society. It would be a society resolutely dedicated to rationality and achievement, in order to master and not succumb to the pace of invention and the certainty of war.

On the one hand, Wells' intellectual 'saints' – his 'power of the thing that is provable right' – established for SF the primacy of empirical materialism: the rationalistic 'God-in-the-image-of-Man' which Lem was to attack in *Solaris*. *The Time Machine* not only centred on a scientist as active and innovative forerunner of the new elite. It also foregrounded in its opening page its own discourse as rational controversy, which, as we learn, is not really about geometry but about the 'misconception' of Social Darwinism. Symptomatically, apart from the narrator, only the typical representatives of Wells' 'Third Force', the medical man and the psychologist, follow the controversy through in search of hypothesis and verification. Despite its pessimistic content, then, the meta-discourse of *The Time Machine* invokes the 'New Republic' of intellectuals and scientists.

On the other hand, there is that pessimism. Suvin has shown how the influence of Wells' teacher, T. H. Huxley –

and in particular his consideration of the implications of evolutionary degeneration and atavism (also referred to in 'Ark in Space') — actually determined the structural relationship of the different parts of *The Time Machine*. Playing upon 'the Social Darwinist preconceptions of a "natural" order of power and of a safe evolutionary progress keeping each "lower" evolutionary rung in its place as prey to the "higher" predator',[45] Wells inverted them. Hence the narrative of *The Time Machine* traces an evolutionary regression in which each 'higher' stage in turn succumbs to its 'inferior' one, until, 'in the suggested extrapolation of a destruction of Earth and/or the solar system, all life would succumb or "become prey" to inorganic being, cosmic processes, or just entropy'.[46]

Wells launched the concept of atavistic and degenerative evolution into SF, where it was popularly taken up. As the narrator says in *The War of the Worlds*, 'without the body the brain would of course become a more selfish intelligence, without any of the emotional substratum of the human being'. The villains of Wells' SF, like the Martians in *The War of the Worlds* and the Selenites of *The First Men in the Moon*, derived from this pessimistic prediction of muscular atrophy and the development of a bloated, emotionless brain: direct forerunners of the Mekon and Davros. In *The Time Machine*, the scientist's otherwise entirely unmotivated emotional attachment to an Eloi girl, and the narrator's fervently final observation on this, that 'even when mind and strength had gone, gratitude and a mutual tenderness still lived on in the heart of men', are signs of Wells' tension. *The Time Machine* which begins with a call to reason, ends with a call to human emotion and community.

But the emphasis on human feelings had little real basis in a rational theory of evolution and human adaptation, and Wells' own intellectual saints were perilously close, as he himself described them in *Anticipations*, to SF's fearful future of ruthless, emotionless rationalism. In the new world state, the intellectual elite would attend to the 'merciful obliteration of weak and silly and pointless things'. The diseased of mind and body would be forbidden to reproduce on pain of death, and all those whose actions or thoughts

proved them to be 'unfitted for free life in the world' would
be 'removed from being'. 'The world is a world, not a charitable institution, and I take it they will have to go.'[47] The
men of the New Republic would have 'little pity and less
benevolence' for the 'helpless and useless', the 'unhappy', or
the 'feeble, ugly and inefficient' — qualities which were to
reappear in Davros's own projected 'universe of peace' in
Doctor Who's 'Genesis of the Daleks' (1975) where the lack
of 'pity' became a central dramatic focus.

The Wellsian tension was to be a powerful ingredient of
popular SF. In Dan Dare's first adventure in 1950, the
opposition of effetely beautiful Eloi and hideously active
Morlocks was reproduced on Venus, divided between the
reptilian/rational Treens and the beautiful and pleasure
loving Therons whom Dare accused of 'reading poetry and
smelling flowers' while children on Earth died of starvation.
In 1963 it was reproduced again in the second *Doctor Who*
adventure, in the conflict between the physically and morally
degenerate Daleks and the Thals, 'pure in body and mind,
who stood for the principles of beauty, creation and, above
all, peace.'[48]

Contrary to this defined opposition, the heroic synthesis
of reason and emotion is always one in process: Wells' time
traveller as scientist, but eternal adventurer: Dan Dare's
Oxbridge trained intellect employed in ceaseless action; the
Doctor as Academy scientist but endless wanderer. Wells'
universal state of reason and harmony is avoided at all costs:
it is the purely logical world of the Time Lords that the
Doctor rejected; it is the universal balance that the Guardian
seeks and the Doctor finally disperses in 'The Key to Time'.
In SF terms, the synthesis is coded as the permanent tension
between harmony (structure represented by the White
Guardian) and chaos (entropy represented by the Black
Guardian) which was powerfully foregrounded in 'The Key
to Time', and in the concluding Tom Baker *Doctor Who*
stories, 'The Keeper of Traken' and 'Logopolis'.

The hero is now a doctor, a scientist *in* the world and *in*
the universe — as 'Realists' like Wells and Chekhov wished
him to be. Harry Levin has pointed out that the doctor was
Realism's new hero: but only because his action-in-the-

world distinguished him from the Romantic villain who, as
scientist, isolated himself in his laboratory, experimented
mysteriously, and became a sinister figure 'coldly or madly
treating humans as guinea pigs: Dr Rappacini, Dr Heidegger,
Dr Jekyll, Dr Moreau'.[49] As that list implies, Wells' confident
vision of *Anticipations* was itself infected by the lurking Romantic fear of universal rationalism as a fixed idea.

SF and fantasy: foregrounding the signifier

Philip Hinchcliffe, with his stress on the Gothic, his conscious
shift away from the buoyant 'interested in gadgetry, technology wins, technology is power' Pertwee image to that of the
ambivalent hero, and his 'scary' interest in monsters from the
Id, was right to call his influence of *Doctor Who* a return to
'fantasy'. The opposition of ego and id, self and other — of
self as taken over by other — which we described as central
themes in *Doctor Who* but which were weakened under Letts
and heavily re-inscribed in the Hinchcliffe period, are also
central to the fantastic mode.

As Rosemary Jackson has noted, the modern fantastic
contains two kinds of myth: 'in the first the source of otherness, of threat, is the self. Danger is seen to originate from
the subject, through excessive knowledge, or rationality, or
the misapplication of the human will. This pattern would be
exemplified by *Frankenstein* and is repeated in H. G. Wells'
The Island of Dr Moreau, R. L. Stevenson's *Dr Jekyll and
Mr Hyde* . . . etc.'[50] In contrast, in the other kind of myth:
'Fear originates in a source external to the subject: the
self suffers an attack of some sort which makes it part of
the other. This is the type of appropriation of the subject
found in *Dracula* and tales of vampirism: it is a sequence of
invasion, metamorphosis and fusion, in which an external
force enters the subject, changes it irreversibly and usually
gives to it the power to initiate similar transformations.'[51] In
Doctor Who, however, there is the theme of demonic rationality, of the Time Lord as cold, super-rational, power-hungry
'other', carried most insistently in the Doctor's doppleganger

relationship with the Master and other deviant Time Lords,
Guardians, and 'Gods' — as in the 'Frankenstein' story 'The
Brain of Morbius' (1976), and as featured in 'the Key to
Time'. On the other hand there is the persistent theme of
the taking-over of human beings by vegetable, animal or
energy forms, as in the Jekyll and Hyde 'Planet of Evil'
(1975), or the 'Dracula' story, 'State of Decay' (1980).
Whether as in 'the Frankenstein type of myth (of which
Faust is a variant), self becomes other through a self-generated
metamorphosis, through the subject's alienation from himself
and consequent splitting or multiplying of identities (structured around themes of 'I')'; or whether as in, 'the Dracula
type of myth . . . otherness is established through a fusion
of self with something outside, producing a new form, an
"other" reality (structured around themes of the "not-I")';
both myths 'push towards a state of undifferentiation of self
from other'.[52] Whereas in 'Cold War' SF oppositions of 'self'
and 'other' redundantly re-establish the certainty of the Law,
of Culture (the maintenance of the Free World, the superiority
of technology) in fantasy these oppositions connote an
absence of Law, of Culture, and of meaning. From *Frankenstein* on, Jackson argues not merely a certain and specific
Law was put in doubt, but *all* laws, all establishments' Faust's
diabolic pact — advanced insistently in *Doctor Who*, as in the
tenth anniversary 'The Three Doctors' (1973)[53] — is the
quest for infinite knowledge, and this is progressively satirised
as absolute knowledge is replaced by its absence. For Omega,
the deviant Time Lord and 'last man' in 'The Three Doctors',
the quest for total knowledge and power leads to physical
absence as his material form disappears and only the will
remains.

In true fantasy this tendency goes further. The fantastic
opposes the entire game of knowing, and of possessing by
naming: of nomination — 'good' and 'evil', heroic identity
and otherness, are no longer accretions of the simple act of
cultural labelling. The demonic is no longer that which
threatens the hero, but that which threatens the concept
'hero' by threatening the difference between it and the image
of the character it is opposed to. It is this state of 'undifferentiation' which science fiction as allegory seeks to ward

off, and yet re-threatens because of its own complicity with the Gothic.

The demonic is that which dissolves the certainty of 'reality' by destroying the system of differences of the language which constitutes it. Even more threatening to simple SF allegory than its 'realist' appropriation of psychologically dense characterisation (the hero who can do good and evil) is this fantastic mode which upsets complex definition as well. Fantasy's central thematic issue is 'an uncertainty as to the nature of the "real", a problematisation of categories of "realism" and "truth", of the "seen" and "known" (in a culture which declares "seeing is believing")'.[54] The inscription of reader's 'hesitation' between empirical and supernatural explanations of narrative events, which Todorov noted as the mark of the fantastic, is thus a 'displacement of fantasy's central thematic issue' — hesitation as to the nature and possibility of a 'real' world inside and outside the text. Distinctions between good and evil, male and female, and (as in Tom Baker's proposal to turn the Doctor's companion into a talking cabbage) 'generic distinctions between animal, vegetable and mineral are blurred in fantasy's attempts to turn over "normal" perceptions and undermine "realistic" ways of seeing'.

The thematic paralleling of themes of 'self' and 'other' across the syntagmatic and paradigmatic planes of the narrative does motivate a potential for 'reading out' to the fantastic in *Doctor Who*, especially in those eras where the bizarre is emphasised — as under Tom Baker where his 'Harpo Marx' in space and time coding threatened an anarchy of nominations. Here, in the scripting of *Doctor Who*, where 'alien-ness' tends to be defined as a negation working against the Doctor's superficially manifested 'humanity', the 'demonic' quality ('something which manifests itself in contradictions') is strong. Goethe's own definition of the incoherence of the diabolic hero which Jackson takes as a forerunner of the 'undifferentiation' of fantasy, is especially appropriate to Tom Baker's and William Hartnell's Doctors:

It was not godlike, for it seemed unreasonable; not human, for it had no understanding; nor devilish, for it was bene-

ficent; nor angelic, for it often betrayed a malicious
pleasure. It resembled chance, for it evolved no consequences; it was like Providence, for it hinted at connection.
All that limits us it seemed to penetrate; it seemed to sport
at will with the necessary elements of our existence; it contracted time and expanded space.[55]

Baker's persona was a reaction against the more unitary and
coherent moralism of Pertwee, when the definition of the
Doctor's character in terms of contradiction (particularly
between rationality and irrationality) had been greatly
weakened. In contrast, Baker developed a Doctor of godlike
knowledge and unreasonable actions — both 'arrogant and
capricious, self-opinionated and irrational', and at the same
time, as Verity Lambert complained, possessing 'this awful
thing of knowing everything and being right about everything'.

When producers of Doctor Who rejected Baker's surfeit
of 'all-knowingness', they were addressing what seemed a
simple dramatic problem. For Lambert, Baker's all-knowingness threatened the hermeneutic code — the mystery — which
she had emphasised; for Nathan-Turner it threatened the
action coding, and weakened the suspense of the cliffhangers. But at another level they were intuitively concerned with something narratively more fundamental; the
collapse of narrative's conventional demarcation of actants
according to a system of differences.

In classical narrative, events are generated by a villainy.
Only the villain must be motivated — by lust, greed or passion
— to obtain the precious object. In contrast, the role of the
hero is 'normal', 'consensual' and 'vulnerable' — he represents the world to which villainy is done. His function is to
restore the precious object, to re-establish the consensus.
In this sense, Davison's 'vulnerable' Doctor is a classic hero;
Baker's — with his tendency to initiate the narrative of events
— is not. An early and influential script editor of Doctor Who,
Dennis Spooner, worried about the Baker era for this reason:

The reason why I could not have cottoned on to doing a

Tom Baker story was that those series always tended to start with the Doctor arriving when there was nothing going on and then he would make it happen. In other words he would initiate the events. If we had any brief at all as writers under Sydney Newman we were told that the Doctor is an observer — a time traveller — looking around, and if he happens to go into history, or indeed into the future, he can never actively interfere with the events in order that he would change them. Most of the stories arose in that once he got into the situation he was forever trying to get out of it . . . Tom Baker, as I saw the shows, would land on a planet, get involved in the story and there would be a hundred points where he could say 'I've had enough of this, let's get back to the Tardis and go'. That never arose in the Hartnell or Troughton stories.[56]

The initiation of events by the Doctor makes him, in narrative terms, comparable to the Master. Hence in 'The Key to Time' the Doctor's active quest for the key motivates the 'mad scientist' moment of 'The Armaggedon Factor'; and in 'Kinda' it is the arrival of the Doctor which allows monstrous villainy to enter a tranquil society.

This reading out towards the fantastic was not because *Doctor Who* is coded — through its central themes — as fantastic. The themes of 'self' and 'other' do not, as Jackson implies, originate in the fantastic mode. Both science fiction (especially in its 'Gothic' variants) and the fantastic were deeply imbued in the nineteenth century with the discourse of Romanticism. The 'fantasy' of *Doctor Who* is *enabled* by this Romantic presence of 'self' and 'other' themes in both SF and the fantastic, and *generated* by specific material practices. An example of this was the first producer's emphasis on the problem of naming (Doctor Who?) and her confusing of traditional narrative by introducing both a hero who always wants to escape (the Doctor) and a hero who wants to stay and help (Ian), so that the Doctor can be both self-seeking anti-hero as solipsistically concerned with himself as the Master later was[57] and yet at the same time a heroic liberator of the oppressed. The Romantic presence was

strongly reinforced by the Hinchliffe/Baker tendency to the
Gothic; and later still by the 'authorial' presence of Tom
Baker at the height of his ratings success under Graham
Williams, allowing him to inflect the programme in terms of
his own 'bizarre' and 'fantastic' humour. These were, however,
generic tendencies which the more 'straight' SF orientation
of the programme would encompass or reject according to
the conditions of production at any particular conjuncture.
Baker's genuinely fantastic desire to subvert generic distinctions by changing his companion into a talking cabbage
was, for instance, vetoed by Graham Williams in the interests
of programme continuity and plausibility, and his anarchic
and negating humour was 'toned down' by the next producer,
John Nathan-Turner, in the cause of undistracted action-
drama. And further, the thing which enabled Baker to
flourish before this was not so much the generic coding of
Doctor Who as fantastic, but rather the specific connection
between the programme as institution (with all its organisational and extra-organisational constraints) and the discourse
of 'meta' SF with the arrival of Douglas Adams as script
editor, as we shall see in the next chapter.

It is also the case that generically (in 'serious' SF) there
has been a tendency against the 'undifferentiation' of fantasy.
Even where, as in works by Vonnegut, Lem and Le Guin, the
cultural imperialism of humankind in trying to 'name' and
explain alien forms is put into question, this is generally from
a position of cultural perspectivism. As the 'absent paradigm'
is constructed, and the relation of the new language to the
new culture is perceived, the gap between signifier and signified is closed, as in 'realistic' narrative.

In contrast, in the fantastic it is left open. Borrowing the
extravagance of the marvellous and the ordinariness of the
mimetic, the fantastic locates the reader in a tense hesitation
between the two and, through its reluctance 'to present
definitive versions of "truth" or "reality", draws attention
to its own practice as a linguistic system'.[58]

As we shall see, in certain 'meta' works of SF like those of
Vonnegut and Adams, there is a tendency in this direction
too, so that Doug Adams' demystification of a *Hitch Hiker's
Guide to the Galaxy* and Vonnegut's demystification of a

Pocket History of Mars as authoritative and transparent accounts of the 'truth' applies to the process of narration as well as to the narrated events. Vonnegut's development from his SF period into his reputation as a 'modernist' is therefore not surprising. But more often in recent SF as in Le Guin and Lem — and to an extent this is true of Vonnegut and Adams too — it is the anthropocentrism of SF's process of nomination which is challenged, rather than the myth of naming itself.

Rather than emphasise fantasy's 'negative ethics of un-differentiation' and the silence of language, the concern for language, translation and communication has generally been on behalf of 'a fresh look at our own culture through the construction of another', and of a perspectivism which has been central to SF as genre at least as early as Wells' *The War of the Worlds*, where the beastliness of Martians to Earth people is compared with that of white Earth people to black Tasmanians. As Jackson notes, SF tends to have an allegorical rather than subversive relationship to the notion of 'the real'.

The fantastic, through its foregrounding of the signifier, subverts the process of naming itself; 'serious' SF on the other hand (with the partial exception of meta-SF) only subverts its own generic description of the universe in 'scientific' (but actually anthropocentric) terms. Popular SF, however, does draw strongly on Gothic fantasy. SF does not occupy a fixed and static 'allegorical' mode as Jackson seems to imply. In *Doctor Who* there have been developments from the early 'perpetuated hermeneutic' of the wanderer without a home (coded in contradiction to the 'human') towards a greater Gothic/fantastic dimension — of the Doctor who has a home but cannot find there a unified self. The 'absent paradigm' of home and culture has been filled up and made concrete since the Hartnell years, but the ensuing identity of the Doctor has been coded variously according to the dominance of the naturalist/referential (under Pertwee) and the Gothic/fantastic (under Baker). If, as Jackson says, fantasy occupies a site of hesitation between the mimetic and the marvellous, then equally science fiction exists in the potential for con-tinuing narrative interplay between the mimetic and the fantastic. That this can be so depends on the crossing of SF texts, such as *Doctor Who*, by the discourses of Positivism and Romanticism.

Romantic Gothic: the disruption of the unified subject

Science fiction's anthropocentric imperialism ('Conquest', or, more liberally, 'Communication') is the ultimate resort of what Stanislav Lem has described as nineteenth-century positivism: the Wellsian reduction of all social contradiction into a check-list of 'unknowns' in which all that is necessary is to 'keep our eyes open and establish priorities'. As a character in Lem's *Solaris* says, humankind's real quest is to communicate with itself.

> We don't want to conquer the cosmos; we simply want to extend the boundaries of the Earth to the frontiers of the cosmos . . . We think of ourselves as the Knights of the Holy Contact. This is another lie. We are only seeking Man. We have no need of other worlds. We need mirrors.[59]

The *Doctor Who* which some audience members perceive is precisely that 'knight and squire' of galactic contact, as the Doctor and his companion carry scientific values of 'achievement' and 'inquiry' to the far reaches of the universe. Whereas Lem's *Solaris* attacks the empirical materialism on which so much of the scientific world view (and science fiction) is based, and which, as Stephen Potts has put it, has located in the universe a new, rationalistic God-in-the-image-of-Man,[60] the linear narrative drive of *Doctor Who* is frequently on behalf of that scientific world view, and it is only the Gothic doppelganger effect which disturbs it. In Hinchcliffe's 'Masque of Mandragola' the threat of villainy is precisely against that process of human rationalism itself. Situated at the turning point between the 'dark ages' of necromancy and the scientific rationalism of Leonardo and Galileo, the Renaissance itself is the subject of attack. The Renaissance perspective — for the first time placing humankind as the source and centre of terrestrial vision — will in the end, as the Mandragola predicts, create a universe in his image. 'Unchecked, man's curiosity might lead him away from this planet until ultimately the Galaxy itself might not contain him.' This Lem-type critique of galactic imperialism[61] is, however, quickly recuperated by conventional narrative (it is the Mandragola who instigate villainy by wanting the universe for themselves) and programme ideology (the Time Lord's liberal perspectivism). As the Doctor says: 'I can't let you interfere with Earth's progress . . . It's part of a Time Lord's job to insist on justice for *all* species . . . Mandragola will . . . take away from Man the only thing worth having — purpose . . . The ability granted to every intelligent species to shape its own destiny.'

The Baker Doctor's 'all-knowingness' depends on two quite different dimensions. First, on a cultural perspectivism which, superficially, seeks to avoid the sin of Solaristics: 'To create the universe in the image of Earth, to see in the multifarious faces of God no more than a reflection of ourselves'.[62] Since, however, *Doctor Who* seldom examines seriously the possibility of what other cultures might be like but rather inscribes the universe in terms of 'human' spontaneity and democracy, this is hardly the critique of naïve positivistic thought that Lem stands for. Yet there is a deeper disturbance of the conventional action narrative carried by the paradigmatic set established in 'The Masque of Mandragola' (as in most *Doctor Who* narratives) between the Doctor and villain as themselves ominously dangerous scientists.

The subversion of the narrative's 'knowledge' is similar to that in the musical genre as Rick Altman describes it, where 'instead of focusing all its interests on a single, central character, following the trajectory of his progress', the linear psychological mode of classical narrativity (and the conventional outcome) is upset by a 'dual-focus structure' built around 'parallel stars . . . and radically divergent values', which 'requires the viewer to be sensitive . . . to simultaneity and comparison'.[63] However, whereas Altman ascribes the structure of the musical simplistically to the consensual operations of 'culture', and takes no account of either conditions of production/reception or of discursive practices operating *within* generic forms, we want here to argue that the 'dual-focus structure' of *Doctor Who*'s narrative depends on the operation within science fiction of discursive practices other than empirical materialism.

Certainly *Doctor Who* conforms in one narrative dimension, as Lem's 'Solaristics' does, to the process of nomination — the resort of Foucault's 'classical episteme' of empirical materialism: the quest 'to ascribe a name to things, and in that name to name their being'.[64] Extra-terrestrial cultures are named in terms of the language of anthropomorphism. Alien monsters exist, as in *Doctor Who*, to define by their difference what is 'essentially' and 'organically' and 'spiritually' human.

But it is the case that SF has always also been composed of discourses more unsettling than Positivism. And not simply SF, but 'classical' thinking itself was subject to differences and contradictions which Foucault's account suppresses. As David Morse notes, the process of 'meticulous nomination' was certainly not the only feature of classical discourse. In contrast to the conservative position which argued that only the social self — the 'I' constructed as a 'subject' and inscribed within the symbolic order — was rational, the Romantic discourse emphasised that the social self, with its ready-made identity, overlaid the 'authentic' self with hypocrisy and powerlessness. This was not a simplistic resort to the creative and solipsistic autonomy of the 'self' which recent critics have generally asserted. While not replacing the social self with the 'I' of fancy and imagination, Romantic discourse saw them as dialectically related and potentially reconcilable. Two selves were postulated within the individual: the deep disordered self and the social self. It was the contradiction between these two selves which produced insincerity and inauthenticity; and it was the programme of every Romantic work to overcome this contradiction by a psychic movement bringing them back into alignment.

With a rupture from his social environment, in contact with nature and spiritual isolation the individual . . . identifies thoughts, moods, feelings, sensations that can only be his own, he becomes overwhelmed by the sheer presence of his own being. But this self-discovery is attended by guilt and uncertainty, for it seems to involve a narcissistic and morbid self-preoccupation . . . The moment of rupture can only be validated by a moment of return in which the individual . . . re-establishes contact with the world, purges himself of egotism and vanity, and, from simply revelling in his sense of himself as luxuriantly given and gratuitous becomes a teacher and a wise man, a dispenser of painfully acquired but necessary wisdom. The world can learn from his mistakes. Self-discovery is necessary, but so is the discovery of others. . .[65]

This dialectic of 'self' and 'other' defines the Romantic problematic, its wandering hero, *and Doctor Who.* The Doctor, par excellence, plays out that narrative of rupture, wandering and return, of social hypocrisy (among the Time Lords), self-preoccupation and vanity (Hartnell as time traveller), wisdom (the 'all-knowing' Baker) and the discovery of others (in liberating the oppressed).

At the same time, the Romantic discourse generated a certain kind of 'Gothic' villain, which is also a familiar of *Doctor Who.* The shift from the universal social/rational subject to the disordered self gave the Romantic discourse a problem of definition and legitimation. Who was to say that the creative revolt against social masks and hypocrisy was authentic? Who was to know at what point the anti-institutional thrust became solipsistic, or turned to paranoia and madness? The indefinably close shadow of the Romantic hero-wanderer became the pure scientist, narrowly seeking in his privatised laboratory for a truth which in effect was his own ego.

To convert the world into one's own passion for identity was the ultimate threat – and was to generate a host of Gothic and SF villains, from the laboratories of Frankenstein and Jekyll to *Doctor Who*'s Davros, who seeks to control from his bunker the entire universe as an extension of his own ego. Because the dividing line between heroic revolt and manic villainy could never be demarcated – except by re-invoking institutionalised definitions – Romantic Gothic generated a degree of angst, guilt and alienation around its central narrative oppositions which attached doubt to its heroic performances and emotional sympathy to its villainous ones.

The impossibility of definition turned Romantic narrative

into a quest for nomination. Who was the hero? Who was the villain? Since its inception *Doctor Who* has drawn deeply on this quest, even in the Pertwee era. In 'the Three Doctors', for instance, there is a strong association between Pertwee's Doctor and the villain Omega. The hero who thinks a universe and the villain who wills one are both deviants in the eyes of the Time Lords, and both are denied their freedom. The Doctor at the end gains his freedom, while his opponent disintegrates – the only freedom available to him. But, via the Doctor, emotional sympathy is generated for Omega's plight, and the Doctor's freedom is itself ambiguous, since it represents the Tardis drive by means of which the Time Lords will send him searching through space and time forever.

In the opening stories of 1963 the Doctor was located in terms of difference rather than definition. He was not hero because of his ego and solipsistic self-interest. At the same time he was not villain because, as hero-wanderer, he accidentally intervened in the social universe on the side of good. The Doctor's characterisation was formed in those interstices between solipsism and chance intervention, in contrast to the villain's fixed idea of controlling the universe. And while destroying the original hermeneutic, the introduction of Gallifrey worked to maintain heroic ambivalence in another way, by generating another typically Gothic device: the double. A succession of 'deviant' dopplegangers of the Doctor – Time Lords who have rebelled against the static complacency of their society – have populated the programme. Their fate is literal solipsism: incarceration (as in 'The Three Doctors' and 'The Brain of Morbius') in a world of their own manic will. Madness and incarceration are sometimes sympathetically handled, as is typical of Romantic discourse. For, as Morse says, where social behaviour is dominated by 'false appearance and seeming', (as on the world of Gallifrey), and 'when every gesture and act may be tainted by insincerity and feigning, then madness becomes a mode of behaviour that is transparent in its very incoherence'. Hence sincerity and madness were connected, and the 'emergent institution of the private madhouse was associated with fraudulent and forcible usurpation of power, for confinement was a method whereby property could be appropriated and harmful truths suppressed'.[66]

In 'The Three Doctors', Omega's possession which the Time Lords have appropriated is his technological genius — he has been the engineer of time travel itself — and his reward is to be confined to his madhouse of anti-matter for ever. The Doctor's sympathy and sorrow over his fate is a mark of his own rejection of the social conformity of Gallifrey (a sign which was later to be markedly developed in the Hinchcliffe era).

On the one hand, the Romantic outcast stands for the human spirit against the dull and consensual state of contingency. On the other hand, he betrays that spark the closer he moves, in his invention and scientism, to a cold rationalism. To leave the status quo for the solipsism of the laboratory was simply to replace the hypocritical self with the insanely interiorised one. One disguised its self as the world; the other converted the world (or in *Doctor Who* the universe) into its quest for self. In each case the health dialectic of self and social was betrayed. Rather than being a constituent of the subject in process, responding to experience, reason would then itself become an unquestioned deity. Reason 'left to itself would become transformed into unreason if not activated by a succession of stimulae. Thus reason itself is not the guarantor of sanity, but rather experience is ... Sanity is not given within the subject but is maintained and constituted through the contact of the subject with the external world.'[67]

The eternal prison of the evil Time Lords is at once a mark of their betrayal by the world of contingency and a metaphor for their own rationalistic madness. The central distinction between the two forms of Time Lord revolt in *Doctor Who* (which otherwise are united by their rejection of social hypocrisy) is between reason based on experience and intuition (the position of the ever-wandering Doctor), and manic reason as the fixed idea of controlling the universe (the position of the ever-incarcerated villains). Only the constant flux of experience, the capacity as it were, to be born again and again, can ward off this threat of the madness of rationalism. In this quest for experience the Doctor is a prodigal son of the Time Lords: as Morse argues, it is the repenting and prodigal heroes, rather than the tragic Oedipus or Othello, which derive from Romanticism. 'Such figures not only serve to manifest the extraordinary power of human feeling and the importance of the ties that bind us to others . . . but also show man's almost endless capacity for regeneration and renewal. The human personality is seen not as monolithic and integral but as composed of endless layers that must be stripped away, of husks that must be shed; it is a procession of identities linked only by their place of transformation, the continued capacity to feel and the capacity to use such feeling to be born anew.'[68]

The Doctor's constant renewal, his tendency (especially under Hartnell and Baker) to be defined by contraries, the prolongation of this character-definition by means of a succession of doubles (most persistently, the Master, a literal alter-ego of the Doctor both at the Academy and in rejecting it), the ultimate and only definition of heroism as the point of tension between stasis and solipsism, between social hypocrisy and the tyranny of madness. All these categories make the Doctor a quintessential Romantic hero and are central to the discourses of knowing and unknowing of Doctor Who.

Discourses of cognition and romanticism

The Romantic Gothic, it is argued here, is a constituent part of the science fiction genre, and in particular of Doctor Who. What this means is that science fiction cannot be defined only in relation to theories of cognition, science and 'realism', as most SF theorists have tried to do. SF's other tendency is towards the unsettling, destabilising qualities of Gothic fantasy and the uncanny. As Jackson has pointed out, following Freud's theory of fantasy, there are two levels of meaning to the German term for the uncanny, 'das Unheimlich'. At the first level, the un-negated version 'Das Heimlich' 'signifies that which is homely familiar, friendly, cheerful, comfortable, intimate . . . its negation therefore summons up the unfamiliar, uncomfortable, strange, alien'.[69] This is precisely the familiar/

unfamiliar characterisation of the Doctor which Doug Adams describes, and was especially emphasised in the Baker era:

Adams: There's got to be something about the character which on the one hand is quite homely and accessible; but that the closer you get to that accessibility, the further away it then seems to be.

However, this de-familiarisation of the Doctor extends to his identification with the villain — and therefore to the other sense of 'uncanny'. ' "Das Heimlich" also means that which is concealed from others — all that is hidden, secreted, obscured. Its negation, 'das Unheimlich, then functions to dis-cover, reveal, expose areas normally kept out of sight . . . and, by doing so, effects a disturbing transformation of the familiar into the unfamiliar.'

This ambivalence is played out across the syntagmatic and paradigmatic planes of the narrative — which we can now define as between the quest for nomination (through cognition, control: 'knowing') and the madness of 'un-knowing' (the villain's positing of desire as desirable because he desires it).

Doctor Who as science fiction must be understood in terms of both: (i) its drive towards the coherent, signified as a verifiable empirical world (the world of Pertwee's Doctor with its quest of scientism — the universe as balanced, organic, understood); and (ii) its recognition of incoherence in the fictionality of 'naming' the ego (the world of Baker's Doctor and its mark of Romanticism — the constantly regenerated selves, the dopplegangers).

Science fiction differs from Realism and Gothic fantasy through this continued tension. On the one hand, its emphasis on cognition and the belief that the universe is a knowable and natural phenomenon distinguishes it from Romantic Gothic (and from fantasy). On the other hand, its constant anxiety about the scientific process itself — the easy transformation of scientific experiment into the solipsistic quest in which conventional distinctions between heroism and villainy are estranged and made ambiguous — distinguishes it from Realism.

In one respect the legacy of Wellsian 'authorship' has been the contrast of the New Republic of intellectuals with the degenerate world of capitalism — as Walter Hirsch has pointed out, businessmen have been the major villains of SF, while the good scientist has been its consistent hero.[70] Alternatively, the cerebral Positivist vision has been crossed by the Romantic one: the hero as outcast against the too cerebral, emotionless villain — himself (or itself) invoked, as in *The War of the Worlds* and in *Doctor Who*'s 'The Daleks', as a potential future of humanity.

In 'Ark in Space' it has become the literal future of humanity. Finding the cyrogenically suspended humans in their ark, refugees from an Earth destroyed by solar flares, Baker's Doctor evokes the Positivist evolutionary vision:

> Homo Sapiens — what an inventive, invincible species! It's only a few million years since they crawled up out of the mud and learned to walk — puny, defenceless bipeds. They survived flood, famine and plague. They've survived cosmic war and holocausts. Now, here they are, out among the stars, waiting to begin a new life, ready to sit out eternity. They are indomitable, indomitable.

What he finds when they wake up, however, is an emotionless and humourless intellectualism, and a society ranked rigidly in functional hierarchies: 'First Med Tech' Vira, 'Commander' Noah, 'Technician' Dune.

> *Vira*:   (contemplating coldly the unconscious Sarah) 'Is she of value?
> *Harry*:   Of value! She's a human being, like ourselves! What kind of question is that?
> *Vira*:   (To Doctor) Your friend is a Romantic.'
> *Doctor*:   Perhaps we both are.

The future of Earth in 'Ark in Space' is predicated closely in terms of Wells intellectual saints. There is no room for the 'weak and silly', and the ark is not a charitable institution for the wandering Doctor.

Vira: There are three of them. Another male called the Doctor, and that female . . . '
Noah: There was a regressive faction among the volunteers for colony 9.
Vira: "With a zero-zero survival predict — *one* generation.
Noah: Even so, our genetic pool has been balanced, cross matched, compact evaluated. Three random units could threaten our survival.
Vira: The council can decide Noah. The plan had a 7% stretch factor . . . (to Harry after Noah goes out). If you are space travellers as you claim, you should leave now.
Harry: I say, that's a bit brusque isn't it?
Vira: Noah will not permit contamination of the genetic pool. All regressive transmitters have been eliminated.'

As Carter has pointed out, many SF writers of the Gernsback era tended to follow that other evolutionary perspective set by Wells.[71] The 'bad' scientist has complemented the business-man as SF's (and *Doctor Who*'s) other staple villain, again following Wells in his novelistic trajectory from the good Time Traveller, through the sadistic Dr Moreau to the tyran-nically mad Griffin in *The Invisible Man*. *Doctor Who*'s central evolutionary debate, between 'machines' which 'must dominate ruthlessly' and 'humans' who will survive if they 'deserve to survive' as creatures of 'reason and compassion' (in the end Noah saves the future of Earth by drawing on his latent feeling and leading the Wirrn who have taken him over to destruction), is founded on that determining debate of the SF genre between the discourses of Romanticism and 'scienti-fic' realism.

In the Wellsian absence of a genuine socialism, the defining point in SF's quest for freedom became the controversy over human emotions. The resort was to Romanticism against Wells' own solipsistic rationalism which replaced his early tendency to analysis of social contradiction and class struggle.[72] It was appropriate that in 'The Sun Makers', where capitalism and class exploitation were propounded only to be displaced by the familiar conflict between 'in-human' bureaucracy and 'human' spontaneity, Tom Baker's Doctor should humorously (as the sign of his 'humanity') misquote Marx's 'All you have to lose is your chains.'

Tom Baker

Chapter 4

Send-up: Authorship and Organisation

> *Doctor*:   I am asking you to help yourself. Nothing will
> change round here unless you change it. . . .
> *Gaudry*:   It's crazy talk. Rebellion? Who would support
> you?
> *Doctor*:   Given the chance to breathe clean air for a few
> hours they might. Have you thought of that?
> *Mandrell*:   What have we got to lose?
> *Doctor*:   Only your claims.
> *Bisham*:   Well put, Doctor!
> *Doctor*:   (smiling) Oh, it was nothing. I have a gift for the
> apt phrase.

Tom Baker's pastiche of Marx in 'The Sun Makers' is actually
in calling on the oppressed to throw off their (tax) 'claims'.
This kind of 'apt phrase' as comic 'in-joke' became Baker's
signature as the fourth Doctor — especially during the three
years when *Doctor Who* was produced by Graham Williams.
It was comedy relying on a certain privileged information. In
'The Horns of Nimon' (1979) the maze-like lair refers back to
the one built by King Minos for the Minotaur (like the Nimon,
half-bull, half-man). As with the Nimon/minos near-anagram,
the Antheans led by Seth are based on the Athenians led by
Theseus. The Doctor's reference at the end to the colour of
Seth's spaceship relates to the fact that Theseus forgot to
follow his father's request that he should paint his returning

ship white to mark his success — a slip that was to prove fatal
for Aegeus.

This was a feature of the Williams/Baker years which the
next producer, John Nathan-Turner (who was production
unit manager under Williams) particularly disliked; complaining that the use, for instance, of the *Doctor Who* production
office telephone number for a computer in one story was a
private joke which was lost on the majority of the audience.
'I think that some of those mythical stories are terrific. But
if you are going to do them, I really think you've not got to
be tempted by a sort of in-joke of the whole thing. In "Underworld" Jason's character was called Jackson, and the spaceship
was called P7E — Persephone! And I just think that that's not
very clever at all. I don't see any reason not to use myths,
legends, Bible, whatever, because I think that there's no substitute for a good story, and if it's a good story, use it. But I
think that one's not got to ram it home to a small percentage
of your audience what you are doing.' Graham Williams dis-
agreed. 'After all, for those who knew it, it would mean
something; for those who didn't, it wouldn't detract anything.
I think if the story had depended upon knowing . . . the
original myth and legend, then it would have been too "In" —
it would have been a bad thing. But as a story, I think it
stands on its own . . . Then if you know about the original,
you get the bonus of the "P7E".'

The disagreement over audiences and dramatic values
between Williams and Nathan-Turner itself raised quite dramatically the ways in which an institution like *Doctor Who* can
vary according to different production and professional practices. This chapter will look at ways in which variations within
professional ideology materially affect production practices;
and further, at ways in which professional values that are
ostensibly identical can themselves by inflected differently
according to pressure from within and outside the television
industry.

Intertextuality and audience space

Orwell's and Huxley's science fiction dystopias provided
Williams' 'The Sun Makers' with the story of a society domin-

ated by a rapacious 'Big Brother' who controls everybody's movements by means of omni-present cameras, and keeps them timid with specially manufactured gas as he collects his oppressive taxes. A different SF coding was laid over these by director Pennant Roberts, who recast the dystopic themes visually and dramatically in reference to Fritz Lang's classic science fiction film, *Metropolis*. The visual drama of Leela about to be steamed alive by the Collector in a half-cylindrical, transparent chamber was borrowed from Lang's laboratory scene where Rotwang reproduces the unconscious Maria in an identical chamber. The revolt of underground workers against their capitalist masters is also taken directly from *Metropolis*, as is the image of workers grappling desperately with the clock-like dials of machines out of control.

The direct motivation for the story was far more pragmatic: writer Robert Holmes' temporary annoyance with his tax man. Intentional comment of this kind does not, of course, provide the meaning of a programme in any simplistic way. Even where producers are aware of them, they are very quickly re-coded according to the professional values of good drama, appropriate television, and so on. External references like these, however, help locate the programme both in terms of its institutional need for novelty-within-continuity, and its perceived audience, and therefore its notion of the appropriate level at which to negotiate the SF genre.

Williams: You couldn't, I don't think, go into the Orwellian side of that monolothic society as much as Orwell did. Nor did we want to. It was enough that there was the over-burdening of tax. And that depression provided us with the villain of the piece. Everything else was a mere device to tell that story. And so one used the taxation system instead of common-or-garden slavery. You could substitute slavery for it quite easily, and it wouldn't make a scrap of difference to the story.

Tulloch: Some of my students felt it was markedly politically oriented.

Williams: Well, it was. But it wasn't party-politicised.

Tulloch: No, but as a system — like a capitalist system?

Williams: Well, taxation, I think, extends beyond the

capitalist system — because the Government has to be paid for. You could say it was a classically Roman civilisation with as much force as you could say it was an American, British or German civilisation. I think that drawing attention to the fact of a society that has allowed its aims to become so confused that taxation is an end in itself rather than a means of providing services for the entire community is no bad achievement in a popular science fiction programme. Yet that's what we did. I don't think we ever intentionally set up to stand on a soap box and say 'this is the message of the programme'. What we tried to do on each and every occasion was to ask people to examine the issues as side issues, not as the main story which is an action-thriller adventure . . . I wanted, more than anything else, that the programme shouldn't carry with it the sententious elements of American programmes, where you have Spock and Captain Kirk discussing for 49 and 50 minutes the fact that, in their terms, one should never kill, one should never interfere in a developing civilisation. That message was obviously desperately important to the makers of *Star Trek* to get over. We rather hoped that any message of that nature that *we* wanted — or felt collectively was a fair and accurate depiction of the circumstances — would be born out of the programme, rather than the programme being based on it.

Williams' attitude to politics in *Doctor Who* — 'a fair and accurate depiction of the circumstances' while avoiding 'party politicising' -- represents the media ideology of balance and neutrality.[1] However, there is a good deal more to professional ideology than the question of political balance as Williams reply indicates.

First, there is the question of promoting difference within continuity in a television institution conceived as 'serious' as well as popular. The 'Orwellian' theme inflects the programme in terms of serious SF, yet is itself transmitted via the Holmes signature as a light-hearted rebuke of any system which has lost sight of its democratic function. One of the lines which always get a laugh is when the Collector, having allowed the workers an (unpaid) holiday to watch Leela being steamed alive, awaits with anticipation her amplified screams, with the words, 'This is where I get a real feeling of job satisfaction'.

One interesting effect of this attempt to be both serious and popular is that by narrowing down the Orwellian critique of both socialism and capitalism to the specificity of a particular system (which, pace the producer, is a world dominated by one trans-global company dedicated entirely to profits) a space is opened in the narrative for some audiences to interpret the programme as anti-capitalist. Jeremy Bentham argued that 'The Sun Makers' was 'heavily laced with left-wing propaganda'.[2] Clearly the operation of professional values which are much more specific to *Doctor Who* than balance and neutrality can operate to direct the programme – for some audiences – including those not normally inclined to a political reading, like the fans – precisely in the direction of political comment.

Secondly, there is the question of tailoring the programme to implied audiences. Williams was concerned to keep social comment as a 'side issue' of the 'action-thriller adventure' because he felt that there was a 'bedrock audience loyalty' of between six and eight million viewers 'which we should feed and take notice of'. Other references – to politics, to serious SF, to classic cinema, to history, to myth and so on – were designed to 'grab on the wing' another audience in order to build *Doctor Who*'s following from the six million bedrock to anything up to fourteen million, which Philip Hinchcliffe had achieved with 'Ark in Space'. In one respect the programme worked for narrative unity and coherence by relegating such references to what Nathan-Turner called 'in-group' asides, and Williams called audience 'bonuses'. Alternatively, the programme has always – and especially in the Williams' era – made its appeal to audience 'sophistication' by means of an allegorical mode of address.

The reason for the common, but very differently valued, use by fans and students of the terms 'pantomime' and 'slapstick' for the Williams era – despite his own apparent intentions – has a lot to do with the very overt emphasis on allegory and intertextuality in some of his shows. Basically allegory, as a mode that works at two levels – a literal one, complete in itself where the drama is enacted, and a metaphorical one, carrying a 'message' — is ideal for *Doctor Who*, since it should allow both the strong sense of narrative desired by producers for the bedrock audience and the 'intellectual suggestiveness' required for the 'bonus' audience.

The double meaning implicit in allegory has to be indicated by some device to alert the target reader/viewer. In *Doctor Who* this is often done by a play on names and parallel situations. Sanders (the name already recalling 'films of Empire') puts on a pith helmet in 'Kinda', a tale of 'Raj' type militarism and imperialism; there is a reference to Troy in 'The Armaggedon Factor', as the miniaturised Doctor, concealed inside K-9, enters the enemy's lair to rescue his princess; and an allusion to 'Morton's Fork' in 'The Sun Makers', a tale of a quasi-monarchical capitalist who exploits the people through a rapacious tax collector. In some cases, as in the Morton's Fork example (where capitalism is safely referred to the manageable past of Henry VII) the intertextual reference operates by generating new meanings. 'Ark in Space', for instance, seems to depend for its writers' meaning on a crucial difference which it develops out of the Bible story it is based on. In each case the captain of the ark is called Noah, and in each his task is to repopulate an Earth destroyed by cataclysm. In the Bible tale there is a perfect consensual harmony between man and beasts, a healthy potential for symbiosis and natural balance in the future world. In 'Ark in Space', on the contrary, humans are defiled by beasts — a process, as the Doctor specifically says, of 'symbiotic atavism' in which the human race will be absorbed and the Earth become a place of aliens. Clearly the SF postulation of two potentials for Earth, as garden or desert, and for humankind, as organic or alien, relies on the system of parallel and difference between the two texts.

However, whether or not intertextuality operates semantically for some audiences, all producers of *Doctor Who* agree that it must not operate in contradiction to the authenticating and rhetorical conventions of the 'bedrock' audience. For them any intertextual reference in *Doctor Who* must be re-tied to the fictional world in so far as its foregrounding devices have (as in the 'Ark in Space' example) a direct relevance to the dominant generic and narrative values of the programme.

Intertextuality in *Doctor Who* is, quite apart from any semantic function it might have, also a mode of address. Even at the most simplistic level — of recognition of references to Greek myth, Shakespeare, the Bible, history, Lang's *Metropolis*, 'specialised' sciences etc — the programme seeks to establish a 'complicit' relationship with its audience, which is much closer to the conventions of theatrical vaudeville than to those of dramatic 'realism'. In the case of the tertiary educated audience — a significant target group for *Doctor Who* — these 'double meanings' (where the 'allegorical' reference is in fact to another 'high art' text or to an entire mode, such as melodrama) can have as much to do with the pleasure derived from the text as its 'scary' dramatic qualities have for a younger audience or its *intra*-textual references have for fans.

> *Peter Holland*: Part of the way the programme *does* appeal to me now, is the trendy, sophisticated 'get the reference' game . . . when the Doctor comes to the cave in 'Kinda' and says, 'Such stuff as dreams are made of' I thought, when I saw them playing chess, straight away of Ferdinand and Miranda playing chess in *The Tempest*. Now whether I want to take that further and say, 'this is a sort of *Tempest* story' I don't know yet. But those sort of references are planted for me to pick up quite deliberately. They are looking for an audience that will get the reference.

Nathan-Turner (who produced 'Kinda') was happy to use Shakespearian or other 'bonuses' provided they did not weaken the drama. Williams' sin against the programme — in the eyes of other producers, directors and fans — was his tendency to signify other texts (whether high art, melodrama or pantomime) too overtly, to make *Doctor Who* (through the use of John Cleese in 'City of Death') into, as Ian Levine put it, 'a slap-stick *Fawlty Towers* in space' — or in our terms to destroy *Doctor Who* as allegory by destroying its basic story. Yet a student audience which likes *Doctor Who* primarily as pantomime (and the current student generation have become so used to the *Monty Python/Fawlty Towers* comedy syndrome that one class seriously believed Peter Watkins'

Culloden to be a *'Monty Python* in history') quite unsurpris-
ingly also likes the Graham Williams' era of the programme.
The producers' quest for a 'bonus' audience opens the possibility, among an important target audience, for a 'point of
resistance' to conventional narrative closure.

Intertextual references are, however, the site and stake of a
much larger target audience than the 'sophisticated' — for
Williams nothing less than the entire audience above the
'bedrock'. In the first place, Williams quickly began to orien-
tate the programme beyond the young children he was in-
structed to address.

> *Williams*: We discovered that very much the largest single
> sector of our audience was between 26 and 36, and almost
> as large a segment was between 36 and 46. So the adult
> audience very much outnumbered the children — which
> was our gut reaction to start with. We thought it was
> *terribly* dangerous to start playing down to what we would
> imagine kids would want . . . I reckoned it was being made
> for the aware and hopefully imaginative sixteen-year-olds
> who could really latch on to the possibilities. We never
> tried to take a theme to its logical conclusion. We almost
> always would stop somewhere and say 'you work out the
> rest of it'. I think spoon-feeding is a dreadful cliché-ridden
> operation.

This call to the audience to 'work' was never intended to
prevent conventional narrative closure. The 'white ship'
example in 'The Horns of Nimon' rather signified itself as a
specialised mode of address — and for those without the
cultural capital to recognise it, it could be recuperated by the
narrative as part of the Doctor's 'zany' character. What
Williams did do was to play more consciously on intertextuality — specifically on the potential for relating to parallel
narrative development in 'source' texts, frequently recreating
identical images and narrative set ups from, for example, *The
Prisoner of Zenda* in 'The Androids of Tara' and *Metropolis*
in 'The Sun Makers'.

In 'The Sun Makers, the shots of machine operatives
desperately losing control of mounting pressure gauges work,

like they do in *Metropolis*, for suspense – and in this case build up the episode's cliffhanger. But in making reference to *Metropolis* they also establish, clearly and consciously, *Doctor Who* as different. Whereas in Lang's film the 'narrative skid'[3] in these shots ties the action into religious allegory (by means of 'crucifixion' at the machines), 'The Sun Makers' establishes its own nomination – *'This is Doctor Who'* – by its parodic mode of address. The Doctor relates to the workers with incongruous humour (rather than empathy as in *Metropolis*)[4] by means of 'apt' quips like 'Don't call me, I'll call you', as he enters the dangerously unstable machine complex.

In 'The Sun Makers' the references to *Metropolis* – as well as references to 'gangster' torture conventions – were designed for the 'great big audience of people who actually do enjoy the visual medium nowadays' (such as the audience for 'classic' movies) and who, like the *Doctor Who* fans but on a wider front, could pick up and enjoy 'buff' references. Indeed, Williams entire 'audience beyond the bedrock' conception was built up on this notion of popular but sophisticated intertextual reference.

Williams: What I *did* take as my barometer, more consciously than anything else I think, were the book stands. Because I used to make an investigation almost every week, by going around the popular book stalls . . . and seeing what paperbacks were shifting – across the board, not just science fiction – and then paid attention to what science fiction was going . . . You could see · waves coming and going: of interest in yukky violence, in big business, in family sagas, in historical romances . . . I'd say, OK. Well, is there anything there that we can do? No, we can't do sickly romance. It's not our bag really, so we'll just have to forget that strand . . . Yukky violence isn't our bag either. *But* that sort of historical romance, yes . . . we can work that in in some way. . . . I reckoned that if people were committed enough to go out and buy the book, then they were likely to be committed enough to notice what was going on in the programme. And it is for *that* sort – if you like, the book-buying public – that we aimed the little one-offs, the little asides that we were talking about.

Hence the 'entire *concept* of "The Key to Time" came out of the success of, and my own enjoyment in, reading science fiction sagas that had been selling terribly well'.

Parody and drama: space 'send-up'

Williams' intertextual tendency was to establish his signature as producer and capture the 'bonus' audience by 'spoof'. 'Something like "City of Death" − that was a very intentional rip-off if you like, as was "Androids of Tara" − definitely spoofed the whole series.' In Williams' last season as producer, under the impact of Doug Adams as script editor, the 'parody' signature became still more ambitious. Whereas Williams was happy enough to see in Duggan (the 'spoof' detective of 'The City of Death') a simple 'send-up' of *Bulldog Drummond*, Adams began to question the conventions of popular television 'realism'. For instance, the trivialisation of the Daleks in Adams first story as script editor, 'Destiny of the Daleks' (1979), was a humorously logical comment on *Doctor Who*'s commitment to 'plausibility' and 'realism'. When the Doctor tells the Daleks that if they really are the master race of the universe they should follow him up a rope ladder, and then later immobilises a Dalek by throwing his hat over its antenna before rolling it down a corridor to destruction, he is doing no more than pointing to the extreme implausibility of these ball-bearing monsters for anything other than the most un-sophisticated child audience.

This, however, drew attention to the bare bones of the action drama − and demystified the show's most venerable villains which angered the fans on the grounds of continuity as well as 'realism'. Philip Hinchcliffe had recognised the problem of their implausibility, but his response was to enfold the Daleks as horrifically as possible within his 'Gothic' signature in 'Genesis of the Daleks'. 'The great problem with those Daleks stories is not to make them silly. David Maloney directed that one, and he worked extremely hard to make the Daleks powerful − you know, so that they are not just idiots running around . . . You can't dwell on those Daleks. You've really got to edit them together and make them more power-

ful and make them more menancing than they are by the way
you shoot it.'

Hinchcliffe's attitude to the Daleks was very similar to that
of the fans, who recognised — and objected to — the Daleks
being turned into 'bumbling idiots' as early as 'The Chase' in
1965. As fan Paul Mount wrote:

> With Dennis Spooner as story editor many of the preceding
> serials of the second season had possessed a lighter, less
> tense air than those of the first season under David Whit-
> taker. This trend continues noticeably with 'The Chase'.
> The old adage 'familiarity breeds contempt' is temptingly
> applicable to the Daleks in this adventure. During their
> first two serials they had been taken totally seriously, as
> objects of horror and destruction. It appears that the only
> logical step to take now is to debase them a little — ridicule
> them and turn them into objects of fun. The Daleks . . . are
> thwarted at every turn; outwitted by the faster-thinking,
> faster-moving humanoids of the story and made to look
> like lumbering fools at almost every opportunity. Yet the
> magic of it is that, at the end of it all, the Daleks retain
> their dignity — their charisma and genius carrying them
> through the excesses of the plot.[5]

So, despite their 'silly spluttering and coughing sounds . . .
spoiling the effect' of the drama in places, the Daleks retained
their dignity and the narrative its tension — which is not what
the fans thought of Graham Williams 'Destiny of the Daleks'.
Working with Douglas Adams as script editor in this 1979
story, Williams conditions of production were quite different
from Verity Lambert's when working with Dennis Spooner in
1965, and the coding of 'comedy' was consequently quite
different.

Spooner had met Sydney Newman while writing for *The
Avengers*, which Newman co-created, and he had met the
Dalek creator Terry Nation on the *Val Parnell Star Time*
when he was writing comedy script for Harry Worth — so his
appearance as writer and script editor for *Doctor Who* was
not surprising (he and Nation had the same agent), and nor
was his comic inflection of the programme. Both Spooner

and Nation had graduated from joke scripts to situation comedy pieces 'because they were easier, and on television, paid more money'.[6] From here both moved on to more serious drama, which helps account for their successful combination on 'The Chase'.

But Spooner's initial comic intervention in *Doctor Who*, as writer of 'The Reign of Terror' was within the standardised framework of 'good' drama. In the midst of the horrors of the French Revolution he introduced a comic gaoler.

> 'The Reign of Terror' was three hours long, six half hour episodes, and you know there are going to be places in episode two where you don't want to go further into the story because you don't want that to happen until episode four. So if you can introduce a character with an element of humour then it becomes a marvellous way of padding the show without boring the audience or breaking up the plot. The audience will always watch 'a funny bit' and quite like it . . . You have to be careful, though. I mean you only have to look at Chandler's Philip Marlow to know how you can even let the humour take over at the end whereas at the beginning it was just put in to vary the process.'[7]

Exactly that kind of 'spoof' detective whose 'humour' took over from the drama was what Graham Williams and Doug Adams were accused of in their 1979 story, 'The City of Death' — and Spooner himself was generally thought to have gone too far in making his 1965 'The Romans'. For fan Paul Mount this story, the 'first broad use of humour since the series began', was a 'well-intentioned disaster' which helped the demise of the historical adventures.[8] Like Williams, Spooner explained the genesis of 'The Romans' in terms of intertextual sources. 'Verity wanted to try a comedy, as we'd tried virtually everything else in the show; but I don't think that pure comedy works in *Doctor Who*. There had been a classic Nero in *Quo Vadis*, so I suppose we were sending up *Quo Vadis*. There was this "Carry On . . . " film in production — *Carry on Cleo* — and at that time I virtually lived next door to Jim Dale who was in the film. When I was writing "The Romans", I went down to Pinewood to watch Jim in the filming; so my story was heavily influenced by *Carry On Cleo*. We had the same researcher, and the "Carry On . . ." films were never very serious with their research . . . Gertan Klauber was in both; that wasn't a concidence — that's where it all came from!'[9]

Ironically, Jim Dale was asked years later to consider the part of the Doctor at the end of the Pertwee era, which, had he taken it, would have meant there would have been no Baker/Williams 'apt phrase' period of *Doctor Who*. But in any case, by that time well-intentioned comic 'disasters' were no longer acceptable — the programme had become an institution. As Spooner says of his attempts at comedy, at that early stage of the show parameters had not been established, and they could get away with far more.

> With the second series of *Doctor Who* we knew that whatever we could establish would mark the boundaries for a long time to come. 'The Romans' was done for comedy and in 'The Web Planet' we wanted to see how far we could go with being weird . . . The story got very good figures . . . but we all decided not to do anything like that again. Not because of the story content, but because of the sheer cost and technical problems involved, plus the fact that . . . we ended up with something that wasn't that sensational compared with 'The Dalek Invasion of Earth'. That story looked a far more realistic show because it was recognisable with Daleks going over London Bridge. It set a precedent that has been followed ever since for the Daleks.[10]

The precedent for Pertwee's 'monster on the toilet seat in Tooting Bec' had been established in 'The Dalek Invasion of Earth' (1964), at the expense of the 'spoof' Dalek precedent of 'The Chase'. Graham Williams' 'mistake' was to ignore Spooner's advice that in an institution like *Doctor Who* once a precedent is established 'you cannot change it'. But then Williams' decision to do a 'spoof' 'Destiny of the Daleks' was no more a purely voluntaristic act than Spooner's was.

Mrs Whitehouse: the space for comedy

When Graham Williams took over as producer of *Doctor Who* it was at the forefront of critical attention from Mary Whitehouse's National Viewers' and Listeners' Association. The liking of Gothic Horror by the former producer, Philip Hinchcliffe, and his script editor, Robert Holmes, had led to the public criticism of 'Genesis of the Daleks', 'The Brain of Morbius', 'The Seeds of Doom' and 'The Deadly Assassin' (1976). 'The Talons of Weng Chiang' (1977) came in for special abuse for its racism, violence and sexuality. This was the high point of a long-term campaign against *Doctor Who* for its 'corrupting' influence in de-sensitising children to violence. For Mrs Whitehouse, 'strangulation — by hand, by claw, by obscene vegetable matter — is the latest gimmick, sufficiently close up so that they get the point. And just for a little variety, show the children how to make a Molotov Cocktail.'[11] The response of the BBC was to prohibit easily imitated methods of violence from the programme, and to discourage the portrayal of horror through everyday household objects. Teddy bears or dolls which turned into monstrous aliens, and death — or the suggestion of death — by means of scissors, 'garotting or slicing with razors', were henceforth consciously avoided. The result eventually was (what Graham Williams called) 'the extremely left-handed compliment indeed of a psychiatrist in Mary Whitehouse's organisation saying that the level of violence in *Doctor Who* was perfectly acceptable because it was so fantastic'.

Williams took the Whitehouse attack very seriously. 'The violence and the pretty ladies — one was very conscious that the microscope was there, that the spotlight was on us.' Williams felt that the poor audience figures at the beginning of his period as producer were directly attributable to the Whitehouse-inspired public debate about *Doctor Who* in the press, Parliament, and in letters to the BBC Board of Governors. Though as a parent he personally felt that children 'loved the violence', Williams decided that the programme could not live with this 'emotional attack'. A new direction for the programme — away from the Gothic tendency of the previous regime — was necessary. The turn to comedy was 'entirely, directly' related to the Whitehouse attack. 'It was replacing the violence . . . that was a very, very major part of the thinking.' Hence Williams' new signature of 'suspense following light relief' was established, 'because in a thriller situation, if you can't have the nastics, it's a vacuum — you've got to put something in there'. Another influence was the massive success of *Star Wars*.[12]

Williams: I was up against it, because my boss was saying, 'What are we going to do about *Star Wars* coming out, and *Star Trek* coming back?' And my point of view was that we didn't have the money or the expertise to do it. Neither did *they* have our — I thought it was a British — television strength, which is in building and creating — writing, acting, directing — character, and pretty quirky character at that. And again, all this, as you can see, added up to the humour and that sort of treatment. If we didn't go for the hardware, we had to go for something. And we went for character. Then if you're going to have character, you can't have people just talking to each other. You could either play it very doom-laden, and weighty and pompous, or you could have people who took themselves very seriously but the Doctor doesn't have to take them seriously as well.

The terrain had been prepared for the arrival of Douglas Adams.

Meta-space and realism: 'The City of Death'

Tom Baker had been consistently witty under his first producer, Philip Hinchcliffe. But there the humour had been incorporated as part of the discourse of human spontaneity within the Gothic mode. For example, in 'The Masque of Mandragola' the Doctor says, 'Had a hard day in the catacombs' as, playing with his yo-yo on the underground altar, he is approached slowly and ominously from behind by the frighteningly masked and cowled space villain. Hinchcliffe's mixture of the fearsome and comic in stories, where men take on the appearance of robots ('The Robots of Death') or

sprout tendrils like plants ('The Seeds of Doom'), and where
the Doctor can laugh in the face of these excrescences and
parodies of the human form, was genuinely in the tradition
of the grotesque; a laughter at cosmic fear which promotes
relief and anxiety together.[13]

What enabled Baker to 'go over the top' in the Williams era
was the conjuncture of the new (Whitehouse induced) comedy
coding with the arrival as script editor of Douglas Adams.
Adams (with his favourite SF writers, Kurt Vonnegut and
Robert Sheckley) was part of the movement of modernist
(or 'meta') SF which, as Ebert describes, 'acquires its narrative
force from laying bare the conventions of science fiction and
subverting its transparent language of mimesis and believability. Instead of using a language which is only a means for
achieving other ends, such as telling an appealing and suspense-
ful story, it employs a self-reflexive discourse acutely aware
of its own aesthetic status and artificiality. Not only language
but also other components of fiction such as "character",
"plot", and "point of view" are handled with aesthetic self-
consciousness in a manner that makes it impossible to take
them for anything but what they actually are: created literary
characters, made-up plots and so forth.'[14]

This meta-SF approach accounts for the accenting of the
Daleks' implausibility as 'monsters' in 'Destiny of the Daleks'
and has led in recent SF to a self-reflexive play with themes,
conventions and narrative models. In *The Sirens of Titan*, for
instance, Vonnegut parodied not only the entire 'Wellsian'
Martian invasion theme and the genre's anthropocentric
imperialism, but the very claim to present an authoritative
future history. In *Sirens* the history of humankind becomes
meaningless in its own anthropocentric terms — since its great
achievements, such as Stonehenge and the Palace of the
League of Nations in Geneva, are no more than signs motivated by the robotic civilization of Tralfamadore, 150 thous-
and light years away from Earth, giving encouragement to
one of their emissaries stranded on Titan on the way to an
even more distant galaxy with a message of 'Greetings'. Similarly, in Doug Adams' *Doctor Who* story, 'The City of Death',
all humankind's inventions — the wheel, the pyramids, scientific research and exploration — have been motivated by the

alien Jaggeroths in order to speed forward the time when their sole surviving member may go back 40 million years to prevent the explosion which both destroyed his space-travelling race and began life on Earth.

In these stories SF's fusing of science (and the will to 'communicate') with galactic imperialism is parodied via central themes and conventions of the genre itself, and the very presumption of the genre to tell an authentic future 'history' — whether utopian or dystopic — is focused on self-reflexively. As Patrick Parrinder has said of *The Sirens of Titan*, the central concept, 'a parody of serious science, is explained to the reader by means of an extract from *A Child's Cyclopedia of Wonders and Things to Do* — a travesty of SF's normal convention of scientific explanation'.[15]

In Douglas Adams' *Hitch Hiker's Guide to the Galaxy* this process is taken further, as the absurd events of the SF narration are punctuated by 'scientific' explanations (of personae and locales) contained in the computerised pocket-book, 'The Hitch Hiker's Guide to the Galaxy', which is, in fact, no more than a hotch-potch of casual speculations put together by a series of worn out, bemused and often irate travellers, whose 'authorial' perspective on events is no more 'objective' and god-like than that of Doug Adams within his book of the same name. In Vonnegut's and Adams' works not only is human history meaningless except as a sign in an alien communication system (in *Hitch Hiker* the Earth's history is a series of computer experiments designed to answer 'the Ultimate Question of Life, the Universe, and Everything' for 'a race of hyper-intelligent, pan-dimensional beings' impossibly distant in the galaxy), but the absurd anthropocentrism of asking such questions and answering them via narratives of grand human events is put into focus. In *Sirens of Titan* Rumfoord's arbitrary 'Pocket History of Mars' (generated by determinations outside both the author's power and knowledge) throws doubt on the whole history of SF authorship deriving from Wells' tale of the Martian invasion of Earth.

As Ebert has explained, the development of 'modernist' SF has derived in part from attempts to 'energize' the stale, 'automized' and no longer effective conventions of the genre. When Doug Adams argued that his intention was not to 'send up' *Doctor Who* but rather to critique its stale 'aliens seek to rule the universe' SF theme, he was drawing on this meta-SF tendency, which came to be seen by his critics as self-reflexive because generically (rather than in terms of *Doctor Who* itself) that is what it was.

At the same time, Adams was never a pure 'modernist': certainly not in *Doctor Who* where he was consciously adhering to television's 'realist' discourse of 'plausible' motivation. 'I wasn't so keen on something just being a spoof or parody of something else. I thought "All right, we'll take an element from something, but then actually build it solidly into the story, so that whatever aspects we decide to give this character actually become embedded in the story and become part of the way the story is worked out." If something's there just for the sake of poking fun at something else, I think it's dull, it's boring.' As Christine Brooke-Rose has pointed out, recent SF has worked to 'draw attention to the signifiers over and above the signified, to the text over and above the supposed referent. I say "over and above" not "rather than", for its transparency does not, as in "modernist" experiments (Joyce, Woolf, etc.) obscure and ambiguate the signified. On the contrary, there is a clear plot, easily followed.[16]

In fact, the degree to which this tendency is developed depends on the material practices of the medium within which the SF story is encoded. Adams' *Hitch Hiker*, for instance, goes further towards obscuring the signified than his *Doctor Who* stories 'The Pirate Planet' and 'The City of Death', where the Doctor's (and author's) critique of the 'aliens take over the universe' theme is enfolded within a 'realistic' and plausible motivation of villainy. Thus in 'The City of Death' the trajectory of the narrative is conventional, as the Doctor acts to stop the Jaggeroth's attempt to prevent the birth of humankind. But the defeat of the villain is by means of one punch to the jaw from a detective, who is a parody of the 'hard-boiled dick' genre. As Brooke-Rose comments, this kind of ironic treatment of conventions of popular 'realist' fiction — in 'The City of Death' of the heroic human action of SF via parody of the detective genre — consists of the humorous use of generic clichés in a kind of knowing wink to the reader/viewer. In this case it worked outside the institutional continuity of the programme, and hence was a wink which *Doctor Who* fans clearly did not enjoy.

'City of Death', in fact, belongs to what SF writer Robert Sheckley calls the 'most venerable of all' the perennially popular science fiction sub-genres, 'The End of The World'. In his edited compilation, *After the Fall*, Sheckley plays on the end of the world theme with satiric and whimsical levity: 'Although we will not go so far as to call it a laughing matter, still, it does seem that the destruction of ourselves and everything we hold dear could be considered with some levity, especially since we are only reading about it rather than undergoing it.'[17]

In 'City of Death', Adams produced an 'upbeat end of the world story' of that kind. He intersperses the horror with laughter, for instance: the running joke about art 'authenticity'; the introduction of a pastiche American, the 'hard-boiled dick' Duggan who, in contrast to the Doctor's wit and logic, tries to counter every situation with a punch; and, most memorably, by the brief insertion of John Cleese and Eleanor Bron. In the last episode the Doctor, Romana and Duggan rush frantically back to the Tardis to try to reach the Jaggeroth ship before the Count. As they reach the gallery the Tardis is being contemplated by two art critics, played by Cleese and Bron:

> *Cleese*: For me the most curious thing about the piece is its wonderful a-functionalism.
> *Bron*: Yes — I see what you mean. Divorced from its function and seen purely as a work of art, its structure of line and colour is obviously counterpointed by the redundant vestiges of its function.
> *Cleese*: And since it has no call to be here the art lies in the fact that it is here.

(The Doctor and his companions rush past them and enter the Tardis. The door closes and, with the critics still contemplating it, the Tardis dematerialises.)

> *Bron*: (now staring at the empty gallery space left by the

vanished Tardis): Exquisite. Absolutely exquisite. (Cleese
nods sagely in agreement, and with a gesture signifies
'superb').

This interlude is very carefully tied into the narrative by
Adams in a number of ways. First, by re-presenting the discourse about art 'authenticity'. Secondly, by continuing the
interplay of 'up-beat' levity and dramatic horror, placed as it
is between the frantic chase and the final defeat of the Count.
Moments before there had been some humour at the Doctor's
inability to catch a Parisian taxi to take him back to the
Tardis and the beginnings of time. Adams believes this tension
between comedy and horror heightened the drama, 'The
story . . . was worked out in a considerable amount of detail,
and actually held a terrifying idea at the bottom of it.' Hence
Adams inserted the taxi scene, quickly followed by the art
critics. 'The Doctor rushes through on his terrible, urgent
mission, dematerialises, and the critics — just to demonstrate
the fact that they couldn't even begin to understand the level
of problem with which they are confronted — don't even
realise that anything strange has happened. They just think it
is part of the artistic experience.' Thirdly, despite the absurd
intervention of Cleese and Bron, their appearance, like the
rest of the story, is coded for 'realism'. It was important to
Adams that the incident should be motivated realistically, as
well as dramatically: 'The thing about the way the Doctor
works is that there should always be a fierce logic behind
what he does. Now logic can sometimes appear to be absolutely manic. So, for instance, I thought, "Now he's landed in
Paris at the beginning of the story, where would he hide the
police box?" Becuase we tend to forget, you see, the fact
that he's still wandering around in this police box, which
tends to be taken for granted — and if you operate strictly
within the context of the stories, people shouldn't be taking
this for granted. So, I thought, "where's he going to park it in
Paris? All right, he'll park it in a modern art gallery where he
hopes it will go unnoticed." '
      Adams solved his problem far more innovatively and
'realistically' in 'The City of Death' than many other writers,
who either tend to ignore the problem or else place the

incoming Tardis in some disused quarry from where the Doctor walks to his adventure.[18] In doing so, Adams plausibly motivated the appearance of his art critics. Hence Adams maintained the 'realist' motivation which has remained unchanged since the first episode of *Doctor Who*, even though its coding has varied — from the hermeneutic 'mystery' coding of Totters junkyard to the 'upbeat' humour of the Parisian art gallery.

Graham Williams nominated 'The City of Death', as his favourite production during his three years at the helm of *Doctor Who*.[19] His successor as producer, John Nathan-Turner, however did not like it, complaining of Williams' tendency to 'undergraduate humour'.

Nathan-Turner: I much prefer wit rather than silliness, and I think that the show had deteriorated on an adventure level into a kind of spoofy, comic-strip — particularly from Tom Baker as the Doctor, who, in a way, set himself up as all-knowing, all-conquering. And in fact what we've done with Tom's last season was to play down the humour. This worked quite well — and with the new Doctor we are making him much more fallible, much more inquisitive. Because every episode ends with the Doctor or his companions in jeopardy, and unless there is a kind of vulnerable aspect to the Doctor's character — I think you push into the foreground the feeling that 'Oh, he'll definitely be alright next week'. And I think that part of the appeal of the show that keeps people watching it is this thing — or *should* be — 'how does he get out of this situation? How does he stop the rock from falling on his head and crushing his skull?

Tulloch: So have you a notion of the audience you are appealing to there, with this slight change of direction? And do you think you might be losing any other target groups that you had?

Nathan-Turner: No. You see, I think that the silliness and the jelly babies and that whole sort of thing that preceded my era was over-playing to what is actually 35% of the audience . . . the under 16s.

Tulloch: So you saw the silliness as relating to the child

audience rather than say the undergraduate audience, even
though you said it was undergraduate humour.
Nathan-Turner: Yes. Well, I think there are two things. I
think there's the undergraduate humour plus childish
silliness . . . Peter Davison has comic elements. At times I
think he's quite Troughton-esque — in the way that he
reacts to flicking on a button — a kind of wide-eyed surprise.
And he's also witty. It's just the distinction between wit
and slapstick really. I didn't like the slapstick element that
had crept into the show, and I don't honestly feel that the
audience as a whole liked it.

It was quickly clear from the discussion that Nathan-Turner's
'adventure' values were as 'realist' as Adams' — dense characterisation (the Doctor was to be vulnerable as well as knowing,
humorous as well as serious), audience identification, traditional narrative designs of 'lack', suspension and resolution —
and yet that he also saw himself as rejecting the direction on
the Williams/Adams period and 'getting back' to the 'true'
traditions of the programme which had been disturbed by a
period of 'send up'. The history of *Doctor Who* did include
slapstick send-up and in-jokes: in 1965 'The Feast of Seven',
the only episode ever transmitted on Christmas Day, had a
'Keystone Cop' parody as the Doctor, Steven and Sarah are
pursued across a succession of Hollywood film sets to furious
piano accompaniment and slides like 'Meanwhile, in the
Sheik's tent.' But the fan historians, wondering that this 'did
not damage the show's reputation', allowed it as a one-off
eccentricity. 'This was Christmas Day, after all, and *Doctor
Who* was just entering into the spirit of things.'[20] Nathan-
Turner's emphasis on dramatic realism and programme continuity was, however, seen as the norm by the fans who
strongly disliked the 'spoof' of the Williams era.

Nathan-Turner's tendency to run together 'undergraduate'
and 'childish' humour as undesirable was determined by his
concern not to undercut the audience's suspension of disbelief:

Tulloch: The Williams era was very melodramatic, and
yet it seemed to me to be sending up the melodrama. I
thought that it might actually be oriented towards not just

a 'silly' audience, but in fact a more sophisticated one which actually liked that play on melodrama. Now, is that reading something into it that wasn't there?

Nathan-Turner: No, I think it probably was there, and I just think that that undercuts the drama. I mean, that's my own personal feeling — and it is why I have cut it out. You can't have a villain that cracks jokes in *Doctor Who*. And we did have one. Once again, it seems as though I'm knocking the previous regime, and I suppose I am in a way — we did have villains who cracked jokes. I don't think the Doctor as a character can take them seriously, and the viewer as part of the audience can get involved successfully, if the baddies crack jokes.

Nathan-Turner's insistence on traditional 'adventure' and audience identification led him to disapprove of the Cleese/ Bron episode in 'The City of Death' as something inserted and drawing attention to itself. 'When somebody walks on for thirty seconds which the audience spends saying, "Oh look! It's John Cleese", or "It's John whatisname — er, Oh, you know, the man from *Fawlty Towers*, blah, blah, blah", you've lost a scene! Either they're in it or they're not.' Douglas Adams rejected this criticism. 'To my mind you don't, or you shouldn't have lost the drama, because it is a moment — one hopes, if one's done one's job properly — of great tension and impact. You suddenly encounter something totally and utterly unexpected, almost as if you think you have changed channels, and you don't understand what it's doing there. And then when the Doctor suddenly arrives in that scene . . . you realise you were on the same track all the time. It's a surprise. It's in a way a funny surprise. But it's not meant to be a surprise which is actually going to undermine it.'

Adams was prepared to admit cases of trivial humour which slipped into the programme while he was script editor. 'In order to get yourself out of a situation which is going to take you twenty minutes if you do it properly, and you've got to get out of it in twenty seconds, you might then do something foolish. Like I remember in 'The Creature from the Pit', the Doctor is hanging in the pit by a rope and he pulls out a book

on mountain climbing, but its been written in Tibetan. So he
pulls out a book of teach-yourself-Tibetan. That sort of thing
is not so good, and was usually a product of desperation at
that point.' And he also argued that on occasion there was
insufficient control of production, so that lead actors could
'go over the top'. 'Very often a director and particularly
actors, seeing parts of humour in a script, think "Ah well
we're all sending this up"; and you suddenly get the silly
voices and the mannered acting – and your tension is gone.
Because they are just picking up the cues from bits they see
as funny, and actually beginning to undermine the whole
thing. I think that for the sort of scripts I was after to work
properly, they needed to be done absolutely for real, absolutely deadpan. Then the humour would be part of it and not be
something which is undermining it.'

To some extent Adams even agreed with Nathan-Turner's
evaluation of the part played by Tom Baker. 'Tom and I got
on terribly well, and had a great deal of respect for each
other. On the other hand, I must say I sometimes thought he
was too prepared to go silly and chuck in a piece of business
which I felt was structurally wrong at whatever point it was.
Of course, it is very easy for a writer to say that something
they have written has been misinterpreted. It's the cry of
writers throughout the ages. But there were times when I
thought, "If we could just do this bit really properly – for
real. Then we wouldn't be pulling the rug out from underneath
it." '

But he denied the widespread accusation among other
producers, directors, and fans of *Doctor Who* that he was
intentionally 'sending up' the BBC's longest running television
institution. And even when he admitted an element of parody – such as in the case of Duggan the detective in 'The
City of Death' – he argued that it was to enhance the complexity and plausibility of the programme rather than to
undercut it.

Tulloch:　Surely with Duggan in 'The City of Death' you
will admit you were spoofing something – parodying, if
you like, the 'hard-boiled' detective genre? – when, for

instance, Duggan saves the world at the end with one punch.

Adams: Well, you see there are different ways in which you can save the universe with one punch, if you see what I mean. Now there's one way — you know "With one bound Jack is free" — meaning you are just to skip all the issues, and have somebody knock someone out and just forget all about the threads of the plot. On the other hand, you can bring the threads of the plot together in such a way that they all cross over at one particular point, where, if one person stops one other person doing one thing, then you are clear . . . And therefore I would say that is not a cheat. In a way it's a *parody* of the sorts of cheat you get when you watch something like that *Flash Gordon* movie made recently, where nothing actually makes any kind of sense at any level at all . . . "The City of Death" was meant to be not the comedy of parody but the comedy of character. There was never any point at which one was actually — well certainly there was never a point at which *I* was trying to send up *Doctor Who* at all . . . Duggan's character is the "hit first ask questions afterwards" type. But every point at which he does that, there is actually a logical reason why he himself would react in that particular way, and why his reacting in that way then has some effect on the plot. So it's never actually thrown in gratuitously or at random, which is what I was trying to avoid the whole time . . . For instance, in my "Pirate Planet" there were things that I didn't like in the production . . . The captain is meant to be this ferocious, pirate-like character. He's over the top, but you discover if you follow the plot that there is a reason why he's behaving in this utterly over-the-top way — so that people will *think* he's just crazy when in fact he's up to something deadly serious. And behind the bluster lies a shrewd mind actually calculating the effects of his bluster . . . Bruce Purchase was encouraged, I think, to camp the part up, and we therefore lost in the end the sense that here was a man who was genuinely dangerous behind the bluster of being dangerous . . . That comes when you build into a script something which is half joke, half real. You can on the one hand see the point of the joke, on the other hand be thereby doubly nervous of the reality of what it means. But then if somebody else shoves in another joke on top of that, the whole thing topples down.

For John Nathan-Turner, Douglas Adams 'was very, very keen on two things: on the juvenile silliness and the sending up. And this was very much reflected in that era of the programme.' Adams' position, as we have seen, was rather more sophisticated than that. Indeed, if he was trying to send up anything it was what he saw as the unmotivated — and therefore 'unrealistic' — villains-seek-to-control-the-universe scenario of so many *Doctor Who* productions, including Nathan-Turner's.

Adams: One thing I think we were trying to solve continually, which I feel they have put aside in the recent *Doctor Who*'s I've seen . . . is really coming to grips with what in any story the final threat is, what the villain actually wants . . . I think that far too many plots in the past — and now — simply revolve around somebody just wanting to take over the universe, which for me actually carries no threat, means nothing at all . . . The threat in "Pirate Planet" was actually in the end quite a horrific one because when this planet dematerialises, it materialises round *another* planet . . . I mean it is squeezing another planet to death regardless of whether there are people on it or whatever. The idea behind that was that they need more and more power to feed these time-dam things. In fact each planet was not going to be enough, then suns were not going to be enough, then the whole solar system was not going to be enough energy in the entire galaxy to do it. So this was something that was happening piecemeal, and at each point was a terrible, deadly threat to a particular world, which actually was going to be destroyed for a very specific purpose . . . In the case of 'The City of Death' again the villain there was trying to solve a problem which was very, very important to him, because he was the sole-survivor of his race. And in order to save his race again he was going to have to reverse the explosion in which they died, which happened to be the explosion which started off life on Earth . . . So we were trying to find real and genuine motivation behind these things. Sometimes that leads one into over-complexity. But now that they have brought back the Master, I can see all sorts of ways it suddenly makes a lot of *Doctor Who* plotting much, much simpler. OK, you've got somebody who walks around in a black beard and moustache and is an obvious baddy, so that anything he does is bad. He is the guy in the black hat. He wants to take over the universe. One can take that for granted, and then get on with everything else. But to my mind that in the end means "boring" because why does a guy want to take over the universe? . . . At the end of "Logopolis" suddenly you had the Master broadcasting a message to the entire universe, which to me just doesn't mean anything. There's nothing you can visualise there, and there's nothing that actually has any meaning in any real world.

From this dispute among *Doctor Who* professionals, two things are particularly clear. First, that Nathan Turner, Adams, and his producer Graham Williams all justified their inflections of the programme in terms of dominant 'professional' values — that is, in terms of 'good drama', 'plausibility' and 'realism'. But that secondly, each oriented this justification in a different way according to his particular professional interests. John Nathan-Turner understood 'drama'[21] in terms of the roots of the programme itself — a return to something it had once been and had 'lost' in the Williams era, a respect for the institution of *Doctor Who* as a series and for its 'continuity' which endeared him to the fans. Graham Williams rejected the 'Oh yeah, that's a real gas — carry on and trip over the carpet as you go out' caricature of his era by Nathan-Turner, and himself justified the comedy in terms of cinema's most recognised 'auteur' — Hitchcock. 'We felt, in the classic sense, that comedy relief sets up the tragedy. Thus we hoped — and Hitchcock uses the same thing to wonderful effect — to cut the ground really from under your feet before you take the moment of tension ... To provide a cliffhanger, we've already said to the audience, "It's OK folks, only a gas . . . it's only a giggle", and then suddenly it's for real.'

Douglas Adams tried to orient the programme in the 'comedy of character' direction of 'complex' drama, and as a writer appealed to literature's most exalted 'auteur':

> You should never, by introducing a gag, undermine the tension of what's going on . . . A particular dramatic device Shakespeare used, which I think is one of the most fantastically impressive pieces of theatre imaginable, is that in *Macbeth* when the worst has happened . . . Duncan has been murdered by Macbeth. It's a terrible crime against nature and you've got Macduff there at the gates — banging on the castle gates trying to be let in. It's a moment of terrific tension, terror; and at that moment you suddenly get this comic character coming on stage — the character of the Porter, telling jokes about French tailors . . . At the moment of highest tension — and not to undermine the tension but in fact to key it up still further — you bring in a moment of humour.

Given the TV industry background of Nathan-Turner and Williams and the Cambridge 'Eng Lit' one of Adams, their respective legitimating references are not particularly surprising. The question is, how do the conditions of production of *Doctor Who* allow 'high art' and 'serious drama' interventions to take place at all — since it is undoubtedly these which permit a whole range of critical (and pleasurable) readings to take place. In this respect Australian 'popular culture' academic John Docker (following Benjamin) described the Cleese/Bron episode as demystifying the 'aura' of 'high art', and English drama academic Peter Holland interpretated the 'chess' playing episode of 'Kinda' in terms of Shakespeare's *The Tempest*.

We are not making a simplistic claim for 'authorship' — as between the personal and 'autonomous' signatures of Adams, Bailey, Williams and Nathan-Turner, for example — although it does seem to be the case, as Barry Letts pointed out, that *Doctor Who* producers have more control over the 'ideas' in the programme than many others in BBC television. It is also the case that from time to time high art writers like Douglas Adams and Christopher Bailey contribute to *Doctor Who* and create problems for the programme as institution — 'Kinda' director Peter Grimwade accused Bailey of trying to do *Play of the Month* in the guise of *Doctor Who*. Both Bailey and Adams had been educated at St John's College, Cambridge, in English, and both inflected their writing for *Doctor Who* in terms of 'serious' SF ('Ursula Le Guin' in one case, meta-SF in the other).

Television is a terrain in which a limited space for 'authorship' may be negotiated, but always in terms of already existing discursive practices (such as *Play of the Month* and 'serious' SF) and material practices (of production and reception) inside and outside the institution of the BBC.

High art and mass entertainment: the space for authorship

There was a certain appropriateness in the Parisian 'Art' context of 'The City of Death', with is play on notions of artistic 'authenticity' and criticism, since Tom Baker's 'bohemian' look — his features concealed behind a wide brimmed hat and scarf — had been based on a portrait by Toulouse Lautrec. However, there was another way in which the production drew on 'Art'. In *Hitch Hiker's Guide to the Galaxy*, Arthur Dent attempts to save his life by his reference to the monstrous Vogon's poetry: 'Interesting rhythmic devices . . . which contrives through the medium of the verse structure to sublimate this, transcend that, and come to terms with the fundamental dichotomies of the other.'[22] This passage, which clearly draws on Adams' particular cultural competence in 'Lit Crit' (whose academic discourse he is, among other things, satirising), is extremely similar to Bron's 'Art' discourse in 'The City of Death'.

Both fuse the satiric and dramatic in comparable ways within the narrative of events. And, further, they both draw playfully on recognisable 'academic' discourses designed to appeal to the large number of adult viewers with considerable 'intellectual capital' — the tertiary educated audience of *Doctor Who* and *Hitch Hiker's Guide to the Galaxy*. These are audience members who might be expected to watch programmes about art, in which the views that Bron and Cleese only slightly parody could well be expressed. At the same time the satire works — through the effect of 'actor as text' — via a recognisable tradition of television comedy represented by John Cleese and the 'arty/intellectual' image of Eleanor Bron (as carried by films such as *Women in Love*). Audience members with this particular cultural 'competence' are perfectly capable of appropriating these effects and of being articulate about them in discussion of the programme. What this represents is the curious admixture of popular ratings orientation with high art seriousness and style which marks some British television institutions. And *Doctor Who*'s ability to cross that institutional interface between 'serious' and 'popular' is a central reason for its successful incorporation of many different audience groups.

In addressing this issue of British television's mixture of 'artistic' and 'popular', Graham Murdock has pointed out that analysts of the role of the writer in television drama have tended to start either from the notion of 'authentic' and 'creative' authorship, or from the notion of the craftsman utterly enmeshed within the cramping restriction of a ratings-oriented industry. Representing the Leavisian 'Great Tradition' of television 'artists' would be Dennis Potter, whereas the 'craft' tradition is represented by writers of *Upstairs, Downstairs* who 'were given the story outline . . . told where it would fit in the series and whether it was to be a "comedy, tragedy or drama", and provided with detailed sketches of the main characters.'[23] Grimwade's contrast of *Play of the Month* and *Doctor Who* rests on the same distinction.

Murdock traces the history of the conjoint perceptions of 'authorship' and 'mass market' from the beginnings of commercial publishing dedicated to dual ('mass' and 'prestige') markets.

This division between the 'primary' and 'secondary' sectors of production and the consequent tension between entrepreneurship and patronage, is common to all the major branches of the cultural industries, and it provides one of the keys to understanding the way in which authorship has

become institutionalised within television drama production
. . . By the time that television got under way in the mid
1950s . . . the major ideological and institutional divisions
within the cultural industries were already firmly established, and television drama was obliged to accommodate
to them. In pursuit of maximum audiences, the popular
series and serials took over the performer orientation of
Hollywood and the entertainment industry. From the titles
onwards (*Dixon, Quatermass, Callan, Lillie*) the whole form
of presentation explicitly invited viewers to identify with
the central characters and to get involved with their dilem-
mas week by week. In contrast, single play production
derived its ethos primarily from the 'serious' theatre and
worked from the beginning with the ideology of authorship.[24]

As a popular series, *Doctor Who* is inescapably wedded to
ratings and stardom. And yet the 'popular/serious' opposition
is clouded by two considerations: the origins of the programme as 'educational' as well as 'entertaining' and 'adult' as well
as 'children's' drama, so that a considerable 'serious' audience
has been built up over the years; and more importantly, by
the fact that SF as genre challenges the 'popular/serious'
interface of the culture industries.

As a long-running series, always on the look-out for novel
stories, the programme does incorporate the possibility of
authorship, and on occasion the theme itself can refer to the
'art versus craft' debate. John Nathan-Turner mentioned one
such case. 'We did a story last year called "Warrior's Gate".
Most of it was set on board a decrepit spaceship that was on
its last legs with a crew of people who really have no interest
whatsoever in the job that they were doing on board the ship
. . . And, talking to the writer while he was working on the
script and while we were briefing him . . . I suddenly realised,
because he was working at Granada television, that this whole
set up — the spaceship with people who were just there to
earn a living — was actually his appreciation of Granada
television.'[25]

In this case the personal signature was completely hidden —
to the producer's satisfaction — behind the action-drama

story, and probably recognised by, at most, a few cognoscenti. In Adams' case, precisely because the suspension of disbelief itself was questioned, the personal signature was widely recognised and resented by many. Adams 'meta-SF' comedy of character, and Bailey's 'Ursula Le Guin' interiorised drama tended to appropriate a space for authorship in terms of the 'serious creativity' formula.

On the other hand, there is a space for authorship which, quite unlike the obtrusive creativity approach is appreciated by fans because (like genre authorship) it works within and expands the mythology of the institution. Here authorship is seen to be closer to the craftsman dimension, yet creativity is perceived in the degree to which conventions are adjusted and recirculated for the obvious pleasure of millions. Jeremy Bentham writes that 'Robert Holmes belief that the series is always at its best when its sources are showing is evident from his *Doctor Who* story, "Spearhead from Space", which plagiarises *Quatermass* to the detail. However, borrowing previously used ideas and converting them into the *Doctor Who* genre has been a practice used in the programme since the Daleks merged together two of H. G. Wells' immortal creations, namely, the Morlocks and the Martian Fighting Machines. The appeal of any *Doctor Who* serial has always been judged by how well it carries over to the millions watching on their television screens. By that token, Robert Holmes need have no worries.'[25] Here the sense is of the continued expansion (but never breaching) of the mythology of the programme as institution. Referring to Holmes as 'The Grand Master' of *Doctor Who* (to which he has contributed as writer or script editor for fifteen years), Bentham notes his:

> Consistent expansion into areas of thought previously considered unreachable for a series like *Doctor Who*. Fifteen years ago, if a writer had suggested to the production team doing a non-monster story as a satire on the tax-collection system, chances are the the writer would have been quickly recommended to take up another job. Yet, in 1977 'The Sun Makers' shattered several long-cherished taboos for what could be done within a series that now refuses to fall into any conventional category or format . . . It was not

aimed at children and it does not simplify the dialogue to make it understandable to a younger audience. In many respects it fulfilled one of the major functions of science fiction: to project a possible future world . . . The money grubbing little mcglomaniac and sycophantic crawler anxious to win promotion are uncomfortable burlesques of the current rat-race in British society.[26]

But whereas for some followers of the programme it is precisely these two features — its function as 'serious' SF and its function as 'serious' social reference — which locates *Doctor Who* across the interface of 'creativity' and 'mass entertainment' and helps maintain the considerable 'quality' audience which the programme has built up over the years. For fans like Bentham the 'auteur' quality of Holmes is his constant renewal and recreation of the programme's *originating* tensions between science fiction and history, fantasy and realism, space and time, morality and humour.

Typical of genre approaches to 'creativity', Bentham finds Holmes' signature in his ability to re-combine already existing elements in ways which are at the same time transformations of the programme. 'Witty' aphorisms are approved of in Holmes — Bentham likes the lines in 'Carnival of Monsters': 'No vapourisation without representation' and 'If you can't stand the cold, stay out of the freezer' — but only because they are combined with a deep seriousness about the 'genre' and its conventional suspension of disbelief. In the same story Bentham notes Holmes' careful researching of the 'upper crust terms of speech used by wealthy property owners in the British Empire colonies' and 'the secret Romany language of the circus and carnival owners. The inclusion of such material in a *Doctor Who* story is evidence that the writer does care about what he is writing.'[27]

The central accusation by fans of Graham Williams was that he 'didn't care', and Bentham discussed his 'unforgiveable' Romana regeneration sequence in 'Destiny of the Daleks' in relation to the careful 'generic' continuity established by Holmes. Hence the programme's return (after the Williams' era) to encouraging authorship-within-continuity and within 'generic mythology' is supported by the most serious fans.

On the other hand, the same fans also draw a distinction between the programme and 'American high gloss ratings television which *Doctor Who* isn't'. Jeremy Bentham and Ian Levine distinguish between the 'ideas', 'character' and 'ingenuity' of *Doctor Who* on the one hand and the 'plastic', 'identical' and 'totally ineffectual' American '35 mm film gloss' of *Fantastic Journey, Buck Rogers* and *Battlestar Gallactica.*

So that, even while 'star' orientation is a strong (and probably increasing) feature of *Doctor Who*, its sense of itself as a peculiarly 'British' and 'quality' show works (through the duplicity of science fiction as both 'serious' and 'mass') to blur the conventional 'high/low' culture interface. Producer Philip Hinchcliffe explained the success of the programme, too, in terms of its peculiar 'cultural' quality:

> We have that special relationship with our audience — *Doctor Who* producers and *Doctor Who* people. We've not been obliged to observe the strictly commercial criteria that say a producer on American television has had to observe when everything has to be reduced and ironed out and made to actually work . . . We can toss in things that don't have to be totally explained. We haven't got somebody saying, ('Hey, what is this line about?') . . . That's not the way British television works . . . Certainly not the way the BBC works . . . So it's a peculiarly British institution and a reflection if you like of British society, or British audiences and British television . . . If the Americans had been given the basic format of the Doctor they would have given you a wonderfully logically worked out 'quirky' hero who was always the same, and you would have been able to see around all the eccentricity and predict it; whereas what we have done is leave it a bit rough around the edges . . . The reason we get away with it is because our audiences are more indulgent . . . We suddenly woke up and realised that it wasn't just a kids' programme but there was something in this sort of Englishness that was valuable and was prized by the audience . . . that sort of slightly English comedy . . .

It is arguable that not only the 'English' quirkiness of the Doctor but also the frequent replacement of the star has laid stress on the *idea* of the character (and the 'liberal' perspectivism he has always stood for) rather than on the star persona itself. There is a public uncertainty of location as between 'star' and 'quality' orientation, between 'ratings' and *The Guardian*'s definition of the programme in terms of British 'culture'.

Even at its most ratings conscious *Doctor Who* continues to encourage this distinction of 'character' and 'innovation' in overt contrast to American SF. It is clear that Nathan-Turner was keen to uphold the 'quality' reputation of the series, and continued to encourage philosophical debate and literary references providing that they did not 'get in the way' of the pace of the show. As Barry Letts said of Nathan-Turner's 'Logopolis':

Another aspect of *Who* which should come up regularly, though not necessarily in every story, is the exploring of new science fiction concepts, new ideas. They are very difficult to find, and at times one does quite deliberately go in for something which is pure space opera — warring aliens and all that sort of thing, because that is part of science fiction . . . But the concepts in 'Logopolis' are absolutely fascinating. They were thought up by Chris Bidmead . . . The science fiction concept is that of a race who, by the use of abstruse and esoteric mathematics, form themselves into a giant computer . . . and affect the actual structure of the universe by their use of mathematics. They have direct control of the universe, of entropy . . . According to the laws of thermodynamics you can never end up with a more structured system, but rather lose structure when you get energy changes. In 'Logopolis' entropy is somehow linked ultradimensionally together, so that the entropy of the universe is not just entropy of the individual parts of it, but is somehow an accelerated entropy which could run through the whole fabric of the universe, and the whole fabric of the universe could collapse. These chaps who are working on very far out mathe-

matical computations are actually at this moment holding
the universe in being by doing this. It's a lovely concept
and is very far away from the sort of stuff you get in *Star
Trek* or *Space 99*.[28]

Because science fiction has a legitimated 'serious' dimension,
and because of the self-consciously 'British quality' aspect of
Doctor Who the programme inhabits a site across the margins
of the dual production system that Murdock describes.
'Logopolis' pleased both the fans through its 'in-house'
references to the history of the programme and the more
serious SF audience with its commitment to scientific ideas.
While certainly working within the 'ethos of entertainment
which promises excitement and emotional engagement rather
than intellectual challenge'[29] (and Doug Adams rejected
'Logopolis' for its lack of 'realistic' motivation), it is arguable
that the space for authorship which the programme leaves
open can *both* provide (on occasion, and always tightly
circumscribed) the intellectual provocation and ideological
challenge (as for instance in Barry Letts' 'The Green Death')
which Murdock argues is institutionally the preserve of
'serious' drama, *and* the 'generic' innovation which serious
fans see in the work of Robert Holmes. The intention of the
programme — and it is a conscious one — is to blend the two
without the obtrusiveness of taking authorship — as in the
case of Doug Adams — 'over the top'.

Intentionality, ideology and analysis:
the space between professional discourses

In a critical postscript to his own research on the BBC television programme, *Nationwide*, David Morley has described
the 'slide towards intentionality' in recent use of the 'encod-
ing/decoding' model of communication by media analysts.
His worry is that by examining the subjective intentions of
the 'senders' and authors of media messages, the actual prop-
erties and meanings of television texts which 'escape the
conscious mind of its author' are lost, so that 'the model

implicitly slides towards a confusion of textual meaning with authorial intention'.[30]

Clearly, meanings of texts do generally escape the conscious mind of authors (producers, writers, etc). For instance, Philip Hinchcliffe's choice of Jckyll and Hyde as a source for 'Planet of Evil' located the programme within a process of cultural transmission (the themes of self and other, image and doppleganger, presence and absence) with all the potential inflections which that Gothic theme had received via the history of science fiction as genre even prior to its incorporation within the institution and production practices of *Doctor Who*. And this choice of metamorphosis as a theme was itself overdetermined by its centrality in the *history* of *Doctor Who* as institution which itself draws on the discourses of Romanticism, fantasy and 'realist' science fiction. Generic codes, technological determinants, professional values, institutional constraints, authorial ideologies, acting styles, musical, design and many other codes all meet in the transmitted text.[31] So that, as Doug Adams rather ruefully put it 'unfortunately television is something which involves dozens and dozens of people at every particular stage, and the final work is not one person's vision'.

Yet, as Morley notes, 'the complication is that broadcasters do, indeed, have intentions: intentions to "communicate effectively", "ensure balance", "entertain and inform" etc. We must recognise that this level of conscious intention and activity is itself framed by a whole set of unconscious ideological practices.'[32]

Morley is right to worry about television research which leaves aside professional values and ideologies, and which tends to equate the 'preferred' meaning of a text with producers' intentions. Notions of 'balance', 'realism' and so on do carry ideological implications: for instance, reproducing the two-party consensus of parliamentary politics,[33] and, as we saw earlier, of the BBC as a television institution. On the other hand, though, these ideological implications are by no means always unconscious and unintentional. In 'The Green Death' there was an overt 'message':

Dicks: There was a time when Barry got terribly agitated

about the ecology, and the world was all going to hell, and
he got really gloomy and depressed about it . . . We were
sitting talking about it, and Barry was grumbling about it
and saying, 'Well, what can I do?'; and I said, 'Well, what
you ought to do is use the position where you are to legit-
imately express these feelings'. And so we worked out an
ecology story — which I was perfectly happy about because
it was a good story — you know, we didn't sell our birthright for a pot of message. And Barry was happy about it,
because it gave him a chance to have an influence in expressing things he was interested in.
Letts: I must say . . . I expected when it came out there'd
be an outcry. I expected people to say, 'My God, they are
using *Doctor Who* for political purposes', because it was
very rude about big business and all the rest of it. And it
didn't get a peep out of anybody.[34]

What the Letts/Dick discussions indicate is that producers
can intentionally inflect a programme in terms of particular
political interests, but always mediated by implicit ideological
(liberal/consensual) values, which Dicks clearly saw as feeding
through into the representation of the Doctor himself. General
ideological positions were in turn mediated by 'professional'
values of 'good drama' — not 'selling one's birthright for a
pot of message' as Dicks put it. This was equally clear in the
case of another foregrounded 'political' statement in 'The
Monster of Peladon': 'Women's Liberation'.

Letts: Speaking personally, I'm very much in favour of
women's lib. I don't like the great extremists who would
like to castrate all the men and throw them in the nearest
ocean . . . I think that's bloody stupid. But I honestly do
think that women have been conditioned to second class
status, and I think that's a very bad thing, and I'm very
pleased it's being changed. So when Sarah Jane Smith
came into the programme we were very pleased that it
fitted in — now this is the other aspect of it — with the
idea that we wanted a *Doctor Who* assistant who would
strongly initiate things.

Dicks: It was partly a response to the climate of the time as well . . .

Letts: That's right.

Dicks: Because one of the perpetual criticisms we got about the female lead, the female heroines, *from* women was that they never did anything except stand around screaming and wait for the Doctor to come and rescue them. And it was becoming increasingly obvious — in my case it was more pragmatic perhaps than Barry's — that you could no longer get away with this kind of thing, that people didn't want that anymore. They very much wanted a heroine who was stronger — and of course it makes better drama . . . She wouldn't think the Doctor was wonderful, and she would argue . . . She always tended to stand up for herself and go off and do things by herself.

That 'going off and doing things by herself', of course, lead Sarah into further problems from which she had to be saved. The traditional narrative representation had in fact little changed. What we actually have in 'The Monster of Peladon' is the conventionally heroic Doctor and his frightened assistant who has to be rescued from monsters. But this dominant narrative line is crossed by a conscious and overt liberal/left ideological intervention by the producer, and consequently by attempts to foreground Sarah's innovative and 'independent' role — which some audience members noted as being 'too obvious' and 'contradictory'. Conventional dramatic values were drawn on (women being rescued) and mobilised ('conflict' of opposites) to accommodate the producer's and script editor's concern for ratings ('you could no longer get away with this sort of thing') on the one hand, and the producer's 'personal' political message on the other.

Clearly television professionals can be quite aware of their own professional — and wider — ideologies, and to ignore their articulacy on the subject is foolish. At the same time it is important to remember that the researcher's analytical framework — no less than professional ideology — is a discursive practice, and as such carries specific 'competencies' and codes of coherence and relevance.[35]

For instance, in our first interview with John Nathan-Turner relevance was quickly assigned to his criticism of the 'spoof' and 'send-up' features of the Graham Williams era. Previously we had written that Doctor Who in this period used the central features of theatrical melodrama (episodic continuity and spectacle) for pastiche, thereby 'foregrounding melodrama as text' — not in the 'progressive' sense of deconstructing the text, but to establish its unity as a mode of address.[36] This 'self-referentiality' became a focus of our discussion with Nathan-Turner, assigning it coherence and relevance in terms of the 'competence' of media theorists, reading in terms of certain dominant notions of self-reflexivity and anti-naturalism. As we saw in an earlier extract, Nathan-Turner readily assented to this line of questioning, but in terms of his own 'professional' dramatic values. His explanation for the 'hiatus' which had occurred in the continuity of the institution during the Williams period was: (a) the loss of control of Tom Baker's eccentricities by a producer who 'likes that sort of thing, presumably', and (b) the 'sending up' influence of Doug Adams as script editor.

It was possible at that stage to begin to construct a scenario of determinations whereby the 'classic realism' of the traditional Doctor Who text was threatened in that period by what Nathan-Turner saw as an over-proliferation of authorship: by Tom Baker who gained an 'illicit' control and inflected the programme in the direction of the bizarre, and by Douglas Adams pre-empting his enormously successful Hitch Hiker's Guide to the Galaxy.[37]

Plausibly, then, two deeper determinants, not discussed by the producer, could be said to have acted on the history of the programme. First, the insertion of the programme — very consciously for instance in Nathan-Turner's own case[38] within the 'star' syndrome with the result that the major performer (on the basis of the programme's earlier production of him as star) can begin to determine its direction. Second, the crossing of the conventional Doctor Who text by the developing tradition of British intellectual and 'absurd' comedy ('Fringe' — TW3 — Monty Python — Fawlty Towers, etc.), this other intervention determined by the first insofar as Graham Williams pointed out that he brought in Doug Adams to generate an 'explosive mixture' with Tom Baker. 'They liked

each other enormously, and liked their ideas enormously . . .
A lot of it came to the screen. It would have been daft having
put that combination together not to use the result.'

One could then formulate a theory of 'subversion' (motivated by academic 'film theory' discourse) as to how the
complexity of signifying practices within television can
generate, in certain specified conjunctures, a critique of
classic 'realism' via a rhetoric of self-referentiality, and the
manipulation of melodramatic, comedic and science fiction
conventions. This would be a legitimate 'account' of the text
insofar as it is generated by audience members endowed with
a certain 'competence'. Nathan-Turner's is also 'legitimate', if
we define legitimacy in terms of his own professional 'competence', and his insertion within the historical dynamic of
the *Doctor Who* television institution − in other words, the
need to succeed by doing something different (from the
'spoof' era) by doing something the same (the 'return' to the
earlier tradition of drama).

However, there were in fact many other determining discourses at work in the generation of the 'spoof' era, which as
we have seen, Graham Williams and Douglas Adams were
conscious of, but which were unknown to us and, apparently,
to John Nathan-Turner too. In fact, Williams was *also* drawing
very consciously on the programme's continuity to establish
his signature of 'difference'. In order, as he put it, to 'take
the kiss of familiarity off it, we would insert some feeling
that this little section of the script was not to be taken *too*
seriously − because the Doctor has dealt with this situation
a thousand times before and come out of it perfectly well'.

Williams, then, was very conscious of programme continuity.
And the comic inflection was only intended to give the
audience a false sense of security before the dramatic reversal
into shock and horror. So the paradigm which Williams drew
on in legitimating his era was in fact the same as that of
Nathan-Turner − the importance of carefully orchestrated
cliffhangers, drama, and difference within continuity.

I tried very consciously to have a mixture in each of the
stories between the very experienced and the very new
elements of the artistic, technical and creative staff. So

that I'd have a director who was very long in the tooth,
knew exactly what he was doing — or should have done on
his track record — and I'd match him with a designer who
had not done a *Doctor Who* before . . . and let the guys
have their heads. Then, if I had a new director on the show,
I'd make sure he was backed up by a very experienced
costume designer. So that admixture I found very beneficial.

Whereas Nathan-Turner readily assented to our discussion
about melodrama's self-referentiality, Williams — *for the
same professional reasons* — denied it when discussing the
same set of sequences from 'The Armaggedon Factor':

> *Tulloch*:   It's all very melodramatic. It seemed to me to
> be consciously so . . .
> *Williams*:   The real threat came because we set up the
> comedy situation *over* what should be in normal television
> terms a suspense situation. I mean, a *time bomb* in *Doctor
> Who* . . . and all other programmes on television is hardly a
> new thing . . . So . . . by saying 'there we are folks, tension,
> tension, tension, but we are playing it for laughs', they
> think 'well, so what?' And then, as you say, Romana comes
> on and says, 'But there is a *real* threat outside' — then
> you identify with them I think . . .
> *Tulloch*:   But there's still spoof as she is saying that, you
> see — because she is sending it up.
> *Williams*:   I don't think that was intentional . . . I think it
> is just overacting probably.

This of course raised a different critique, which could be
derived from the comments of the fans — and by implication
from Philip Hinchcliffe and Douglas Adams:[39] that Williams
delegated too much control on the show. Williams argued
that his delegation of power was carefully controlled — he
had not, for instance, allowed Tom Baker to replace his
conventional female companions with a talking cabbage. 'I
was very conscious that I was being pushed by a lot of people,
particularly by Tom Baker who wanted to change the programme really quite dramatically. And I reckoned that if you
are going to keep the loyalty of the audience you can't afford

a change of more than about 15 per cent a year . . . otherwise it starts to become a different programme. And you are, after . . . 15 years in many ways fulfilling the audience's expectations of the programme as well as trying to gather to yourself a new generation of viewers.'

Williams in fact argued that he was constantly trying to restrain Baker who believed that in *Doctor Who* anything was admissible. In 'Stones of Blood' (1978), Baker and the director wanted to celebrate the programme's fifteenth anniversary and 100th story by having the Doctor take a birthday cake out of the fridge. *This* kind of self-referentiality was not approved of by Williams (as compared to intra-diegetic self-referencing, whereby the Doctor may refer to previous incidents involved in earlier incarnations), and he prohibited it against considerable opposition. Williams also argued that he liked Baker's humour only insofar as it was the apex of a tendency that had been in *Doctor Who* from the beginning.

> *Tulloch*: And presumably that's one reason why you gave him his head to some extent — because you felt that was something in the programme that could be developed.
> *Williams*: Quite right. As long as it was. I was conscious more than anything else actually in that three years of keeping him on a rein . . . Just like guiding a very strong and fierce horse.
> *Tulloch*: But one that was driving in something like the right direction.
> *Williams*: Yes, that's right.

It was that quest for comedy-within-continuity which presumably led to Williams's choice of Doug Adams as script editor in his *last* year as producer — by then the annual 15% shifts had built up enough for Williams to incorporate the author of *Hitch Hiker*. Adams, too, was restrained. On one occasion he wanted an interiorised 'psychological' exploration of the Doctor, which might have reached further into the Gothic 'threat' of solipsism.

> *Adams*: There was one thing I wanted to do, actually, which Graham was dead against — which was to do a story

that would actually explore the character of the Doctor a
bit more. Because you think, 'well he gets swept from one
event to another, but what in the end does he actually
think about it all?' I wanted to do a story — maybe only
as a short one, as a two-parter — where he decides that he
really is sick and tired of, and can no longer see any point
in, just continually going round pitting himself against this
and pitting himself against that . . . And I wanted him
actually to try to escape out of it, and refuse to have anything to do with whatever problem the universe may throw
at him. But gradually having to return to that because of
something that happened.

Hinchcliffe had allowed Baker a moment of solipsistic with-
drawal in episode 1 of 'Pyramids of Mars' in order to establish
a sombre mood from which the terror of Sutekh developed.
Williams was not prepared to breach programme continuity
by stretching this out to an entire story. He *was* prepared to
put his signature on the programme by challenging the 'swept
from one event to another' tradition — though not in the
direction of dramatic interiorisation that Adams wanted. 'I
got a bit cheesed off with the Doctor happening to arrive . . .
just at the point a crisis burst. It seemed like an enjoyable
coincidence for all these years. But it was one I thought we
could do something about and turn to our advantage, which
was the genesis of the thought behind 'The Key to Time' . . .
We wanted a very good and sufficient reason for this journey
to wherever he was going . . . so the seeds had been set even
before he joined the story.' It was this rather cautious professional approach to change within continuity, and this degree
of intentionality which opened the way for Doug Adams and
at the same time confined him — determining his blend of
meta-SF and dramatic 'realism'.

   In the last resort it is this professional ideology (working
through the 'serious/soap' possibilities of SF) which generally
prevent a splitting apart of the texts of *Doctor Who* in terms
of the 'primary' and 'secondary' systems of television production. It is not as though in 'The Monster of Peladon' a 'serious'
authorial social comment on feminism and trade unions is
dropped as a contradiction into an otherwise 'mass' oriented

space opera drawing heavily on the suave persona of Jon Pertwee. Certainly producer Barry Letts' own position helps account for the relatively anti-big business story of 'The Green Death' which contrasts strongly with the failure of writer Fay Weldon's attempt to establish a class opposition in *Upstairs, Downstairs* against the more patrician sentiments of that programme's script editor and producer. However, as Murdock rightly stresses, 'these emphases cannot be explained simply in terms of the personal predilections of the more powerful members of the production team. They must also be seen as logical accommodations to the need for ratings success.[40] Terrance Dicks' response to public 'recognition' that the world of colonialism was no longer a 'good thing', signified his belief that a popular television serial must not offend or challenge the public consensus — unless it risks the fate of *Days of Hope*. On the other hand Barry Letts' belief that a 'left-of-centre' position was the 'only possible' one for a 'creative' and 'intelligent' person to take, was a conscious appeal to traditions of a British intellectual and professional strata, some of which make up a significant audience for *Doctor Who*. However, it is clear that though Dicks and Letts referred respectively to the 'mass' and 'serious' sectors of the audience, professional co-operation (since Letts no less than Dicks was concerned with ratings) helped to fuse 'ideas' and 'entertainment'.

Professional ideologies invariably mediate the personal and institutional determinants of the 'primary' and 'secondary' production spheres. It is not simply a matter of one professional ideology for the primary sphere ('ratings') and another for the secondary sphere ('authorship') as Murdock seems to imply. Further professional codings ('realism', 'drama', 'plausibility', 'motivation') cross both spheres, so that in cases of direct contradiction (as in the disagreement between Doug Adams and John Nathan-Turner), differences can themselves be expressed in identical professional terms. Differences between them were not revealed by direct appeals to 'art' or 'ratings' (indeed, as we have seen, Adams 'The City of Death' gently satirises the notion of 'pure' and 'authentic' art) but in the codes of relevance and coherence which structured their respective 'realist' discourses. Whereas Nathan-Turner's emphasis was strongly on the audience excitement (cliffhangers) and emotional engagement (in his choice of star and companions) of 'mass' entertainment, Adams was especially concerned with the rational *explanation* of causes and events and the critique of popular SF conventions more appropriate to 'serious' drama.

The Dicks/Letts examples, and the Nathan-Turner/Williams/ Adams ones, indicate, (i) that working close to the interface of primary/secondary production (if primarily on the 'mass entertainment' side) — *Doctor Who* as a series opens out the potential for inscribing different 'mass'/'serious' notions of narrative 'realism' and authorship — and hence different audiences; (ii) that the potential for disruption between these institutionalised practices is generally contained within an over-riding 'professional' practice (the ideology of 'good drama' etc.) and a more localised programme practice ('continuity') — though at the cost of some audiences recognising 'contradictions' in textual coherence; (iii) that the ambiguity of the programme's location can lead to a choice of production personnel (especially at the scriptwriting level) which generates problems for its 'continuity' as an institution (at least in the eyes of serious fans and many television professionals) but that even here a similar rhetoric is employed to legitimate divergent professional practices; (iv) that though the 'serious/soap' possibilities of SF operate in general to unify the programme, they can also lead to distinct and disturbing shifts and eras in *Doctor Who*, particularly given the career concern of new producers to establish the success of their signature. In the case of Graham Williams this shift was initiated by pressures from outside the BBC.

A whole range of institutional factors, then, had crossed to generate the 'personal' signature of the Graham Williams era of production: the ambiguous location of the programme within the BBC as institution, the impact of Mary Whitehouse, the threat of cinema space opera, the search, via the bookstalls, for a way to predict ratings, the producer's perception of the 'strength' of British film and television (from Ealing through to *Fawlty Towers*) in creating quirky characterisation, the personal charisma and taste for the bizarre of Tom Baker, the arrival of Douglas Adams to complement Baker, the 'tension' within the *Doctor Who* concept of the rational and irrational. It was these institutional pressures and discursive practices — rather than the personal maliciousness or carelessness which so many of the fans complained of — which generated what Nathan-Turner called the 'spoofy comic strip' Williams signature. And just because the determinants were so complex, the 'comedy' inflection was probably harder to handle than the 'Gothic Horror' of the Hinchcliffe era, required tighter handling than Williams was able to give it, and was all too easily 'sent over the top' by actors and production personnel. On the other hand, when working as Williams and Adams wanted it (as in 'The City of Death', written by Adams, and Williams' personal favourite among his productions) it clearly was popular, not only with some of Graham Williams bitterest critics among the fans,[41] but with the wider audience, more of whom watched this story than any other *Doctor Who*.

Peter Davison

Chapter 5

Cliffhanger: Circulating Stars and Satellites

As the fifth Doctor, Peter Davison was the youngest, the 'dishiest' the most marketed, the most visible. The *Radio Times* of 17–23 October 1981, said, giving him its cover photo:

> He's one of the busiest around, but you would never guess from his unassuming manner that Peter Davison is an actor. For the next few months he will be all but hogging the television screen — first as Brian, the well-intentioned but disaster-prone anti-hero of the comedy series *Sink or Swim*, then in his familiar role as the lady-killing vet, Tristan Farnon in the third series of *All Creatures Great and Small*; and after *that*, in his long-awaited debut as the fifth and dishiest *Doctor Who* . . . With episodes of *Sink or Swim* and *Doctor Who* in production simultaneously, Peter has found himself playing one role in the morning, and the other the same afternoon.

As well as these parts Davison could be regularly seen on television quiz and chat shows. In Australia in 1982 his first series of *Doctor Who* was followed half an hour later on Thursday nights by *All Creatures*, the two parts separated only by the ABC national news. In England in late 1981 Peter Davison as the Doctor was *on* the national news. As the

Radio Times put it in introducing the 'New Who' in the first
week of January 1982:

> People watching television one evening last autumn would
> have seen an unlikely duo. *The Nine O'Clock News* that
> night starred two actors — Ronald Reagan and Peter
> Davison. Only one of them got the part of Doctor Who.
> The enduring Doctor has, over the years, become a kind of
> lovable national monument. The tension and speculation
> that surround the election of each new actor to that part is
> not unlike that surrounding the election of the American
> president. But that it should qualify for inclusion in a
> major news bulletin amazed the 30-year-old victor, Peter
> Davison. 'I was staggered to see it announced on the news
> ... I really had no idea that *Doctor Who* was so important.'

The new Doctor's producer made him important by injecting
an already circulating star image into the programme. Publicity
and marketing was something producer John Nathan-Turner
was very conscious of. His new Doctor was designed to
'appeal': 'I wanted to bring down the age of the Doctor. That
was the first consideration. I wanted somebody who was
equally at home in what you might call straight drama and
who could also play witty lines . . . So that he is able to bring
the whimsical nature of the Doctor, plus a very distinct touch
of drama to it — you know, *belief*. He is a very sincere actor,
very intelligent actor, and added to which he brings a huge
female following. He is a very, very popular lad, particularly
with the ladies.'

The star

John Ellis has argued for a basic definition of a star as 'a performer in a particular medium whose figure enters into subsidiary forms of circulation, and then feeds back into future
performances'.[1] He distinguishes between the star image in
the classical cinema industry and in current day television. In
cinema:

Marketing creates, by various means, a 'narrative image', a sense of what the particular film narrative is . . . It does not provide a plot synopsis, it gives ingredients which seem rather incompatible. Hence a film poster will provide an image or two (a couple embracing, a view of a particular location) and then a slogan in the form of a paradox (e.g. 'They wanted happiness, they found love'). This slogan, these images, will be spread about the press, about the city. They provide a sense of the terrain on which the film works (clearly that of 'melodrama'), but not of what actually happens. The completion of the narrative image is found in the cinema. The narrative image produces an inadequate knowledge of the film, it teases and excites curiosity (or warns against the film for those who profess not to like melodrama). The star's image is a component in this process . . . Star images are paradoxical. They are composed, like narrative images, of clues rather than complete. The star image is an *incoherent* image. It shows the star both as an ordinary person and as an extraordinary person. It is also an *incomplete* image.'[2]

In contrast, Ellis argues that the star image in television is less glamorous, more immediate and 'ordinary' because it lacks cinema's photo effect: 'that almost intolerable sense that the figures (and everything else) that are present on the screen are nevertheless absent, elsewhere'. On the other hand, television 'pretends to actuality, to immediacy . . . and uses the techniques of direct address . . . The television performer appears regularly for a series which itself is constituted on the basis of repetition of a particular character and/or situation. The television performer appears in subsidiary forms of circulation (newspapers, magazines) mostly during the time that the series of performances is being broadcast . . . presenting them as much more of an immediate presence.'[3]

But Ellis forgets the effect of the career trajectory of the television star, and is wrong to assume that there is 'no way' the image in circulation is 'a promise of television as the synthesis of its disparate parts'. Take, for example the marketing of *Doctor Who*. He rightly stresses the 'immediacy' effect of television, but ignores the fact that television — and a long-

running series in particular — is as much to do with 'monu-
ments' and institutions as to do with immediacy. The 'immediacy' effect which, as we have seen, was a potent factor
in the circulation of William Hartnell's image as the first
Doctor, is deeply compromised by the time of the fifth
Doctor with the effect of the programme as institution.

As the *Radio Times* says, the choice of a new Doctor is
both a television event and part of a 'monumental' history;
and a producer as shrewd as John Nathan-Turner is able in
pre-transmission publicity to play on that to produce precisely
the 'tease' of inadequate knowledge, the paradox of the
incompatible (Davison as vulnerable and heroic), the use of
star image already in circulation (Davison as ladies' man'
from *All Creatures* to arouse puzzled expectation ('a sexy
Doctor!?') — all working as a potent 'invitation' to the programme still to come.

This potential to draw on the 'lacks' of the star image — its
paradoxes and incoherence — to promise closure and synthesis
in the coming show is particularly the case in *Doctor Who
where there is* a continuous change of Doctors, each being
similar but different. It was especially open to manipulation
in the case of Peter Davison because of the unusually long gap
between Tom Baker's last performance and his first one,
during which time Nathan-Turner produced ' "hinting" texts
for newspapers, along the lines of "more vulnerable, more
heroic, more youthful" . . . a kind of tease, because they
don't know how vulnerable, how heroic, how youthful'.

Authenticating the hero: Peter Davison as the Doctor

Peter Davison's much marketed persona was described by
director Peter Grimwade as 'a profound innocence' — and
certainly that is an organising feature of his performances in
All Creatures Great and Small, Sink or Swim and *Doctor Who*.
For Grimwade who has had contact with *Doctor Who* over
many years, this use of the 'personality' of the lead actor has
been a constant feature of the show, bringing 'freshness' to
the institution, and a particular 'human' weakness to create a
tension with the institutionalised omniscience of the lead

character. John Nathan-Turner agreed with Grimwade's assessment: 'there are certain attributes of the character of the Doctor which are inherent whoever plays it, obviously. But I think, yes it's a true assessment — that every single actor who has played the part has brought a lot of himself . . . Certainly I briefed Peter to bring a lot of himself . . . I wanted basically "Peter Davison/Doctor" with added attributes.'

Grimwade argued that Peter Davison's human 'vulnerability' established the authenticity of the character, making him a 'shrewder boy-next-door' — a familiar 'star' function, as Richard Dyer notes: 'It is the star's really seeming to be what he/she is supposed to be that secures his/her star status, "star quality" or charisma. Authenticity is both a quality necessary to the star phenomenon to make it work, and also the quality that guarantees the authenticity of the other particular values a star embodies (such as girl-next-door-ness etc).'[4] As Dyer argues, in recent times 'the criteria governing performance have shifted from whether the performance is well done to whether it is truthful . . . with the referent of truthfulness not being falsifiable statements but the person's 'person'. All the major discourses of contemporary Western society address themselves to people as individuals, as free and separate human beings who are, in their separateness, the source of all social arrangements. Once individuals, in this sense, become the pivot of the whole ensemble of discourses that make sense of society, it is not surprising that it comes to matter very much whether those individuals are indeed functioning as they appear to be. If the individual is the guarantor of the social order, then he or she must be worthy of that role.'[5]

Yet, Dyer argues, there have been contrary and disturbing tendencies in modern Western thought which have acted to 'dislodge the security with which the individual holds his/her place as the guarantor of discourse'. Various intellectual trends within Western culture — Marxism, behaviourism, psycho-analysis, linguistics and modernism — have respectively achieved a wide public currency in suggesting that 'what we do, say, think and feel, and what happens in the world, are not due to us as we know ourselves but to economic forces, instincts, unconscious motivations, habits and patterns of speech'.[6] In addition the rise of mass media (particularly

advertising) and mass totalitarianism have generated the guid-
ing concept of 'Manipulation', determining 'vast profits and
despotic power on the one hand, and a docile populace on
the other'.

The defence of individualism in the context of totalitarianism and a 'docile populace' is, as we have seen, a centrally
recurring narrative theme in Doctor Who. But Dyer is more
concerned here with the relationship of this paradox to stardom itself.

> What is particularly fascinating about the mass media and
> totalitarianism is that, even as they are being identified as
> destroying the individual, they are also largely in the busi-
> ness of promoting the individual and the claims of human-
> ism. To get back to stars, no aspect of the media can be
> more obviously attended by hype than the production of
> stars; there is nothing sophisticated about knowing they
> are manufactured and promoted . . . Even the media knows
> it, as films like A Star is Born show. Yet in the very same
> breath as audiences and producers alike acknowledge stars
> as hype they are declaring this or that star as the genuine
> article.'[7]

That 'very same breath' is, of course, the determining discourse of the Radio Times 'you would never guess from his
unassuming manner that Peter Davison is an actor'.

How is the star image authenticated as somehow more real
than just an image? At an obvious level, Dyer argues, by referring back 'the question of the star's authenticity . . . to her/his
existence in the real world'. So, for instance, discussions of
Jon Pertwee's Bondian Doctor always relate to his 'real'
physicality and daring: 'skin-diving, water-skiing and roaring
his tiny motor bike around the mountains'.[8] In contrast to
Pertwee's former 'masks' — 'the polished radio performer
with an incredible range of funny voices'[9] — there was now
this 'real' Jon Pertwee who, in his own words, 'hadn't really
found myself before Doctor Who'.[10]

However, this referring back to the 'real me', can itself lead
to problems. In the first place, as Dyer argues, because it relies

on a rhetoric of authenticity, 'it has its own in-built instability — yesterday's markers of sincerity and authenticity are today's signs of hype and artifice'.[11] In the early 1970s reference back to the 'real' Pertwee may have been a necessary counter to the potential accusation that the confident third Doctor was nothing more than Bondian hype. But fashions in 'sincerity' and 'authenticity' changed, and Nathan-Turner was referring to something very different in an age of recession when he spoke of Davison's vulnerability carrying 'belief'.

Secondly, this very overt emphasis on actors playing themselves in *Doctor Who* can conflict with their own professional ideology. As Burns has pointed out, actors acquire a pride in their skills which are often seen as opaque to the public, and are concerned with artistic 'integrity'.[11] Though this may manifest itself in a variety of ways (Jon Pertwee, for instance, distinguished between a 'Royal Shakespeare' and his own 'working' type of actor) professional actors have a personal obligation to uphold their status as actors, partly because of the desire to succeed, and in interview tend to reject the identification of their parts with their 'natural' selves.

Pertwee was very conscious of historical trends external to the programme: as he said 'fashion sense' and 'martial arts' were 'very much in', and so 'I was able to wear beautiful clothes' and adopt 'Venusian Aikido . . . as a form of attack and defence'. Pertwee relied on popular media conventions to 'be himself'. Nathan-Turner, unlike Pertwee, was very conscious of the history of the programme (in particular, of course, in his precedessor's era) and of the problem for an actor on becoming the fifth Doctor in a long-term institution with such defined, yet at the same time undefined, parameters. In contrast to the Bondian persona of Pertwee, Nathan-Turner drew on a 'real life' photograph of Davison at a charity cricket match for his authenticating image.

Nathan-Turner: I think 'the Doctor' — as a character on a piece of paper and by the fact that he has been re-cast over the years — is a very scant outline . . . you hope for a persona from the actor you cast to carry it. You hope for a *lot* of that person, and a few more attributes besides. Imagine yourself as Peter Davison taking on the role of

Doctor Who when he has been preceded by four enormous personas in the part. So much of all of them has been themselves. I've never worked with William Hartnell, but I've been fortunate enough to work with Patrick Troughton, Jon Pertwee and Tom Baker, and a lot of their portrayal of the Doctor has been themselves. And I think all of them have been equally successful because of that very reason. But do bear in mind from an actor that they take a character outline and build upon it. Always, every actor takes something of themselves and builds upon it. But there's very little to build upon as an actor if you come in as the fifth actor to play the part with the same brief: 'the hero'.

Yet, however much Nathan-Turner appealed to a photo of the 'real' Davison to authenticate his new Doctor, it was his professional 'needs' as producer of action drama which in fact determined the new star image. He wanted Davison to be 'youthful, heroic' because this was to be action-drama not 'cod' send-up; and he wanted him to be vulnerable because this would make the dramatic cliffhangers more plausible. Nathan-Turner's choice of Peter Davison as the Doctor was therefore determined by his notion of realistic action drama, and his belief that, fundamentally and originally, that was what *Doctor Who* was.

Peter Davison's selection also depended on the actor's good fortune in being in a successful show with the future producer of *Doctor Who*. As Davison said, 'In television really you are so much at the whim of the next producer . . . You just need one producer to say . . . "I think he'd be good", and you are away.' Nathan-Turner was faced with the considerable problem of replacing that seven year monument, Tom Baker. His solution was to counter Baker's strongly self-reflexive style (the 'send up' persona) with an intertextual one, to challenge Baker's intensity of popularity with so many audiences ('The Doctor as he should be') with the television extensiveness of Davison's stardom. At the same time by tying Davison back to past Doctors through motifs of acting style, he sought to anchor that intertextuality in the institutional history of *Doctor Who* and thereby outflank Baker's seven year reign.

Davison's part as the Doctor resulted from the interaction

of the star as circulating 'text' (the sense of the Doctor's 'universal innocence' deriving from Davison's public image in *All Creatures*, and *Sink or Swim*) and Nathan-Turner's application of 'professional' values to his own considerable experience of *Doctor Who*. The producer was to draw on the star image of Davison that was in public circulation and use it to 'go back', via its youthful vigour and innocent vulnerability, to the 'drama' of *Doctor Who*.

However, Davison's performance also drew on his own knowledge of *Doctor Who*. Unlike Pertwee, he had watched the programme as 'a dedicated Doctor-fan' and so was an ideal choice for a producer who wanted to return to the roots of the show. Davison would bring 'something of himself' (actually his star image) to the part; but he would also be able to locate his role within the history of *Doctor Who* as institution.

> *Davison*:   There is no way that I could do it anything like Tom Baker. So the difference takes care of itself. It's the continuity, as far as similarity, that is the difficult thing. And that I try to get by watching the old *Doctor Whos* and also by bringing in maybe little things that they did. And this bearing in mind that one is playing a part that has been played by four other people. It's not like any other part because you haven't actually got a *character*. You know, you can't say 'this character feels like this', or 'this character comes from this background'. There is no background that you can relate to at all.

There was, though, a particular background to work against: the 'over-the-top' persona of Tom Baker. In making a break with the immediate past of *Doctor Who*, Davison, like Nathan-Turner, stressed programme continuity.

> *Davison*:   To a certain extent there was very little continuity in the other Doctors. Now I'm trying to kind of get *some* continuity, because . . . I feel as if I had some sort of inferiority complex when I started because I *was* the youngest. And I felt — because Tom Baker had done it for *seven years*, which is an awfully long time — that I had to

really ignore Tom. He is probably the person that I've
thought least about in terms of the way I did it, because,
again, I think that really takes care of itself. There are lots
of children who don't know any other Doctor Who; they
only know Tom Baker . . . I did feel on occasions that
Doctor Who lost its impact because, instead of going from
a funny or a light relief moment to a crisis, the crises were
treated as light moments, which I don't think you can
actually do.

In his sense of 'continuity', 'drama', and mixture of 'pace'
and 'wit', Davison was very much Nathan-Turner's Doctor.
And yet, like Pertwee, as an actor he had some doubts about
the 'playing it as himself' tag: 'I think it is very hard to say
what my own personality is really. John Nathan-Turner once
at a conference in America said that he wanted someone who
didn't just act but who brought their own personality to it . . .
I don't know whether I do that. To me, to be quite honest
with you, it is very much an instinctive thing rather than a
thought process . . . The parts that I have done have always
had a certain light touch to them, rather than straightforward
heaviness.'

Like Pertwee, Davison preferred to think of his 'personality'
in terms of a kind of acting persona, which conflicted in one
important detail with Nathan-Turner's 'professional' need as
a producer of 'action-drama':

Davison: I think there are at the moment *some* differences
in the way John sees it and the way I see it . . . He'll say to
the press, 'Oh, I think this new Doctor Who will be more
heroic' . . . They are not the words that I would have
chosen. Which is why somebody in America asked me how
I can be heroic and also vulnerable at the same time . . . I
think he is not so heroic. He is more a victim of circumstances, and it comes out of necessity largely. That comes
out of a preference, from my point of view, of having
stories in which the Doctor is in the middle of the muddle
rather than the outsider who comes in and sorts everyone
else's problems out.

'Like Tristan, but brave':[12] the notion of drawing on his innocence, vulnerable sexiness and idleness for a character who never works but bums around the universe with attractive female companions has a certain appropriateness for *Doctor Who*. But there are other problems too resulting from the confusion of 'personal' and 'acting' persona. Davison's star image in both *All Creatures* and *Sink or Swim* had been constructed narratively as a 'tall poppies' relationship with a more abrasive sparring partner: in each case his brother. The action tended to be theirs, the rather vulnerable response Davison's. In this sense one could argue that the return of the Master as a regular character was demanded by the intertextual effect of Davison's star image. Once again he had an acerbic and stronger alter-ego to act off. But in this case the response could not be coded for humour, as it was in *All Creatures* and *Sink or Swim*, since now the alter-ego was a villain, and villains could not, in Nathan-Turner's action-drama regime, be funny. The result, as read by many audience members, was an uncertainty of response from Davison who was unused, and rather unwilling, to play the hero.

The problem was compounded by the deference conceded to the star during production. Davison himself said that he believed in the character itself 'taking over' the part, as had happened with Tristan. Yet the pattern of deference between permanent star and transitory directors is such, on a long-running series like *Doctor Who*, that *neither* may really know how the part is developing.

Davison: There *is* a problem with my doing things, you are quite right there. They *are* treated with a sort of deference, which is not always a good thing. Because it means that you are maybe allowed to get away with things or do things which you shouldn't be allowed to get away with. Now I am used in the past to people stopping me if I am doing something which they think is . . . over-the-top or not enough and saying . . . 'Do that again'. But I get the feeling in this, on the part of directors — because directors come in and there *you* are, 'the Doctor' — that they are actually fairly reluctant to give you notes. You sometimes

actually have to coax notes out of directors, which is a
new experience. It's a shame . . . I remember saying to
John Black when we did the first one (which is the second
story that will go out) 'Don't be afraid to say what you
think is right and what you think is wrong', because he
wasn't until I said that, at all. He was just leaving it to me.
And I didn't know what I was doing.

It was the positive filling out of the role of the Doctor
rather than the vetoing of what he must not do (not be too
sexy, not to be all-knowing, not go 'over-the-top') that was
the difficult part of character construction — and audience
criticisms of Peter Davison that he was 'always wandering
around looking lost with his mouth open', and that he was
too schoolmasterly and hectoring (*'Don't* wander off, Adric.
How many times . . . ') were directly related to this.

In this situation of, as Davison says, having 'little to go on',
Doctor Who has tended to adopt television's 'similar but different' strategy, working within the character-mythology of
the show. But even at this level of continuity there have been
problems. Davison felt that 'there was very little continuity
in the other Doctors', and yet Tom Baker clearly found the
continuity of the part both a restraint and challenge.

> *Baker:*   One of the problems about playing the Doctor . . .
> is that it's not an acting part in the sense that the character
> is very, very severely limited. There are boundaries over
> which the Doctor can't go . . . The hero in melodrama
> always adopts a moral viewpoint; he is totally predictable.
> So how can you surprise people? You have to be inventive
> within the limitations of predictability, and that's the fun.
> The jelly babies were my idea . . . [13]

The point is that Baker and Davison interpreted the continuity
of the part with different emphases. Baker recognised the
Doctor's asexual, anti-acquisitive moralism, and played the
upright hero part for what it was, *as melodrama*, using his
jelly babies and toothy grin to have 'fun' with melodramatic
conventions. Not surprisingly audiences spoke of the 'panto-

mime' effect of, for instance, 'The Horns of Nimon'. The jelly babies and 'fun', however, generated the too 'spoofy' and 'all-knowing' hero that Nathan-Turner did not like. Now continuity was to be drawn on in quite a different way – in terms of the programme as institution. To the delight of the fans, Davison began to erase the recent Baker signature, and return the show (with his three companions – as in the 1963 series) to its roots and history.[14] The Doctor's problematic regeneration had Davison incorporating mannerisms of Hartnell, Troughton and Pertwee, with Baker's mark, symtomatically, confined to abandoned clothes and unravelled scarf scattered around the Tardis. After stressing continuity thus in 'Castravalva' (1982), Davison continued in later stories to incorporate the history of the programme in his performance. There was in it something of the tetchiness of the first Doctor and much of the panic of the second (Troughton is his own personal favourite). There was also, in his emphasis on the vulnerability of a man 'out on his own' a return to the mood of the very first ('exiles from our own planet') episode in 1963.

All of this, of course, emphasises the enormous 'performer' orientation of *Doctor Who* as popular drama. Each new star establishes the 'digression' on which a long-term series depends, and each tries to maintain 'continuity' in his own way. As we have said 'idiosyncrasy' itself is a powerful narrative device for establishing programme continuity, while at the same time *Doctor Who* mobilises different narrative codes with different strengths in different eras: for example, the emphasis on the hermeneutic under Hartnell (Doctor Who?), the cultural/proairetic under Pertwee (the tendency to social comment of stories set on Earth), the reflexive under Baker (with Adams' meta-SF), the proairetic under Davison (the 'return' to action drama).

These themselves are crossed by a variety of cultural archetypes of hero: the Doctor as scientist and Romantic visionary; the Doctor as Trickster who defeats by guile and running away; the Doctor as Bondian superhero in a technologically confident world; the Doctor as rampant 'university' youth, complete with scarf, 'challenging the old values, the old certainties of society' (which is how Hinchcliffe saw

Baker), the Doctor as vulnerable hero in a vulnerable world
of recession.

Despite offering more than one meaning, the star image is
structured, and its elements of signification often reinforce
each other, as Dyer argues is the case with John Wayne; or,
in the case of *Doctor Who*, Jon Pertwee's 'I ride motor cycles
. . . I like good food and wine . . . I'm a lover of clothes and
adventure and women'. But in other cases the elements of the
star image 'may be to some degree in opposition or contradiction, in which case the star's image is characterised by attempts
to negotiate, reconcile or mask the difference between the
elements, or else simply hold them in tension'.[15] This contradiction of hero-image in *Doctor Who* is, we have already
argued, a central narrative and generic device, which draws on
SF's founding discourses. Here it is suggested that this tension
is mobilised via the phenomenon of star-as-text. The doppleganger effect is only possible in *Doctor Who* because Hartnell
can plausibily 'be' both sympathetic hero and selfish anti-hero
(drawing on his 1930s to 1960s 'comic', 'tough' and 'pathetic-
ally human' personae),[16] and Baker can interact so quickly
between his 'all-knowing' and manically villainous star image.
And even Peter Davison, whose doppleganger derives mainly
from his action-drama opposition to the Master, draws on the
contradiction of naïve innocence (foregrounded in one *Radio
Times* publicity article) and 'sexiness' (foregrounded in another
three months before).

Despite the apparent galaxy of possibilities for an SF hero,
one reason why the Romantic image has always been near the
surface is that, apart from the high technology/optimistic/all-
American hero type (which the show has tended to work
against for perceived market reasons), 'playing for realism of
performance' has meant that there have been few possible
models, given the middle-of-the-market tendency of the television industry. There has been no black, female or working
class Doctor. All Doctors and companions have either been
English or outer-space English (until Nathan-Turner brought
in an Australian actress to play Tegan), and given the increasing orientation of this 'typically' English programme to the
American market, are likely to remain so in the lead parts.

Satellites

Nathan-Turner: We come now to the change in the line-up
of companions. We've got the young heroic Doctor who
hopefully appeals to everyone, especially the ladies. We
have a female companion called Tegan, who is 24, nice
figure, nice legs who appeals to the men. And we have two
young companions, Adric and Nyssa, who are both 18—19
and are there for audience identification — the younger
audience.'

On location for 'Black Orchid' (1982), there was a photo-call
for the star and his companions. 'Black Orchid' was, with the
exception of 'Castravalva', the only story in Peter Davison's
first season to involve an expensive beyond outer-London
location (it was shot near Tunbridge Wells) and so justified
a photo call[17] — as did its spectacular setting, an English
stately home (exteriors only) in the rolling hills and woods
of Sussex.

On 12 October 1981 the *Daily Mirror* and *Daily Star* printed
nearly identical photographs: the Doctor masked and dressed
as a clown, with arms folded standing in front of the Tardis
and the stately front door of Buckhurst Park. On either side
of him, presenting him as 'star', are his two female companions, Tegan and Nyssa. These satellite women gesture invit-
ingly (as 'dancing girls') and expansively from the frame, and
themselves form a frame for the mystery/star persona.

The *Daily Star* presented its photo as a 'tease', with its
anchorage 'Guess who's the clown?' to be answered on another
page. The *Daily Mirror* had its cropped close-up of the star
beneath its main photo, separated by the anchorage: 'IT's
WHO: Here's a man of mystery — a TV star masquerading
with a couple of dancing girls. Actually, it's Peter Davison,
the new Doctor Who.'

Three months before the first television viewing of the new
Doctor Peter Davison is still unseen, masked from the public,
a mystery. John Nathan-Turner's publicity is challenging
what Ellis describes as the 'immediacy', 'direct address' and
'ordinariness' effect of the conventional television star persona

by manipulating the institutional advantage of *Doctor Who*. Each new Doctor is, in advance, a mystery, and so for this reason too 'Black Orchid' and its masked Doctor is appropriate for a photo-call, offering an incomplete image as an invitation to the programme still to come.

But these pre-transmission publicity images also signify in other important ways. Davison's arms are folded, not around his female companions — the producer has vetoed that kind of press photograph because of the sexual connotations of his new, young Doctor. And yet clearly the photographs in subsidiary circulation can only offer a masked face to the public because the persona of Davison as star is already *known* (as the *Daily Star* says in its tease). The 'dancing girl' frame inevitably draws on the 'dishy' Davison-as-Tristan persona which Nathan-Turner clearly wanted. The star's arms are folded, but the posture is still determinedly and conventionally 'male' (compare the images in Marianne Wex's photo-essay, ' "Feminine" and "Masculine": Body Language').[18] Similarly, the companions' 'dancing girls' posture draws on a long history of the commodity circulation of the 'feminine' starlet representation:[19] teasingly 'there' (on stage, on film, on television) for the possession of the invited male viewer, just as the female star is located within the diegetic space of the narrative for the possession of the male star.[20]

In the publicity photograph one female companion is masked, the other is not. Nyssa, the non-terran aristocrat is mistaken in the story for the daughter of an English Lord. Here the *Doctor Who* doppleganger motif is elaborated: it is Nyssa's double who is being strangled by the solipsistically incarcerated and mad 'Doctor'. But Tegan — as appropriate to her 'down-to-Earth' Australian character — is unmasked. When asked why he chose an Australian for the part of the Doctor's main female companion, John Nathan-Turner said; 'I personally find it a bit difficult to keep accepting him picking up Earth England girls.' So on the grounds of realism and plausibility (and probably dramatic contrast as well, because her predecessor Lalla Ward carried her own English aristocracy origins very overtly as Romana) the 'typically' earthy Australian, Tegan, was born.

In fact, though, the 'active' Tegan also relates to a long-term history of companions of *Doctor Who*. The programme's producers are quite blunt about the limitations of the character part.

> The function of the companion I'm sad to say, is and always has been, a stereotype . . . The companion is a story-telling device. That is not being cynical — it's a fact. You have to have her there. It is a very cardboard figure. (Graham Williams)

> Somebody who could say 'Doctor, what is all this about?' So that the Doctor could then say, 'Oh well, now in simple terms it is so and so . . . ' — you see, to explain to the audience what is happening. (Barry Letts)

Because of the unusually dominating presence of the scientist Doctor over his stereotyped 'plot device' female companions, there is, as fan Jeremy Bentham admits; 'a strong male chauvinist element in *Doctor Who*. There don't tend to be many women actresses (in comparison to the many men) appearing in *Doctor Who* apart from this screaming companion.'

There was at least one attempt to inject a charismatic female *villain*, into *Doctor Who* in the Letts/Pertwee story 'Colony in Space'.

> *Letts*:   The IMC miners first officer was a very thinly disguised brutal killer, despite his smart black uniform. Now, we thought it would be a good idea to change that character slightly and make it a woman rather than a man. After all, women in *Doctor Who* tended to be there for one reason only: to scream at the monsters. So it seemed a good excuse to have a really evil villainess. We cast Susan Jameson in the role and this was even publicised in one of the newspapers. Then, one morning I got a phone call from my head of department. Apparently he had read the scripts and was afraid that the public might find the notion of a female killer in a black, jack-booted uniform rather 'kinky' . . . and so I was asked to change the role back to a male.[21]

The kinky, black-clad and jack-booted villainess had to wait for Servelan in the 'adult' time-slotted *Blake's Seven*, but producers of *Doctor Who* have in recent years been concerned to get away — generally unsuccessfully[22] — from the screaming companion. Carole Ann Ford, who played Susan, the first female companion, pointed out that, 'Susan was originally going to be quite a tough little girl — a bit like *The Avengers* lady, using judo and karate — but having telepathic communication with the Doctor. Then they decided they wanted me to be a normal teenage girl so that other teenage girls could easily identify with me . . . I was doing one of *The Wednesday Plays* when Waris Hussein, the original director of *Doctor Who*, spotted me. He was up in the control box and I was on the set — screaming. I think they chose me because they wanted a good screamer. I certainly did an awful lot of it!'[23]

Susan had, however, been strongly enfolded within the hermeneutic coding of the first episode, and this, together with her visible physical as well as mental maturing (her rebelliousness against the Doctor, for example) carried the 'drama' of the part during her time as companion. With her replacement by Maureen O'Brien as Vicki, the least successful aspect of 'the screamer' began to dominate the companion role. O'Brien, who later went off to be probably the most successful career performer of any of the Doctor's companions, said of the part; 'I found the role limiting to say the least . . . To look frightened and scream a lot is not very demanding to an actor.'[24]

The conception of the *Doctor Who* female companion has oscillated between two limitations — passive/screamer and active/initiator — ever since,[25] and producers have inflected the 'stereotypes' according to contemporary trends and fashions. The selection of Jackie Lane as Dodo — (Vicki's successor as long-term companion) — was influenced by the success of stars like Michael Caine and Twiggy in making the Cockney accent fashionable. Dodo was to be a close replacement of Susan, a surrogate granddaughter for the Doctor. But she was also to be a 'contemporary' Cockney waif with nothing of the mysterious alien about her — and special episodes were written in the 'present day' to mark her introduction in 'The Massacre' (1966) and her departure in 'The War

Machines' (1966).[26] Similarly, Katy Manning, who played Jo Grant, represented 'Chelsea Road' 1960s, Elizabeth Sladen as Sarah Jane Smith 'Women's Lib' 1970s and Janet Fielding as Tegan the independent 1981 'cosmopolitan' professional lady.

All the companions who followed Dodo in the Hartnell and Troughton years mentioned screaming as their inevitable fate[27] – though Zoe was able to appear as a scientific equal to the Doctor – not so much because of her 'computer' lines, but because Troughton's Doctor, like Zoe, tended to get frightened and run. As Wendy Padbury said, 'Zoe . . . was supposed to be ageless even if she did look young. She was originally intended to be a computerised type of lady without many human emotions. At the start she was different from the other girls the Doctor had been involved with – a bit more in control. I suppose. But it didn't take long for her to become a jibbering wreck, screaming in a corner like everybody else.'

Katy Manning's Jo was part of a determined policy by producer Barry Letts and script editor Terrance Dicks to get beyond the stereotype, although she still ended up a screamer. Letts and Dicks explained their reason for replacing the first Pertwee companion Liz Shaw with Jo Grant.

Dicks: We saw lots of people, and really I think probably had a slightly different character in mind. Then Katy Manning turned up for the interview and she was late, desperately nervous, short-sighted and had a hacking cough because she smoked too much. She was generally in a *terrible* state and made a complete shambles of the whole thing. But she was just so lovable – you know, there was a quality of personality that came out. So when we got her, we used that quality.

Letts: I was saying earlier that when we were choosing Tom Baker, we were looking for somebody with a personality, and possibly an eccentric in their own right. I always said the same thing about the *Doctor Who* girls. When I was asking around the agents and so on, I was saying 'the last thing that I want is just a pretty doll or somebody who can just stand there and scream. We have got to have somebody who has got a strong personality in their own right, and it doesn't all *that* matter what that personality is, because that can be incorporated in the part *given* that we have this basic idea. And the basic idea was this: the assistant that I had inherited was Caroline John who played Liz Shaw (in the first Jon Pertwee season) . . . a polymath who could answer practically any question on any discipline . . . Caroline is a very good actress, and has played at the National and all this sort of thing, so the fact that we dropped her after a season has got nothing to do with her ability. It had to do with the designing of the character who was supposed to be a brilliant Cambridge scientist . . . So the consequence was that when anything came up, she discussed it with the Doctor more or less as an equal. We didn't have anybody who could say, 'Doctor, what's all this about?'

So they were looking for someone with 'strength of personality in their own right' and 'gutsy' performance and this is certainly the period with — for many fans and producers of the show — the best liked and remembered female companions, Jo Grant and Sarah Jane Smith. There was, however, a marked difference between these two, to the extent that the appearance of Liz Sladen as Sarah is often taken to mark a new era of the programme in its search for more positive female roles. The difference was planned by Letts and Dicks in line with Letts' liking for 'women's lib', Dicks' response to pressure from women, and their joint wish for a companion who would conflict with the Doctor and strongly initiate the drama.

Nevertheless, as the Australian *Doctor Who* Fan Club pointed out, Sarah lapsed from her 'feminist' stance to the extent that a group of young Sydney mothers argued:

'Sarah was the worst. She was quite an hysterical type. She used to annoy me.'
'Yes me too!'
'She used to carry on so, a real scatterbrain.'
'She was screaming all the time, even the children complained about her.'[28]

In constructing the part of Leela, Philip Hinchcliffe was

quite aware that Jo and Sarah Jane were 'screamers' like the rest. 'They were extremely emancipated feminine women, but as soon as they got into the programme you had to drag all that in by the scruff of its neck, because although they had the accoutrements of their era, which was the late 'Swinging Sixties', basically they were acting out *The Perils of Pauline* every week. That's the basic dichotomy of those characters.' The long-term aim for an *Avengers*-type lady in leathers was finally achieved in Sarah Jane's replacement by the savage 'huntress' Leela (who nevertheless was still the female = intuition companion in contrast to the male = reason Doctor).

The audience group of young mothers argued that this was the only female companion that their little girls identified with while playing – and certainly Hinchcliffe designed Leela precisely for this reason (after 'talking to the little girl who lived next door'). Yet Leela's very brief huntress leathers, cleavage and (in 'The Talons of Weng Chiang') wet, see-through Victorian underwear were there to capture the adult male.

If this was a 'positive' female role in any sense, it was one that, in the opinion of the next producer Graham Williams, 'didn't work terribly well'. And, significantly, super-buff Ian Levine (for once agreeing with Williams), who felt that it was 'inconceivable' for the Doctor's 'charisma' to be conveyed by a woman, also found that Leela – the only female companion who ever challenged the Doctor for heroic identification – 'never worked' for him as a companion.

Hinchcliffe, whose approach to *Doctor Who* was always consciously intertextual, had intended to get round the contradiction of the strong woman who must nevertheless defer to the Doctor (in her 'what's happening' role) by constructing an Eliza Doolittle character who could ask questions as part of the 'civilising' process. However, the male-oriented huntress intervened, and the idea was not followed up by Williams who replaced the 'instinctive' huntress with the 'intellectual' Romana. Williams argued that after the woman of instinct, 'the only remaining stereotype' was the 'Ice Goddess'. But in making Romana a Time Lady, he created a companion which other producers most wanted to avoid, the brilliant scientist.

He quickly found that he had to 'soften' the part because of actress Mary Tamm's 'wanting to be liked', and when she left and was replaced by Lalla Ward as Romana 2 'it didn't seem to make much sense in doing another Ice Goddess. The companion is a story-telling device.'

Nevertheless, Williams defended his cerebral 'Ice Goddess' companion on conventional dramatic grounds. 'I think it is more interesting to see an intellectual person scream with terror, because you would normally think that there is a better reason behind it than just screaming. It must be something to be really worried about.' The potential of a positive woman who was of equal intelligence to the Doctor was opened out by Graham Williams' Romana, but was quickly closed off again both by Williams' dramatic 'need' for the conventional screamer and by the underlying Romantic discourse of the programme. Since, although having higher marks from the Academy than the Doctor, Romana was his inferior because solipsistically 'bookish' and lacking his 'experience'. Under John Nathan-Turner that potential, displaced on to the photogenically 'pretty' Nyssa, was entirely erased.

We have quoted at some length statements made by producers, writers and female performers because what was clearly revealed in all the discussions we had about gender differences was that the fundamental problems about female representation are engaged with in a limited manner. Although the performers display some awareness of the problems, the 'sympathetic' nature of the male makers of *Doctor Who* is in itself patronising, and ultimately such questions are subsumed within the more urgent 'professional' concerns i.e., dramatic 'conflict', the narrative operations of the series and problems of audience identification. Furthermore these concerns are invariably articulated and dealt with in very conventional terms.

A new producer − returning to the roots

As a number of *Doctor Who* producers, such as Verity Lambert and Philip Hinchcliffe, argued, one of the reasons for the success of *Doctor Who* has been the appointment of young and ambitious producers to the show, willing and eager to take risks to impose their signature on the programme and thereby giving it an ever renewed 'freshness'. From his very first story, 'The Leisure Hive', John Nathan-Turner provided this kind of renewed 'difference'. Beginning with the explosively updated titles and signature tune, 'The Leisure Hive' (1980) visually signified the difference of a new regime in terms of 'style'. The first episode begins with a slow 'artistic' pan from Brighton's Palace Pier along a windswept beach with empty, flapping deckchairs and colourful tents, by way of the equivalent 'tent'-shaped Tardis to the first visible figure, the deeply wrapped, scarfed and hatted Doctor slumped in a deckchair. All four episodes of 'The Leisure Hive' are specularly 'arty' in camera work and strong on the special effects which Nathan-Turner was to use with such bravura. They also pulled Tom Baker back from the 'manic' to the ominously serious performance of forboding and 'wit' which was to be the feature of his final season, culminating in 'Logopolis'. Nathan-Turner's policy, in getting away from the directors and performances of the former regime, was to provide as much variety in visual style and story-line as possible. 'I think we on the programme have to do different things instead of always playing safe. It's no good doing seven space operas . . . We must try and ring the changes – in this second season do a totally historical story, do a sci-fi. historical story, do an alien story like 'Kinda' where people have psychological problems . . . ' Similarly, in his first season, the stories incorporated, 'a whole variety of themes right from the monster story, "Full Circle", to the art nouveau trappings of "The Keeper of Traken". "Meglos" was intended, right from the start, as a very traditional story because I felt there was room for such a production in the series.'[29]

Above all, Nathan-Turner emphasised the professional trappings of television entertainment – 'tighter pace', 'dramatic impact' and 'visual style', the three qualities tied together, he believed, in differentiating his regime from his predecessor's. For instance, in 'The Leisure Hive', he justified the considerable expense of booking an extra day of studio recording in order to 'demonstrate very visually' how the show had changed. At the same time Tom Baker's 'more

stylised' costume was designed to draw his image away from
the 'slapstick elements' of the Williams era.[30] Combining
'American' style technology and pace with 'historical English'
location, and at the same time negating his predecessor's
signature, the first episode of 'The Leisure Hive' strongly
established the new Nathan-Turner regime.

Yet it did so by emphasing programme continuity as well
as 'difference'. The opening of 'The Leisure Hive' with
Romana and the Doctor on the beach at Brighton invokes the
memory of Graham Williams' first story, when the Doctor
tried to take Leela there but failed. Indeed, the fans saw
similarity with the past as part of the new producer's 'difference'. Commenting on Nathan-Turner's first season, *Doctor
Who Monthly* noted 'the superb continuity linking the serials
not only with each other but with other serials long past.
And not just verbal continuity (such as Gallifrey's co-ordinates
of ten zero eleven, zero zero by zero two in "Pyramids of
Mars" being rementioned) but visual continuity too. The
Master in "The Keeper of Traken" looked exactly as he did
in "The Deadly Assassin". Little touches as well; the Doctor's
"Weng Chiang" coat hooked onto a coat hanger; Romana's
school hat from "City of Death" tossed casually aside. Small
inclusions like this do not further the story at all but they do
contribute nicely to an essential unity in the series that has
been all but ignored in recent years.'[31]

On the one hand there was to be continuity — Nathan-
Turner went to some trouble to find the supposedly junked
Master's costume from 'Deadly Assassin'. On the other hand
there was to be that symptomatic difference from the
Williams era. Anthony Ainley's Master was to look very like
the Roger Delgado original; but, Nathan-Turner insisted, 'with
slightly less humour than Roger had portrayed. My own taste
in humour is for wit rather than belly-laughs and this will be
reflected in the Master.'[32] Central to the rejection of his
predecessor's era, was the phasing out of Romana and K-9.

> *Nathan-Turner*:   What I inherited was the Doctor, Romana
> and K-9, and I thought that that was really a *ludicrous*
> line-up. Because you had the Doctor who was a Time Lord,
> Romana who was a Time Lady and the dog who was a

computer, and I wondered why they just didn't wink at each other and say 'It's method number 38'. There was no reason for the Doctor ever to have to explain anything to Romana. So that all conversation between them either became very bitchy to impart the plot, or else it was an unreasonable scene where the Doctor has to say, 'Well, there's part of your education that you don't know about, and here it is . . . ' They were all too knowing, that earlier line-up of the Doctor, Romana and the dog. That's why they went.

'All-knowingness', reduced the drama of the cliffhangers for Nathan-Turner. Hence they were replaced by 'vulnerability'.[33] Hence, too, the destruction of the sonic screwdriver (which could instantly release the Doctor from almost any tight situation) in 'The Visitation' for, as Nathan-Turner frequently told the fans, despite his adherence to programme history, if continuity conflicted with suspense and drama it would have to take second place.

In this, his second season, Nathan-Turner also re-introduced the 1963 element of Doctor and companions who don't always 'get on with one another', but – very consciously – for 'character' rather than 'bitchy' reasons.

Female companions: Tegan and Nyssa

John Nathan-Turner's new female companions Tegan and Nyssa were a contrasting pair, taking the programme back to its roots when it had two female companions back in 1963. Tegan (like Barbara) was a professional woman, was older than the other female companion, and was 'of her year' (Tegan's 1981/Barbara's 1963). And as with Barbara and Ian, Tegan's 'bitching' relationship with the Doctor was generated by his inability to return her to that time. Nyssa, like Susan, was put into the programme for children to identify with. Nyssa and Susan were 'SF' companions, marked by special powers. Just as Susan's telepathy and extra-sensory perception enabled her mind to become sensitised by psychic energy in 'The Sensorites' (1964), so too Nyssa could act as a medium between the Doctor and the Zeraphin in 'Time Flight' (1982) because her special sensory perception was catalysed by psychic energy.

At the same time, there were important differences between the two periods of companions, despite Nathan-Turner's interest to 'get back to the dramatic roots of the programme'. The narrative 'character' of Barbara was determined by the 'educational' discourse of the original programme, itself a residual feature of the BBC's 'high culture' orientation. Tegan, in contrast with 'nice figure, nice legs' marked the ratings end of the 'commercialised' BBC spectrum which, as we saw in Chapter 1, generated *Doctor Who* in the first place.

Instead of the sexuality which was explicit in that 'nice figure, nice legs' concept yet repressed in the programme (even in 'Kinda' where the writer tried to bring it to the fore), Tegan's 'overly aggressive personality problem' was emphasised. In this sense Tegan was more a return to Sarah Jane Smith — like her an aggressive, impulsive 'professional' who nevertheless would get into scrapes as a result of her independent 'feminism'. For instance, air hostess Tegan was led into the Tardis in the first place because of her 'liberated' refusal to let her aunt rely on the men at the garage to change a punctured tyre — though this was done for 'dramatic' rather than personal 'political' reasons.

Tulloch: In one episode my audience groups have seen, Sarah Jane Smith talks about 'women's lib' to the Queen of Peladon. They said there had been some development in the role of the female companion, even though some of them said it was tokenism. Do you think that has happened?
Nathan-Turner: I don't think it's tokenism. Certainly the feminists would like Tegan. It just makes for greater drama between your regulars if you've got an aggressive girl who tends to think she knows best. It's not tokenism in any way. It just makes for a better line-up if there is friction.
Tulloch: You are talking in terms of dramatic motivation, which is consistent with what you have said all along.
Nathan-Turner: I feel that every answer to every question is 'dramatic motivation' really.

Nathan-Turner's concern was for 'character' motivation to speed along the pace of the programme and hence, through 'conflict', to heighten the drama. He disliked the repetition of every *Doctor Who* story opening with an unmotivated perambulation outside the Tardis.

> *Nathan-Turner*: We sit down with a blank sheet of paper and we create a character, and we must have motivation for the way they think, and the way they behave, to create dramatic situations. Tegan . . . I see her as *Doctor Who*'s J.R. — a kind of independent, bossy girl, who says, 'I want to go back to Heathrow. For goodness sake get me on my plane. *Now* look what you have done' — which speeds scenes along. It stops this thing of 'Oh well, here we are. Let's go out and have a walk.'
>
> *Tulloch*: Some people see *Doctor Who* as a programme of 'ideas'. But in a programme of 'ideas' there is obviously a danger of losing 'pace'. Has that been something in your mind?
>
> *Nathan-Turner*: I would combine with the ideas, the characterisation which we lay a lot of store by. I think the show is much more pacey now simply because we don't have lethargic Tardis scenes that just spin on and on. There is always a dramatic progression in terms of the structure of the script.

So, for instance, in 'The Visitation' a row between Tegan and the Doctor over his inability to return her to her plane (the Tardis has arrived at Heathrow 300 years too early) projects the angry Tegan outside the Tardis to cool off; and similarly in 'Earthshock' a row between Adric and the Doctor over the latter's refusal to return the boy to E-space, sends the Doctor impetuously outside to sulk.

The juxtaposition of 'ideas' and 'characterisation' is clearly a significant one for the programme, in so far as Douglas Adams, in responding to Nathan-Turner's criticism of his period on the show, argued that, on the contrary, it was *Nathan-Turner*'s productions that were slow: 'In comparison with what we were doing, the new ones are terribly, terribly slow. We seem to have endless, endless wanderings round and round the same point. I think that, in the time we were there, there was this sheer weight of ideas we managed to pack in — the sheer number of events and things going on . . . In contrast, in 'Logopolis' we . . . did seem to spend ages and ages wandering around and around and around the interior of the Tardis.'

Doug Adams' comments on 'Logopolis' were perhaps unfair, given that the story was about the renewal of the Tardis, whose state of entropy was endangering the Doctor and his companions, and hence one might expect a number of Tardis scenes. However, Adams general point would be shared by a lot of audience members: that in stories such as 'Four to Doomsday' and 'The Visitation', quite apart from 'Logopolis', there were what seemed like endless chases through woods and corridors because of the number of relatively undifferentiated companions.

Nathan-Turner rightly emphasised the importance of strong characterisation in avoiding this kind of problem. His choice of Janet Fielding for the role of Tegan is interesting in this context, in so far as she had an impressive background, not in television, but in experimental theatre. With a degree in political science and journalism from the University of Queensland, Janet Fielding had joined Albert Hunt's 'Brechtian' Popular Theatre Group in Australia.

Fielding: The show we brought over from Australia to England was about the history of racism in Australia and was about an hour in length. It was done as a revival meeting-cum-variety show, and the thing that kept on cropping up was that a lot of people colonising Australia used Christianity to subjugate native people, and to *justify* their subjugation of them. So it was a look at racism in the history of Australia and how it affected Aborigines. We used songs, and we used a lot of routines that owed a lot to the Marx Brothers . . . That was all out-front playing, very dynamic, very hard, very little subtlety, there was a need to come over as a much larger than life personality, which for some people is quite easy. For me it was easy.

Janet Fielding's liking for 'out-front, larger than life' playing, 'anarchic' Marx brothers routines, 'political issues that were inherently comic', and the use of metaphor might have suited her better to the Baker-Adams-Williams period of *Doctor Who*.[34] But it was to be the Nathan-Turner regime in which she played companion to the Doctor.

In contrast to Janet Fielding, Sarah Sutton who played Nyssa had considerable television experience before joining *Doctor Who*. The daughter of an airline pilot with no theatrical connections, Sarah Sutton had been directed into acting from the age of seven, joining a ballet school with an agency and her first television work being at the age of eleven in the highly successful *Menace* story, 'Boys and Girls Come out to Play'. After that she played in television and radio consistently, culminating in a part in *Doctor Who*'s 'The Keeper of Traken' which led to her selection as a continuing companion.

Tegan's and Nyssa's roles as 'earthy', aggressive Australian of 1981 and 'unearthly' gentle aristocrat from a 'timeless' planet were supposedly as different as Janet Fielding's and Sarah Sutton's professional backgrounds. Tegan was much more 'up-front' than the quietly photogenic Nyssa, but both were dominated by John Nathan-Turner's 'vulnerability' signature. For much of the time both functioned purely as excuses for 'scrapes' and cliffhangers, though occasionally Tegan's impetuosity (as in 'Earthshock') and Nyssa's scientific understanding (as in 'The Visitation') allowed them a momentary heroic role.

Tegan's part was recognisably within the tradition, starting with Sarah Jane Smith, of, as Nathan-Turner put it, the 'character development that has occurred in the companions in recent years'. As a part with 'realistic' personality problems, allowing her to be both aggressive and 'vulnerable', Tegan was a part that Janet Fielding felt comfortable in, even if it did not give her a lot of scope for her range of acting experience. Nyssa was a more difficult problem, because the 1963 prototype of the 'SF' companion part, Susan, relied on a hermeneutic emphasis which the programme had long since lost.

Tulloch: Obviously in a 'kitchen sink' drama or something of current social 'relevance' an actor will have some model to work against or within, to get 'realism'. But *Doctor Who* is a different sort of show. So what sort of advice do you

give your actors? When you say, 'No, I don't like it that
way', are you still going for 'realism'?

Nathan-Turner: Yes.

Tulloch: What does that mean in an SF programme like
this?

Nathan-Turner: Realism of performance is not to 'cod'
it, not for the villain to verbally twirl his moustache — it's
to play it as just a nasty, evil person rather than a sort of
'cod' villain.

Nathan-Turner's definition of 'realism of performance' derived
from his professional reaction to his predecessor's production
of *Doctor Who* — and the emphasis on 'character' rather than
'cod' melodrama did provide some guidelines for the construction and performance of the parts of the Doctor, Tegan and
the Master. Given, though, that Nyssa was meant to be something of a mystery figure from outer space, the 'realist' performance was more of a problem, and probably the most
successful part for Nyssa during Nathan-Turner's first two
seasons was in 'Time Flight' when, in a brief echo of her
'hermeneutic' prototype, Nyssa's narrative role was defined
in terms of her mysterious ability to mediate between the
'ordinary' and the 'alien'.

For the rest, the performer lent on the professional ideology
of 'intuition' (the distinction Jon Pertwee made between the
'working' and 'Shakesperian' sort of actor) and on the 'technical' nature of the programme and her part within it.

Sutton: If you are doing Shakespeare you have to think
about it a lot more. *Doctor Who* is a technical programme
. . . I don't go and meditate for three hours you know.
You are guided very much by what the character says. We
know that Nyssa is very technical and she's very bright and
she's adventurous and that sort of thing . . . I come from a
planet that doesn't exist . . . I could walk around on my
head if I really wanted to and no one could say, 'people
like her don't do that'. No one can say what Nyssa would
do because there are no such people as Trakenites . . . People
from Liverpool may do one sort of thing, or people from
Birmingham, but people from Traken — who can say?

Yet it is clear that Sarah Sutton could not 'walk on her head' if she wanted to. The production's notions of 'plausibility' (for an aristocrat of any society), 'drama' (as against 'send-up' and farce), and 'realism' (in terms of the second by second interaction of actors who always think of themselves, in motivation, as humans even if their parts are not) worked against it. In this situation the consistency of characterisation was stretched across a number of professional determinants which were both general ('drama', 'realism', 'plausibility') as well as particular to this period of *Doctor Who* (for instance the over-riding concern for 'vulnerability'). Consequently, the minor companion roles could become extraordinarily difficult to play consistently – as was most obviously the case with Adric.

The male companion: Adric

Tom Baker's appearance as the fourth Doctor in 1974 and Peter Davison's arrival as the fifth Doctor in 1981 determined the fate of the two male companions, Harry and Adric. As producer Philip Hinchcliffe explained; 'At the end of Barry Lett's last season as producer, when they knew Jon Pertwee was leaving, and before they searched around to find a new Doctor, there were all kinds of odd ideas floating about. At one point there was an idea, I think, of Richard Hearne or somebody like that to play the Doctor as a doddering old man. And so Barry thought it would be a good idea to have an assistant like in the old days, to do all the running and punching.'

However, the search to replace Tom Baker – at that stage the youngest ever Doctor, and well able to look after himself in a fight, as seen in the swordsman persona of 'The Masque of Mandragora' – ensured the redundancy of the virile male companion, and Harry was reduced to subsidiary verbal repartee with Sarah; he usually gently sending up her 'feminism', she rebuking his penchant for 'the obvious'. For instance, in Hinchcliffe's first *Doctor Who*, 'The Ark in Space' Harry's persona as naval surgeon is drawn on, allowing him the comedic put down of Sarah with the (to her, infuriating) line,

'Come along, nurse Smith'. And yet that kind of repartee threatened to draw attention to the sexist construction of the companion roles — since the fate of Sarah as companion was (as in 'The Monster of Peladon') very often precisely that of nurse to the wounded. Harry was 'eased out', and, as Baker's persona became more bizarre, the task of 'running and punching' was taken on by other actants in the narrative — Leela and K-9. In contrast Nathan-Turner introduced Adric in 1980 in order to rescue the Doctor from the insuperably 'all-knowing' Romana and K-9. As a combination of light-fingered Oliver Twist and precocious mathematical genius, Adric could prick the pomposity of Baker's Doctor by exhibiting his most endearing features (whereas with Davison he tended to bring out his more petulant and 'immature' ones). Baker's Doctor admonished Adric for stealing in their first story together, 'Full Circle', but the Doctor himself had started his career as time traveller by stealing the Tardis. Adric's intention was a careful repetition of that original scenario, in that his desire was to escape from a world which, dominated by the indecisive Deciders, was as riddled with bureaucratic ineptitude and procedure as the Doctor's own rejected world of Gallifrey. As a young 'scientific' deviant, then, Adric was a novitiate of the Doctor, and one who, by means of his super-rational but 'innocent' logic, could draw attention to the Doctor's special superiority — his experience *and* his fallibility.

Adric was another of John Nathan-Turner's careful inventions as producer. Drawing on the 'investigator and sidekick' convention of television drama (as Bazalgette points out about a popular cop series: 'Kojak is always the teacher, sometimes a harsh one, Crocker is always the innocent'),[35] Adric plausibly motivated the 'what's happening' companion function in the more complex SF narrative that Nathan-Turner liked. Adric was able to give the narrative the required 'difference' and variation by being both a useful scientific helper, as in 'The Keeper of Traken', and, often in the very same action, making the Doctor vulnerable by his innocent interventions (as, again, in 'The Keeper of Traken', 'Four to Doomsday', 'Kinda', etc.). On the one hand he did not threaten the Doctor mentally (as Romana did); on the other hand he added the physical threat which Nathan-Turner had hitherto found lacking in the 'invulnerable' Baker. As Matthew Waterhouse put it; 'For a while the Doctor went around with the Time Lady Romana and a sort of robot computer hound, K-9, and the three of them were all geniuses, all terribly clever. John felt he would like to put a bit of fallibility back into the companions, so he dragged me in.'

Adric had other functions as well. He was part of Nathan-Turner's strategy to 'crack' the ratings problem by providing differentiated audience identification. Adric was consequently signified as 'child' by constantly getting into trouble and being ever-hungry. In addition, Nathan-Turner carefully orchestrated his introduction to *Doctor Who* via the 'E-space' trilogy, 'Full Circle', 'State of Decay' and 'Warriors' Gate', to give some 'shape' to his generically diffuse first season as producer. Nathan-Turner was as concerned to achieve the series' 'shape' as the serial's 'cliffhanger' and, while disliking Williams' 'umbrella' concept in 'The Key to Time' (which took up the entire sixteenth season of *Doctor Who*), was able to bring together the blend of 'series/serials' by means of the 'Adric' trilogy, the first two of which ended with an 'Adric' cliffhanger: 'What we did in my first season, for I think the first time, was to cliffhanger *out* of stories . . . Do the wrap-up, and then cliffhanger out as well.'[36]

The 'companion cliffhanger' could be used to introduce new assistants (as with Adric at the end of 'Full Circle', and Nyssa at the end of 'The Keeper of Traken') or to suspend the enigma of whether they really were ongoing companions. As Matthew Waterhouse explained; 'They didn't confirm that I was going to stay on after 'Full Circle' . . . They didn't know for sure until we got to 'Warriors' Gate'. The first two stories were left open so that I could leave. At the end of 'State of Decay' . . . Tom Baker drags me into the Tardis and says, "Right, we are taking you home kiddo", and then the Tardis dematerialises and it was open-ended whether I would be in the next story.'

John Nathan-Turner was, in fact, more interested in phasing out the 'invulnerable' duo of Romana and K-9, which was done at the end of 'Warrior's Gate'. So the more 'fallible' Adric was kept on to seal over the transition of companions from Romana/K-9 to Tegan/Nyssa. His task in the next story,

'The Keeper of Traken', was to work with (and so introduce)
Nyssa as a worthy 'scientific' companion to the Doctor, and
in 'Logopolis' to foreground the independent/vulnerable/
abrasive 'get me back to Heathrow' persona of Tegan. Adric
performed the narrative function of introducing the other
companions in their 'differences'. He also located them
according to the appropriate hierarchy of 'scientific' discourse.
As a novitiate of the Doctor, Adric was superior in the companion's 'what's happening' function to Tegan. Hence he acted
as a transition point in the dialogue between scientific ignorance and wisdom. Similarly, while their different competencies
in scientific knowledge demarcate Nyssa and Tegan in terms
of different interpretations of the world, so Adric's mathematics and his earlier status as companion marks him as
superior to Nyssa in the Tardis.

In this narrative certainty as to a hierarchy of 'knowledge'
Adric was located in terms of SF's Postivist discourse. But in
his 'vulnerability' function he tended, in his more 'successful'
(i.e. conspicuous) parts to be located in terms of the Romantic
'doppleganger'.[38] So, in 'Kinda', Adric's preoccupied intellectual curiosity leads to his possession by a robotic and
death-dealing war-machine; and, more centrally, in 'Castravalva' it is actually Adric's advanced computational competence which motivates the narrative collision between the
Doctor's experiential (time travelling) persona and the doppleganger's manically solipsistic scientism, as the Master literally
creates a world in the image of his own power-lust.

It is clear that the character 'space' that Adric inhabited
was crossed by a range of generic, narrative and professional
discourses, not least of which was his function in Nathan-
Turner's first season in tying the series format together, and
cementing the transition from one era of companions to
another.

Writing about *The Sweeney*, Phillip Drummond has pointed
out that it must:

Obey the general conditions for the television series — less
overflowing, more strictly episodic than the amorphous
'serial' (for instance, *Coronation Street* or *Crossroads*), but
nonetheless insufficiently discrete to impede the elabora-

tion of a (more or less) continuous internal 'mythology' and hermeneutic for the series as a whole, particularly focussed by the perpetuity of certain characters. Thus the overarching syntagmatics of the series as a whole, synchronising motifs of the series dispersed along its linearity, may provide a form of 'overdetermination' for intra-episodic narrative and dramatic cruces . . . At the very simplest level, a series may open with a police 'failure' in order to supply added narrative tension to the resolution of succeeding dramas, as though enacting the 'rescue' of the series itself . . . the defeat of the police in one episode may necessitate the subsequent return of the criminals for capture in a later episode (hence the inter-relation, hinted at by titles, of such episodes as 'Golden Fleece' and 'Trojan Bus'); episodes preoccupied with personal crises among the regular characters may be grouped to form a 'testing' area within the serial-narrative (for example, within four episodes: Regan's attempt to clear himself of maltreating a witness in 'Big Brother'; Carter's loss of his wife in 'Hit and Run'; Haskin's framing in 'Golden Fleece'). The place of the episode 'Golden Fleece' within two of the patterns already traced may suggest some of the complexity of constructing detailed progressions for the series as a whole.[37]

The introduction of Adric in the E-space trilogy was an attempt to bind together the 'non-discrete yet episodic' paradox of the episodic serial format by means of a localised mythology — the alternative universe which was to be 'explained' later (in 'Logopolis') in terms of *Doctor Who*'s own version of SF's primary debate of structure versus entropy. The new diegetic world of Adric was therefore located in the series' 'over-arching syntagmatics', and the transition from the 'invulnerable' universe of Romana/K-9 to the 'vulnerable' one of Tegan/Nyssa was established by a clustering of 'personal crisis' episodes of the kind Drummond noted in *The Sweeney*. Each of the new companions was introduced into the fatherly custodianship of the Doctor by the death of his/her closest companion in the diegetic world: Adric through the death of his brother; Nyssa through the death of her father; and Tegan through the death of her aunt. Furthermore, if the 'personal crisis' syndrome marked the unity and continuity of the new companions, something else just as important marked their difference (in addition to their coding in the hierarchy of 'knowledge'). Nyssa's father and Tegan's aunt were killed by the Master, unlike Adric's brother — and the Master as 'invulnerable' doppleganger to Peter Davison's vulnerable fifth Doctor was a primary effect of John Nathan-Turner's new 'action drama' signature.

The Master was indeed the mark of the Doctor's (and series') 'failure' — in two ways. First, in terms of the diegesis, the Master's success marked the failure of the series to attain proper closure. From here on, Nathan-Turner would attempt to cliffhanger out of entire seasons, with the apparent loss of Tegan at the end of the second season, and the death of Baker's Doctor (coupled with the puzzle of the new Doctor) at the end of his first season, necessitating the return of the series itself for the Master to be punished (and the mysterious fifth Doctor to be fully revealed). Secondly, in terms of professional production values, the return of a 'real' (as against 'spoof') villain in the Master marked the transition from the Williams' era to Nathan-Turner's. The 'defeat' of Tom Baker by the Master in 'Logopolis' was also the defeat and replacement of the star's seven year regime. The placing of 'The Keeper of Traken' in the middle of the 'Crises of companions' trajectory, and at the beginning of the 'defeat of old hero by renewed villain' one, both suggests (like Drummond's example of 'Golden Fleece') the syntagmatic complexity of Nathan-Turner's first series and locates it in terms of similarity/difference between the Doctor's new companions. Because, at this point, with Nathan-Turner's desire to replace the invulnerable Baker/Doctor and Romana with the vulnerable Davison/Doctor and Tegan about to be achieved, the rationale for Adric's existence, in effect, disappeared.

Furthermore, Nathan-Turner's 'up-market' strategy of introducing big name stars began to populate the narrative in a way that had never happened in the early days of three companions. So in 'Kinda', 'The Visitation', 'Earthshock' and 'Time Flight' guest stars fulfilled the 'what's happening'/ 'running and punching' function in addition to the regular companions. The over-cluttered narrative had to be reprieved and Adric, whose youthful mistakes were introduced — together with the continual breakdowns of K-9, and the mysterious failure of the sonic screwdriver in 'The Keeper of Traken' — to make the fourth Doctor more fragile, was not long to outlive the disappearance of Baker, K-9 and the screwdriver.

The arrival of Tom Baker's Doctor has 'eased out' Harry; the arrival of Peter Davison now led to the phasing out of Adric. The fact that Baker had reigned for the five and half years between Harry and Adric without a male companion indicates the uncertainty of tenure of male assistants in *Doctor Who*. Whereas female companions have been a constant, the male companion has, as Philip Hinchcliffe said, largely existed to fill a 'running and punching' role. This was established as a convention with Verity Lambert's first male companion Ian (William Russell), who was a virile adjunct to the elderly William Hartnell, and was carried on through space pilot Steven Taylor (Peter Purves), Cockney midshipman Ben Jackson (Michael Craze) and Scottish Highlander soldier, Jamie McCrimmon (Frazer Hines) to the initial conception of naval-surgeon Harry Sullivan (Ian Marter).

The 'punching' role of the male companion has only survived at all because the Doctor has been, philosophically, a pacifist. In practice this has meant redundancy for the male companion role in any period when *Doctor Who*, for whatever 'up-dating' motive of programming, has located its 'action' either in the Doctor or in the female companions. During the Bond/Holmes inflection of *Doctor Who*, when Jon Pertwee performed his chase/karate stunts himself, there was no room for a male companion (who was replaced by the 'Moriarty' figure of the Master); and nor was there during the period of the savage Leela. Further, where male companions were accompanied by 'active' females (as for example Steven by *Avengers*-type space agent Sara Kingdom, and Harry by 'feminist' Sarah-Jane Smith) they were reduced to little more than cyphers.

The best-remembered male companions have been Ian (in the Hartnell era) and Jamie (in the Troughton one), and their success relied on their appropriation by the dominant narrative discourse of the respective Doctors. It was, as we saw in Chapter 1, the 'successful' displacement of the hermeneutic by the proiaretic code of action which marked the 'success' of Ian as character-actant. And similarly, Jamie was 'successful' (surviving almost the entire three years of Troughton's Doctor) because his 'up-front' physicality allowed Troughton to disappear into the mystery of the 'performance'. Not only was Jamie's 'running and punching' narratively more appropriate in this period than any other because Troughton's Doctor was the only one who never fought physically (at the time when 'monsters' clustered around the Doctor in greater profusion than before or since), but in addition the ever-kilted Jamie signified an unchanging, stereotyped acting-persona against which Troughton could perform — in the early stories, for instance, impersonating a washerwoman ('The Highlanders', 1966) and a gypsy musician ('The Underwater Menance', 1967).

Nathan-Turner's construction of Adric was thus much more sophisticated and closely tailored to programme 'needs'. Adric was the first non-terran male companion, and so could draw on a generic potential denied to his predecessors. Yet, by most accounts, both internal to the production team and in the wider audience, the part failed. The common explanation was Matthew Waterhouse's inexperience as an actor. With only one professional acting part behind him (a very minor role in To Serve Them All My Days), Waterhouse was the first to admit his inexperience.[38] Unlike the acting careers of Janet Fielding and Sarah Sutton there had been no professional preparation for the part of Adric. Without even an agent, Waterhouse was a Doctor Who buff with enormously detailed knowledge of the programme and vague ambitions to be an actor when he read in the gossip column of the Evening News that the programme was looking for a boy actor. He contacted Nathan-Turner directly and got the part. As he said, 'If I was to be in any job in the world, any programme in the world, for me it is Doctor Who . . . I'd rather have done Doctor Who than a film or a great stage play or anything . . . My notion of Doctor Who is based on the entire history of it, because it is my favourite programme and I know a lot about it and I read a lot about it.'

Yet inexperience was only part of Waterhouse's problem.

His knowledge of the programme was little help to him in the role. As his was a non-terran character, there were no precedents which he could adapt, and no 'realistic' models he could appropriate. Unlike Sarah Sutton, he did not see 'realism of performance' as even a potential of his part: 'No, realism isn't important. I mean, my character I assume is basically designed so that teenagers and children can have somebody to identify with. That is important . . . My character varies from story to story almost. In one story I am a mathematical genius, and in the next I'm just being stupid.'

Stretched as it was across a whole range of programme 'needs' — child-identity, narrative 'vulnerability', series continuity, science fiction 'alieness' and so on — the part of Adric was, as Waterhouse said, a matter of the moment and hardly coherent. In one story Adric's 'boyish' relationship with the villain would be entirely innocent — he would endanger the Doctor by being 'taken in' by the rogue's plausibility as in 'Four to Doomsday'. But this might be preceded and followed by stories where being 'taken in' is a perceptive and intelligent posture which Adric adopts to try and defeat the villain and rescue the Doctor and his companions (as in 'State of Decay' and 'Kinda'). The fact is that Waterhouse probably received less deference than any of the other regular actors, and there was less concern for the continuity of his part.

Because of the 'SF' coding of the character, Adric was also stretched between the 'scientific' and the 'Romantic' poles of the genre, his 'alien' qualities signified by logic, reason, mathematics, and his 'boyish' ones in terms of his vulnerability to science's doppleganger, the *idée fixe* of power (the Master in 'Castravalva', Monarch in 'Four to Doomsday'). Adric was vulnerable to the Master's and Monarch's megalomanic solipsism because of his lack of the intuition and experience which, in the Doctor, is the mark of the Romantic hero. In 'Castravalva' and 'Four to Doomsday' Adric motivates the flow of the narrative because he lacks the experience which separates reason from madness. He is that site of ambivalence in Romanticism's quest for an 'authentic' reason. In 'Four to Doomsday' there is the perfect rationally solipsistic villain, Monarch, who is trying to travel back to before the origins

of the universe in order to meet himself-as-god. In contrast
there is the Doctor who relies on his experience (as wanderer),
intuition (suspicion of Monarch's friendship) and ability to
adapt to the flux of experience (use of a cricket ball to project
him in space). But his vulnerability is in his neophyte Adric,
in so far as experience not reason is the guarantor of sanity.

   This location of the new 'vulnerability' signature of *Doctor
Who* in the Romantic discourse was a potentially rewarding
one for an actor. Adric for a while could play the new (but
inexperienced) scientist-as-rebel in the (dangerous) image of
the Doctor. Indeed the concept of the next male companion
after Adric, Turlough, drew on this potential more firmly by
making him an ally of the Doctor's supreme enemy, the Black
Guardian. But in Adric's case other codings of character split
it apart, or else made it trivial. The 'scientific' coding of
Adric (the 'pass the sodium chloride please' of 'Four to
Doomsday') and the 'boyish' coding (Adric with the piled up
plate of food in 'Black Orchid') were recipes for the repetitive
and banal. Further, the character of Adric existed to fill a
production need, in particular the transition from invulnerable
to vulnerable Doctors.

   With the arrival of the 'dishy' and 'vulnerable' fifth Doctor,
the representation of Adric as 'SF' hero was circulated across
the audiences of a new child/adult television time slot. Peter
Davison not only stole the mark of vulnerability; he also, as
'star' designed to 'bring in the ladies', relegated Adric the
more surely to his 'child identity' role, a reactive part which
had to be fitted to whatever 'boy in trouble' tasks were
expected of it. As the three companions (Tegan included)
increasingly became 'children' to the Doctor (because of
Nathan-Turner's worry about the emphasis on Davison's
virility), so Adric became 'redundant' – and by the time of
'The Visitation' there were just too many 'children' running
around and getting caught by villains.

   Adric's final identity in 'Earthshock' drew not on character,
but on programme continuity: Adric holding the rope of his
dead brother as he himself dies, with musical motifs from
'Full Circle' whimsically returning the programme full circle.
At the same time as drawing on *Doctor Who*'s history (with
clips from Hartnell's, Troughton's and Baker's conflicts with

Cybermen) 'Earthshock' established programme history, by having its credits roll silent over a close-up of Adric's broken star of mathematical excellence. Adric's death, totally unexpected by the audience, was the ultimate in cliffhangers, suggesting, as Nathan-Turner wanted it to, that if the Doctor's neophyte companion could die, then perhaps at some time the rock would fall on the head of the Doctor.

In an important sense the dominant discursive practices of the Nathan-Turner regime — 'vulnerability' and programme continuity — established Adric first as a marker of programme transition and then as an absence. Ironically, Adric's complaint to the Doctor in 'Earthshock', 'I'm tired of being an outsider' drew as much resonance from the actor's professional marginality as from the part he inhabited. For some in the production team nothing so became Adric's part as his leaving of it.

Circulation

John Nathan-Turner's period as producer is marked not only by the programme 'returning to its roots' and by a fine attention being paid to the detail and continuity of its history, but also by a carefully orchestrated strategy in relation to projecting and constructing a differentiated audience. Matters such as pre-transmission publicity, scheduling and international marketing were of crucial importance.

Pre-transmission publicity

Nathan-Turner: Because it was announced in October 1980 that Peter was going to be the new Doctor, we tried during that year, after the initial announcement and its subsequent publicity, to embroider on the publicity so that people accepted Peter as the Doctor even before he actually appeared as the character . . . And so we have encouraged people who have rung up and said 'Can Peter appear on such-and-such show?' to introduce him as the new Doctor Who . . . And then, during our production period, which ran from April 1981 till now (February 1982), we've once again employed the same tactics. We've had photo-calls on location, photo-calls in the studio, all of which the new Doctor Who has been attached to, as a kind of label . . . It's been quite successful really . . . It's a very difficult thing bridging the gap from one Doctor to the other, particularly when, as this time, we've been off the air for nine months.

In this circumstance of subsidiary circulation between (and not during) the seasons being broadcast (and especially in the case of the 'teasing' gap between Doctors), the star effect was similar to that in the cinema where, as Ellis says, the actual performance was a special, rare event because the subsidiary circulation of the image was commonplace. In this way an institution like *Doctor Who* avoids the banality effect caused by the 'repetition of a particular character' on television.[39]

It is the establishing of the new Doctor which is crucial: once the 'charisma' is accepted, as in the case of Tom Baker's seven years as lead actor, the programme-as-institution tends to carry the audience. Though Davison's new Doctor did not get a *Radio Times* front cover at the beginning of his first season in January 1982, Nathan-Turner pointed to the success of his pre-transmission strategy in that Davison had been given a colour cover for the new series of *Sink or Swim* in the previous October, and a considerable part of the accompanying article was a 'tease' for the forthcoming *Doctor Who*. Further, Davison's constant television exposure was seen by Nathan-Turner as 'a kind of plus for the programme and anticipation. We've tried always to get in the fact that we are going out in January. So I think it's all worked to one end really.' That 'end' was high ratings, and the success of Nathan-Turner's pre-transmission strategy can be judged by the fact that the first audience figures for the new Doctor were a very high eleven million.

Time slot

The lack of a total coherence to the *Crossroads* narrative . . . by offering multiple small segments in a serial stripped over three ... nights each week at 6.35 or 5.15 pm (according to area) can be seen to fit into the professional ideology of a toddler's truce as well as the stipulations about time-bands and suitable programming made by the IBA. The toddlers' truce ... was based on the idea of no programme transmissions between 6.00 and 7.00 pm so that children could be put to bed. Its use is seen to necessitate programmes which consist of multiple short items that a non-static household is able to absorb selectively. That is, the belief that people will put the television on for programmes that do not require constant attention, whereas they would not for a long and involving narrative, was important to the genesis of *Tonight* (and its successor *Nationwide*), and can be seen to fit the *Crossroads* narrative structure. *Crossroads* can also be scheduled at earlier times because it fits the IBA stipulation about the need to cater for a very differentiated audience with a large proportion of children watching alone at either of its transmission times. If this is compared to the audience expected to be watching at 7.30 — a static family audience with the mother present and central in determining channel selection, able to absorb a more coherent narrative and the need to aggregate a large audience to induce high advertising expenditure — it is clear that the *Coronation Street* narrative fits these requirements. *Hazell* or *The Sweeney*, on the other hand, are both designed for the action series slot at 9.00 pm — programmes with greater dramatic licence because the responsibility for what children should watch is believed to lie with parents ... After 9.00 pm there is an attempt to aggregate a different audience based on the 'adult'.[40]

From 1963 until 1982 *Doctor Who* was placed in a 'family' viewing slot on a Saturday, usually starting somewhere between 5.15 and 6.00 pm. Possibly because of the different family pattern of time allocation on a Saturday (*The Guardian*, for example, expected fathers to have just finished watching Saturday afternoon sport and families were thought now to be having tea around the television), and certainly because of his commitment to the 'action drama' of *Doctor Who*, John Nathan-Turner had no intention of making concessions to the

Crossroads type of audience who, as he put it, 'can miss it for three months and pick it up . . . On *Doctor Who* we never cater for anybody who has missed the previous episode'. In fact he instituted a 'new' policy of cliffhanging out of entire stories, to tie the separate narratives together more tightly.

Of much more significance to Nathan-Turner than the change in time[41] of the new Peter Davison season was the change of days, and the transmission of *Doctor Who* twice weekly, on Monday and Tuesday at 6.55 pm. Because it is a show with many different audience groups, because 'no kids really have gone to bed by 7 o'clock', because he believed that the show should not over appeal to the children who only made up 35 pcr cent of the audience anyway, and because of his hopes of appropriating for *Doctor Who* the large adult (particularly female) personal following of Peter Davison, Nathan-Turner was more interested in its location in terms of general audience trends and programme 'flow' than in any notion of a 'toddlers' truce format like *Crossroads*.

Nathan-Turner: I think the change of days is absolutely right for the show at this time. What has normally been following us is the Saturday evening sledgehammer, which is a show called *The Generation Game* that has been running for about ten years. It started off with Bruce Forsyth who was incredibly popular, and we were, as it were, the stepping stone to the evening's viewing. We were the first thing virtually, and then in came the blockbuster and on from there. Hopefully you'd grab the audience for the whole evening like that . . . I think that the tea-time slot on Saturday has really been outgrown by public taste — not by the programme, but by public taste . . . Because of our new transmission bi-weekly it was decided to put Larry Grayson's *Generation Game* which had always been in the top twenty programmes in our old slot. And it's failed . . . I think it only proves what I felt, after an initial horror at being told that the programme was being moved . . . I thought it through and decided it would be the best thing for the programme. This seems awfully easy to say now that we've had our first audience figures in, which for episode one of Peter Davison, in 'Castravalva' is almost

11 million. It's a combination of things — the fact that it's not a 'tea and crumpets and *Doctor Who*' slot anymore . . . and the fact that Peter has a huge following in the public, particularly among the female viewers.

So that whereas Graham Williams watched the popular book-stalls, John Nathan-Turner watched the ratings of surrounding shows and imported a star who already had a big following.[42]

The high pressure marketing of the initial Davison season was undoubtedly influenced by the relative failure of Nathan-Turner's first season as producer of *Doctor Who*, which was also Tom Baker's last as star of the show. Faced with competition on the commercial channel from *Buck Rogers*, the audience figures were poor, although they began to recover when *Doctor Who* was moved to an earlier time slot (by which time *Buck Rogers*, which itself had lost its early popularity, was off the air anyway). As Jeremy Bentham noted gloomily to fans in early 1982:

Despite the recovery staged towards the end of last season the overall ratings from 'The Leisure Hive' through to 'Logopolis' were not good. In fact the staggering and unexpected figures of 7,000,000 accorded to the (BBC 2) re-run of (Jon Pertwee's) 'Carnival of Monsters' was way in excess of average figures for the first four stories in the final Tom Baker series. With the last two Graham Williams' seasons also having netted poor figures a question mark now stands over the world's longest-running science fiction series. One of the prime reasons for moving *Doctor Who* out of its traditional Saturday slot and into a twice weekly weekday line-up was to see if the series will merit continuation beyond its twentieth season. For if the new series fails to attract figures of around 10,000,000 or more then a serious possibility exists that the programme will end at its twentieth anniversary.[43]

A little later, however, Bentham was able to write jubilantly,

On the ratings front, *Doctor Who* has gone from strength to strength. The first episode of 'Castravalva' netted 10½

million viewers. Subsequent episodes show a moderate
slump to the still successful figure of 9.4 million . . . From
there, though, the trend was ever upwards until, with 'The
Visitation' figures were holding at just below eleven million
. . . The letter-writing public clearly favours a return to a
Saturday slot, but with the weekday dates netting totals
around eleven million viewers, Milne and Hart may be
reluctant to risk a drop in audience figures by returning to
the traditional venue.[44]

And so, it can be assumed, would John Nathan-Turner. Not
only would the new time slot give him the opportunity to
innovate in future seasons, but it also removed *Doctor Who*
from the continuing war being waged between the BBC and
commercial television over Saturday night audiences. As
Richard Paterson explains:

A striking example of the schedulers' notion of the family
audience was London Weekend Television's thinking in
launching *Bruce Forsyth's Big Night* in their 1978 Autumn
season in an attempt to counter the BBC's domination of
Saturday nights. The innovative form of the programme
was based on research into viewing habits during that evening. Taking six discussion groups based on families in
class C1 and C2 (the main group of consumers that needs
to be aggregated into the audience; research shows that
members of social classes D and E watch commercial television anyway), it indicated that the male of the household
controls the choice of channel on Saturday afternoons up
until 16.00; at this point — while wrestling is transmitted —
there is some family negotiation. After 17.15, it was found,
the choice depends mainly on the male and the children,
with women apparently busy doing domestic tasks and
given little say. Having completed these, though, the woman
again becomes significant between 19.30 and 20.00 and is
a major influence in the negotiations which continue
through the evening. (Hence the radical changes in the
second version (*Bruce Forsyth's Big Night* when its transmission was brought forward from 19.25 to 18.00). The
children were found to remain involved in negotiations

after the mythical cut-off – at least until *Match of the Day* is broadcast, when once again it is the male who chooses. Late programmes generate a special – predominantly young – audience; thus *All You Need is Love*, Tony Palmer's history of popular music, was able to aggregate a large but demographically specific audience.[45]

The complex irony of the fact that London Weekend Television's research completely overlooks the possibility (or, we would argue, the necessity) that it is television schedules that *construct* audiences thereby helping to re-inforce the leisure activities and habits of, in particular, nuclear families is unremarked upon by Paterson. However, his argument nevertheless supports Nathan-Turner's contention that the child audience will continue to be an important factor in switching over to *Doctor Who* at 18.55 and gives some context to his strategy to 'crack' the problem of the family audience by carefully locating a point of appeal for men, women and children separately, rather than promoting the generalised 'family' image the show once had. It is also likely that BBC controllers considered the poor ratings *Doctor Who* was receiving from the Autumn of 1978 in the light of commercial television's new aggressive strategy to capture the Saturday night audience (with *Bruce Forsyth's Big Night* in Autumn 1978, with *Buck Rogers* set against *Doctor Who* in 1980, and with ITV's contentious challenge to the BBC's late evening *Match of the Day*). It is conceivable that *Doctor Who* was moved to *allow* Larry Grayson's *Generation Game* to capture the audience for the BBC at an earlier time on Saturday. Certainly, the decision to move *Doctor Who* would have been as much to do with the controllers' notion of Saturday evening flow as with concern for the future of a particular programme. (In fact this example indicates the key significance accorded the 'art' of scheduling.) But it did allow Nathan-Turner the potential for more manouverability with his up-marketing strategy, illustrating Paterson's point that 'innovation in programme making may . . . depend less on the "creative" moment . . . than . . . the moment of circulation which influences the type and size of audience'.[46] In addition there was the unique advantage for producers of *Doctor Who* that the

programme *already* appealed to demographically specific
audiences (such as the young adults who might also watch
All You Need Is Love and in Australia the late Saturday night
Blake's Seven). So it already challenged the notion of the
uniform 'family' audience.

In this sense, *Doctor Who* should be well adapted to
respond to the changing conceptions of audience that new
media technology will bring. Paterson argued that; 'as channels multiply, as satellite broadcasting gets underway, as
videocassettes and discs become widely available and the
number of television sets in each household increases, patterns
of viewing and selection and the range of potential target
audiences are bound to look quite different. This will in turn
require new marketing strategies; and it may even mean the
end of "the family" as we — or rather as Mrs Whitehouse and
the schedulers — know it.'

One of Nathan-Turner's considerable strengths as a producer, according to one of his directors, was in television
'politics' and the prediction of future trends. He was very
aware of the potential disruption of conventional notions of
scheduling which imminent technological change would bring,
and argued that the widespread marketing of videocassettes
would entirely alter the pattern of television 'flow' and *The
Guardian's* concept of an 'English' afternoon and evening's
family viewing. He was keen to innovate — notably with a
new series *K-9*, starring the mechanical dog and former
Doctor Who companion Elisabeth Sladen, aimed at a different
audience. There had also been negotiations with an American
company to make a film of *Doctor Who* which fell through
when Tom Baker left. And in particular, Nathan-Turner was
extremely conscious of the expanding possibilities for manipulation of the American market.

International marketing

The centrality of market pressures and entertainment values
to series production has been further reinforced in the last
decade by the growing significance of international sales to
the economics of television. In a period of rapidly rising

production costs, selling programmes in overseas markets, particularly the massive American market, has become an important way of boosting revenues, and series are among the most popular exports since they are easy for networks to schedule. At the same time, the need to find material that will be intelligible and attractive in a wide range of markets places extra constraints on the popular series' ideological and thematic range . . . One option is to give the overseas networks the one fiction commodity they can't get anywhere else – authentically English historical sagas. The breakthrough in this area came with the BBC's adaptation of *The Forsyte Saga* and the series on the lives of Elizabeth I and Henry VIII. But the commercial companies were quick to follow and historical series now make a very substantial contribution to their export effort. The best sellers for 1979, for example, include London Weekend's *Lillie* and *Thomas and Sarah* (a spin-off from *Upstairs, Downstairs*); *Jennie* and *Edward and Mrs Simpson* from Thames; Granada's adaptation of *Hard Times*, and the Anglia-Trident version of the life of Dickens. As these instances suggest, the drive for overseas sales has certain effects on the range and treatment of historical themes. Programmes are obliged to trade-off the most pervasive images of historic England and to work with the dominant 'great man' theory of history. This produces, among other things, a concentration on periods that are already internationally familiar from popular fiction and feature films (most recently the reigns of Victoria and Edward), an emphasis on those social groups who are thought of as quintessentially English, the royal family and the aristocracy, and a marked preference for biographical approaches and explanations. (Graham Murdock)[47]

The most notable recent example of this has been the 'critical' (and international) success of *Brideshead Revisited*, in which even the General Strike of 1926 is reduced to the personal 'tragedy' of a British aristocratic family. Clearly *Doctor Who* with its relatively low budget and established constituency cannot enter far into this very expensive territory. None the less, in his second season John Nathan-Turner's favourite story, 'Black Orchid', marked a return to 'pure' history for *Doctor Who*, and, set in 1925, was about the personal tragedy of a British aristocratic family, was set on location at a stately home, and introduced the 'Victorian/Regency' dressed Doctor to the familiar milieu (village cricket, cocktails and garden party) of conventional 'British upper-class' representation. In fact, *Doctor Who*'s 'very English' signature actually draws on its 'cheap and cheerful' effects as Philip Hinchcliffe suggests. Whether or not it adds the extra dimension of British history, *Doctor Who* is already recognised by foreign audiences as an English institution, and is marketable as such (which is one reason why the 'Southern Counties' accent and presence of the Doctor is likely to continue).

It is certainly the case that Nathan-Turner was very keen to exploit the American market, making frequent visits there, often during very busy production schedules, and occasionally at considerable personal inconvenience (such as his two-day trip to Tulsa with Peter Davison during the US air traffic controllers' strike).

Nathan-Turner: It's many years since a totally historical story has been done, like my 'Black Orchid' set in 1925; and the reason for doing the 1925 story was to see how popular it is. Now, I like it — it's probably . . . my favourite of this season. I want to see what the audience reaction is to it . . . and if its a good reaction index, then we will do more.

Tulloch: Have you any idea of widening the market, into new areas — film, the video-cassette market and so on?

Nathan-Turner: Yes, I have lots of ideas. The only problem is that different departments of the BBC organise them, and so, as they do the deals and as they do the marketing aspect, it's very difficult to do anything more than suggest. But one thing I am very keen on is doing as many promotional trips as I can. A week on Thursday, on 4 February, I'm flying to Florida to do a convention — not with Peter Davison sadly, whom I'd like to take, but unfortunately he's tied up with another programme. I'm doing possibly one in the North-East of the States in May or June. I'm definitely going to Chicago in July. I'm definitely going to Ottawa in August – all of which are promotional visits, lecturing and doing panels as they call them in the States.

In terms of international publicity, Nathan-Turner's policy was highly successful, with Australia's *Daily Mirror* reporting on the 10,000 fans flocking to the July convention in Chicago and quoting the organiser's comments: 'This convention has established *Doctor Who* as a legitimate cult figure in America. It drew far greater audiences than *Brideshead Revisited* and it is as popular, if not more popular than other British exports such as *Monty Python*. We have simply been swamped.'[48]

Though *Doctor Who* was selling in thirty-nine countries in 1982, Nathan-Turner, with his emphasis on an action-adventure format, was obviously looking especially to the American market, and the interest in historical stories was very different from the paternalistic concern to educate of the original *Doctor Who*. On the other hand, he had no intention of diversifying at the expense of the institutionalised British audience for which the programme is primarily intended. Quite apart from any conscious or unconscious orientation to the American market, the making of 'Black Orchid' also depended on more local professional considerations: the reduction in the number of *Doctor Who* episodes decreed for the 1982 season (from 26 to 24 – thus generating the two-part 'Black Orchid'); Nathan-Turner's sense of responsibility as a BBC producer (giving inexperienced directors a chance with 'relatively simple' two-parters); and, probably above all, his acceptance of television's repetitive plurality, 'producing always variety, always the same thing'. That much at least had not changed since 1963.

If one defines the existence and determination of cultural artefacts through three crucial states – those of production, circulation, consumption (as we do in this book), there is an interesting feature of circulation which is revealed when television programmes are internationally marketed. Through our discussion of the scheduling of *Doctor Who* in Britain it is clear that transmission times are debated and worried about at great length by the TV producers and executives involved in the process of constructing the schedules. And the time slot anticipated or proposed for a programme directly influences production (a 'family' show, not too much sex or violence, etc.). Thus scheduling strategies not only help to construct audiences but also act as one level of determination on production.

This clearly is not the case when the programme is scheduled on foreign systems. It is difficult to draw international comparisons without engaging in a lengthy account of the complexities of different countries' broadcasting systems, but an example will indicate the significance of the difference. In Britain the majority of TV programmes are broadcast nationally and simultaneously. In the USA ninety-two stations bought the programme, all of which scheduled it at different times. Dallas, for example, transmitted *Doctor Who* at 10.30 in the evening and the director of the publicity firm promoting the programme in the USA resented the suggestion that *Doctor Who* was intended as a children's programme! In Australia, in contrast, the ABC regards *Doctor Who* as a children's programme (they have no 'family' category) and consequently screen it at 6.30 before the 7.00 pm national news (from 7.30 a 'parental guidance recommended' category applies; from 8.30 an 'adults only' category). Since *Doctor Who* is not categorised as either 'PGR' or 'AO', and since under current censorship regulations the ABC has to take the most serious classification to cover a whole series or serial (*Brideshead Revisited* had to have an 'AO' for the entire series because of a nude scene in one episode), individual *Doctor Who* stories can get into difficulties. 'Black Orchid' had the attempted saving of Nyssa from the 'clown' by a waiter (and his subsequent strangling) cut, leading to a crude edit from Nyssa struggling to Nyssa fainting (which she originally did on seeing the murder). 'Planet of the Spiders' was held up by censorship for years; 'The Deadly Assassin' (1976) was not shown at all; while Hinchcliffe's emphatically Gothic story 'The Brain of Morbius' (1976) was (uniquely) screened as a feature movie late in the evening in the 'AO' slot.

In Sydney the 6.30 screening competes with all the commercial news programmes, so any household wanting to watch the news as well as *Doctor Who* would be led to watch the ABC news. Rather than this necessarily being a competitive strategy to build up an evening's following (the ABC has very small percentage figures compared with the BBC – *Doctor Who*, for example, ranging from 7 per cent to 11 per cent TV households in Melbourne and Sydney for the new Peter Davison series to 4 per cent to 8 per cent for third or fourth repeats of Tom Baker), members of the ABC Audience Research section suspected that many young viewers tuned in to *Doctor Who* because they did not want to watch the news – and so would not watch ABC news after it either.

Scheduling of *Doctor Who* will vary in detail according to the complexities of different broadcasting systems. What is clear is that in order to insert itself in such very different scheduling categories and time slots internationally *Doctor Who* must continue to inscribe quite different audience groups within its narratives. When the US trade magazine *Variety* carried a front page picture advertisement 'Guess Who?' on 25 August 1982, its publicity anchorage was in terms of general audience size and market:

> Once upon a time BBC-TV started to produce a half-hour sci-fi series which is now a world wide phenomenon – seen weekly by some 93 million viewers in 39 countries – and which is still in production after 20 years, and now successfully invading the United States. Very enthusiastic and loyal fan clubs are springing up everywhere from coast-to-coast. Also, local publicity will astound you . . . And those Program Directors who do Guess Who – and act not – will live happily ever after.

But the picture that Lionheart Television International (a Division of Public Media Inc) chose for its advertisement seemed designed for a specific 'adult' audience: not the 'eyes' 'n teeth' Baker grin (and interestingly it was Tom Baker not Peter Davison who was featured), but a serious, soft-focus, dreamy, young and Byronic Baker, locked in frame and distantly penetrating gaze with a beautiful alien woman. It was a publicity still from 'The Hand of Fear' (1976) which signified both the sexual Baker and the unsettingly Romantic Doctor – plus – doppleganger. The complexities of international programming had overlaid the marketing energy of John Nathan-Turner with the signature of Philip Hinchcliffe.

**Mary Morris (*left*) as Panna and Sarah Prince as Karuna
in 'Kinda'**

Chapter 6

'Kinda': Conditions of Production and Performance

Every performance of *Doctor Who* relies on a competence in cultural, televisual and dramatic codes on the part of both performers and viewers. Even in an 'SF' show like *Doctor Who*, actors are very concerned to draw on everyday norms to establish plausibility and 'reality'. So, during recording of 'Kinda', Richard Todd asked the director whether he could have the button of his tunic undone in the last scene with Hindle. This small, unrehearsed change in costumic coding is typical of the way actors continuously think through their parts in terms of everyday notions of plausibility. Todd was drawing here on a recognisable (cultural) convention for 'being relaxed'. He was also replacing with this small sign his earlier 'camp' performance in rehearsal where Sanders and Hindle, now visibly 'close to nature', exit arm in arm holding a flower. This had been cut at the producer's run in rehearsal, because it signified a dramatic sub-code which John Nathan-Turner did not like: 'send up'.

Although televisual norms (of 'realism', 'transparency', etc.) had remained relatively unchanged under the previous producer (with, however, a tendency for a more pantomimic presentation, as, for instance, in 'The Horns of Nimon' where the Doctor and his companions constantly 'hid' from the monsters while remaining clearly in view), dramatic sub-codes had been shifted into a different register. Codes of heroism and villainy had, Nathan-Turner complained, been altered to

the extent that dramatic enigmas and resolutions had been
weakened by an invulnerable Doctor and comic villains.
Histrionic codes of performance which might have seemed
realistic in Victorian melodrama, and which, as Elam notes,
only survive today in the form of parodic 'quotes', were
being drawn on by actors (often, apparently against the producer's intentions) to 'camp the part up'.[1] In addition, with
the arrival of Douglas Adams new codes of dramatic performance (deriving from meta-SF) were emerging. This process of
code-breaking Eco calls 'undercoding' in so far as the new
code is not sufficiently within an audience's 'competence' to
decode the performance as the producers intend. As Elam
points out, every time we try to understand a novel dramatic
experience by means of imprecise terms ('bizarre', 'experimental', 'avant-garde', 'theatre of the absurd', 'send-up')
'either through ignorance of the specific generic rules in force
or because they scarcely exist, we are applying a loose sub-
code produced by undercoding'.[2] This was the case with
Adams' new 'meta-SF' coding, which Graham Williams explained as 'theatre of the absurd', fans disliked as 'send-up',
and many tertiary students liked as 'bizarre' or 'black' comedy.

It is important in this fluid situation of code-making and
breaking that the 'coherence' of a particular performance is
rescued by means of 'overcoding'. Here 'idiolectal' factors —
'the ensemble of personal, psychological, ideological and
stylistic traits which makes a written text recognisably
"Strindbergian" (even in imitation), an acting method "Giel-
gudian" or an overall performance text "Brechtian" ' — are
important.[3] In the Williams period of *Doctor Who* this 'idiolectal' coding (providing 'distinctiveness' to an undercoded
text) was performed — monumentally — by Tom Baker, to
the extent that even the most prosaic features of cultural
coding and kinesic gesture such as 'Hullo, I'm the Doctor'
were, as fans complained, overcoded in that idiosyncratic
jumble-mumbled 'Hullo, I'm the Doctor, this is Romana,
K-9'.

Richard Todd's final 'camp' scene gestured, the producer
thought, to this 'send-up' period, and he cut it. However, it
would be misleading to infer from this that the 'preferred
meaning' of a performed text depends simply on the intention-

ality of the producer (or star). Elam is right to argue that a 'performance brings about a multiplication of communicational factors' drawing together a variety of sources of dramatic information: writer, director, designer, composer, costume designer, lighting designer, etc., each, in different areas, involved in 'the forms that signals take and the encoding of the messages'.[4]

What Elam calls the semiotic 'thickness' (multiple codes) of a performed text varies according to the 'redundancy' (high predictability) of 'auxiliary' performance codes. Thus, for instance, if the sets, music and so on were simply to reinforce the actors' performance without adding to it or inflecting it in the direction of new associations, but simply overlaid the acted 'pace' and 'drama' with their own, they would be relatively redundant, serving only to bind together the text's temporal unfolding. On the other hand, in the Williams/Adams story, 'The City of Death', the use of music and sets in the scenes featuring the Count and Countess was more entropic, drawing on motifs which some audience members recognised as 'very forties', and therefore potentially re-locating the 'stolen art' theme in terms of, say, The Maltese Falcon. It is unlikely, in fact, that, 'auxiliary' codes are ever completely redundant. Even where they are not intentionally 'referencing out' to other texts, they are usually still intertextual (as we saw earlier in the case of Nyssa's costume). Costume designers and set designers draw on their own (relatively autonomous) code system, and a particular set in part derives its meaning from differences within that code. Sometimes, as in 'The Sun Makers' where some of the designs for Megropolis derive directly from Lang's Metropolis, the intertextual reference is overt and related to the theme. In other cases the references derive from a more general intertextual repetoire. In 'Kinda' the 'New Tahiti' reference of the 'source' text (The Word For World Is Forest) was mediated by the 'Christian' and 'Garden of Eden' inflections of Christopher Bailey's script in production, before generating the familiar 'Gauguin' costuming, setting, fruit and flowers[5] which some audience members recognised and interpreted as a 'typical' Doctor Who reference — even though it is unlikely that this reading had been intended by the designer. As we will see, in looking at 'Kinda', every performance text is marked by a potential heterogeneity of 'meanings' (attached to its various codes) which it is the task of the dominant member of the production team to make coherent by mobilising 'professional' values.

Christianising Buddhism: 'Kinda'

SF's spiritual past

In Wells there had been tension between optimistic belief in human potential for changing social oppression (on behalf of the greater sophistication and complexity of the organism) and a pessimistic sense of the future as a hideous return, via atavistic evolution, to the unidimensionality and barbarism of the distant past. This distant past is also a representative past in SF. As Hanzo has noted, the restoration of monsters from a primeval situation (of brutally primitive tribes, of Hitlerian-style thuggery) constitute a perpetual concern of SF as 'the historic past is recovered and preserved again and again . . . Without exaggeration it can be said that much science fiction drifts as though in a kind of archaic field of temporal magnetism towards what we might call a hyperpast, a veritable black hole of pastness, of prehistoric and geologic time, the time of the antehuman.'[6]

This endless recycling of the historical past is that of 'Fallen man, condemned to a cyclic pattern of history on Earth'[7] from which the only historical (non-cyclical) alternative in SF is the inhuman linear development of an ever more perfect technology. Thus humankind is rescued from a past beset by monsters only to plunge it into a future controlled by equally alien machines.

But, Hanzo argues, there is another constituent 'past' in SF — the search for a lost common consciousness, 'new forms of community, new modes of love, new systems of communication, new domains of consciousness'.[8] This is the 'buried past of the unconscious' where 'man lives in what appears to be the ideal unity with the other . . . which psychologically recovers that original unit that, in the life of every individual, is remembered unconsciously as the identity with the mother'.[9] The 'nebulously childlike universe where the unity of musical harmony prevails' in *Close Encounters of the Third Kind*; the 'inevitable return to an unconscious suprapersonal unity whenever the force is invoked' in *Star Wars*; the final 'supernal, childlike innocence' of *2001*; the return of the Earth itself to the unconscious unity of its lifeless origins in *The Time Machine* — signify for Hanzo the memory of a loss, and the desire to replace this original unity. The quest for a past as psychological state is a desperate denial of the guilt and anxiety aroused by the emergence of an individuating consciousness.

Hanzo derives the structural possibility of SF as genre — its conditions for establishing meaning — from these two pasts. The 'historical' and 'psychological' pasts define SF's possibilities of interpretation, describe its 'empty meanings' which a host of historical inflections will fill. For these 'are two very different pasts, though they may be mixed in various degrees, but by definition they are mutually annihilating'. To 'discover the end of time is to destroy history, and to be abandoned to history is to suffer the primeval loss forever'.[10]

Much of science fiction is indeed structured by these two pasts. *Doctor Who*'s '*Kinda*', for example, describes how suprapersonal communion is threatened with transformation into the bestial past (and future) of history through the impact of Earth's linear-technological history. Hanzo chooses to interpret SF's psychological' past according to the discourse of Freudian psychoanalysis, which he calls 'a kind of mythic tale'. However, the structure he describes — as fallen man is condemned to a depraved and cyclic history after eating of the tree of knowledge, until finally saved from historicity by spiritual integration — suggests a different mythical tale. And indeed Hanzo's own examples — his suggestion that the 'apocalyptic visual' of ultimate undifferentiation is 'science fiction as scripture', his reference to the Fall, and his recognition that in 'dozens of similar fictional developments, the future returns quietly to some scene whose simplicity, grace, and human oneness identify it as that garden from which we all descend'[11] — all suggest a Christian discourse determining the 'sin' of the individuating consciousness.

Hanzo's two 'pasts' are coded by two discourses of profound significance for science fiction: one is the past of
evolutionary struggle generated by 'scientific' Darwinism; the
other is the past of spiritual communion, the Christian garden
beyond the Fall. While emphasising the roots of SF in scientific
empiricism, we must also remember that religion is not an
embarrassment in SF as it is in other 'naturalist' genres.
Indeed, a Christian 'spiritual' response to Darwin is central to
the debate in the late nineteenth-century (Gothic) precursor
of SF. Central Gothic themes which were to feed SF, such as
the split between scientist and monster in *Dracula*, were
Christian allegories of 'what would happen were materialism
to be as successful in shaping the moral basis of the human
community as it has been successful in elucidating the physical
basis of life'.[12] As Blinderman has argued, Stoker's *Dracula*
draws on Darwin and degeneration theory to present 'a contest between two evolutionary options: the ameliorative,
progressive, Christian congregation, or the Social Darwinian
superman in the form of the ultimate parasitic degenerate,
Count Dracula'.[13] Dracula was the degenerate messiah replacing the kingdom of the spirit with the carnal kingdom of
human history, and drawing on all the sexual and onanistic
resources Christians associated with that monster from the
past, Darwin's ape. Dracula was the degenerate parasite,
replacing Christian compassion for one's neighbour with a
leech-like existence on more active human beings; and Dracula
was the sign of a materialist kinship replacing Christian im-
morality and spirituality with the dreadful 'assimilation' of
all things, as scientifically rendered in Huxley's 'On the
Physical Basis of Life': 'I might sup upon lobster, and the
matter of life of the crustacean would undergo the same
wonderful metamorphosis into humanity. And were I to . . .
undergo shipwreck, the crustacean might . . . return the
compliment and demonstrate our common nature by turning
my protoplasm into living lobster.'[14] This 'desire' in Dracula
was not simply, as Jackson argues, to 'lose a separative human
consciousness' and 'violate the most cherished of human
unities: the unity of "character" '.[15] It was also the desire to
rupture the special spiritual unity of person with person in
the image of God.

It is important to stress the connections between Protestantism and Romanticism (which we noted in Chapter 1), because
it is through the intertextual connections of Romantic-Gothic
and SF that Christianity so readily resurfaces — as in the
parasitic assimilation of more active human beings by the
Dukkha in 'Kinda', and the consequent threat to the entire
fabric of spiritual unity. Yet in its original form 'Kinda' was
a Buddhist allegory. SF as genre provided the 'structural
possibility' of the Christian inflection, but professional and
organisational factors determined it.

Authorship and production

It is a matter of exploring the way in which notions of
authorship operate as both an ideology and a practice in
different types of production, and unravelling their recip-
rocal relationship to organisational forms and to pressures
which shape them. (Graham Murdock)[16]

On the one hand the television performance will be moulded
in accordance with the professional and personal interests of
the more powerful members of the production team. As
producer Barry Letts said, 'Obviously each incarnation of the
Doctor will reflect the personalities of the producer and the
script editor concerned'. On the other hand, as Murdock says,
quoting Terry Eagleton, 'The text is always an expression of
general ideologies as actively mediated through the writer's
personal authorial ideology, which is structured in turn by his
or her class background, professional career and present
situation'.[17]

In the case of Christopher Bailey, writer of 'Kinda', the
most central 'authorial ideology' was his Buddhism. But it
would certainly be inadequate to read off 'Kinda' as a Buddhist tale in its transmitted form. If anything, it became a
Christian allegory. Yet that allegory was in no sense the result
of personal intentionality or the simple 'expression' of the
values of the more powerful members of the production team,
as we have suggested was the case in *The Eagle*. In so far as
general or specifically 'authorial' ideologies are inscribed in

television 'texts', they are generally the result of a complex interplay of a whole range of professional and other discursive practices which are often non-conscious and taken for granted, and which respond to the daily pressures both within broadcasting organisations (such as ratings) and outside them (such as the various public 'censorship' groups).

In the first place, Bailey's 'Kinda' depended on the space for authorship opened up by the location of *Doctor Who*-as-institution within the BBC. As we shall see, the potential for serious SF attracted Christopher Bailey, with his 'literary' background, into writing for the programme. Secondly, this space for authorship was severely limited by dominant production codes. As previously mentioned, the pressure of Mary Whitehouse's National Viewers' and Listeners' Association had helped shift *Doctor Who* from the 'Gothic Horror' orientation of its Philip Hinchcliffe years to the 'satiric/comic' Graham Williams period. John Nathan-Turner, the producer of 'Kinda', in turn reacted against the 'childish humour' and restored the programme, as he saw it, to its history as 'good action drama'. Fan-historian Jeremy Bentham wrote that one of the major qualities John Nathan-Turner brought to the show was 'an appreciation of the fan's point of view, a legacy from his own youth as a devout film-goer when he would write copiously to movie companies in the United States'.[18] Nathan-Turner himself argued in support of this 'buff' orientation: 'I think continuity is very important. You might as well take time to get it right rather than needlessly get it wrong.'[19] The emphasis on continuity ran as a minor theme throughout his first season as producer, with reminders of the Doctor's hermit mentor in 'State of Decay', of Leela, Andred and the first K-9 in 'Full Circle', the return of the Master in 'The Keeper of Traken' (which was not in Johnny Byrne's original script but was added by the producer and script editor), and the entire theme of 'Logopolis' 'revolving around the myth of *Doctor Who*'.

Nathan-Turner's orientation as producer was strongly influenced by his own professional background. He felt that his three years (as actor and stage manager) in the theatre, followed by thirteen years at the BBC working up through every production job (floor assistant, floor manager, production assistant, and production unit manager) before producing *Doctor Who*, gave him an advantage over the type who 'gets a degree and does a little bit of directing and then . . . straight in as a producer. Some people come clean in to produce, never having worked in television at all.' In contrast, he had the experience, in the gallery and on the studio floor to 'understand the problems of actors' and to 'know exactly what's required of my team'.

The decision to get rid of K-9 had been motivated not simply by a producer's concern for better drama, but also by an understanding of an actor's difficulties: 'To make dialogue with K-9 work an actor either has to go down on his hands and knees to speak to him, or else the camera angle has to be very high to have both actor and dog in the same shot. The first instance robs a scene of serious dignity. You can't be dignified squatting on haunches no matter how good the actor. The second ploy stops the camera from detecting eye movement in the actor, and eye contact and expression is what acting is all about.'[20]

His thoroughly 'professional' identification with the television industry was also evident in his 'very visual' signature and use of the latest television technology. His first production, 'The Leisure Hive', replaced 'slapstick' with a 'glossy' stylised look and in his second story, 'Meglos', the new process of 'Scene-Sync' (with linked cameras panning and tilting along a CSO background) was used for the first time to portray the huge screens on the planet Zolpha-Thura.[21]

Though wanting to use every televisual and dramatic means for spectacle and suspense, Nathan-Turner was sufficiently influenced by the past of *Doctor Who* not to go too far with horror. The producer argued that 'with *Doctor Who* the intention is to scare, but not to horrify. To keep everyone on the edges of their seats but without giving them lasting nightmares at night.'[22] None the less desire for dramatic 'variety' did lead to Gothic themes — a monster story in 'Full Circle' and a vampire one in 'State of Decay' — the latter bringing renewed outside pressure and questions in Parliament: 'We did get into a bit of trouble from the RSPCA and the Institute for Terrestrial Ecology over our showing of vampire bats. They've spent years trying to educate the public to the idea

that bats are just mice with wings and then along we come
and rekindle the old phobias.'[23] However, these were not
pressure groups with the potency of Mary Whitehouse or
Scotland Yard, and could be more or less ignored.

Christopher Bailey's 'Kinda', while also being 'different',
could be guaranteed — with its Buddhist theme — not to
generate this kind of 'violence' and 'horror' problem (though
apparently a thrashing scene of Adric by Hindle was omitted),[24] would be in continuity with the Doctor's perennial
anti-killing position, and had potential for effects and strong
visual style in the Wherever. It was within these parameters
and constraints, of the BBC as institution, industry and
profession that Bailey completed the 'Kinda' story for John
Nathan-Turner's second season as producer of Doctor Who.

Christopher Bailey's professional background — as one
who did 'come in with a degree' to television work — was
quite different from John Nathan-Turner's. Like Doug
Adams, Bailey's 'high literature' training oriented him towards
'quality' SF, but in his case the 'sophisticated' socio-political
allegory of Ursula Le Guin rather than satire: 'I don't go
along with the Douglas Adams school of science fiction
where you sneer at it and are clever. But the fact is that
millions of people round the world read science fiction that
contains very, very sophisticated concepts . . . And that could
be your audience for Doctor Who. I think they underestimate
the audience . . . If you look at writers like Ursula Le Guin,
they are dealing with very, very advanced ideas. The gadgetry
school of science fiction in novels ended thirty years ago —
it's a fifties thing.'

Although John Nathan-Turner would certainly have denied
that he was uninterested in 'concepts', it is the case that he
(like the fans) was more closely oriented to what Ebert has
called film and TV 'parascience fiction'[25] (in distinction to
'meta' and 'literary' SF).

Bailey: The analogy I used at one fairly 'hairy' stage in
the writing, when I was being asked to explain something
totally, was that . . . if it was a Doctor Who version of
Little Red Riding Hood . . . they'd . . . say, 'Now how is
that wolf able to impersonate a grandmother?' . . . And

then somebody would say, 'Well of course, it's the mind-transfer fibrulator on the wall' . . . Things get explained too much — or not really explained. There's a sense in which . . . you . . . throw together a few words about the 'ambivalent time and space condenser', and a sort of pseudo-explanation of what's going on.

An example of 'pseudo-explanation' which Bailey could have mentioned in 'Kinda' was the use of the 'delta-wave augmenter' to keep Nyssa in 'induced D-sleep' and therefore out of almost the entire story. It was not, however, the use of 'gobbledygook' in itself Bailey was objecting too. Rather it was the emphasis on, and time given to, details of naturalistic plausibility (in which effects and gadgetry often play a part) rather than to more complex ideas. During the sypher dub of 'Kinda', for instance, there was some concern that Hindle is heard shouting 'Put the lights on' as the Doctor and Todd escape down a lit corridor in episode 3. Somebody suggested that the line was funny enough (in terms of Hindle's paranoia) to retain given that the public would only see it once. At this stage the line was kept in, because the final, satisfied conclusion of the discussion was that the light could be rationalised as coming through the open airlock door. However, the producer later cut the line on the basis of 'realism'. Minor though the case may be such attention to detail is crucial to what Raymond Williams has called the 'naturalist habit' of everyday television. Here the demand of 'high naturalism' to locate drama within a 'real' (rather than divine or metaphysical) world has become 'a naturalised assumption of an immediately negotiable everyday world, presented through conventions which are not seen as conventions'. However fanciful the programme concepts may be, humans must, in the last resort, act as 'realistically' as they would in a contemporary drama — or else have their actions explained realistically according to some pseudo-scientific 'gobbledygook' as Bailey said. Realistic motivation and plausibility is the glue which binds a performance together, and establishes the coherence of its preferred meaning.

As Kristin Thompson has said, a film or television work 'displays a struggle by the unifying structures to "contain" the diverse elements that make up its whole system. Motivation is the primary tool by which the work makes its own devices seem reasonable. At that point where motivation fails, excess begins.[26] Under the pressure of time, television professionals sometimes have to take short-cuts which threaten to expose the elements of programme construction to a degree that would be unacceptable in film-making. During the rehearsal of 'Castravalva' John Nathan-Turner worried about the naturalistic view of the courtyard which the camera picked up behind the collapsing Doctor, since there had just been a POV shot, from the point of view of the Doctor and companions, of the courtyard appearing as a jigsaw mosaic. He suggested that Tegan should draw a curtain — though neither this nor the other suggestion of closing the shutters seemed a particularly plausible response to the collapse of the Doctor. The director Fiona Cumming said that drawing the curtain would make it seem like night, thus affecting the lighting of a number of scenes after it. Finally, they agreed that the shutters be closed, and the courtyard seen through the shutters could be rationalised as the realistic-looking part of the jigsaw effect, with the unrealistic part hidden. The solution was obviously not satisfactory from the point of view of their 'realist' values, because it still required the implausible closing of the shutters.[27] But under the pressure of time it was the minimal acceptable solution — given that there could be no question of removing the special effect.

The role of the producer in all this is as a kind of gallery censor during 'rehearse-record' days. Here the producer, sitting side-by-side with the director watching the monitors will quickly overrule an actor's actual on-screen interpretation. For example, during recording of 'Castravalva', Nathan-Turner forcefully pointed out to the director, and through her to the actor, that given the Murgrave's pink hat and make-up, the acting must be very restrained in order to avoid the character seeming to be 'in drag'. Similarly, it was the producer who vetoed a hand gesture from an otherwise hidden Peter Davison as 'too Monty Python'. In each case, John Nathan-Turner was acting quickly to prevent a self-referencing 'excess' in the programme by ironing out the kind of on-screen 'spoof' by actors of which Doug Adams had complained. Clearly, John

Nathan-Turner had a tighter control during production than his predecessor.

One result of this was a tendency to play down actors' 'interpretation' — a tendency which worried Christopher Bailey: 'I think actors' ability is a resource — in a way it's the biggest resource, never mind about writers — that this programme doesn't use . . . As soon as they've got the lights and everything set up, it's "OK now we'll have the actors. Give us a performance".'

An example of strict control of performers to prevent them 'going over the top' during the rehearsals of 'Kinda' was in Janet Fielding's interpretation of her part once her body has been taken over by the Mara. Her initial interpretation was to play the part sensuously, in a snake-like, sibilant way. This was rejected by both the producer and the director, Peter Grimwade. 'I've got to make a show that is pacey. If it doesn't work the way it is suggested on the page it's got to go . . . One's got to get the idea of Tegan taken over by a demonic presence, and if the way that she does it — which is sort of sibilant, pretending to be a snake — sounds like Janet Fielding doing a Bette Davies imitation, then it's got to go, because it's not believable and its not convincing.'

Grimwade's conception of 'Tegan taken over by a demonic presence' is indicative of the principles and professional values behind the changes that were made. Bailey's original concept had been one in which the standard 'hero-chase-monsters' format was replaced by an interiorised villainy. There were to be no dramatic snakes; rather, the visitors to the paradise world of the Kinda were to bring with them their own cultural repressions — aggression in the case of the colonists, sensuality in the case of the beautiful Tegan. And in turn, when this 'villainy' was passed on via Tegan, it would express itself in Aris as the quality most repressed in Kinda culture — leadership and individuation. Consequently, Bailey felt that Janet Fielding's interiorised, sensuous villainy 'would have been perfect'. 'What we have now is a snake which moves from arm to arm, which is very, very obvious . . . Its hammering the point into the ground in terms of technology. The idea that you can do it through an actor is not on . . . Simon Rouse plays Hindle as a madman . . . purely out of him as an actor.

There were no snakes and disappearing boxes. The production team got his acting power there, but they seemed quite surprised.'

Several of the actors in 'Kinda' complained during recording at the over-hectic pace, at not being given enough information, at being abused for mistakes where were due to lack of guidance, at sudden changes in performance. Some personalised their criticisms, but Lee Cornes argued that the phenomenon of 'actors as lumps' was typical of television.

Since there seemed a considerable shift in opinion by some actors between rehearsals and recording as to their treatment by the director, we asked Peter Grimwade about it.

Tulloch: Seeing you in rehearsal and then seeing you in recording was almost like a Jekyll and Hyde situation. In rehearsal you seemed to be a director with enormous time and sympathy for actors, and they said so. And then in recording you seemed to have no time for actors – there just wasn't time.

Grimwade: That's television. That's absolutely true, which is why rehearsal in television is so important. You have the time with the actors in rehearsal. Once you get into the studio (I warned the actors . . . but they always tend to feel they may be being a bit neglected in the studio) particularly on *Doctor Who, but* particularly on *Doctor Who*, it's 'beat the clock' . . . It happens on any television programme, but on *Doctor Who* it's exaggerated. John is pushing the show out as well, and getting as much in as he possibly can. He's *absolutely* pushing the system to breaking point – which I agree with as well, because I think that's what it's about . . . Get as much in, get as much event, as much excitement, as many effects as everything will stand . . . Yes, I'm afraid you are absolutely right about that. But that is the way time is allocated, and that is why rehearsal *is* so important, because that's when there is the time, that's where you *must* give the actors the time. But in the studio there *is* no time, and if you spend time thinking, and talking, and being relaxed and able to accept things, you don't get the show in. It's no good *how* nice it's all been on the studio floor with the actors, if that is not on tape then the whole thing is a waste of time . . . Communication between the actor and the director once we are in recording and you've got the glass window of the gallery between you, is up to the floor manager. I think the floor manager has very much got to be able to cope with the neurosis of the actor, and to pick it up and know exactly how to deal with it and to reassure.

During the recording of 'Kinda' floor manager Ann Fagetter had, like director Peter Grimwade, a great deal of pressure to deal with: including complaints from the cast about the temperature on the studio floor; a 'Kinda' baby that came close enough to choking on an apple to upset some of the cast; and the problem during the first two days of covering the studio floor with leaves, when the nature of the set, and the director's shooting style made access to monitors, on which she could see the actual site of the problem, almost impossible. At the end of the first day's recording (of the second 'Kinda' session) there was a strong debate between producer, director and floor manager as to how things could be speeded up, since a number of scenes planned for the day had not been recorded. The producer felt that the floor manager's lack of access to monitors wasted time, since she had to be told from the gallery where to shovel leaves. The floor manager argued that it was impossible to put in more monitors, since the camera would pick them up. The camera had, in fact, picked up some cables, which only the floor manager (but, unusually, nobody in the gallery) had seen, but had not passed the information on because it was so close to the end of recording time. The producer said they would probably have to 'buy' that shot, and hope they would be seen as tree roots. The director said a reduction of his problematic long shots would minimise the effect of greenery in this 'paradise' setting. The floor manager said that perhaps the way to speed things up was to change the floor manager, and complained that some of the cast had stood around without being recorded all evening.

This kind of abrasive debate is the result of the incredible time pressure Doctor Who is under. It is also a thoroughly 'professional' debate, not only because the participants argue

professionally from their own experience, but also because
the assumptions underlying it are already predetermined by
the professional values of television. Minor differences aside,[28]
Doctor Who directors were dominated by the unquestioned
professional values of 'pace', 'events', 'effects' and 'believability'.

Grimwade was quite clear about the 'serious drama' preten-
sions of Bailey, and rejected them as inappropriate to *Doctor
Who*.

> *Grimwade*:   I would say that we all disagree with the
> writer in that respect, because the writer wants to do *Play
> of the Month* and he happens to be writing it in the *Doctor
> Who* slot. He'd be very happy if we could cut the Doctor
> out. I think he is a very untypical writer in that respect,
> and he's using the programme as a peg for a particular style
> of writing . . . But I've got to make a show that is pacey.

Grimwade's attribution of Bailey as *Play of the Month*, and
Bailey's complaint about the production as 'gadgetry school'
represent, of course, the institutionalised practices within the
BBC of 'serious drama' and 'popular entertainment'. It is a
useful distinction, but, as Murdock says, it oversimplifies,
because it tends to make too rigid a distinction between
'control' and 'creativity' in the actual production practices of
television professionals – and this is especially so in *Doctor
Who*. Bailey's case was not a simple matter of personal
'creativity' and 'expressivity' hampered by 'writing it in the
Doctor Who slot'. His position was determined by 'constraints', one of which – his concern for science fiction as a
serious genre – might have seemed very appropriate to *Doctor
Who* which, as Terrance Dicks described it, is 'a very intellectual show . . . concealed under the guise of an action-adventure
programme for the family'. Equally, despite admitting that
'I would go and direct traffic if I'm needed to, because one's
got to eat', Grimwade was not simply an 'effect' of production
constraints.

It is true that Grimwade saw the job of the inexperienced
director in terms of conforming to the needs of the industry
and of particular producers. He said, for instance, that he

would have been happy to direct *Doctor Who* under Graham Williams, even though he did not like his 'send-up' inflection of the programme any more than Nathan-Turner did. He described the difficulty of getting directing jobs after completing the BBC directors' course — the lobbying, the vicious circle of not being attractive to time-harassed producers because of inexperience.

In this situation television professionals are subject to control by chance and personal connections. Grimwade's break came because he had known John Nathan-Turner for a long time — they had once worked in the same department — and the latter had seen his episode of *The Omega Factor* and liked it. But the point is that Nathan-Turner liked his work because he was a 'professional' director in the producer's sense — oriented to action, drama and 'pace'. Like Nathan-Turner, Grimwade was experienced in television, having worked as assistant film editor, production assistant, floor manager and assistant director. In particular, his experience with 'one of two rather good editors' on television drama gave him a 'craft' in pace and visual rhythm which would have appealed to Nathan-Turner, rather more than the long, wordy scenes which Christopher Bailey originally wrote for 'Kinda' and which 'had' to be shortened and inter-cut with other action scenes.

Rather than being 'controlled' by his producer, then, Peter Grimwade was offered a space to assert his own professional values — which he did very successfully. Looking in his first season for good action directors with the strong sense of visual style and effect which was to be his personal 'signature', Nathan-Turner offered Grimwade his first *Doctor Who* directing job on 'Full Circle'. This drew special praise from *Doctor Who Monthly*: 'It is often said that if you notice the director's handywork in a production then something is wrong with the story. On the basis of "Full Circle' I would dispute this. The slow motion rising of the Marshmen from the lake was a cinematic play, but it made for one of the best episode endings in a very long time.'[29] 'Logopolis', his second *Doctor Who*, was a considerable success for Peter Grimwade. Voted by the fans as the best of a highly rated season it also received an accolade from *Time Out*. ' "Logopolis", with its excellent performances throughout, its mind-boggling concepts and its exemplary direction by Peter Grimwade shows just how good a *Doctor Who* story can be.'[30]

In the 1982 season Grimwade was sufficiently established to be offered the difficult job of directing the 'very unusual' and 'very untypical' 'Kinda', which he was pleased to do 'because it was not the sort of story that I'd done before, and was more of a challenge – it was different'. Far from being 'controlled' by the production system in the sense of being its 'effect', seeing Grimwade rehearsing 'Kinda' one was aware of a director working vigorously within his professional values of 'pace', 'realism' and 'believability', while allowing actors the space for their own improvisations.

> *Grimwade*:   Everyone thinks, 'Oh, well, *Doctor Who* is so easy – there's no serious, deep psychology to it.' But to get it believable, to get it convincing, to get it paced you have to work very, very hard. Because the material is not so easy to realise, you've got to work out why things are happening to justify it. If we just did it in the way that American series, with all their money, do the filmed science fiction stuff, it would no longer have any kind of appeal at all. I think that our strength in a way – and this is just talking about the performance side – is the fact that we rehearsed very intensely, very seriously, for what, in comparative terms, is quite a long time. And I think one does come out with characters of integrity. They are believable. You've got, on the whole, very good actors giving totally committed performances, even though on the printed page it's a bit cod, it's a bit shallow, and it's a bit tinsely . . . I think that is why John Nathan-Turner is very keen that one gets very, very good actors to play all the parts. Not just because it's nice presentation if you've got a star name on the front, but because you need the weight. The thinner a character is written, the stronger in a way it needs to be played in order to convince – it's got to be real and believable.

So Grimwade himself distinguished between *Doctor Who* and the expensive 'hardware' and 'gadgetry' school of American science fiction. He was negotiating a space — a limited 'authorial' space — between the 'shallow' characterisation of 'American series' and the overample characterisation of the original *Play of the Month* 'Kinda'. He was trying to make this 'very untypical *Doctor Who* story . . . work within the format'. ' "Kinda" goes in for much deeper characterisation of the non-regulars and it tends to concentrate on the characterisation of these people in the dome — almost to a fault, whereby . . . you neglect the basic adventure format. The difficulty was to make sure that it all worked in terms of a straightforward adventure story, with all these kinds of extra resonances that were coming from the writer.'

Action-adventure 'integrity' is catered for by prolonged debate over the 'realism' of the detailed, moment-by-moment interactions. During rehearsals of 'Kinda', for instance, actors spent a lot of time in the acting pairs that the script tended to divide them into (Tegan and Aris, the Doctor and Todd, Sanders and Hindle) discussing the believability of a particular voice inflection, gesture or reaction. It is this process which Peter Grimwade says must be worked at intensely in order to raise *Doctor Who* above the shallow characterisation of American series.

The visual effects designer on 'Kinda', Peter Logan confirmed this emphasis on acting.

Logan: The acting has always been the first consideration because even in the studio it is the effects and the hardware that is left out if there is a case of time problems. I have often been told by a director on an occasion when I have been standing around in the studio just waiting to do an effect, 'Sorry we can't do the effect. We will have to scrub around that' because we are getting to the end of recording time. When queried, I have always been told, 'Well, it's the acting that is the most important thing. The hardware is secondary' . . . It is an irritant, but on the other hand I have exactly the same irritant on other programmes, because I think the BBC as a whole will turn round and say, 'The actors as far as we are concerned are more important than any of the props or the hardware.'

This is, in fact, what happened to Logan during the recording of 'Kinda' when, because of serious time pressure, Peter Grimwade only could allow literally a few seconds to recording the elaborate collapsing pillar effect that Logan had spent a lot of time preparing and then, as time actually ran out during the recording of Panna superimposed at the top of a collapsing pillar, Grimwade opted to replace the effect in the edited episode with a close-up of Mary Morris' expressive facial gesture. In any case, Logan far preferred Graham Williams' much despised (by the fans) 'Destiny of the Daleks' to 'Kinda' for professional reasons.

> *Logan*:   I like to think that if I am allotted to a *Doctor Who* or any other fictitious programme that there are going to be a lot of effects, a lot of models, a lot of locations . . . 'Kinda' has no locations so you can't do any work outside. It has no models to speak of. There is one static model which is purely the environment in which they are living, the space dome . . . But it doesn't *do* anything and this is where I feel that I am cheated. And there is very little in the way of explosives or pyrotechnics other than the machine that they travel about in . . . Out of say half a dozen *Doctor Who*'s that are produced by this department per year, only two have a big budget which means that people can build spacecraft and do a lot of model shooting, or there are locations which is of course a lot of money involving lots of people going out with the film crew and props to actually film on location, as in 'Destiny of the Daleks' . . . 'Destiny' was in my opinion a very good story. It also involved quite a lot of hardware and quite a lot of foresight, if you like, in the preparation of the spaceship . . . One gets a preconceived idea of a spaceship that you would like to have in the programme, and then when you read later on in the script that this machine has to bury itself in the ground all those preconceived ideas go out of the window, and you have to start re-designing, re-thinking some form of vehicle that can not only fly through space but be capable of burying itself in the earth, which is why it turned out to be conical shaped at the bottom that could screw itself into the ground, which we had to do as a model

shot. And it had to look as though it could do that in the model . . . Because it turned out as it did I felt satisfied. I felt that that particular story fully achieved what I was aiming at. Whereas with 'Kinda' I feel cheated because I feel that my assistants could do just as well with some of the hardware that was necessary as I could. I feel that I am really superfluous because I'm not really applying my mind in what is required.

'Kinda' in particular demanded 'acting' before 'effects' since it focussed on the inner drama of characterisation, in addition to the drama of action. *Doctor Who* script editor Eric Saward was very clear about this in terms of perceived audiences when discussing 'Kinda'. 'It's true that we wanted snakes and things to be hard and positive and originally Chris Bailey didn't . . . We are attempting to appeal to a very broad audience of all ages, of all backgrounds . . . All the Buddhist stuff in Chris's script, all the symbolism and so on — it's there if you can get it . . . if you know about it. But when children are sitting there, they want a bit of something that will help them along too.'

Saward is adhering here to basic rules of audience aggregation among television professionals. Paul Espinosa has described these as 'text-building practices relating to producer perceptions about the audience'.[31] Such rules as 'engaging the audience' by providing 'believable' and 'realistic' characters to identify with, as 'meeting the audience expectations of the show' by consistent and positive presentation of leading characters (which Grimwade complained Bailey would have been only too happy to ignore by 'leaving the Doctor out altogether'), and as 'not dividing the audience' (as, Nathan-Turner argued, 'in' references to Greek myth or the *Doctor Who* telephone number did) are all readily discernible in *Doctor Who*.

At the same time, though, *Doctor Who* differs from Espinosa's example of *The Lou Grant Show* in being what Eric Saward calls a 'specialised' programme or, as we have described it, one which works close to the 'serious' interface of popular television drama. *Doctor Who* tries to negotiate this 'generic' terrain between the 'superficial' characterisation of American

TV series and the 'so in, so incestuous' Graham Williams era of the programme which, in Saward's opinion 'insulted its audience'.

However, if it is too simplistic on the one hand to assign Peter Grimwade and the production team to the 'gadgetry school' of American SF series, so too is it to define Christopher Bailey's 'fault' in terms of inappropriately overlaying *Doctor Who* with *Play of the Month*. To see what *kind* of 'quality' drama Bailey was intending, we need to look more carefully at the intertextual relations of 'Kinda' with 'serious' SF, and at the kind of 'psychological drama' Bailey was himself attempting by developing Hindle in an interiorised way in 'neglect of the basic adventure format'.

Christopher Bailey and Ursula Le Guin

All members of the *Doctor Who* production team defined their show in distinction to the 'hardware' style of *Star Wars* and American television SF. They pointed out that it was impossible to complete in terms of spectacle because of budget restrictions, and that in any case *Doctor Who* has a quality which would be lost through this kind of emulation. What the particular 'SF' quality of *Doctor Who* is was harder to define. Eric Saward initially defined its 'genre' quality in familiar terms. 'Chris Bailey's is perhaps not the sort of script that comes in everyday for us. But last season we had one by the then script editor, Chris Bidmead, called "Logopolis", which had a very interesting idea. The city of logic where things are literally constructed out of mathematical computations . . . If you could get at it, it was a good idea, quite an original idea. But still it moved well enough, it was pacey enough for really anybody if they weren't particularly interested in the concept.' But he also defined the 'best science fiction' as an 'ideal' towards which, *Doctor Who* looked. 'The best science fiction really is that where you don't have to go to gobbledygook, where you've got a created race, an alien race that exists and has its own values, its own ideas and so on, and it has created its own life form. It's very difficult to do, and it isn't very often done in our show. Although it is pulled off occasionally in novels. Ideally that is the sort of science fiction we are looking for.'

In 'Kinda' Bailey was offering *Doctor Who* precisely this kind of 'conjectural' SF via its apparent model in Le Guin's novel, *The Word For World Is Forest.*

In both 'Kinda' and *The Word For World Is Forest* there is: (1) an Earth-type advance exploration mission containing scientists and military which is preparing colonisation and exploitation of a planet referred to as 'Paradise'; (2) a division between the 'by-the-book' rigidity of the military and the cultural perspectivism of the scientists; (3) a taking of 'hostages' and 'servants' by the military from among the local 'primitives'; (4) a narrative recognition that the locals, far from being primitive, have a highly advanced culture in terms of eliminating divisive aggression and individualistic assertion; (5) a relationship of this community in some 'organic' way with the forest; (6) a contrast between the psychological equilibrium of the 'primitives' and the psychological disequilibrium of the colonists; (7) a manifestation of this disequilibrium in terms of a divorce between subconscious urges and conscious rationalisations which justify aggression and exploitation; (8) an alien world of hypnotic quality 'that made you day-dream'; (9) a representation of the central conflict of good and evil in terms of a debate about the assumed superiority of individualistic achievement and linear progress in contrast to communal harmony and a static history; (10) a narrative valuation of the quietest stance (although this is offset in 'Kinda' by the mediating position of the Doctor as 'wanderer' between linear exploitation and communal stasis); (11) a representation of the forces of evil in terms of biology (sexuality) and history (evolution); (12) the creation — through the arrival of the colonists and their interaction with the natives — of an antagonistic and destructively individualistic 'God' or 'leader' whose stigma is that of marking the once harmonious community as for ever open to the violence of the 'outside'.

To say that Bailey was 'influenced' by Le Guin is, on the one hand, simply to say what is common in *Doctor Who*: that it frequently operates as a conscious re-working of other texts. But it is also to state a difference, since the intertextual

reference was an authorial attempt to mark *Doctor Who* in
terms of Saward's 'ideal' possibility: 'conjectural' SF. Obviously Bailey's intervention drew on his own competencies
in terms of 'serious' literature. But rather than simply creating
a schism between *Play of the Month* and 'popular' drama,
there was a potential meeting point between Bailey's SF
inflection of 'sophisticated' literature and Saward's own
programme 'ideal'. Without that it is unlikely that 'Kinda'
would have been comissioned or that, given the 'problems'
involved in bringing it to air, there could have been negotiations with Bailey about the possibility of doing a further
script for the next season.

Bailey: Buddhism and Jungian archetypes

We have discussed Bailey's 'high art' and 'sophisticated SF'
orientation first in order to emphasise that the general ideologies of 'authors' (in this case Bailey's Buddhism) operate
through production practices, and especially through dominant organisational, professional and generic forms. However,
it is the case that Bailey's Buddhism also had a direct influence
on 'Kinda', transforming its Le Guin reference in significant
ways.

> *Bailey*: One way Buddhism percolates through is that I
> tried to set myself to write it without people being killed
> all along the way. Very often this type of programme gets
> its tension over a pile of dead bodies . . . The original idea
> was the wheel of life — a Tibetan concept — the wheel
> which continues to revolve and on which we are all broken.
> The aim of Buddhist practice 'is to stop the wheel; and the
> 'Paradise' that the Kinda inhabit is a paradise in which that
> wheel has been stopped, and the threat is that the wheel
> will start again.

Bailey also left interpretative markers in his script by means of
Kinda names: Dukkha, Anatta, Anicca, Mara, Panna, Karuna
and the box of Jana (Jhana). According to the First Truth of
Buddhism, 'Dukkha' (suffering, insubstantiality) describes the

world's sickness, cured only by the Buddhist method, and in particular by 'jhana' (meditation). 'Suffering' in 'Kinda' was not to result from killing but is the result of human striving for definition, of the desire to control identity, experience, and the world itself. The attempt at material control of the world (the project of Sanders and Hindle) or to fix identity (the desire of Tegan) is to submit to the wheel of life which is the place of lust, malevolence and greed, controlled by demons (mara). The futile attempt to control and define life in a linear way leads to complete self-frustration, and to the 'Round of birth-and-death'. 'Man's identification with his idea of himself gives him a spacious and precarious sense of permanence . . . Convention . . . encourages him to associate his idea of himself with equally abstract and symbolic roles and stereotypes, since these will help him to form an idea of himself which will be definite and intelligible. But to the degree that he identifies with the fixed idea, he becomes aware of "life" as something which flows past him — faster and faster as he grows older . . . The more he attempts to clutch the world, the more he feels it as a process in motion.'[32] As with Tegan in the darkness of the Wherever, attempts at 'definition, setting bounds, delineation — these are always acts of division and thus of duality, for as soon as a boundary is defined it has two sides'.[33] The process then of naming and definition (Tegan's two selves, Sanders' 'sir' and Aris' 'I am Aris — he who has voice') is illusion and the source of suffering (dukkha).

The world of Buddha (as in the organic communal world of the Kinda) is totally impossible to categorise and difficult to define conceptually — and therefore is quite opaque to the soldiers' 'by-the-book' attempts to control it. 'Anicca' (impermanance) is the Buddhist doctrine that the more one tries to control and define the world, the more it recedes from the grasp and changes; and 'Anatta' (egolessness) is the doctrine that any attempt to define one's enduring ego is equally an illusion because there is no self which is separate from the flux and transition of experience (hence Anatta's and Anicca's 'game' with notions of perception and ego-identity).

Against the soldiers attempt to fix and define the world via cultural stereotypes ('Thank you, *Sir*'), stand Panna and

Karuna. By means of jhana (the box of jana), the fatal wheel of time may be stopped in the 'clear awareness there is neither past nor future, but just this one moment'.[34] Panna is the one who, through intuitive wisdom, sees the nature of reality as transient and gives birth to 'karuna' (active compassion) for all who are still trapped in the ignorance of quest and definition. So Sanders, by means of the box of jana (given to him by Panna via karuna) is brought to 'nirvana', the escape from an eternal fixation with defining one's life (i.e. as a colonist, moving from planet to planet) and therefore from the cycle of birth and death.

The central 'Buddhist' opposition in Bailey's story, then, is between the stereotyped 'by the book' world of definition and fixed idea (the colonist world of the dome), and the strangely static yet transient world of the Kinda, the conflict between linear historicism and holistic integration generating the worlds of enigma (dukkha/unsubstantiality) and action (mara/temptation). In the transmitted version, however, Bailey complained, 'you tend to lose the original ideas you had . . . The things that to me seemed interesting about the story were often on the margins, little things that were lingered over, and not so much of the chasing around corridors. I would have liked to have that lingering and the strangeness in the atmosphere. I think that the atmosphere in the forest is not as strange as it should have been.'

That strangeness was crucial to the conjectural world of 'Kinda', commenting – as in Le Guin's *The Word For World Is Forest* – on the terran world of linear development and material exploitation. A further problem for Bailey was the representation of the Doctor, since, for the sake of programme continuity, he has to be a hero, whereas in Le Guin's novel the nearest thing to a hero is Selver, one of the 'primitives', who, because he kills in self-protection, is fatally infected with terran values (his equivalent in 'Kinda', but not as 'hero' is Aris). However, the moral ambivalence of Le Guin's hero is to some extent reproduced in 'Kinda', since it is the Doctor (via Tegan) who actually generates the narrative's 'villainy'.

While not wanting to get rid of the Doctor completely, as Peter Grimwade suggested, Bailey did want to get rid of him as action-hero, and he drew on Jungian concepts to do so. 'There have been lots of Doctors, and in the hierarchy of heroes in Jungian psychology . . . there is a definite level of hero. The lowest level of hero is the simple sort of Luke Skywalker type of 'good guy' – you know, Flash Gordon. And the highest level of the hero is the wise old man, who has insight and wisdom into things. If you look at the development of *Doctor Who*, it has developed from the very highest level *down* the scale to the simplest sort of hero.'

So, unlike John Nathan-Turner, Bailey was attracted to the 'all-knowing' wisdom of Tom Baker, for whom 'Kinda' had originally been written. 'I did consider the Doctor to be more of a sage than he now is, and so I had him helping the Kinda, but helping them in full knowledge that something was just being postponed.' With the departure of Baker, and under pressure from the production team he removed lines emphasising the Doctor's wisdom, such as, 'the Doctor pointing out the way in which the wheel can't stop . . . The whole thing originally was based on the idea of inside and outside . . . and that the Kinda world was artificial in the sense that they have tried to stop time, and they have created an inside. An outside will always break in, and time will always tell.' The idea was cut out, Bailey complained, because 'nobody was chasing anybody'.

Bailey matched the Doctor with another Jungian type of hero on the Kinda side: the Trickster. 'Its very much based on a concept out of Jung . . . There is a figure called, I think, Hare in North American Indian mythology, who performed that function in relation to their society that the Trickster performs in relation to the Kinda society, i.e. one of maintaining the values of the society, but not by preaching or by leading or by ruling, but just by bringing things back to sanity by ridicule and clowning.'

If heroic action on both sides – by the soldiers and by Aris – was initially intended to be satirised by two worldly wise heroes – the Doctor and the Trickster – so too was 'villainy' to be taken out of the realm of meglomania. Like Doug Adams, Bailey was concerned to motivate villainy in a more sophisticated way than the 'desire to rule the universe syndrome' which Nathan-Turner had strongly reinforced by bringing back the Master. Unlike Adams, though, Bailey looked to an interiorised personal/cultural villainy, again drawing on a combination of Jung and Buddhism.

> *Bailey*:   Originally Tegan was taken over by a force from within which, in fact, is just one aspect of herself — called the Mara — but which has ended up pretty near to being a full-blooded demon . . . In Buddhism there is no evil. There is no devil. So it is very difficult to write for *Doctor Who . . .* In my original version the Mara was a very ambivalent thing. In Tegan, she became quite mischievous and sexy — quite flirty and lascivious. And Aris . . . became filled with the desire for revenge. The Mara took a different form depending on whom the force was occupying. And the snake didn't exist. But in the process of brightening it up, colouring it up — which I guess needs doing — the Mara got red eyes and an evil laugh. It interests me because it now fits in with a Christian notion of evil — that evil is the devil.'

However, this Christian inflection of 'villainy' (the snake/devil in the Garden of Eden) which was motivated by the professional pressures of 'pace', 'adventure' and 'effects', was only possibly because Bailey had in fact, created a villain. He seems to have drawn on another Jungian notion (the Shadow) to locate Buddhism's Mara in a Jungian notion of the unconscious. Jung had perceived two related archetypes of the collective unconscious: the persona (the socialised being in which the individual personality is totally submerged by its ordained role); and the repressed 'other' side of the persona, the 'shadow'. Jung argued that in its collective aspect, the shadow (itself, of course, a central Gothic figure of evil) frequently expressed itself as a devil — and in Tegan's 'take-over' by the Mara in 'Kinda', Bailey seems to have fused this archetype with another Jungian notion — the animus (the 'male' element in the unconscious of women, signified by the desire for power, aggression etc.).

   In so far as it is repressed the shadow is a villain from within the unconscious of everyone, motivating Bailey's preferred 'interiorised drama'. At the same time, the repressed side of the unconscious depends for its content on what is socially prohibited. So in Bailey's original version, evil was to be a cultural phenomenon: the repressed side of Tegan's terran identity (sexuality) and of Aris's Kinda culture (drive, leadership) would emerge as separate villainies, generating the action. On the one hand, Aris's villainy is motivated by terran colonisation and militarism, and the narrative resolution is the liberal-minded defeat of this greater exploitation. But on the other hand, Tegan's villainy is motivated by the Doctor's travelling. The Doctor himself, is in this sense, the eternal shadow of flux and chaos underlying the Kinda persona of harmony and stasis. In this version, 'Kinda' would have drawn on the deepest SF/Gothic roots of *Doctor Who*: its narrative tension between anthropocentric closure and 'undifferentiation'.

It is the Trickster, though, who might have played out this narrative tension in 'Kinda' — as he did in the original Trickster myth cycle. The Red Indian Trickster satire was fundamentally at the expense of an ordered and inward-looking society. It was not only war that the Winnebago's Trickster ridiculed, but also peace. Hence not only the younger war leader from the 'lower' Bear clan (the equivalent to Aris) was satirised, but also the 'upper' Thunderbird chief who, like Panna, stood for wisdom and peace.

Essentially the Trickster represented a universe of excess and disorder in criticism of the strictures of the given social order and its ritualised distinction between peace and war, order and chaos. As in Romantic discourse, the Trickster ritually rehearsed the threat of undifferentiation. His actions — unbridled sexuality, endless wandering and voracious appetite — were of an excess beyond the powers of nomination. Radin argues that the Trickster represents not only the undifferentiated and distant past, but likewise the undifferentiated present within every individual.[35] Karl Kerényi sees the Trickster as 'the spirit of disorder, the enemy of boundaries',[36] and Jung calls him 'a faithful copy of an absolutely undifferentiated human consciousness'.[37]

But the Trickster cycle also addressed the task of differentiating between humankind, the gods above them and the animals beneath. On the one hand, humankind had to be distinguished from subhuman forces (with whom the Trickster quickly became identified), hence there was generated the Hare/Trickster figure who evolved in the myth cycle as a benefactor and culture hero, who secured fire, food, cultivation, education, the regulation of the seasons, and, in addition, freed the world from monsters. On the other hand, humankind had to be distinguished from gods, and so by his absurd and excessive activities, the Trickster established human weaknesses. 'Because of him men die . . . because of him men steal . . . because of him men abuse women . . . lie and are lazy and unreliable.'[38]

The fundamental function of the Trickster myth among North American Indians was human nomination – but nomination in terms of difference from gods and monsters. In establishing these boundaries, the Trickster opened up the perspective of disorder. As Kerényi argues: 'Disorder belongs to the totality of life, and the spirit of this disorder is the trickster. His function in an archaic society, or rather the function of his mythology, of the tales told about him, is to add disorder to order and so make a whole, to render possible, within the fixed bounds of what is permitted, an experience of what is not permitted.'[39]

What Jung was especially interested in was the process of bringing this disorder to consciousness. For Jung, the Trickster's counter-social tendencies represent a collective form of the 'shadow'. Clearly Jung, like Bailey, felt there was much to be said for this earlier collective stage of consciousness since, because the stories of the Trickster myth were not disagreeable to the Winnebago consciousness, they were not repressed.

In contrast, in modern civilisation the darkness and evil of the past have not vanished, but have been repressed and withdrawn into the unconscious. 'The so-called civilised man has forgotten the trickster' and 'never suspects that his own hidden and apparently harmless shadow has qualities whose dangerousness exceeds his wildest dreams. As soon as people get together in masses and submerge the individual, the shadow is mobilised, and, as history shows, may even be personified and incarnated.'[40] Since 'the individual shadow is never absent as a component of personality, the collective figure can construct itself out of it continually. Not always, of course, as a mythological figure, but, in consequence of the increasing repression and neglect of the original mythologems, as a corresponding projection on other social groups and nations.'[41]

Hence, for Jung, the 'military mind' loses the power of introspection and projects all its own weaknesses outwards. 'In this way his code of ethics is replaced by a knowledge of what is permitted or forbidden or ordered. How, under these circumstances, can one expect a soldier to subject an order received from a superior to ethical scrutiny? It still hasn't occurred to him that he might be capable of spontaneous ethical impulses, and of performing them – even when no one is looking.'[42] And so, of course, we have the 'by-the-book' soldiers of 'Kinda'. By way of Buddhism and Jung, Chris Bailey has added a psychological theory to Le Guin's 'brutalising colonists versus civilised primitives' theme, which helps to generate his preferred 'interiorised' drama. The 'conflict' is not simply between different ('advanced' and 'primitive') cultures, but within cultures, as each in their different way struggle with their own unconscious.

Among the soldiers – especially Hindle – the 'shadow' is both repressed and projected outward against the Kinda people. The Kinda, in contrast, maintain their paradise by way of the Trickster who makes conscious the unconscious, and so 'holds the earlier low intellectual level before the eyes of the more highly developed' so that they 'shall not forget how things looked yesterday'.[43] By externalising the shadow and ridiculing it, the Trickster deprives it of its dangerously repressed 'energy'.

It seems clear from Christopher Bailey's comments that he originally intended the Doctor to represent a third, and higher, Jungian archetype than either the repressed 'civilised man' or the primitive (because endogamous and solipsistic) consciousness of the Kinda. This higher archetype was to be the 'wise old man', which is the summit for Jung of human development and individuation. Unlike the action-heroes (soldiers, businessmen, etc.) of early adulthood who repress parts of themselves on the drive to power, pleasure and success, the 'mature' man has accepted the 'inferior' parts of himself. He has learnt to live with the elements of his unconscious. 'In this journey the traveller must first meet with his shadow, and learn to live with this formidable and often terrifying aspect of himself: there is no wholeness without a recognition of the opposites.'[44]

If Bailey did intend the Doctor as 'wise old man' it was as a reaction to the action-drama formula he disliked. Yet in this ultimate figure of 'wholeness' and repose there is no drama at all. In contrast to the interiorised drama of Hindle and the exteriorised one of the Kinda, the Doctor would have sunk from view, as Peter Grimwade said. It is arguable, of course, that the Doctor's hostile-yet-sympathetic relationship with his own 'shadows' is a dramatisation of the 'mature' recognition that the self, like the universe, depends on the conscious interplay of the forces of light and darkness, yin and yang, outside and inside. Yet the drama of *Doctor Who* inheres in the endless journey, rather than the final reward of wisdom. The Trickster's failure to protect his enclosed social order is the failure of mythology in the face of external aggression. But that penetration from outside is not simply the result of colonisation; it stems from the Doctor's own excessive (Trickster-like) wandering too.

In this sense, the Trickster is a reflection of the Doctor himself — especially in the mediating role both play between stasis and change. What Radin calls the outstanding characteristic of the Trickster-hero — his two-fold function of benefactor and buffoon — has been the single most significant characteristic of the Doctor too. It has been marked in different eras — most notably in Troughton and Baker, least in Pertwee — but it persists even under the current, action-oriented, anti-satire regime.

Panna: No male can open the Box of Jana without being driven out of his mind. It's well known . . . Unless . . . is he an idiot?
Todd (amused): Are you?
Doctor: I've been called one many times!
Panna: Be quiet, idiot!

As Radin says of the Red Indian Trickster, so too the Doctor represents the potential of the 'undifferentiated', remaining 'everything to every man . . . hero, buffoon, he who was before good and evil, denier, affirmer, destroyer, and creator'.[45] Even in eras of *Doctor Who* which emphasise the 'action-drama' hero, this 'negative' Doctor who denies boundaries still resurfaces. In 'Kinda' it is the Doctor who destroys a culture through his wanderlust, a contradiction which Peter Grimwade noted and tried to efface:

> *Grimwade*:   The whole trouble is caused by the Doctor. If Tegan hadn't landed with the Doctor, nothing would have ever happened. It would all have worked out quite happily. So in fact it's the Doctor's intervention that caused the problem, and he is only getting himself out of a problem that he has created . . . I would say that that is a weakness if one really went into it . . . You conceal all that a little bit. You play it all down and you don't realise that that is the case.

Grimwade's 'action' formula was playing down the generic effect of Romanticism.

Music and pictures: 'Doctor Who' as melodrama

> Today melodrama dominates cinema and television screens . . . In 1976 at the end of a lecture on melodrama David Mayer showed an episode which illustrated many points he had been making. The episode was the current instalment of *Doctor Who*.[46]
>
> (Louis James)

The connection between melodrama and Romanticism was particularly close, especially in the presentation of simple people in wild, unaffected landscapes to highlight authentic passions, and in the use of music directly to reflect and effect emotional states. When James mentions the role of music in the melodrama *Frankenstein* as affecting the feeling of the monster and soothing his intention to kill, he is in fact also rehearsing a scene between the Doctor and Aggedor in 'The Monster of Peladon'. Twentieth-century 'serious' drama's quest to be music-free is as Mayer says, 'a comparatively new practice, not a long established tradition . . . As the term informs us, melody is part of melodrama's appeal'[47] — as it certainly is in *Doctor Who* where, as in Peter Howell's work on 'Kinda', about fifteen minutes out of twenty-five requires incidental music.

> *Howell*:   I think it requires less effort from the audience to enjoy it properly after the music has been added because it actually helps them along the way. You inveigle them into almost relying on the music as a sort of security because it is confirming what they are looking at. And then of course you give them a kick up the pants because in fact you put in a shock at the right moment.

As in traditional melodrama, music in *Doctor Who* works dramatically by underlying and presenting the conflict of rapidly changing emotional states — so that it is often more by means of incidental music than by interiorised acting that emotional change is expressed.

> *Howell*:   The music is normally, the way I write it, really dealing second by second with the character's actual emotional response to the situation . . . I have just done a short little cue where Panna has died and Karuna gets telepathic waves to the effect that she's now Panna . . . When you actually come to write the music for it you start asking yourself, "Well, what are the various different things that people are thinking?" The music actually starts when she comes into the cave, so in fact the Doctor's been thinking, 'Well, right, Panna is dead.' . . . The situation is basically very sad. Karuna goes up to the stick, takes hold of it and you've obviously got to have music saying 'Hello, what's going on here?' . . . You would expect her to come back and grieve. But she doesn't — 'something peculiar is happening'. And then from the sadness of that, she says, 'Of course I'm not dead' — and we have 'sheer wonderment'. 'How can Panna not be dead, and how can this woman say

she's actually taken it all over?' So it is all those split second things.

This is typically the use of music in melodrama, where as Mayer describes it, 'music is an affecting and effecting device to underline and emphasise the emotional content of a play's action . . . maintaining the momentum of the play's headlong rush from sensation to sensation, from crisis to emotional crisis.'[48] In 'Kinda' this short cue re-defines the emotional shock of the previous cliffhanger ('I think she's dead') in terms of the new episode's 'epic' theme: the grand, cyclical history of the Kinda. Hence Bailey's 'Buddhist' theme (the movement from Panna/wisdom to Karuna/compassion) is invoked here by the incidental music while the dialogue remains silent or in puzzlement.

This is typical of the semiotic 'thickness' of performance discourse, which, as Elam says, is marked diachronically (i.e. in its temporal unfolding) 'by the discontinuity of its various levels . . . Not all the contributory systems will be operative at every point in the performance: each message and signal will at times fall to a zero level, so that, while theatrical discourse at large is a constant, its actual make-up is subject to continual change.'[49] Here, for example, the musical channel of communication replaces, cues, determines the visual and linguistic channels in presenting information; whereas, as we will see, in the dome scenes which are dominated by a 'realist' rather than melodramatic performance code, the music tends to fall silent.

What has motivated this temporary hegemony of a 'melodramatic' over a 'realist' mode is the clustering of other conventional melodramatic devices around the cliffhanger (repeated at the beginning of this final episode): the use of primitive landscape to highlight the Kinda's 'true' passion; the swift scenic mood change from 'significant' static tableau (the cave sequence of the Doctor, Todd and Panna) to its violent destruction (in the future/past 'vision' scene); the pantomimic/acrobatic performance of the Trickster, establishing drama through physical style.[50]

What is interesting in the 'death of Panna' sequence is the way in which other performance codes, too, allow the 'Budd-

hist' sub-text a rare moment of motivational force in order to
justify 'realistically' the actors' interpretation.

> *Grimwade*:   I didn't tell the actors very seriously that
> 'Kinda' had a Buddhist line to it . . . It can't be important
> because you are not doing a tale for Buddhists. Yet having
> done a little bit of homework just for my own interest,
> there were one or two moments when I thought, 'Well,
> that is the right way to play that, because that is what is
> motivating the writer at that point and therefore it would
> be wrong to do it another way' . . . For instance, when
> Panna is dead. In rehearsal the actors very much wanted
> Karuna to 'pretend to be Panna and put on Mary Morris'
> voice'. But I said, 'No, I don't think it works like that
> because in fact the idea is there are two of them, there are
> two elements of wisdom and love/compassion which are
> complementary. But at the same time they are the same
> thing, and because Panna is dead and because Karuna
> represents love and compassion she *is* Panna because
> through love and compassion you therefore have wisdom.
> So she must emphasise as much the other side as Panna's
> side. To pretend to be Panna is simply apeing, as if she is
> possessed by the spirit of the old woman rather than having
> the attributes of the old woman, but in a different way'.

The thing which has brought popular melodrama into the
domain of intellectual condescension among 'high art' critics
has been the notion that 'melodramatic music, just as melodramatic incidents, characters and dialogue, could be readily
assembled from ready-made parts'.[51] Heilman has argued
that tragedy was more profound because it explored the crisis
of inner personality whereas melodrama presented only
'types'.[52] It was clearly this comparison that Chris Bailey had
in mind when criticising the production of his script. In contrast to the drama of inner personality he had written, there
was now (despite momentary resort to Buddhist characterisation) this drama of global collapse, strong on effects and
conveyed by types. He complained, while watching the
recording of Panna and Karuna signalling to the Doctor, of
the stereotype of the 'mysterious', signified by the slow,

beckoning hand gestures. Yet melodrama has never been just a matter of ham acting and hackneyed typing. Melodrama's representation of character was originally coded 'realistically' according to strict rules that the audience was well aware of and which were located in 'scientific' theories about the way physical expression conveyed moral and emotional states.

It is not a coincidence that where, in 'Kinda', the acting foregrounded 'internal' drama (to the satisfaction of Bailey) as in Hindle's madness, Peter Howell omitted emotion-amplifying music on the grounds that 'the acting is very, very good'. Two drama conventions, melodrama and 'serious' psychological realism, are allowed here to co-exist side by side — and what in fact allows them to cohere is the re-coding of melodramatic 'realism' within current, 'professional' TV realist conventions. Whereas original audiences of popular melodrama were content to enter a game (where expectations of role-types were set up and fulfilled) based on their understanding of psychological reality, modern audiences live on the other side of theories of the unconscious of Freud and Jung. External expression is no longer seen as innocently representing inner feelings. Hindle's outburst is not authenticated by nature so much as catalysed by it; and the Trickster's pantomime now acts out the very different game of the cultural unconscious.

The tension between conventional melodrama and modern 'serious' drama is mediated by professional 'realism' which dominantly overlays the codes of each with its own. Bailey's 'Jungian' theme is easily appropriated by professional conventions which draw implicitly on modern theories of the unconscious and psychological realism. Hence the production recuperates Bailey's 'high art' intentions. But melodrama is 'tamed' in a similar way. Although the use of music is essentially melodramatic, the 'realistic' basis of its traditional emphasis (the science of the passions) is now gone. Whereas the 'agitatios', 'pateticos' and 'passionatos' could on the stage be related to melodramatic moods and gestures quite transparently, now any motif or theme conventionally expressing an emotion would draw attention to itself. Incidental music in *Doctor Who* must do the job of music in melodrama, but —

according to current conventions of realism — without foregrounding itself.

Howell: I don't like using themes in incidental music
because I think they draw attention to the music. Incidental
music should be exactly what it says. If you put a tune in
it is becoming featured music, and it is sticking out. I think
it is much better to associate instrumental sounds with
people without actually necessarily associating a known
tune. So the Mara is identified by a bowed cymbal sound
. . . worked like a percussion instrument into the music to
help it identify . . . If instead I had put in a bit with a
marvellous, memorable tune that sounds like Mars from
'The Planets' I'd have basically been starting a variety
show.

Essentially, Howell's is the same 'realist adventure drama'
position that the producer Nathan-Turner espoused in criticising Williams' 'The City of Death' for becoming a variety act
starring John Cleese and Eleanor Bron. *Doctor Who* is not then
simply in the line of theatrical melodrama, any more than
'Kinda' is serious drama. Each of these is filtered through a
series of current professional codings: the dominating code of
dramatic 'realism' as we have been discussing, but also others
depending on the particular professional values of individual
contributors to the programme, such as Peter Howell. He,
especially, was concerned to emphasise the fact that the
composition of incidental music should not be reduced to its
'SF' location in the BBC Radiophonic Workshop.

Howell: We might be doing the music here now, but that
doesn't alter the function of the music . . . it is incidental
music, as ever was. Which means that you can't necessarily
do way-out whizz-bang electronic music if in fact that goes
against the convention of incidental music. You've got to
try and work in these new sounds . . . but you've got to be
careful not to do it simply for the sake of making it electronic music, so that people can turn round and say 'Oh,
it's *Doctor Who*'.
Tulloch: Is there a difference then from visual technical

developments? *Doctor Who* tends to absorb the latest television technology there. You are saying you don't throw in whatever new electronic music development there is just because it is an SF sort of programme.

Howell: That's right . . . I think you have not got to use the new box of tricks that has come out just for the sake of it . . . in case what you are really doing is just acting like an advert for a music shop down Charing Cross Road.

Professionally, Howell sees his task as relying sufficiently on musical conventions to make the audience see the point, while innovating (with the 'new box of tricks') to avoid staleness.

Tulloch: Do you think there are conventions for the sort of music you do which you lock into rather spontaneously? One tended, for example, to get an awful lot of that same church organ effect in 'medieval' *Doctor Who* stories.

Howell: I think if you do more than two stories a year, or whatever your own limitation is, you get so stale you are likely to lock on to those conventions, you are right. Inevitably you have got to reflect what is happening on the screen. If they have decided to use monks and some quasi-religious fraternity . . . you've got to actually reflect that in the music . . . If you were very original about it and didn't use one of the recognised ways nobody would be getting the message that was intended in the incidental music anyway. So it is a very difficult path you tread between signposting all the events with recognised and readable signposts, but doing it in such a way that people don't turn around and say 'Yes, but we've heard it all before'. So you have got to try and find new ways of doing it. In "Meglos", where there was a monk-like atmosphere I'd like to think I got around it by actually using the "fifths" bit, where you use that chant and plain song idea, but because I did it all with a voice synthesiser it had a completely different tonal colour than you would normally expect.

This was Peter Howell's own particular version of television's 'similar but different' requirement, relying on a perceived tension between 'realist' and 'SF' musical conventions. Bailey's 'Kinda' eased Howell's problem because of the 'freshness' and 'originality' of the story. But Howell still, of course, drew on conventions (such as 'primitive idyllic' versus 'savage barbarian') to structure his composition. What is especially interesting here is the way in which the writer's 'authorship' intervenes in this process.

There were, as Howell saw it, three basic centres for musical emphasis in 'Kinda': the dome, the Mara, and the simple Kinda people. Playing down the dome music allowed him to structure his incidental music in terms of an opposition between the Mara and the Kinda. This would, he argued, locate the drama in musical terms. The opposition would be *his* signature.

> 'I quite like to have a different mood for each lot of incidental music I do . . . And the mood was definitely created in 'Kinda' by two things: by the windchimes and the soft sounds they created (and therefore the soft, slightly lyrical attitude of the Kinda themselves in their normal state); and in complete contrast, by the harshness of the Wherever and the Mara . . . You have got chimes, which are derived from brushing and pinging a bit of cut glass that has then been worked on tape, and you've got the Mara which . . . is the bowed cymbal — again actually not electronic but a noise. So you have got these contrasting things.'

The conventional 'lyrical' idyll versus 'monstrous' dark places opposition (itself derived conventionally from pastoral romance)[53] is nevertheless complicated by Bailey's Buddhist values. 'The business about Panna and the wheel turning caused the lyrical side of the Kinda to also have a slightly epic quality . . . I wouldn't say it's the "Exodus" theme, but it certainly allows you to go a bit further in that direction.'

Interestingly, this could, on rare occasions, allow Howell to work against the 'action-drama' coding of the director. For instance, Grimwade's vision of the future/past destruction of the 'Kinda' established conflict and pace by fast intercutting between the horrified faces of Todd and the Doctor, the helpless Panna, the electronically distorted dance of the

Trickster, and various signifiers of time running down: a sundial, a metronome, an alarm clock, a digital clock, an egg timer, a flickering candle — an effect which Howell found banal. 'If I had latched on to those clocks and candles I would have been doing nursery rhymes. So you had to forget about that and concentrate on the more epic quality of the end. I had the idea of having a loud, incisive metronome tick . . . Normally speaking, when you are getting more excited, as with heart beats, you always speed things up. But I slowed it down, because in fact it was time coming back to zero. So, as a change, the tempo of the piece actually gets broader and larger . . . the epic idea . . . It opens out.'

Peter Howell's own professional values of 'freshness within convention' were therefore not a matter of autonomous 'creativity', but were rather a site for the interplay of conventions from melodrama, action-realism and 'serious' drama. Howell saw his contribution as drawing out what is already in the finished programme (since he always works only on the finally edited tape). But because the finished programme is itself a complex of different 'realist' modes, there is always space for finding 'difference' and contradiction within the formula.

Design and setting: marketable realism

The opening titles and music of 'Kinda' immediately presents Nathan-Turner's 'up-dating' signature. We flash through a star-field[54] (replacing the 'old-fashioned' time tunnel) and into the first visual as Howell's 'fresh but not ridiculously new'[55] signature tune gives way to natural sound. The initial scene is a building engulfed as much by the dominant bird sounds as by the forest around. We have arrived, by way of space and time, at another world in a series now nineteen years old.

The Dome (external)

The opening shots establish programme continuity as well as story difference. First, in the general sense of depending on programme formula — of which there are basically two: the 'discovery' principle where one starts off in the interior of the Tardis and discovers a new world subjectively through the eyes of the crew as they wander out; and the 'premise' principle which introduces an alien culture with which, we know from experience, the Doctor will become involved.[56] Secondly, through the particular coding of beautiful landscapes in *Doctor Who*, each containing a hidden threat which the first episode will quickly reveal. In 'Kinda' the premise of a colonial culture (markedly designated as 'British Raj') is combined with the threat of the encroaching forest to generate the familiar 'mineral exploitation' theme of *Doctor Who*, but now in an 'oddball' (*Play of the Month*) guise, since the encroaching forest will signify the creeping madness of the one-dimensional, linearly 'rational' militaristic mind.

When Hindle later complains, 'Seeds, and spores and things. Everywhere. Getting hold. Rooting. Thrusting. Branching. Blocking out the light', we know that the threat is within him, and that his solution of exploding the forest (and the Kinda culture) is an alibi for the conflict in his own psyche. None the less, though the ultimate madness is psychological, its determinant is cultural. As in the first episode of *Doctor Who* in 1963, that culture is earmarked as 'British'. As Peter Grimwade said, 'They are not just from Earth. They're from England. They have got English names. They have got attitudes of the Raj — that's why the pith helmets are there.'

But unlike 'An Unearthly Child', 'Kinda' appropriates British 'history' not the British 'here-and-now'. 'Britain, 1963' had been used simply as a point of transition to establish the hermeneutic coding: the original Doctor Who? Now, in 1981, 'British history', signified by stock colonial types (Sanders 'of the River') and well-rehearsed colonial situations (civilising the primitives through stiff upper lip) could be sure to appeal (as 'authentically English historical saga') to an international (and hopefully American) market. So whereas the 'ordinary' British school of 1963 is not presented as 'social analysis', the colonial military class of 'Kinda' is. From this basis a compromise could be struck between the *Play of the Month* tendencies of Bailey and the marketing orientation of Nathan-Turner.

For Bailey, the 'Raj' situation of a small, 'advanced' out-post located on the edge of a vast 'uncivilised' terrain, would generate the interiorised drama of mental oppression. As designer Malcolm Thornton described, the dome had to be related visually to the forest as an alien presence, 'an intrusion into the calm and peace of the forest'. Yet he designed the inside of the dome to give the sense of the colonists as them-selves oppressed by the vastness of 'the forest looming outside . . . I wanted to get the feel of the package, the kit of parts, dropped on the forest, but then the forest all the time impos-ing itself on them when they were inside . . . The main feature of the interior being that whichever way you look you were always aware of the forest.' For Bailey, then, the relation of dome and forest was a metaphor for the rational/irrational conflict within the military-colonial mind. For Nathan-Turner the dome was, because of the psychological complexity of the acting parts, a perfect site to display his guest stars — and Peter Grimwade's camera style, which tended to reduce the oppressive effect of the forest, supported the producer's inflection.

The Dome (internal)

An internal door is violently wrenched aside to reveal, in MCU, the military commander, Sanders. The first face of 'Kinda' is the face of its most famous guest star. Nathan-Turner's preferred (initial) reading, as we know, is 'That's Richard Todd'. But it is essential to his 'action-drama' signa-ture that the star is immediately enfolded 'realistically' within the diegesis.

Everything is done here to avoid the overly emphatic 'Cleese-type' star persona. There is the stern contemptuous expression and tunic-zipping gesture signifying instantly the military type. There is also the 'transparency' effect of choos-ing Richard Todd to play this part because of his personal similarity, as Grimwade saw it, to the 'Raj' type. Thirdly, the dome interior is carefully designed in minute shabby detail to establish the story as 'realistic' and 'believable' — a plausible place for a colonising mind rather than a studio setting for a star.

Thornton: It was a matter of working out the style of
the dome structure in a realistic way. What sort of structure
could have come out of packages dropped from a space
craft on to a planet without knowing too much of the
environment or conditions of the planet. It was designing
something that could be reasonably believable. I thought
along the lines of a space-frame structure slung in to a
plug-in pod system which provided the different areas
required for the dome . . . I wanted to give the feel that it
was a sophisticated construction that could be dropped in
crates on to any planet and assembled.

This, however, is action-drama, not documentary. The first
establishing shot of the interior is coded for 'suspense' and
'threat': an angled crane shot expressionistically lit of Hindle
sprawled asleep, defenceless but gripping his gun. Sanders
turns on the light to establish the 'realistic' world of the
dome. But also to demonstrate (since every detail of the
drama must be plausibly motivated) that it could be dark and
ominous around Hindle because it is only just dawn (indicated
by the dawn chorus and Sanders dressing). So the opening
gesture (displaying yet hiding the star) signifies in a dual way
the military mind and the plausibility of the 'threat' scene.

This, then, is action-realism. In the foreground there is a
puzzle — two empty chairs and a mask. In the second dome
scene one chair will be accounted for: the scientist Todd,
another visible 'star' (Nerys Hughes, who is quickly enfolded
within the familiar 'authoritarian v. scientist' discourse of
Doctor Who). But the other chair, marked 'Roberts' will
remain empty, motivating the major puzzle of the first episode
('where's Roberts?'), promoting a potential (but false) explanation for the strange people of the Wherever scene, and
generating the conventional programme scenario: missing
exploration member/suspect Doctor (cf. 'Planet of Evil').
This in turn will motivate the suspended enigma of episode 1:
Hindle, now awake but still with gun in hand, threatening the
Doctor.

The other mystery, the mask, is not withheld but immediately used to hint at the 'serious' coding of 'Kinda'. The
contrast of officious leaders with others of their crew is con-

ventional in *Doctor Who* ('Planet of Evil', 'Warriors Gate', etc.). But in 'Kinda' it is marked by an 'anthropological' discourse (Todd's comment on the mask to Sanders) and by 'serious psychological drama'. Sanders puts on the native mask shouts 'Boo', and the frightened Hindle awakens with a cry. 'What's the matter boy? Bad dreams?': the Jungian theme is broached. Unlike the later Kinda use of the mask, this is used to frighten, control and divide. But this is action-drama and the pace will not linger. We cut immediately leaving the broader audience to recognise simply that this is the familiar world of trouble and anxiety which (inevitably) the Doctor will enter.

The Tardis (exterior)

We cut appropriately to Tegan because it is Tegan who will activate the potential of 'bad dreams'. Her dreaming alone will generate the 'villainy'. She ambles from the forest in an open blouse – a hint of the (controlled) sensuousness of the next episode when, overtaken by the Mara, she sways her hips through the forest. As she pauses for the conventional Doctor's-family-of-companions Tardis scene we should remember that Tegan is there to market the programme via her 'nice figure, nice legs'. Adric and Nyssa are (typically) presented using their minds. Adric's mental powers (and Tegan's typical mistake) enable him to clear the draughts board. But that action also established 'Kinda's continuity with the cliffhanger out of 'Four to Doomsday'. There are problems within the Doctor's domesticated world (as Tegan will exemplify in 'Kinda'): Nyssa has collapsed at the end of the previous episode and in her dizzy state is not the usual intellectual match for Adric.

The sequence is replete with Nathan-Turner's signature: (a) pace – no lengthy Tardis interior scene[57] followed by 'Well, here we are, let's go out and have a walk' (Tegan already having her walk, moves straight into the resolution of the suspended enigma); (b) vulnerability – the Doctor's mistake in immediately displacing the sonic screwdriver from the action ties the resolution of the cliffhanger into the drama of the action to come (signalled by the first sound of the ominous 'wheel of time' music); (c) continuity — Tegan's impatient 'I suppose we're stuck here now while she sleeps' re-establishing her 'Get me back to Heathrow' impatience, while Adric's response (smiling at the forest) of 'It's so beautiful' is a reminder of his forest world of 'Full Circle'; (d) visual style — exact formal reversal in the cut to the dome, as the 2-shot (facing out to forest) of Tegan and Adric is replaced by the 2-shot of Sanders and Hindle (facing away from forest).

The Forest

Unlike Peter Howell, designer Malcolm Thornton came into contact with 'Kinda' at an early script stage and worked closely with the director to establish a 'realistic' visual topography. As with Howell, professional values of dramatic conflict and opposition determine his thinking, in this case between the 'alien' dome and the 'natural' forest. He came close here to the feeling in Le Guin of the oppression felt by 'rational' colonists in an 'excessively tranquil' world that was entirely organic. But much of the 'conjectural' quality of Le Guin which Bailey wanted — the 'absent paradigm' sense of nature as culture was lost because of the commitment of studio 'realism'. For Bailey, Thornton's forest was not strange enough.

> *Thornton*: We felt that it shouldn't — it needn't — look too exotic or strange, as though set on a planet unknown to us all. We felt that if we pushed just the lush, paradise, calm feeling, but then added as much interesting colour to it as we could get, it would make a sufficient point about the forest and the lives that the Kinda led within that forest. I made the decision to add in the glade area a rock pool and a waterfall, to suggest a completely different area to the paths and the densely jungled area of the forest . . . When Aris arrives and makes his stand we find him in the glade, trying to take control — that made a nice contrast with the peaceful feel of the glade up to that point. He burst in on it and upset that calm — as, almost, the dome had upset the calm of the forest.

From this familiar professional starting point of 'drama', 'contrast', 'conflict', 'realism', Thornton developed an entire topography. The Windchimes, again like the dome seen as an 'alien' intrusion in the forest, were, despite being mysterious, designed to appear 'realistic'. 'We very much wanted to give the feel of an Aeolian Harp . . . the wind passing through and the strange sort of harmonic sounds that they then gave off . . . The actual profile . . . was based on us thinking about what physically would seem fairly realistic in terms of a structure that would make these sounds.' And similarly, notions of topographical realism (transition from forest to foothills to mountains) and contrast established Panna's cave setting.

> *Thornton*:   We suggested the cave up on a higher level, beyond the tree line possibly, to which the Doctor had to go with Karuna up to Panna's cave. We felt it was a nice contrast having been in the dense green for so long to move away from that . . . to take advantage of the rock situation we had established within the forest, and try to set up a situation where the Doctor could be seen coming up into this framed picture — sky and tree-line — from which he would then move into the well of the cave, which could be a nice darkened area. Not necessarily too mysterious and threatening, but just a contrast to the brightness and lightness outside.

The visual contrast could be motivated realistically by the fact that Panna was blind and did not need light to find her way around. 'And that device of seeing them framed in the mouth of the cave was then useful later on to lay in our effects in that nicely framed area.'

Effects, contrast, drama, realism: Malcolm Thornton was very much a professional in Peter Grimwade's sense. The particular device Thornton mentions of using the cave mouth as a picture tableau which is quickly destroyed by the dynamic of destruction is, as we said, a typically melodramatic device. Yet here it was established within a realistic topography and according to either plausibly naturalistic (Panna's blindness) or 'SF' (the Mara's world of destruction) motivation. As in

the case of Howell's music, the 'realist' effect was in fact
wedded to SF by using the 'box of tricks' — here CSO and
special effects combined to suggest the Doctor and Todd
passing from the cave through some terrible black wave.

The Wherever

> The Tardis is standing in a small clearing. Nearby, Adric
> and Nyssa sit, in the morning sunshine, at a small table
> playing draughts. We get Tegan's POV of this as she returns
> from a morning stroll. It is exactly the same POV as her
> POV of the caravan/chess players at the top of scene eigh-
> teen.
>
> ('Kinda' Rehearsal Script)

Bailey's script offers the potential for an unusual narrative
development of the *Doctor Who* doppleganger paradigm, as
the story folds back on itself (to the Tardis set up) as though
to start again, but in a 'Wherever' world populated by malicious doubles of the Doctor and his companions. Thornton
recognised this sufficiently to design the 'gypsy caravan' as
an 'alien' double of the Tardis. However, Thornton's 'space
and time' parallel tended to direct the programme away from
this potential.

> *Thornton*:   We really had nothing to go on . . . What does
> it mean? Is it a space craft? . . . The more we thought about
> it, we felt it was almost some sort of energy. It was a meta-
> physical thing . . . I designed a very simple structure. In
> proportion it was very similar to the Tardis . . . It was
> really a physical structure that we wanted to look as strange
> as possible but had some sort of tie-up, however vague it
> might be, with space/time travel and energy — as the Tardis,
> almost. We had the idea of a light inside it, pulsating out,
> and then putting . . . on the outside odd period mouldings,
> odd images of centuries before or since . . . that just caught
> the light . . . There was the odd image of a jumbo jet and
> so on painted in to be not that recognisable. But they were

glimpses of time gone by or time to come. We just pushed the look of that as far as we could go technically to try and make the whole thing look as strange as possible.

It seems clear that the Wherever sequences in 'Kinda' created the greatest problems of uncertainty and ambiguity for designer and director — separated as it was from the 'realist' topography of contrasts which had constructed the rest of Deva Loka. In the bare and empty blackness of the CSO Wherever sets, props like the 'caravan' and costumes like the 'Elizabethan' clothes worn by Anatta and Anicca foregrounded their connotative or symbolising function, as most audience groups readily recognised — though without ever (including a Buddhist group)[58] understanding what (in Bailey's terms) they were connoting. It was only in the Wherever that set, props and costumes acquired an 'action force' almost equivalent to the actors.[59] The potential was indicated here of a reversal of television's dominant naturalist habit — where 'star' actors attract the audience's attention to their own performance and sets are hierarchically subordinated to a transparently functional status. And clearly Bailey would have liked the sets to be made 'strange' elsewhere in the production. But in a Nathan-Turner production that was not to be, and even in the Wherever the familiar emphasis on pushing 'as far as we could go technically', and the 'continuity' emphasis on space and time, drew away from that potential and tended to recuperate the sequences as 'Nathan-Turner visual style'.

Instead of Bailey's 'conjectural' emphasis, the 'Kinda' studio was dominated by a dedication to naturalism and technical effects. The first day of the second studio session was delayed by two things: the superimposition of the snake from Tegan's to Aris' arm, and the constant demand of the producer for a more realistic forest floor.

Thornton: The floor of the forest was one of the biggest problems . . . We had the very difficult problem of the cameras moving on that studio floor, pushing their way through dressing, leaves and grass turfs. And also the problem of the TSS when it was in the forest coming towards camera, pushing its way through piles of leaves . . . so that in a long shot . . . you could see a clear path cut behind it. *Nathan-Turner*: You either shoot a forest through foreground forestry, and everything is kind of played deep in the set and people walk right to camera and deliver their lines and move on, or you try to open the whole thing up and create areas for the actors to act in, which thereby means that part of the floor is exposed . . . I think perhaps on 'Kinda' the ambitions of the director to get so many different angles in what was really basically a small set to create a huge jungle has resulted in creating avenues for the camera which were exposed in other shots as being blank floor. I think that is a lesson that both the director concerned and I learned for the future.

During recording there were constant delays as the producer rejected takes because 'it just looks like a studio floor', and, after several minutes spent sweeping leaves across, 'now is just looks like a studio floor with a few leaves on'. The problem was exacerbated, as Thornton said, by the fact that, 'because we were pretty well shooting 360°', there were problems masking as many as four cameras and the floor monitors which 'give off that blue glow, even if they are facing away from camera and are masked.' So there were few floor monitors, and the floor manager was unable to see the bare floor patches which the producer, who was up in the gallery, was complaining about.

When designing for Grimwade on 'Logopolis', Thornton's problems had been ones which could be catered for in advance of the recording session: a set which would decay and collapse; the cost in man-hours to build it, and so on. 'Because Logopolis was basically traditional footage going up to 12 to 14 feet, one could pre-plan it a lot more. You knew where your solid surfaces started and ended, you knew where you were going to shoot off . . . With 'Kinda' you are planning greenery that you don't know the precise height and shape of until you actually get the tall trees and bushes into the studio.' Despite Thornton's care at the plant hire company to try and match his model, precious time was therefore lost coming to terms with the actual set during recording. 'We had to cut a few high shots because we would never have been able to take such wide shots and dress the floor at the same time. So the first night we were overrunning, and the producer and I . . . overnight ordered seven dozen bags of green and dried leaves, and spent the next two days dressing the forest floor to shot . . . It was watching cameras most of the time, watching for shoot offs, dressing to shot.'

It is arguable that this degree of commitment to 'realism' affected not only the production values on that first day of recording (as under time pressure continuity and other mistakes were made in the Adric/Doctor/TSS scenes) but also on later days. For instance, the snake climax was allowed to go through into transmission with a wire clearly seen between its jaws. Grimwade never made up the time to use the complicated, time-consuming electronic effects he had planned for this sequence. Moreover, episode 3 of 'Kinda' ran a few minutes short and had to be made up by rather static conversational filler recorded later at the 'Earthshock' studio (also directed by Grimwade).

Nathan-Turner argued that this was nothing to do with studio time lost, but rather was due to the failure of certain set pieces (such as the TSS fight with Aris and one of the Trickster's sequences) to 'expand in the studio' as they had expected. On the other hand, Lee Cornes who played the Trickster argued that those particular scenes had contracted because of time shortage and lack of planning. 'The scene with Aris when I mimic him with the doll . . . got cut to Aris looking at one spot and seeing me virtually at his shoulder with ten extras, not being able to move or do anything basically . . . What we did in rehearsal was completely removed – we didn't even block it in again. The director said, "You can't do this, you can't do that, shoot it", literally – with a minor rehearsal that was so confusing as to be pointless . . . If he'd said, "Have half an hour to think of something", then OK, but he didn't . . . It's pressure of time, and not thinking through the event beforehand, and no thorough co-ordination with what the set is really like.'

Of all the various audience groups who watched 'Kinda', only other television producers complained of 'forest paths that looked like a studio floor with leaves on'[60] – and,

ironically, the very attempts Nathan-Turner made to redress
that led to the continuity and production value problems
which the same producers commented on very unfavourably.

Acting: regulating the performance

We have been looking at some of the key performance codings
which combined to generate the 'semiotic thickness' of 'Kinda'
as a communicational act. As Elam says, we can account for
the co-operation between different codes in the production
of a performed text by means of 'two major trans-systemic
considerations'. The first is the 'sharing of semantic content
by different kinds of signal'. Peter Howell's concern that the
incidental music should underpin the action and not obtrude
as a 'variety act'; Malcolm Thornton's concern to create a
naturalistically plausible topographic world; Dick Mills'
determination that on special sound effects 'if the creature is
obviously living, albeit it has got ten heads and green blood
and breathes fire, it is still a living object, so I try to make it
from living (acoustic) rather than electronic sounds' – are all
examples of the professional commitment to 'realism' of
performance, a deeply ingrained determination to efface the
signs of the coding process. The very nature of performance
which, as it unfolds, is discontinuous in its emphasis of different textual codes – now relying on actors' language, now on
gesture, now on incidental music, sets, props, special sounds
or effects to carry its messages – means that the unity of a
text depends on professional commitment to 'the phenomenon of transcodification, whereby a given bit of semantic
information can be translated from one system to another.'[61]
     Yet global professional values are inflected differently in
different eras of performance – it is this which makes *Doctor
Who* an unfolding text. And in the period of John Nathan-
Turner, the commitment to circulating stars might have
threatened the second area of textual unity that Elam mentions: 'the semantic and stylistic coherence of theatrical discourse in its temporal unfolding'.[62] In the last resort it is the
director (and producer) who have responsibility for textual
'coherence', and one of the major threats to this that they

face – especially in Nathan-Turner's star-oriented *Doctor Who* – comes from the actors, because these will bring with them to the show a wole range of histrionic sub-codes. Nerys Hughes carried a popular television image as a 'situation comedy' persona from *The Liver Birds*. Richard Todd carried with him his 'stiff upper lip British hero' persona. Lee Cornes was attracted to the part of the Trickster because of his professional interest in mime and 'visual' comedy. Janet Fielding as Tegan had an earlier 'Brechtian' career dealing with exploitation of primitives by British colonists – potentially significant to her role in '*Kinda*'. These, and others (including Peter Davison himself) carried to the '*Kinda*' narrative an intertextual history which, as Elam puts it, can perform by 'drawing attention to the performer's idiolectal traits (common to all his performances) . . . Not infrequently the primary "meaning" of a given representation for its audience is the very presence of its favourite performer, i.e. the performance text becomes the "vehicle" for the actor rather than vice versa).'[63]

So a performance littered with stars and other 'specialist' performers runs the risk, as it unfolds, of being crossed by an entire generic range of histrionic sub codes. In the case of 'novitiate' actors, this is obviously less of a problem than with stars who often only exist as performers in terms of an intertextual image-career. Adrian Mills, for example, who was very conscious of the status of *Doctor Who* as an institution and who was delighted to be in a programme which would give him exposure at its new evening viewing time, was eager to draw on the experience of the director (whom he found very approachable) and older stars like Mary Morris for professional advice, and he used the 'luxury of a week and a half rehearsal before three days in the studio' to absorb the advice he solicited. By and large that advice was minor and detailed – notably Grimwade's caution not to 'peak' too early, and to lose his Liverpool accent, because 'We can't have a planet miles from anywhere . . . where the savages talk in Liverpuddlian'. For the rest, the values of 'realist' motivation Mills inculcated at drama school – 'Why am I doing that? What makes me want to attack the dome, or the Doctor?' – could be relied upon to produce an acceptable attitude to performance. 'It's like living in the country and having a dual carriageway stuck next to you — you rebel, it's inevitable.' It was this 'plausibility' coding, drawing on 'things that have happened to you in your own life' rather than the author's Buddhist ideas (which Mills had heard very little about) that ensured his commitment to the 'realist' values of the production.

Similarly, Lee Cornes who had only been given a brief story-line description of the part by Grimwade, and felt that the writer probably intended more with it, thought that such knowledge would have made the part unplayable. 'I don't think you need to wrestle with my function within the tribe. It is quite clear. It's to alleviate tension by all means possible and . . . entertain for social reasons.' Further 'Buddhist' information would have detracted from a part that is 'so fluid and imaginative that you could actually see anything into it. And yet basically it combines all the classic ingredients of goodies and baddies, comedy and drama . . . That's the appeal of it . . . I didn't go and identify with the great ideas, because I was seeing it as a story.' This commitment to the action rather than 'ideas', and also his concern never to be located within a particular histrionic code (the Trickster was not to be just 'clown' or 'pantomime' or 'gymnast' or 'acrobat'), meant that Cornes could be given considerable freedom to interpret the part. But this was only after auditions in which Grimwade rejected aspirants to the part who threatened to turn it into a self-referencing variety act — one turned the table over at audition and did gymnastics; another acted like a monkey, throwing things at the director. As Cornes said, 'It actually is a drama role, and I felt some conflict in the fact that this probably doesn't look very funny. But if I had made it any bigger or tried to do a trick it would have pulled away from my drama function.'

In most cases, then, an actor's professional values, competence and career interests will ensure textual coherence. The case of the star is more complicated. Nerys Hughes was chosen for 'Kinda' as a recognisable star face, in a part (as cool and crisp scientist) which was, she said, very foreign to her own personality, let alone to her persona in The Liver Birds. The solution lay in 'realism'. 'Actors have got to be real. It is my first, most important aim, to find the reality of whatever I've done . . . Even in futuristic science fiction I've got to find my own reality. I have to think that I'm Todd. I have to imagine inside myself that I am this scientific person, and that's the only way I can play it.' Committed to 'serious' theatre and television, and finding her *Doctor Who* part 'one-dimensional', Nerys Hughes nevertheless saw no fundamental difference in the way to approach her parts. 'Actors who are thinking behind the eyes . . . are living it, being it.' . . . 'The first thing I did was a television series called *Diary of a Young Man*, which I was terribly lucky with because Ken Loach directed it . . . It was the first of its kind in those days of being very real, very earthy. And Michael Blakemore, directing the last play I did, *The Wild Duck*, instead of making Ibsen something heavy and trying to be symbolic all the time, just made it real, so that all the symbolism came out of the natural comedy.'

For this actress any comedy in her part must be 'real' too — if a joke is signalled, as we did sometimes in *Liver Birds*, you push a bit harder and make it even more unreal.' Like most of the other actors, she was clearly imbued with Nathan-Turner's signature. Hence she agreed with his critique of the Baker era, and had no intention of bringing 'unreal' comedy into the show. 'I don't see anything wrong with humour, because humour is in life. But to actually make a series sending itself up, parodying itself, that's no good either.'

A more direct way of incorporating stars unobtrusively is by co-opting an appropriate intertextual 'idiolect' for a part — In particular, Stratford John's 'Barlow' mixture of ruthlessness and gauche charm for Monarch in 'Four to Doomsday', and Richard Todd's 'British imperial hero' role for Sanders in 'Kinda'. In the latter case a combination of national ('very British'), generic ('stiff upper lip war hero') and historical (early post war) histrionic sub-codes could themselves be foregrounded as 'dated' to extract an underplayed humour.

Yet Richard Todd, who was attracted to his 'vignette' part in order to get television experience, had originally conceived the part very differently, and this created some early problems in rehearsal.

Every actor likes to do something which is widening his

scope . . . And in my particular case with this it was a
chance to get away from doing a straight role or a dramatic
role or a romantic role. I thought it was a good exercise,
purely as an actor, because there is a certain difficulty in
walking the tight rope between burlesque and reality in a
thing of this sort.

Possibly influenced by what he saw of the programme during
the Tom Baker years, Richard Todd had accepted the part of
Sanders as a cnance to do comedy.

Todd: I did realise when I first came into rehearsal that
it wasn't exactly their concept of the character because it
was slightly a send up, slightly a burlesque . . . a sort of
Colonel Blimp of the British Raj type . . . That is not what
was wanted . . . It has been made very clear to me by the
producer and the director that one has to seek for reality . . .
The comedy has to arise out of the reality and not be
played for comedy as such, because if you play it for
comedy there is a tendency to send up. It is no longer a
funny part. If there is any humour in it at all it is simply
out of the pompous stupidity of the man . . . I still have to
find a way of playing a slightly ridiculous character, but to
play him believably . . . You don't have to play it for fun,
but it is funny to see this man who has been a typically
severe, pompous, rather waffling army man suddenly
ameliorate and become almost whimsy at the end . . . That
is where the humour lies — for the audience, not for the
actor . . . I believe from what I've gleaned in the last few
weeks that there was a tendency for the programme to get
slightly glib and slightly send-up. It was beginning to lose
reality, and people were playing it for laughs.

Richard Todd made it clear that one of the things he liked
about playing in *Doctor Who* was that there is no star billing,
so avoiding 'all that jockeying for position which . . . so many
actors are very, very sensitive about. This programme works
on the policy, much as the Royal Shakespeare Company does,
of no cast system, no star system, even though they have
their leading men. It is status that enables the RSC to do

that, and that's what *Doctor Who* has . . . William Hartnell and Patrick Troughton and Jon Pertwee and Tom Baker and now Peter Davison have played the Doctor, but the star of the series is the series.'

That is certainly the case. But perhaps there is a danger in this venerable institution of atrophy — that in gaining its 'reality' it is losing its 'laughs'. John Nathan-Turner is conscious of the problem, and chose as his star someone who had television recognition as both dramatic and funny. Yet most of the tertiary educated and science fiction audiences interviewed denied his assertion that he had replaced 'slapstick' with 'wit'. There is no particular answer to that conundrum since the recognition of comedy relies, like any other textual 'meaning', on the range of cultural competences in any particular audience. But what does seem certain, given the enshrined tradition of television 'realism', is that future producers of *Doctor Who* will continue to claim that 'education' 'comedy', 'ideas', 'send-up' or 'wit' is in the service of programme coherence. And that coherence is now totally bound up with the mythology of two decades of adventure.

The Chief Dalek

Appendix I

The People who made *Doctor Who*

Both Appendix I and Appendix II (pp. 306—15)
were prepared by **Jeremy Bentham,** former Associate Editor
and writer for the publication *Doctor Who Monthly*.

The Doctor played by William Hartnell
Produced by Verity Lambert and Mervyn Pinfield
Script-Editor: David Whitaker

Code	Serial Title	Writers	Directors	Designers
A	AN UNEARTHLY CHILD (The Tribe of Gum)	Anthony Coburn (C. E. Webber)	Waris Hussein	Peter Brachacki
B	THE DALEKS	Terry Nation	Christopher Barry Richard Martin	Barry Newbery Raymond Cusick
C	BEYOND THE SUN (The Edge of Destruction)	David Whitaker	Richard Martin Frank Cox	Jeremy Davies Raymond Cusick
D	MARCO POLO	John Lucarotti	Waris Hussein John Crocket	Barry Newbery
E	THE KEYS OF MARINUS	Terry Nation	John Gorrie	Raymond Cusick
F	THE AZTECS	John Lucarotti	John Crocket	Barry Newbery
G	THE SENSORITES	Peter R. Newman	Mervyn Pinfield Frank Cox	Raymond Cusick
H	THE REIGN OF TERROR	Dennis Spooner	Henric Hirsch	Roderick Laing
J	PLANET OF GIANTS	Louis Marks	Mervyn Pinfield Douglas Camfield	Raymond Cusick
K	THE DALEK INVASION OF EARTH	Terry Nation	Richard Martin	Spencer Chapman

Script-Editor: Dennis Spooner

Code	Serial Title	Writers	Directors	Designers
L	THE RESCUE	David Whitaker	Christopher Barry	Raymond Cusick
M	THE ROMANS	Dennis Spooner	Christopher Barry	Raymond Cusick

Produced by Verity Lambert

Code	Serial Title	Writers	Directors	Designers
N	THE WEB PLANET	Bill Strutton	Richard Martin	John Wood
P	THE CRUSADE	David Whitaker	Douglas Camfield	Barry Newbery

		Writer	Director	Designer
Q	THE SPACE MUSEUM	Glyn Jones	Mervyn Pinfield	Spencer Chapman
R	THE CHASE	Terry Nation	Richard Martin	Raymond Cusick / John Wood

Script-Editor: Donald Tosh

		Writer	Director	Designer
S	THE TIME MEDDLER	Dennis Spooner	Douglas Camfield	Barry Newbery
T	GALAXY FOUR	William Emms	Derek Martinus	Richard Hunt
T/A	MISSION TO THE UNKNOWN	Terry Nation	Derek Martinus	Richard Hunt / Raymond Cusick

Produced by John Wiles

		Writer	Director	Designer
U	THE MYTH MAKERS	Donald Cotton	Michael Leeston-Smith	John Wood
V	THE DALEKS' MASTER PLAN	Terry Nation / Dennis Spooner	Douglas Camfield	Raymond Cusick / Barry Newbery
W	THE MASSACRE	John Lucarotti / Donald Tosh	Paddy Russell	Michael Young

Script-Editor: Gerry Davis

		Writer	Director	Designer
X	THE ARK	Paul Erickson / Lesley Scott	Michael Imison	Barry Newbery

Produced by Innes Lloyd

		Writer	Director	Designer
Y	THE CELESTIAL TOYMAKER	Brian Hayles	Bill Sellars	John Wood
Z	THE GUN FIGHTERS	Donald Cotton	Rex Tucker	Barry Newbery
AA	THE SAVAGES	Ian Stuart Black	Christopher Barry	Stuart Walker
BB	THE WAR MACHINES	Ian Stuart Black (Kit Pedler)	Michael Ferguson	Raymond London
CC	THE SMUGGLERS	Brian Hayles	Julia Smith	Richard Hunt
DD	THE TENTH PLANET	Kit Pedler / Gerry Davis	Derek Martinus	Peter Kindred

Code	Serial title	Writers	Directors	Designers
		The Doctor played by Patrick Troughton		
EE	THE POWER OF THE DALEKS	Terry Nation (Dennis Spooner)	Christopher Barry	Derek Dodd
FF	THE HIGHLANDERS	Elwyn Jones Gerry Davis	Hugh David	Geoffrey Kirkland
GG	THE UNDERWATER MENACE	Geoffrey Orme	Julia Smith	Jack Robinson
HH	THE MOONBASE	Kit Pedler	Morris Barry	Colin Shaw
JJ	THE MACRA TERROR	Ian Stuart Black	John Davies	Kenneth Sharp
KK	THE FACELESS ONES	David Ellis Malcolm Hulke	Gerry Mill	Geoffrey Kirkland
		Script-Editors: Gerry Davis and Peter Bryant		
LL	THE EVIL OF THE DALEKS	David Whitaker	Derek Martinus	Chris Thompson
		Produced by Peter Bryant **Script-Editor: Victor Pemberton**		
MM	THE TOMB OF THE CYBERMEN	Kit Pedler Gerry Davis	Morris Barry	Martin Johnson
		Produced by Innes Lloyd **Script-Editor: Peter Bryant**		
NN	THE ABOMINABLE SNOWMEN	Mervyn Haisman Henry Lincoln	Gerald Blake	Malcolm Middleton
OO	THE ICE WARRIORS	Brian Hayles	Derek Martinus	Jeremy Davies
PP	THE ENEMY OF THE WORLD	David Whitaker	Barry Letts	Christopher Pemsel

Produced by Peter Bryant
Script-Editor: Derrick Sherwin

QQ	THE WEB OF FEAR	Mervyn Haisman Henry Lincoln	Douglas Camfield	David Myerscough-Jones
RR	FURY FROM THE DEEP	Victor Pemberton	Hugh David	Peter Kindred
SS	THE WHEEL IN SPACE	David Whitaker (Kit Pedler)	Tristan de Vere Cole	Derek Dodd
TT	THE DOMINATORS	Mervyn Haisman Henry Lincoln	Morris Barry	Barry Newbery
UU	THE MIND ROBBER	Peter Ling	David Maloney	Evan Hercules

Script-Editor: Terrance Dicks

VV	THE INVASION	Derrick Sherwin (Kit Pedler)	Douglas Camfield	Richard Hunt
WW	THE KROTONS	Robert Holmes	David Maloney	Raymond London
XX	THE SEEDS OF DEATH	Brian Hayles	Michael Ferguson	Paul Allen
YY	THE SPACE PIRATES	Robert Holmes	Michael Hart	Ian Watson

Produced by Derrick Sherwin

ZZ	THE WAR GAMES	Malcolm Hulke Terrance Dicks	David Maloney	Roger Cheveley

The Doctor played by Jon Pertwee

AAA	SPEARHEAD FROM SPACE	Robert Holmes	Derek Martinus	Paul Allen

Code	Serial title	Writers	Directors	Designers
		Produced by Barry Letts		
BBB	DR WHO & THE SILURIANS	Malcolm Hulke	Timothy Combe	Barry Newbery
CCC	THE AMBASSADORS OF DEATH	David Whitaker (Malcolm Hulke)	Michael Ferguson	David Myerscough-Jones
DDD	INFERNO	Don Houghton	Douglas Camfield / Barry Letts	Jeremy Davies
EEE	TERROR OF THE AUTONS	Robert Holmes	Barry Letts	Ian Watson
FFF	THE MIND OF EVIL	Don Houghton	Timothy Combe	Raymond London
GGG	THE CLAWS OF AXOS	Bob Baker / Dave Martin	Michael Ferguson	Kenneth Sharp
HHH	COLONY IN SPACE	Malcolm Hulke	Michael Briant	Tim Gleeson
JJJ	THE DAEMONS	Robert Sloman / Barry Letts	Christopher Barry	Roger Ford
KKK	THE DAY OF THE DALEKS	Louis Marks	Paul Bernard	David Myerscough-Jones
MMM	THE CURSE OF PELADON	Brian Hayles	Lennie Mayne	Gloria Clayton
LLL	THE SEA DEVILS	Malcolm Hulke	Michael Briant	Tony Snoaden
NNN	THE MUTANTS	Bob Baker / Dave Martin	Christopher Barry	Jeremy Bear
OOO	THE TIME MONSTER	Robert Sloman	Paul Bernard	Tim Gleeson
RRR	THE THREE DOCTORS	Bob Baker / Dave Martin	Lennie Mayne	Roger Liminton
PPP	CARNIVAL OF MONSTERS	Robert Holmes	Barry Letts	Roger Liminton
QQQ	FRONTIER IN SPACE	Malcolm Hulke	Paul Bernard	Cynthia Kljuco
SSS	PLANET OF THE DALEKS	Terry Nation	David Maloney / Paul Bernard	John Hurst
TTT	THE GREEN DEATH	Robert Sloman	Michael Briant	John Burrowes
UUU	THE TIME WARRIOR	Robert Holmes	Alan Bromly	Keith Cheetham

WWW	INVASION OF THE DINOSAURS	Malcolm Hulke	Paddy Russell	Richard Morris
XXX	DEATH TO THE DALEKS	Terry Nation	Michael Briant	Colin Green
YYY	THE MONSTER OF PELADON	Brian Hayles	Lennie Mayne	Gloria Clayton
ZZZ	PLANET OF THE SPIDERS	Robert Sloman	Barry Letts	Rochelle Selwyn

The Doctor played by Tom Baker

Script-Editor: Robert Holmes

4A	ROBOT	Terrance Dicks	Christopher Barry	Ian Rawnsley

Produced by Philip Hinchcliffe

4C	THE ARK IN SPACE	Robert Holmes	Rodney Bennett	Roger Murray-Leach
4B	THE SONTARAN EXPERIMENT	Bob Baker Dave Martin	Rodney Bennett	Roger Murray-Leach
4E	GENESIS OF THE DALEKS	Terry Nation	David Maloney	David Spode
4D	REVENGE OF THE CYBERMEN	Gerry Davis	Michael E. Briant	Roger Murray-Leach
4F	TERROR OF THE ZYGONS	Robert Banks Stewart	Douglas Camfield	Nigel Curzon
4H	PLANET OF EVIL	Louis Marks	David Maloney	Roger Murray-Leach
4G	PYRAMIDS OF MARS	Robert Holmes Lewis Greifer	Paddy Russell	Christine Ruscoe
4J	THE ANDROID INVASION	Terry Nation	Barry Letts	Philip Lindley
4K	THE BRAIN OF MORBIUS	Terrance Dicks	Christopher Barry	Barry Newbery
4L	THE SEEDS OF DOOM	Robert Banks Stewart	Douglas Camfield	Roger Murray-Leach Jeremy Bear
4M	THE MASQUE OF MANDRAGORA	Louis Marks	Rodney Bennett	Barry Newbery
4N	THE HAND OF FEAR	Bob Baker Dave Martin	Lennie Mayne	Christine Ruscoe
4P	THE DEADLY ASSASSIN	Robert Holmes	David Maloney	Roger Murray-Leach
4Q	FACE OF EVIL	Chris Boucher	Pennant Roberts	Austin Ruddy
4R	THE ROBOTS OF DEATH	Chris Boucher	Michael E. Briant	Kenneth Sharp
4S	THE TALONS OF WENG-CHIANG	Robert Holmes	David Maloney	Roger Murray-Leach

Code	Serial title	Writers	Directors	Designers
		Produced by Graham Williams		
4V	HORROR OF FANG ROCK	Terrance Dicks	Paddy Russell	Paul Allen
4T	THE INVISIBLE ENEMY	Bob Baker Dave Martin	Derrick Goodwin	Barry Newbery
4X	IMAGE OF THE FENDAHL	Chris Boucher	George Spenton-Foster	Anna Ridley
		Script-Editor: Anthony Read		
4W	THE SUN MAKERS	Robert Holmes	Pennant Roberts	Tony Snoaden
4Y	UNDERWORLD	Bob Baker Dave Martin	Norman Stewart	Dick Coles
4Z	THE INVASION OF TIME	Anthony Read Graham Williams	Gerald Blake	Barbara Gosnold
5A	THE RIBOS OPERATION	Robert Holmes	George Spenton-Foster	Ken Ledsham
5B	THE PIRATE PLANET	Douglas Adams	Pennant Roberts	Jon Pusey
5C	THE STONES OF BLOOD	David Fisher	Darrol Blake	John Stout
5D	THE ANDROIDS OF TARA	David Fisher	Michael Hayes	Valerie Warrender
5E	THE POWER OF KROLL	Robert Holmes	Norman Stewart	Don Giles
5F	THE ARMAGEDDON FACTOR	Bob Baker Dave Martin	Michael Hayes	Richard McManan-Smith
		Script-Editor: Douglas Adams		
5J	DESTINY OF THE DALEKS	Terry Nation	Ken Grieve	Ken Ledsham
5H	CITY OF DEATH	Douglas Adams Graham Williams	Michael Hayes	Richard McManan-Smith
5G	THE CREATURE FROM THE PIT	David Fisher	Christopher Barry	Valerie Warrender

Code	Title	Writer	Director	Designer
5K	NIGHTMARE OF EDEN	Bob Baker	Alan Bromly / Graham Williams	Roger Cann
5L	THE HORNS OF NIMON	Anthony Read	Kenny McBain	Graeme Story

Produced by John Nathan-Turner
Executive Producer: Barry Letts
Script-Editor: Christopher H. Bidmead

Code	Title	Writer	Director	Designer
5N	THE LEISURE HIVE	David Fisher	Lovett Bickford	Tom Yardley-Jones
5Q	MEGLOS	John Flanagan / Andrew McCulloch	Terrence Dudley	Philip Lindley
5R	FULL CIRCLE	Andrew Smith	Peter Grimwade	Janet Budden
5P	STATE OF DECAY	Terrance Dicks	Peter Moffatt	Christine Ruscoe
5S	WARRIORS' GATE	Steve Gallagher	Paul Joyce	Graeme Story
5T	THE KEEPER OF TRAKEN	Johnny Byrne	John Black	Tony Burrough
5V	LOGOPOLIS	Christopher H. Bidmead	Peter Grimwade	Malcolm Thornton

The Doctor played by Peter Davison
Produced by John Nathan-Turner
Script-Editor: Eric Saward

Code	Title	Writer	Director	Designer
5Z	CASTROVALVA	Christopher H. Bidmead	Fiona Cumming	Janet Budden

Script-Editor: Antony Root

Code	Title	Writer	Director	Designer
5W	FOUR TO DOOMSDAY	Terence Dudley	John Black	Tony Burrough

Script-Editor: Eric Saward

Code	Title	Writer	Director	Designer
5Y	KINDA	Christopher Bailey	Peter Grimwade	Malcolm Thornton

Script-Editor: Antony Root

Code	Title	Writer	Director	Designer
5X	THE VISITATION	Eric Saward	Peter Moffatt	Ken Starkey

Code	Serial title	Writers	Directors	Designers
		Script-Editor: Eric Saward		
6A	BLACK ORCHID	Terence Dudley	Ron Jones	Tony Burrough
6B	EARTHSHOCK	Eric Saward	Peter Grimwade	Bernard Lloyd-Jones
6C	TIME-FLIGHT	Peter Grimwade	Ron Jones	Richard McManan-Smith
6E	ARC OF INFINITY	Johnny Byrne	Ron Jones	Marjorie Pratt
6D	SNAKEDANCE	Christopher Bailey	Fiona Cumming	Jan Spoczynski
6F	MAWDRYN UNDEAD	Peter Grimwade	Peter Moffatt	Stephen Scott
6G	TERMINUS	Steve Gallagher	Mary Ridge	Dick Coles
6H	ENLIGHTENMENT	Barbara Clegg	Fiona Cumming	Colin Green
6J	THE KING'S DEMONS	Terence Dudley	Tony Virgo	Ken Ledsham
6K	THE FIVE DOCTORS	Terrance Dicks	Peter Moffatt	Malcolm Thornton

Appendix II

Further Reading on *Doctor Who*

Peter Haining, *Twenty Years of Doctor Who*, W. H. Allen, 1983.

Mark Harris, *The Doctor Who Technical Manual*, Severn House, 1983.

Terrance Dicks and Malcolm Hulke, *The Making of Doctor Who*, W. H. Allen, 1980.

Alan Road, *Doctor Who — The Making of a Television Series*, André Deutsch, 1982.

Graham Rickard, *A Day With A TV Producer*, Wayland, 1980.

Doctor Who Monthly, Marvel Comics.

The British Film Institute hopes to be able to make available a few episodes of *Doctor Who* for hire by teachers who intend to teach about *Doctor Who* in their Television Studies lessons. Any teachers wishing for more information about these programmes and their support documentation should contact the BFI Film and Video Library, 81 Dean Street, London W1V 6AA.

Notes and References

Except where otherwise indicated by footnotes, all quotations from *Doctor Who* professionals and artists are from interviews conducted by John Tulloch between August 1981 and February 1982.

Introduction

1. Cf. Colin MacCabe, 'Realism and the cinema: notes on some Brechtian theses', *Screen*, vol. 15, no. 2, Summer 1974.
2. John Fiske, '*Doctor Who*: ideology and the reading of a popular narrative text', *Australian Journal of Screen Theory*, nos 14–15, 1983.

Chapter 1 Mystery: Television Discourse and Institution

1. BBC Audience Research figures (1979, Analysis 23) indicate the following class breakdown for *Doctor Who* (figures in brackets indicating percentage UK class composition):

   Social Grade A   =   3.7%   (6%)
   Social Grade B   = 22.8% (24%)
   (*Middle Class*) = 26.5% (30%)

   Social Grade CX = 45.7% (40%)
   Social Grade CY = 27.8% (30%)
   (*Working Class*) = 73.5% (70%)

   Australian Broadcasting Commission qualitative audience research findings based on percentage of viewing population 'familiar' with the programme who classify it as either 'particularly enjoy' or 'like' (and defining class rather loosely via social status of residential area) reveals:

   High status   = 26% appreciate
   Middle status = 29% appreciate
   Low status   = 23% appreciate

These figures can be compared with those for *Buck Rogers* in the same month (September 1982, Melbourne) of High = 17%, Middle = 26%, Low = 38%, suggesting that whereas *Doctor Who* is liked generally across classes, *Buck Rogers* has a strong popularity base in the working class. As regards sex of audience, the BBC figures showed 51.5% male (48.5%) and 48.5% female (51.5%)-watchers.

2. Edna Boling, 'Tuning up *Doctor Who*', *Canberra Times*, 10 August 1980, p. 9.

3. *The Guardian*, 4 January 1982, p. 10.

4. Richard Collins, *Television News* (London: British Film Institute, 1976), p. 35.

5. Sarah Hayes, 'The mind stretching and the macabre', *The Times Literary Supplement*, 20 November 1981, p. 1361.

6. Nigel Robinson, *Time Out*, 27 November — 3 December 1981, p. 94.

7. So that Terrance Dicks could speak of the 'fairly lean and economic' Simenon-style of his *Doctor Who* books and speak with satisfaction of their use with slow readers in schools, whereas in contrast Madame Tussauds strongly emphasised the 'fear and horror' aspect in its *Doctor Who* exhibition.

8. Christine Geraghty, 'The continuous serial — a definition', in Richard Dyer *et al.*, *Coronation Street* (London: British Film Institute, 1981), p. 10.

9. Marion Jordan, 'Realism and convention', in Dyer *et al.*, *Coronation Street*, p. 35.

10. Or actually OHO changing immediately to WHO.

11. Stephen Heath & Gillian Skirrow, 'Television, a world in action', *Screen*, vol. 18 no. 2, Summer 1977, p. 19.

12. Ibid., p. 57.

13. Ibid., p. 56.

14. Patrick Parrinder, *Science Fiction: its criticism and teaching* (London: Methuen, 1980), pp. 120—1.

15. Cf. the time machine in the inventor's cluttered laboratory and guest-infested home in Wells's *The Time Machine*.

16. Cf. Gill Davies on Hollywood narrative in 'Teaching about narrative', *Screen Education*, 29, Winter 1978/9, p. 61.

17. Richard Paterson & John Stewart, ' "Street" life' in Dyer *et al.*, (1981), p. 98.

18. See John Tulloch, *Legends on the screen: the narrative film in Australia, 1919—1929* (Sydney: Currency/Australian Film Institute 1981), p. 380.

19. The former is then further codified to differentiate Susan from the Doctor. Susan's ECU's in the opening sequences are shot downward, from the teachers' 'superior' eyeline, emphasising the precocious mystery of a child who knows more than her teachers. The camera angle for the Doctor's ECU's are in contrast upwards, signifying his ominous and arrogant superiority to the teachers (who are generally shot at eyeline and in 2-shot or MCU).

20. Stuart Hall, 'The determination of news photographs', in Stanley
    Cohen and Jock Young (eds) *The Manufacture of News: deviance,
    social problems and the mass media* (London: Constable, 1973),
    p. 178, and Charlotte Brunsdon and David Morley, *Everyday
    Television: 'Nationwide'* (London: British Film Institute 1978),
    pp. 64–5.
21. William Russell was well known on British and US television as the
    star of *Sir Lancelot*.
22. Heath & Skirrow, 'Television, a world in action', p. 15.
23. Tony Skillen, personal communication.
24. Raymond Williams, *Television: Technology and Cultural Form*
    (London: Fontana, 1974), p. 33.
25. Ibid., p. 39.
26. Krishnan Kumar, 'Holding the middle ground: the BBC, the public
    and the professional broadcaster', in James Curran, Michael Gure-
    vitch & Janet Woollacott, *Mass Communication and Society*
    (London, Arnold 1977), p. 232.
27. Ibid., p. 236.
28. Ibid., p. 237.
29. John Tulloch, *Australian Cinema: Industry, Narrative and Meaning*
    (Sydney: Allen & Unwin, 1982), pp. 76–7.
30. Michael Tracey, *The Production of Political Television* (London:
    Routledge, 1977), p. 84.
31. Kumar, 'Holding the middle ground', p. 241.
32. Tracey, *The Production of Political Television*, p. 87, This same
    entertainment/education scenario (this time for 'country folk') also
    informed the BBC's long-running radio series, *The Archers*.
33. Whereas shows like *William Tell* could afford to spend a lot on the
    initial set up, after which it used the same sets, props and costumes
    week after week, *Doctor Who*, moving to a different location every
    few weeks, had to rely on six fairly cheap sets per story, with no
    location shooting in the first season at all. This, *Doctor Who
    Monthly* (no. 56) points out, led to the vital emphasis on good,
    dramatic scripting.
34. 'Marco Polo' contained a four minute monologue on the history of
    the Hashashin murder cult which teachers voiced their praise about.
35. Interview with Bruce Horsefield, 25 September, 1979.
36. Jeremy Bentham, 'The Daleks', *Doctor Who: An Adventure in
    Space and Time* (London: Cybermark), Series B, p. 7.
37. This 'scientific blue print' tradition of SF which was a feature of
    The Eagle generally, as well as being inserted in 'Dan Dare', derives
    from the early, optimistic phase of popular SF when, as Parrinder
    (1980) notes, 'Gernsback and his successors offered a Verne-like
    combination of boyish adventures with nuts, bolts and blueprints'
    (p. 13). This optimism was reflected in 'Dan Dare' graphic designer
    Frank Hampson's belief that 'prognostications about technology
    were too gloomy' after the Second World War. 'Attitudes were so
    pessimistic, with the Bomb, and the Cold War, and rationing at the

front of every mind. I wanted to give hope for the future, to show that rockets and science in general could reveal new worlds, new opportunities.' *Dan Dare, Pilot of the Future in 'The Man From Nowhere'* (Hendrik-Ido-Ambacht: Dragon, 1979), introduction.

38. Ibid., 'Dan Dare and Frank Hampson: Space Fleet Reviewed'.
39. Jeremy Bentham, *Amazing Journeys* (London: Doctor Who Appreciation Society, 1979), p. 18.
40. *Dan Dare, Pilot of the Future* (1979), foreword by Kit Pedler. There was also a relationship between the Mekon and the Daleks who, as Jeremy Bentham has pointed out, in their design board form resembled 'a cross between Dan Dare's Mekon and a skinned, bloated animal'.
41. David Morse, *Perspectives on Romanticism: a transformational analysis* (London: Macmillan, 1981), pp. 143–4.
42. Ibid., p. 173.
43. Ibid., p. 152.
44. Pedler, foreword in *Dan Dare, Pilot of the Future*.
45. In the pilot episode, made because BBC executives wanted to check the viability of a potential costly series, Hartnell's Doctor was more malign and cantankerous. This was toned down at the executives' request for family viewing.
46. In 'Dan Dare: the Red Moon Mystery' – see issue of 18 April, 1952.
47. *The Eagle*, 21 April, 1950, p. 11.
48. *The Eagle*, 29 May, 1953, p. 6.
49. *The Eagle*, 24 August, 1951.
50. Parrinder, *Science Fiction: its criticism and teaching*, p. 30.
51. 'Dan Dare and Frank Hampson' (1979).
52. *The Eagle*, 29 May, 1953, p. 11.
53. Kumar, 'Holding the middleground', p. 245.
54. Ibid., p. 246.
55. Ibid., p. 247.
56. This was equally true of the Hartnell years. In 'Reign of Terror' (1964), the Doctor's position is that of an emphatic 'moderate' between the aristocrats and the more extreme revolutionaries.
57. See the comments of Australian television professionals cited in Chapter 2.
58. BBC Audience Research, Analysis 23, 1979.
59. Shaun Sutton, *The Largest Theatre in the World* (London: BBC, 1981), p. 8.
60. Ibid., p. 7.
61. Ibid., p. 12.
62. Ibid., p. 8.

Chapter 2 Regeneration: Narrative Similarity and Difference

1. Bentham, *Amazing Journeys*, p. 35.
2. Bentham's interpretation, ibid., p. 35.

3. These were apparently unknown to Troughton and gradually tapered, story by story, by the costume designers to reduce the 'clown' effect as his 'overtly maniacal style ... gave way to a gentler, more teasing characterisation', *Doctor Who Monthly*, no. 55, p. 29.

4. Ibid.

5. Troughton was acting in *The Viking Queen* when chosen to play the Doctor and since then he has played a variety of television (*The Wives of Henry VIII, Jenny, Space 1999, The Famous Five, The Sweeney, Treasure Island, All Creatures Great and Small*, etc.) and film (*Scars of Dracula, Sinbad and the Eye of the Tiger, The Omen*) character roles.

6. Elizabeth Burns, *Theatricality: a study of convention in the theatre and in social life* (London: Longman, 1972), p. 155.

7. Letter to author, 5 January 1982.

8. Manuel Alvarado & Edward Buscombe, *Hazell: the making of a TV series* (London: Latimer/British Film Institute, 1978).

9. Quoted from the MacTaggart Lecture given by Jeremy Isaacs at the 1979 Edinburgh International Television Festival.

10. Burns, *Theatricality*, p. 151.

11. Dyer, *et al.*, *Coronation Street*, p. 7.

12. Burns, *Theatricality*, p. 106.

13. Sheila Johnston '*Crossroads*: approaches to popular television fiction' paper given at B.F.I. Summer School, 1981, p. 10.

14. Burns, *Theatricality*, p. 178.

15. The *Radio Times Doctor Who* 10th Anniversary Special Issue (London: BBC, 1973), p. 6.

16. J. Mukařovský, 'An attempt at a structural analysis of a dramatic figure', in John Burbank and Peter Steiner, *Structure, Sign and Function: Selected Essays by Jan Mukařovský* (New Haven: Yale U.P., 1978), pp. 174–5.

17. According to theorists of narrative like Todorov and Propp, classical narratives begin with an initial situation of equilibrium and 'fullness' ('the king had a beautiful daughter') which is disturbed by a 'lack' ('the dragon kidnapped the king's daughter') that must be redressed ('the prince killed the dragon') before the final fulfilment or 'plenitude' of the narrative ('the prince married the king's daughter'). For an elaboration of the implications of this see Tulloch, *Australian Cinema*, ch. 6.

18. Jim Kitses, *Horizons West* (London: Thames & Hudson, 1969), ch. 1.

19. Henry Nash Smith, *Virgin Land* (New York: Random House, 1957).

20. In popular literary SF, Venus, in a modified version of the garden/desert opposition, may conventionally signify steaming 'African' tropics and Mars the 'Wild West', while Earth itself may be an overcrowded, over-urbanised, polluted place from which to escape and 'go native'. See Paul A. Carter, *The Creation of Tomorrow* (New York: Columbia U.P., 1977), p. 84. But this has not been a familiar feature of film SF.

21. The Tardis, in fact, is telepathically attuned to the Doctor's mind.
22. Bentham, *Amazing Journeys*, p. 36.
23. 'Who's Who', *Radio Times*, 24 March, 1979, p. 10.
24. Ibid.
25. Though John Nathan-Turner insisted that Peter Davison was comic as well as serious, the overwhelmingly predominant response in our audience surveys was that the programme had lost much of its 'humour' after Baker.
26. Richard Dyer, *Stars* London, BFI, 1979, pp. 72 ff) discusses the way in which the representations of a star in various media texts constitute a star's 'image career'. These complex, sometimes contradictory representations construct a preferred reading (a star-as-text) that we know as recognisably 'Jane Fonda' in fictional (e.g. film) and 'factual' (e.g. televised public rallies) texts, and it is this rather than any actual person, Jane Fonda, that inhabits her various roles.
27. According to Saussure the meaning of a sign is largely determined by its relationship to other signs. There are two types of relationship: syntagmatic and paradigmatic. Syntagmatic relationships are rules of *combination*: the grammatical rules for instance which allow the linear statement, 'Jane shut the window'; or the vestimentary code which determines the wearing of shoes, socks, trousers and shirt, etc.; or the conventional rules of dining which place the meat course after soup and before pudding, etc. Hence a restaurant menu describes a 'narrative' of eating, beginning with hors d'oeuvres and ending with cheese and/or fruit. Each of these syntagmatic relationships describes a linear relationship, of things which combine at the same time with other things to compose a complete 'text'. In contrast, paradigmatic (or metaphoric) relationships are rules of *selection*: 'Jane' could be replaced by 'Jack', 'shut' by 'banged'; trousers may be selected from a range of colours, fabrics and styles, may be dirty or clean etc.; the main course of a menu offers choices of meat or fish, etc. Here the meaning of the chosen unit is determined mainly in terms of the units which are not selected ('banging' the window rather than 'closing' it), whereas in a syntagmatic relationship meaning is mainly determined by the unit's relationship with other units in the syntagm (a diner who asks for his pudding before his soup will 'signify' in a certain way).
28. F. Dostoyevskii, *The Brothers Karamazov* (Harmondsworth: Penguin, 1958), p. 287.
29. Orrin E. Klapp, 'Heroes, villains and fools as agents of social control', *American Sociological Review*, vol. 19, no. 1 (1954), pp. 56–62.
30. Jerry Palmer, 'Thrillers: the deviant behind the consensus', in I. Taylor & L. Taylor, *Politics and Deviance* (Harmondsworth: Penguin, 1973), pp. 138–56.
31. John Tulloch, 'Cinema and social control: the John Wayne syn-

drome', in *Conflict and Control in the Cinema* (Melbourne: Macmillan, 1977), pp. 253—74.

32. Geoff Hurd, *'The Sweeney* — contradiction and coherence', *Screen Education*, no. 20 (Autumn 1976), p. 51.
33. J. H. Westergaard, 'The myth of classlessness', cited in Hurd, ibid., p. 51.
34. Johnston, *'Crossroads'*, p. 9.
35. Ibid., p. 14.
36. Director Peter Grimwade's description of writer Chris Bailey's 'Kinda'.
37. Johnston, *'Crossroads'*, p. 12.
38. Geraghty, 'The Continuous Serial', p. 17.
39. In Australia the ABC transmits *Doctor Who* stripped across Monday to Thursday at 6.30 p.m. for several months of most years. This leads to several repeats over the years of any one story.
40. Audience group of television professionals interviewed by Liz Stone, Sydney, 29 June 1981.
41. The problems implicit in this distinction between adult and child responses will be examined in another book.
42. Writer Chris Bailey was attempting an interiorised (Jungian) and culture-based notion of villainy to replace the conventional 'chase' of hero and villain. Each relevant character was to reveal its own culturally repressed 'shadow'. For Tegan this was to be her sexuality. Janet Fielding's initial 'sensuous' performance in rehearsal, however, was dismissed by director Peter Grimwade as 'too Bette Davis', and the sexual theme was toned right down. See Chapter 6.
43. For a discussion of contrary and contradictory relations at the level of form of content, see A. J. Greimas & F. Rastier, 'The Interaction of Semiotic Constraints', *Yale French Studies*, no. 41 (1968), pp. 86—105. For the distinction between the levels of analysis of (a) the imminent narrative structure where 'signification is *indifferent* to the modes of its manifestation' and (b) the linguistic structures of narrative, see A. J. Greimas, 'Elements of a Narrative Grammar', *Diacritics*, March 1977, pp. 23—40.
44. Frederic Jameson, *The Prison House of Language* (Princeton U.P., 1972), pp. 67—8.
45. Dostoyevskii, *The Brothers Karamazov*, pp. 298—9.
46. Ibid., p. 164.
47. A. Fletcher, *Allegory: the theory of a symbolic mode* (Ithaca: Cornell U.P., 1964).
48. *Doctor Who Monthly*, no. 50, p. 27.
49. Phillip Drummond, 'Structural and narrative constraints and strategies in *The Sweeney*', *Screen Education*, no. 20 (Autumn 1976), p. 24.

Chapter 3 Establishment: Science Fiction and Fantasy

1. Sean Hogben, 'Dr Who . . . Adventure With Time to Spare', *TV Week*, 25 September, 1982, p. 47.
2. *Doctor Who Monthly*, no. 55, p. 47.
3. Ibid., p. 28.
4. *Doctor Who Monthly*, no. 49, p. 34.
5. See front page story in BBC Staff Journal, *Ariel*, 20 January, 1982.
6. Marc Angenot, 'The absent paradigm: an introduction to the semiotics of science fiction', *Science Fiction Studies*, vol. 6 (1979), p. 10.
7. Ibid.
8. For analyses of the discourses of knowledge presented by TV quiz shows see John Tulloch, 'TV Quiz Shows and the concept of knowledge' *Screen Education*, no. 19 (Summer 1976), pp. 3–13, and John Fiske, 'TV Quiz Shows and the purchase of Cultural Capital', *Australian Journal of Screen Theory*, no. 13, pp. 1–16.
9. Paul Mount, 'The Dalek invasion of Earth', *Doctor Who: An Adventure in Space and Time* (London: Cybermark), Serial K, p. 5.
10. Angenot, 'The Absent Paradigm', p. 10.
11. Ursula K. Le Guin, *The Word For World Is Forest* (London: Panther, 1980), pp. 12–13.
12. In the transmitted television production some of the 'class' speeches were toned down and the reference to the General Strike omitted.
13. Malcolm Hulke, *Doctor Who and the Green Death* (London: Target, 1975), p. 14.
14. Le Guin, *The Word for World is Forest*, p. 52.
15. Ibid., p. 33.
16. Ibid., p. 36.
17. Ibid., p. 41.
18. Ibid., p. 10.
19. Angenot, 'The absent paradigm', p. 12.
20. Ibid., p. 16.
21. *Doctor Who Monthly*, Winter Special 1981, p. 33.
22. Darko Suvin, 'The state of the art in science fiction theory: determining and delimiting the genre', *Science Fiction Studies*, vol. 6, pt. 1 (1979), p. 36.
23. Ibid., p. 37.
24. Ibid.
25. Ibid.
26. Ibid.
27. Ibid., p. 38.
28. Georg Lukács, *The Historical Novel* (London, Peregrine 1969) pp. 218 ff.
29. Marc Angenot & Darko Suvin, 'Not only but also: reflections on cognition and ideology in Science Fiction and SF criticism', *Science Fiction Studies*, vol. 6, pt. 2 (1979), p. 169.

30. We are following here the distinctions made by Terry Lovell between empiricism, realism and conventionalism in *Pictures of Reality: Aesthetics, Politics and Pleasure* (London: British Film Institute, 1980).
31. Angenot & Suvin, 'Not only but also', pp. 170—1.
32. Dyer *et al.*, *Coronation Street*, p. 6.
33. Angenot & Suvin, 'Not only but also', pp. 171—2.
34. Suvin, 'The state of the art in science fiction theory', p. 38.
35. Tzvetan Todorov, *The Fantastic: a structural approach to a literary genre* (Ithaca: Cornell U.P., 1975).
36. Suvin, 'The state of the art in science fiction theory, p. 33.
37. Angenot & Suvin, 'Not only but also', p. 177.
38. We shall take up this issue of the 'semiotic thickness' of performed texts in Chapter 6.
39. Patrick Parrinder, *H. G. Wells* (Edinburgh: Oliver & Boyd, 1970), p. 4.
40. For an analysis of Chekhov's work in terms of his scientific education and evolutionist world view, see John Tulloch, *Chekhov: a structuralist study* (London: Macmillan, 1980).
41. H. G. Wells, *Anticipations* (London: Chapman & Hall, 1902), p. 86.
42. Ibid., p. 173.
43. Ibid., p. 97.
44. Ibid., p. 141.
45. Darko Suvin, *Metamorphoses of science fiction: on the poetics and history of a literary genre* (New Haven: Yale U.P., 1979), p. 233.
46. Ibid., p. 235.
47. Wells, *Anticipations*, p. 317.
48. J. Bentham, 'The Daleks', *Doctor Who: An Adventure in Space and Time* (London: Cybermark), Serial B, p. 7.
49. Harry Levin, 'Science and Fiction', in George E. Slusser, George R. Guffey & Mark Rose, *Bridges to Science Fiction* (Carbondale: Southern Illinois U.P., 1980), p. 6.
50. Rosemary Jackson, *Fantasy: the literature of subversion* (London: Methuen, 1981), p. 58.
51. Ibid.
52. Ibid., p. 59.
53. Throughout this text we have given the date of the first episode of a story as its year of transmission. However, since 'The Three Doctors' actually began on the second last day of 1972 running through to 20 January 1973 (the tenth anniversary year) we have given the latter as its date.
54. Jackson, *Fantasy: the literature of subversion*, p. 49.
55. Ibid., p. 56.
56. *Doctor Who Monthly*, no. 56, p. 24.
57. In his opening story, the Doctor, in an act of pure selfishness, seeks to escape to the Tardis by killing a badly wounded primitive with a stone, but is restrained by Ian.

58. Jackson, *Fantasy: the literature of subversion*, p. 37.
59. Cited in Stephen Potts, 'Dialogues concerning human understanding: empirical views of God from Locke to Lem', in Slusser *et al.* (1980), p. 42.
60. Ibid.
61. There is another example in 'The Invisible Enemy' (1977), where the virus of the nucleus of the swarm which intends to take over humankind tells the Doctor, 'Consider the human species. They send hordes of settlers across space to breed, multiply, conquer and dominate. We have as much right to conquer you as you have to strike out across the stars.' The Doctor's reply typically displaces human guilt: 'But you intend to dominate *both* worlds, the micro and the macrocosm.'
62. Potts, 'Dialogues concerning human understanding', pp. 51–2.
63. Rick Altman (ed), *Genre: The Musical* (London: Routledge, 1981), p. 200.
64. Michel Foucault, *The Order of Things: an archaeology of the human sciences* (London: Tavistock, 1970), p. 120.
65. Morse, *Perspectives in Romanticism*, p. 36.
66. Ibid., p. 45.
67. Ibid., p. 58.
68. Ibid., p. 209.
69. Jackson, *Fantasy: the literature of subversion*, p. 65.
70. Walter Hirsch, 'The image of the scientist in science fiction: a content analysis', *American Journal of Sociology*, vol. 63, no. 5 (1958), pp. 506–12.
71. Carter, *The Creation of Tomorrow*.
72. Wells belonged to that broad intellectual élite who adhered to a Left Romanticism in the early years of this century – see Lovell, *Pictures of Reality*, p. 74.

Chapter 4 Send-up: Authorship and Organisation

1. On this issue see S. Hall, I. Connell and L. Curti, 'The unity of current affairs TV', *Working Papers in Cultural Studies*, no. 9 (1976), pp. 51–94; Peter Golding, 'Media Professionalism in the Third World', in Curran *et al.* (1977), pp. 291–308. For an analysis of professional ideology in relation to fictional forms, see Tulloch, *Australian Cinema*, pp. 101–12.
2. Bentham, *Amazing Journeys*, p. 28.
3. The term is Barthes' (*S/Z*, London, Jonathan Cape 1975, p. 93), suggesting the build up of narrative characterisation via expansion and repetition of meanings – for an elaboration see Tulloch (1982), *Australian Cinema*, p. 236.
4. See John Tulloch, 'Genetic structuralism and the cinema – a look at Fritz Lang's *Metropolis*', *Australian Journal of Screen Theory*, no. 1 (1976), p. 15.

5. Paul Mount, 'The Chase', *Doctor Who: an adventure in space and time* (London: Cybermark), Serial R, p. 5.
6. *Doctor Who Monthly*, no. 56, p. 22.
7. Ibid., p. 23.
8. Mount, 'The Romans', *Doctor Who: an adventure in space and time*, pp. 5–6.
9. Ibid., p. 10.
10. *Doctor Who Monthly*, no. 56, p. 23.
11. Cited in Michael Tracey & David Morrison, *Whitehouse* (London: Macmillan, 1979), p. 85. Whitehouse's organisation was by far the most potent pressure group harrying *Doctor Who*, although there were complaints from Scotland Yard about an auton policeman in 'Terror of the Autons' (1971) and from societies concerned with the representation of bats over the vampire story 'State of Decay' (1981). According to Barry Letts, 'Terror of the Autons' elicited a lot of mail from parents complaining that their children were frightened to take their teddy bears to bed with them (the story featured a troll doll which came to life and strangled people when it got warm), and also critical leading articles in *The Daily Express* and *The Daily Telegraph*. 'For a while we were watched very carefully right up the hierarchy up to the Managing Director of Television. Where we had gone wrong, quite clearly, was making the horror implicit in things which were people's everyday life – in the children's everyday life.'
12. There is some debate as to whether K-9 was a spin-off from *Star Wars*' domesticated robots. John Nathan-Turner, production unit manager in the Williams period, and partly responsible for K-9 becoming a regular in the series, insists that 'we were first'.
13. See Philip Thompson, *The Grotesque* (London: Methuen, 1972) & Mikhail Bakhtin, *Rabelais and His World* (Cambridge: Mass, 1968) cited in John O. Thompson (ed), *Monty Python: complete and utter theory of the grotesque* (London: British Film Institute, 1982), pp. 13–14, 17–19, 42–3.
14. Teresa L. Ebert, 'The convergence of postmodern innovative fiction and science fiction', *Poetics Today*, vol. I, no. 4 (1980), p. 93.
15. Parrinder, *Science Fiction*, p. 117.
16. Christine Brooke-Rose, *A Rhetoric of the Unreal: Studies in narrative and structure* (Cambridge: Cambridge U.P., 1981).
17. Robert Sheckley (ed), *After the Fall* (London: Sphere, 1980), p. vii.
18. *Doctor Who* director Peter Grimwade, while writing 'Earthshock' (1982) noted that since a ten-year-old child has never seen a police box, he only knows the Tardis as the Tardis – hence the astonishment of police in 'Earthshock' at seeing a Metropolitan police box in a gallery at Heathrow is implausible. 'It's not a police box anymore. People would say, "It must be the Doctor" . . . So you have got a sort of convention. You have got to pretend you are in a

world where no one knows who Doctor Who is — even though everyone knows who Doctor Who is.'

19. Possibly partly because this story (aided by a blackout of commercial TV at the time) brought in the highest audience ratings ever for the show.

20. Gary Hopkins, 'Dalek — Death by thy Name', *Doctor Who: An Adventure in Time and Space* (London: Cybermark), Serial V, p. 12.

21. As a former actor, Nathan-Turner was also concerned with the dramatic potential of actors. He complained that K-9 took an element of drama away from actors because in a high camera angle (used to get both a standing actor and K-9 in shot together) one could not see the actor's eyes, and 'eye contact and expression is what acting is all about', (*Doctor Who Monthly*, no. 51, p. 32). Symptomatically, the only aspect of continuity with the decayed Master's form which Nathan-Turner rejected for 'The Keeper of Traken' was the frightening artificial eyes. He relied instead on the actor's own.

22. Douglas Adams, *The Hitch Hiker's Guide to the Galaxy* (London: Pan, 1979), p. 55.

23. Graham Murdock, 'Authorship and Organisation', *Screen Education*, no. 35 (Summer 1980), p. 27.

24. Ibid., pp. 23—4.

25. Bentham, *Amazing Journeys*, p. 26.

26. Ibid., p. 25, 28.

27. Ibid., p. 27.

28. In fact the 'idealist' theme of minds holding the matter of the universe together is by no means new to popular SF. See for instance the discussion of Simak and Jacobi's 'The Street that Wasn't there' in Carter, *The Creation of Tomorrow*, pp. 154—5.

29. Murdock, 'Authorship and Organisation', p. 29.

30. David Morley, 'The *Nationwide* audience: a postscript', *Screen Education*, no. 39 (Summer 1981), p. 4.

31. Producers tend to talk mainly of financial determinants rather than others, as for instance Williams' comments on the restricted budget which led him to experiment with an almost entirely CSO 'set' in 'Underworld'.

32. Morley, 'The *Nationwide* audience', p. 4.

33. See Hall *et al.*, 'The unity of current affairs TV'.

34. But then the transmitted programme was a toned down version of the novel.

35. The notion of an overall semantic and syntactic textual coherence relates to the concept of a 'preferred reading' contained in a text which as Kress puts it 'realises the value-system, world knowledge, ideological system of a given discourse, and of its users'. At the same time 'a crucial factor in the reader's construction of the meaning of a text is the assignment of *relevance* to certain parts of the text . . . Relevance — though initially assigned by the speaker/

writer – may be assigned in quite different ways by the hearer/ reader'. Gunther Kress, 'Media Analysis and the Study of Discourse', *Media Information Australia*, no. 28 (May, 1983).
This issue of relevance is crucial to the process of decoding, understanding and evaluating texts, and will be the focus of another book.

36. John Tulloch, paper at 'Sociology of Literature and Drama' colloquium, University of Sydney, June 1980, a revised version of which appears as 'Dr Who: Similarity and Difference' in *Australian Journal of Screen Theory*, no. 11/12 (1982), pp. 8–24.

37. Adams was in fact finishing off the radio version of *Hitch Hiker* during the first few months of his contract with *Doctor Who*.

38. Nathan-Turner augmented his 'always on television' star Peter Davison with a list of star names to 'up-market' the show. Stratford Johns, Richard Todd, Nerys Hughes, Barbara Murray and Beryl Reid all appeared in the course of a few stories as guest stars.

39. Philip Hinchcliffe for instance argued: 'You really had to sit on Tom Baker . . . Basically I kept a firm control and my directors by and large were very strong . . . But I would have thought that had I come in as producer as Graham Williams did when Tom had been doing it for three years I would have had a terrible time trying to keep the lid on it, and I think that probably that's what happened.' Ian Levine was more blunt: 'Graham Williams was a weak producer. John Nathan-Turner walked in and said "We are not going to have any more of this slap-stick" . . . and Tom Baker was brought into line immediately.' Jeremy Bentham argued that because of the strict constraints on Williams to remove the violent element in the programme, 'he did that by concentrating the programme towards the character of the Doctor himself, this charismatic figure, which in essence gave Tom Baker a lot more control over the programme than perhaps he should have had to the extent that the actor was dictating what the director should show on the screen'.

40. Murdock, 'Authorship and Organisation', p. 28.

41. Ian Levine, for instance, rather grudgingly admitted that he 'liked "City of Death". It is almost a classic, but not quite . . . It was certainly the best in that lamentable season . . . It had a very good premise . . . but too much slap-stick, too much comedy thrown in.'

Chapter 5 Cliffhanger: Circulating Stars and Satellites

1. John Ellis, 'Star/Industry/Image' paper presented at British Film Institute 'Star Signs' Workshop, January 1981, p. 1.
2. Ibid., pp. 2–3.
3. Ibid., pp. 14–15.
4. Richard Dyer, '*A Star Is Born* and the construction of Authenticity' paper presented at BFI 'Star Signs' Workshop, January 1981, p. 2.
5. Ibid., p. 3.
6. Ibid., pp. 4–5.

7. Ibid., p. 5.
8. *The Radio Times Doctor Who* 10th Anniversary Special Issue (London: BBC, 1973), p. 7.
9. Terrance Dicks & Malcolm Hulke, *The Making of Doctor Who* (London: Target, 1976), p. 32.
10. *Radio Times* 10th Anniversary Special, p. 7.
11. Burns, *Theatricality*, p. 155.
12. *Radio Times*, 17–23 January 1981.
13. Tom Baker speaking in 'Whose Doctor Who' BBC *The Lively Arts* documentary 1976, and 'Who's Who' *Radio Times* 24 March, 1979, p. 10. However, Troughton is peeved at this claim, for in fact it was he who introduced the jelly babies.
14. Characteristically, Davison's *Radio Times* publicity authenticated his character's innocence in terms of his *own* 'innocent' insertion in the programme's history: ' "I feel that, over the years, *Doctor Who* has become less vital, no longer struggling for survival, depending on instant, miraculous solutions to problems. The suspense of 'now how is he going to get out of this tight corner?' has been missing. I want to restore that. My Doctor will be flawed . . . I want him to have a sort of reckless innocence." It was as something of an innocent that Peter Davison first made the acquaintance of the Doctor nearly eighteen years ago. He was a little lad of twelve and, for six years, tuned in regularly every Saturday to catch the wanderings of the Time Lord. And as befits a dedicated Doctor-fan, he is able to analyse and dissect with intimate knowledge the character of his four predecessors.'
15. Dyer, *Stars*, p. 72.
16. Hartnell had established a stage and film reputation for comedy and farce in the 1930s, then a 'tough' persona in films (*The Way Ahead*) and TV (*The Army Game*) in the 1940s/1950s, followed by the 'noble but pathetic' talent scout in *This Sporting Life* (1962). Baker has played a series of villains (as Rasputin, in horror stories, as Long John Silver, etc., invariably making much use of his eyes).
17. Location filming has become more rare in *Doctor Who*, as John Nathan-Turner described: 'What has been happening during the last three or four years is that the rate of inflation has been dictated at say 16 per cent, but out budgets have only been increased something like 8 per cent, or sometimes 10 per cent. So effectively we have taken a cut. Since I took over, which is eighteen months ago, we do very little filming. And if we do film, we try to stay within twenty five miles of London, which means that we don't have to spend money putting up actors and production teams. I keep campaigning to get a bit more money. Just enough to go away, because places like Black Park and Birnham Beeches get awfully repetitive. And forever one is having to insert a line like "an Earth-type planet" in order to justify typically outer-London locations. So it is a problem . . . We haven't cut it altogether. We always do about three four-part stories in the season with no filming at all. And then in

others we have less film than before, even though we don't go away.
The old rule used to be that every four-part story had five days
filming . . . We actually had five days on the last one we did, 'The
Visitation' and we got about twenty-five minutes, but that was
going some.'

18. Marianne Wex, ' "Feminine" and "Masculine": body language',
    Screen Education, no. 39 (Summer 1981), p. 54.
19. For an example in early cinema see Tulloch, *Legends on the Screen*,
    pp. 30 ff.
20. Laura Mulvey, 'Visual Pleasure and Narrative Cinema', *Screen*, vol.
    16, no. 3 (Autumn 1975), pp. 6–18.
21. *Doctor Who Monthly*, May 1981, p. 22.
22. It is arguable that Leela was successful in this respect. In the first
    Williams story, 'Horror of Fang Rock', not only was the contrast
    between Leela and the ever-screaming Adelaide humorously marked
    as a *class* contrast (Adelaide being effete and 'kept' plaything of
    the leisure class) rather than it being a 'female' trait, but also one
    of the men is described by Leela as 'frightened one'.
23. *Radio Times Doctor Who*, 10th Anniversary Special, p. 11.
24. Cited in Paul Mount, 'Vicki', in 'The Myth Makers', *Doctor Who:
    An Adventure in Space and Time* (London: Cybermark) Serial U,
    p. 7.
25. For instance Sara Kingdom, the ruthless space agent who accom-
    panied the Doctor during the twelve part 'The Daleks' Master Plan'
    (1965–6) incorporated some of the tough lady *Avengers* image.
26. This, the first entirely 'modern day' story, also introduced Dodo's
    successor Polly as a 'contemporary' mini-skirted companion.
27. See interviews with Anneke Wills (Polly), Deborah Watling (Vic-
    toria), Wendy Padbury (Zoe), Katy Manning (Jo) in *Doctor Who*
    10th Anniversary Special.
28. Group of young mothers, interviewed in Sydney by Liz Stone,
    13 July 1981.
29. *Doctor Who Monthly*, no. 51, p. 30.
30. Ibid.
31. *Doctor Who Monthly*, no. 52, p. 26.
32. *Doctor Who Monthly*, no. 51, p. 33.
33. This was extended further in his third season with the introduction
    of the male companion Turlough who in fact is an ally of the Black
    Guardian.
34. Terrance Dicks said that the first feature of Tom Baker which he
    wrote for was the 'scatter-brained Harpo Marx quality'.
35. Cary Bazalgette, 'Reagan and Carter, Kojak and Crocker, Batman
    and Robin?', *Screen Education*, no. 20 (Autumn 1976), p. 60.
36. In fact, of course, the very first story in 1963 cliffhangered out
    into the first Dalek story by means of a dangerously rising radio-
    activity gauge.
37. Drummond, 'Structural and narrative constraints and strategies in
    The Sweeney', pp. 19–20.

38. 'I'm not really an actor yet . . . Television is a terribly insular world, and it's more insular when you haven't done anything else professionally.'
39. Ellis, 'Star/Industry/Image', pp. 14–15.
40. Richard Paterson, 'The Production Context of *Coronation Street*' in Dyer *et al., Coronation Street*, p. 60.
41. He did, however, have to take careful note of the BBC guidelines on sex and violence. 'It's something I'm watching in the new season because Peter is so young, and it's part of the reason why Tegan is this independent, bossy character. A question that is often asked by the press particularly is about the sleeping arrangements in the Tardis and "does the Doctor ever have affairs with his companions" . . . As I have been quoted in the press as saying about five times, "there's no hanky-panky in the Tardis". But it is something to watch when you've got a young Doctor who is heroic and good looking and he's got two attractive girls around him . . . I don't let them touch each other in press calls. They usually want Peter to put his arms round the two girls, which I don't allow – only because I know the press so well. You can see the sort of caption now: "Doctor Who takes two girls to his heart" . . . I think it just keeps raising the boring old question about the sleeping arrangements in the Tardis, which is why I have brought in, in this season, the girls' room, where the two girls sleep.'
42. In addition he introduced 'star' names in guest roles. 'What I have done to up-market the programme is to try and cast well-known guest artists in either guest villain or guest goodie roles, which brings with them quite a lot of publicity . . . Of course it is costly . . . but it brings us press coverage which thereby brings in audiences. And also it raises the standard of any other artist that is in the programme . . . I distinguish between well-known actors in our business who have a well-known face but not necessarily a name to the public and the type of people that *I* cast so that an audience will say, "That's Barbara Murray!" That's what I aim for . . . The policy used to be good actors who weren't necessarily famous. I want famous good actors . . . The minute I get a couple of very good names, I get calls from agents to say "what about so and so?" who would perhaps never have dreamt of appearing in a *Doctor Who* before, because there is no billing. It is "starring Peter Davison" and that's it. We don't have "and special guest star Stratford Johns" – they are just part of the cast list.'
43. J. Bentham's *Doctor Who* information service ('Freesheet') no. 10, p. 1.
44. Ibid., no. 11, p. 1.
45. Richard Paterson, 'Planning the family: the art of the television schedule', *Screen Education*, no. 35 (Summer 1980), p. 82.
46. Ibid., p. 85.
47. Murdock, *Screen Education*, no. 35 (Summer 1980), pp. 38–9.
48. *Daily Mirror*, 19 July, 1982, p. 2.

Chapter 6 'Kinda': Conditions of Production and
          Performance

1. Keir Elam, *The Semiotics of Theatre and Drama* (London: Methuen, 1980), p. 54.
2. Ibid., p. 55.
3. Ibid.
4. Ibid., p. 37.
5. See, for instance, Gauguin's 'Ia Orana Maria', 1891.
6. Thomas Hanzo, 'The Past of Science Fiction', in Slusser *et al.*, *Bridges to Science Fiction*, pp. 133–4.
7. Ibid., p. 142.
8. Ibid.
9. Ibid., p. 134.
10. Ibid., p. 136.
11. Ibid., p. 142.
12. Charles Blinderman, 'Vampurella: Darwin and Count Dracula', *Massachusetts Review*, Summer 1980, p. 428.
13. Ibid.
14. Cited in Blinderman, 'Vampurella: Darwin and Count Dracula', p. 417.
15. Jackson, *Fantasy* . . . , p. 82.
16. Murdock, 'Authorship and Organisation', p. 20.
17. Ibid., p. 26.
18. *Doctor Who Monthly*, no. 51, p. 29.
19. Ibid., p. 31.
20. Ibid., p. 32.
21. *Doctor Who Monthly*, no. 51, p. 30.
22. Ibid., p. 31.
23. Ibid.
24. According to David Saunders, *Doctor Who* Appreciation Society (London).
25. This 'is a type of writing which is energised by the sudden popularity of science fiction among a new class of readers . . . an adaptation and updating of the old-fashioned space opera type of science fiction for the tastes of middle class consumers whose passion for gadgets is inexhaustible . . . This type of science fiction has the tendency to leave the literary domain altogether and move into TV serials, films and comic strips'. (Ebert, 'The convergence of postmodern innovative fiction and science fiction', p. 92.)
26. Kristin Thompson, 'The concept of cinematic excess', *Cine-Tracts*, vol. I, no. 2, p. 58.
27. This is made more plausible by having the Doctor collapse unnoticed as the two companions close the shutters.
28. Peter Grimwade likes to get down to the studio floor if he can; Fiona Cumming finds the time, and has the eye, to spot new aesthetic shots during recording, such as a lighting effect on a door

in 'Castravalva' 'just like the sacristry door at Iona' which she was keen to emphasise.

29. *Doctor Who Monthly*, no. 52, p. 27.
30. Robinson, *Time Out*, p. 94.
31. Paul Espinosa, 'The audience in the text: ethnographic observations of a Hollywood story conference', *Media, Culture and Society*, vol. 4, no. I (1982), pp. 77–86.
32. Alan Watts, *The Way of Zen* (Harmondsworth: Pelican, 1976), p. 142.
33. Ibid., p. 59.
34. Ibid., p. 75.
35. Paul Radin, *The Trickster: a study in American Indian mythology* (New York: Schocken, 1972), p. 168.
36. Karl Kerényi, 'The Trickster in relation to Greek mythology' in Radin, ibid., p. 185.
37. C. G. Jung, 'On the psychology of the Trickster figure', in Radin, ibid., p. 200.
38. Radin, ibid., p. 147.
39. Kerényi, 'The Trickster in relation to Greek mythology, p. 185.
40. Jung, 'On the psychology of the Trickster figure', p. 206.
41. Ibid., p. 209.
42. Ibid., p. 207.
43. Ibid.
44. Frieda Fordham, *An Introduction to Jung's Psychology* (Harmondsworth. Penguin, 1953), p. 79.
45. Radin, The Trickster, p. 109.
46. Louis James, 'Introduction' and 'Was Jerrold's Black Ey'd Susan more popular than Wordsworth's Lucy?', in D. Bradby, L. James & B. Sharratt, *Performance and Politics in Popular Drama* (Cambridge: Cambridge University Press, 1980), p. 3, 15.
47. David Mayer, 'The music of melodrama', in Bradby *et al.* (1980), pp. 49–50.
48. Ibid., p. 51.
49. Elam (1980), p. 45.
50. In melodrama, 'even death on the stage was ... energetic, "exhibited by violent distortion, groaning, gasping for breath, stretching the body, raising, and then letting it fall" ' (James, p. 12) – very much the sequence of actions performed by Lee Cornes in the envisioned death of the Trickster.
51. Mayer, 'The music of melodrama', in Bradby *et al.*, *Performance and Politics in Popular Drama*, p. 51.
52. James, 'Introduction', in Bradby *et al.*, *Performance and Politics in Popular Drama*, p. 5.
53. Tulloch, *Australian Cinema . . .* , pp. 176 ff.
54. Finding the time-tunnel titles 'old fashioned', Nathan-Turner was not completely successful in replacing them. 'In my new style of titles, which is more of a star field, the *time* aspect has been retained; as the stars and meteorites are flashing by, some of them remain

and gradually join together into what looks like a huge planet which eventually turns out to be the Doctor's face. But judging from the mail, I think that's probably being too subtle and many people don't like the titles because they don't retain this time aspect.'

55. Edna Boling, 'Tuning up Doctor Who', *The Canberra Times*, 10 August 1980, p. 9.

56. For the various permutations on this principle see the 'Cybermark' *Doctor Who* series.

57. At the same time this avoided Tardis console scenes, which, as visual effects designer Peter Logan described, had been a source of disagreement with unions and with the Appreciation Society over the years.

> *Logan*:   There was an attempt to change the Tardis console during my time and I know that it was because of the amount of publicity received by the various Appreciation Societies that it was changed back again to the original console which goes up and down . . . In one of the stories it was changed to a little sort of Victorian eight-sided cabinet with brass rails and hardwood . . . There have always been lines of demarcation as to who should actually operate and move about the Tardis console. It was one of those bones of contention. It used to sit out in the Ring Road and not be moved around because props refused to move it. The console was so big and props always used to say 'No, it's not our job to move it', visual effects said 'Well, we only operate it and make all the things happen on it so therefore it is not really an effect and it should be props', and the scene crew used to side with props and say 'It is certainly nothing to do with us', and in the end it used to be left out in the Ring Road for all and sundry to come along and play with the knobs or whatever. So they decided they would write something different into the story which didn't actually do a lot by way of effects but was small enough to put into a prop cage, and this I think was one of the reasons for the change. Also the mechanical devices which made it go up and down and light up in the middle was also going across lines of demarcation because the electricians even today say it is their job to make it go up and down and not ours, and we are saying, 'No, it is our job to make the effects happen because it is an effect.' And so there is a lot of argument about the whole thing everytime we use it, which is why it's not often in the story now. In fact even in the last three stories that I've been involved in where the Tardis has been used we have had to operate it with a piece of wood underneath making it go up and down. It was these union problems that led to the change. First of all we made it into a twelve-volt motor which operated through a series of gears, because if you work on twelve volts then in theory the electricians haven't got any

jurisdiction over it. The unions say that anything that the electricians deal with should be mains. But then this created a problem because the lights inside were mains, so we changed those to twelve volts. We even used twelve volts to operate the fluorescent tube. Then when we got that into the studio the electricians said 'Oh no, it's still our job' and provided a twelve-volt transformer. But this blew the motor because it was a.c. and not d.c., so we were back to square one making the Tardis go up and down with a piece of wood underneath, pumping like a see-saw . . . We have got it down to pneumatics now. We have got an air bottle . . . and the electricians can't touch it now.

58. A group of Asian undergraduates at the University of New South Wales who were Buddhist and quite aware of the meaning of 'dukkha', 'annata', 'anicca' etc. still did not 'read' the episode of 'Kinda' in which they appeared in a 'Buddhist' way. Concerned to appropriate Western professional values and skills to take back to their countries, these students found *Doctor Who* of no interest because 'too imaginative and unreal' and preferred shows which gave them a 'realistic' understanding of Western culture, such as news and documentary and drama which reflects 'more down to earth problems'. Consequently they did not consider *Doctor Who* sufficiently appropriate to their interests to begin to assign relevance and codes of coherence to their understanding of it. This for them was *Western* television (and therefore was not considered as a forum for Buddhist ideas). Hence the Buddhist clues (played down by the production team — the names 'annata', 'annica', 'dukkha', etc. are not given in the narrative of events, only in the cast list at the end) were not appropriated to generate a reading: the students' Western professional orientation overlaid the producer's 'action-drama' signature to efface the Buddhist allegory.

59. Cf. Elam, *The Semiotics of Theatre and Drama*, p. 16.

60. Audience group of TV professionals, Sydney, 13 October 1982.

61. Elam, *The Semiotics of Theatre and Drama*, p. 84.

62. Ibid.

63. Ibid., pp. 86—7.

Index

This index consists of all titles, names of people and of organisations.